Urban Geography

Critical Introductions to Geography

Critical Introductions to Geography is a series of textbooks for undergraduate courses covering the key geographical subdisciplines and providing broad and introductory treatment with a critical edge. They are designed for the North American and international market and take a lively and engaging approach with a distinct geographical voice that distinguishes them from more traditional and out-dated texts.

Prospective authors interested in the series should contact the series editor:

John Paul Jones III
School of Geography and Development
University of Arizona
jpjones@email.arizona.edu

Published

Cultural Geography
Don Mitchell

Geographies of Globalization
Andrew Herod

Geographies of Media and Communication
Paul C. Adams

Social Geography
Vincent J. Del Casino Jr

Mapping
Jeremy W. Crampton

Research Methods in Geography
Basil Gomez and John Paul Jones III

Political Ecology, Second Edition
Paul Robbins

Geographic Thought
Tim Cresswell

Environment and Society, Second Edition
Paul Robbins, Sarah Moore and John Hintz

Urban Geography
Andrew E.G. Jonas, Eugene McCann, and Mary Thomas

Urban Geography

A Critical Introduction

Andrew E.G. Jonas, Eugene McCann, and Mary Thomas

WILEY Blackwell

This edition first published 2015
© 2015 Andrew E.G. Jonas, Eugene McCann, and Mary Thomas.

Registered Office
John Wiley & Sons, Ltd., The Atrium, Southern Gate, Chichester, West Sussex, PO19 8SQ, UK

Editorial Offices
350 Main Street, Malden, MA 02148-5020, USA
9600 Garsington Road, Oxford, OX4 2DQ, UK
The Atrium, Southern Gate, Chichester, West Sussex, PO19 8SQ, UK

For details of our global editorial offices, for customer services, and for information about how to apply for permission to reuse the copyright material in this book please see our website at www.wiley.com/wiley-blackwell.

The right of Andrew E.G. Jonas, Eugene McCann, and Mary Thomas to be identified as the authors of this work has been asserted in accordance with the UK Copyright, Designs and Patents Act 1988.

All rights reserved. No part of this publication may be reproduced, stored in a retrieval system, or transmitted, in any form or by any means, electronic, mechanical, photocopying, recording or otherwise, except as permitted by the UK Copyright, Designs and Patents Act 1988, without the prior permission of the publisher.

Wiley also publishes its books in a variety of electronic formats. Some content that appears in print may not be available in electronic books.

Designations used by companies to distinguish their products are often claimed as trademarks. All brand names and product names used in this book are trade names, service marks, trademarks or registered trademarks of their respective owners. The publisher is not associated with any product or vendor mentioned in this book.

Limit of Liability/Disclaimer of Warranty: While the publisher and authors have used their best efforts in preparing this book, they make no representations or warranties with respect to the accuracy or completeness of the contents of this book and specifically disclaim any implied warranties of merchantability or fitness for a particular purpose. It is sold on the understanding that the publisher is not engaged in rendering professional services and neither the publisher nor the author shall be liable for damages arising herefrom. If professional advice or other expert assistance is required, the services of a competent professional should be sought.

Library of Congress Cataloging-in-Publication Data

Jonas, Andrew E. G., 1961–
    Urban geography : a critical introduction / Andrew E.G. Jonas, Eugene McCann and Mary Thomas.
        pages   cm
    Includes bibliographical references and index.
    ISBN 978-1-4051-8980-4 (hardback) – ISBN 978-1-4051-8979-8 (paper)   1. Urban geography.
2. Human geography.   I. McCann, Eugene.   II. Thomas, Mary E. (Mary Elizabeth), 1970–
III.   Title.
    GF125.J66 2015
    307.76–dc23

                                                            2014044811

A catalogue record for this book is available from the British Library.

Cover image: The Ashton Canal dissecting the formerly industrial area of Ancoats in Manchester, England. Photo © Eugene McCann

Set in 10/12.5pt Minion by SPi Publisher Services, Pondicherry, India

Printed in the UK

Contents

Contents

List of Figures

List of Tables

List of Boxes

Acknowledgments

The rich scholarship of the generations of critical urban geographers who came before us taught us how to be researchers as well as political thinkers. Their work showed us that the examination of urban space could be firmly insistent on social, political, and economic justice. At the same time, the resistance of the people and groups oppressed by status quo capitalism, political oppression and exclusion, and social inequality around the world motivate us to continue that work. We wrote this textbook to communicate the legacy of critical urban scholarship to students and to highlight how struggles for social justice are central to the study of cities. We also want to encourage students to think about what they can do to further critical thought and activism.

Our own students have always reminded us to stay current, critical, and engaged. They inspire us with their participation and passion. We hope that this book will encourage students everywhere to keep the study of cities firmly in conversation with justice movements and engaged in furthering the quest for more democratic urban spaces and futures.

Acknowledging everyone who has contributed directly or indirectly to the development of this book – and each of our intellectual and political perspectives on urban geography – would take as many words as the book already holds. We do want to note, in general, the debt we owe to the communities of scholars who shape the many approaches to critical urban geography that we discuss in the following pages. There are *many* more people than those whose names appear in the bibliography who have influenced our thinking and who inspire our work and teaching.

We also thank the many friends, colleagues, friends of friends, and strangers who kindly donated photographs from their personal collections for use in this book. We are especially grateful to colleagues and friends who took time out of their busy schedules to comment on drafts of specific chapters and, in some cases, the entire manuscript. We thank the anonymous reviewers who read chapters and provided useful comments. Special thanks to John Paul Jones III (the "critical introduction" series editor) and Justin Vaughan, Ben Thatcher, and Lisa Sharp at Wiley-Blackwell for their patience and support over the years that this book has been in gestation. Sam Affholter provided invaluable help with permissions, as did Alison McIntosh with the bibliography.

Andy Jonas would like to thank (in no particular order) Pauline Deutz, Kevin Cox, Andy Mair, Susan Hanson, Kim England, Andy Wood, David Ley, Kevin Morgan, Bob Lake, David Wilson, Byron Miller, Kevin Ward, the late (and great) Duncan Fuller, Roger Lee, Jane Wills, Maksuder Rahman, Graham Haughton, Aidan While, David Gibbs, Bob Fagan, Phil O'Neill, Pauline McGuirk, Robyn Dowling, Rob Krueger, Stephanie Pincetl, Jim Sullivan, Linda McCarthy, Stephen Hall, Ruth Craggs, David Atkinson, David Sauri, Ugo Rossi, Francesc Muñoz, Andy Goetz, Eric Boschmann, and Marcela Mele.

Eugene McCann thanks Christiana Miewald and Sophie McCann, and (in alphabetical order): Daniela Aiello, Stephanie Campbell, JP Catungal, Sarah Elwood, Bob Lake, Andy Longhurst, Glen Lowry, Felipe Magalhães, Deborah Martin, Alison McIntosh, Ronan Paddison, John Pickles, Jesse Proudfoot, Mark Purcell, Marit Rosol, Jim Rubenstein, Rob Ruzanic, Lynn Saffery, Rich Schein, Nicole Stewart, Rini Sumartojo, Cristina Temenos, Kevin Ward, and Astrid Wood.

Mary Thomas thanks Lisa Bhungalia, Mathew Coleman, Nicole Constable, Lynaya Elliott, Colin McFarlane, Kate Swanson, Sarah Turner, and Max Woodworth, with special thanks to Natalie Oswin for her help with several draft chapters.

Preface

Urban geography is one of the most popular subfields of human geography. Yet very few urban geography textbooks offer comprehensive guides to the wide range of critical approaches to urban geography now practiced by geographers. The aim of this book is to offer you an introductory guide to this rich variety, drawing upon concepts, themes, and examples from urban scholarship conducted in diverse geographical locations.

No doubt you are wondering what *critical* urban geography is all about: what makes our approach to urban geography "critical"? The term critical has an intellectual connotation and a political one. Crucially, these two orientations cannot be separated. Critical human geography (of which critical urban geography is one part) is not an approach that values or strives for detachment from the world it studies. Being a critical geographer is not about being impartial or just reporting objective facts. Nor does it simply entail working within existing intellectual paradigms, while not questioning their foundational assumptions. Being a critical urban geographer is about being *part* of the (urbanized) world that we study. It is about being *partial*, both in the sense of acknowledging that academics will never have a complete understanding of how the world is or should be, and in the sense of being willing to take an intellectual and political stance. Being critical is about questioning taken-for-granted assumptions, both about cities and about urban studies. It means highlighting and/ or participating in attempts to change cities for the better.

Yet, we are not suggesting that being a critical urban geographer means subscribing to any one political or intellectual orthodoxy. Presently the label critical geography is applied to a great variety of intellectual endeavors across the discipline that are broadly concerned with identifying spatial patterns of inequality, injustice, and oppression and with accounting for the social relations and political processes that produce such patterns. In general terms, these approaches also share an explicit opposition to oppression, a commitment to social justice, some form of internationalism or globalism in their outlook, and a commitment to using theory and analysis to achieve social change. From these intellectual and political starting points, critical geographers of various types take seriously their relationships to activism, both in the city in general and also within academic institutions. They pay attention to questions of ethics in their research, many engage in applied or policy-relevant research of one form or another, and all of them take seriously the political and intellectual potential of various forms of teaching and writing.

Today's critical urban geography owes debts to earlier generations of radical, liberal, and progressive scholars who were broadly interested in questions of social justice, inequality, and oppression in the city. Their work sought to connect the study of spatial inequalities – marked differences in income from neighborhood to neighborhood, or geographies of racial segregation, or the prioritization of problematically gendered or heterosexual perspectives on cities, for example – to an analysis of unequal social and capitalist political economic relations. Indeed, it would be difficult to imagine a critical human geography, in general, without the city as a central focus of investigation. Nor is it possible to think of a critical approach to geographical analysis that lacks a radical or progressive view of social change.

Critical urban geographers maintain that (urban) society is fundamentally unequal and uneven, with resources, power, identities, and stigma clustered spatially (rather than evenly spread) across the landscapes of cities. We seek to expose, explain, and engage with these inequalities by putting current conditions in historical, geographical, and social context. We also strive to go beyond common sense understandings to identify the conditions and interests that benefit from and perpetuate inequalities. This, after all, is an introduction to critical urban research.

More concretely still, critical urban geographers see urban built environments as neither natural nor unchanging/unchangeable. Approaching cities as socio-spatial processes (an approach we outline in Chapter 1) is coupled with a critical sensibility that focuses on inequality and difference. This focus allows us to see cities as spatial expressions of unequal societies and as built environments that tend to perpetuate those societies, and, crucially, also as places that can be changed and can nurture change. Central to this critical sensibility is the question, *"cities for whom?"* In order to change cities for the better, we must analyze them in terms of who controls them, who benefits from how they are (unevenly) organized, and how they operate as socio-spatial processes with unequal effects.

Instructors know that teaching an urban geography course, with its necessarily wide scope, is never easy. Similarly, one of our challenges in writing a text like this is to find a balance between offering a comprehensive survey of key critical concepts in urban geography and providing accessible and up-to-date examples of how these concepts can be put into practice. For these reasons, this book places an emphasis on how critical urban geographers have approached the city in terms of marshalling empirical evidence to support critical ideas and concepts, and in turn how new critical ideas have emerged through concrete urban research. In particular, the book pays attention to the variety of ways in which critical urban scholarship is conducted, represented, and disseminated, and how undergraduates, in turn, might themselves engage in critical urban research. Using glossaries and case study boxes, the book highlights many of the key critical concepts and approaches used by urban geographers to inform their research and provide guides to further reading so students can develop their own critical research activities.

The book is designed to fit into a "normal" teaching semester. Each chapter has a particular thematic emphasis. The first two chapters offer a gentle introduction to critical approaches to the city by building upon some familiar models and theories of urban form and process. These chapters are followed by more in-depth coverage of thematic topics, including the urban economy, global cities, labor, planning, place marketing, social reproduction, nature, experience, art and graffiti, urban crises, and alternative urban spaces. Individual chapters strike a careful balance between a depiction of the diversity of ordinary urban geographies and an exposure of the networks, flows, and relationships that increasingly connect cities and urban spaces at the global level. Although we hope that our coverage of critical urban geography themes is comprehensive, instructors will be able to select chapters or particular sections to meet their own teaching requirements.

Today's critical geographers draw upon a wide range of conceptual approaches and social theories, which you will learn about in this book. Critical geography's many fields have spawned research groups, discussion forums, online blogs and scholar webpages, conferences, and many journals publishing the latest thinking. We hope that, in this book, you gain an appreciation of both the key common themes in critical urban geography as well as the rich diversity of approaches in the field.

Andy Jonas, Eugene McCann, and Mary Thomas, June 2014

Chapter 1

Approaching the City

Urban Geography: A Critical Introduction, First Edition. Andrew E.G. Jonas, Eugene McCann, and Mary Thomas.
© 2015 Andrew E.G. Jonas, Eugene McCann, and Mary Thomas. Published 2015 by John Wiley & Sons, Ltd.

1.1   Introduction

Approaching the city. What do we mean by this? Do we hope to kindle some excitement in you? Yes, we do! We assume that you have enrolled in a course about cities, or that you have picked up this book, because you are interested in cities and interested in learning more about their dynamics. If you are like us, you have probably always been drawn to cities and to urbanism – the distinctive ways of life that characterize cities – even before developing an academic interest. You might consider yourself to be an urbanite, someone that has always lived in an urban environment. Or you might be from the suburbs or a rural area, but have moved to the city to attend college or university. Or maybe you are studying in a small town but you expect to move to a city when you graduate. In any case, we guess that you have often approached cities in the most straightforward sense: you have travelled toward one. As your plane broke through the clouds on its final descent, as your bus or car rounded one last bend to reveal a spectacular skyline, or as your train gradually made its way through an ever-intensifying landscape of factories, office and retail parks, houses, and apartments, toward a central station, you probably found yourself stimulated by excitement, expectation, and curiosity; perhaps by nervousness and trepidation or, most likely, by a mixture of all these feelings.

Urbanist (urban scholar) Mike Davis imagines such an approach to Dubai:

> As your jet starts its descent, you are glued to your window. … [T]he plane slowly banks toward the desert mainland [and] you gasp at the even more improbable vision ahead. Out of a chrome forest of skyscrapers soars a new Tower of Babel. It is an impossible half-mile high: taller than the Empire State Building stacked on top of itself. You are still rubbing your eyes with wonderment as the plane lands. … With your adrenaline pumped up … you round off the afternoon with some snowboarding on the local indoor snow mountain (outdoors, the temperature is 105°[F]). (Davis, 2006a: 47–48)

Bright lights, big city

Cities – their bright lights, spectacular buildings, and extreme experiences – have figured centrally in people's imaginations for centuries. They are places of possibility and danger, of hope and disappointment, of power and powerlessness, of glamour and destitution, of production and consumption. They are often seen as different or special – separated off, sometimes behind walls – from the rural areas beyond. They are often seen as sites where new innovations emerge and as places that epitomize new forms of social organization.

For example, scholars like Karl Marx and Friedrich Engels saw the English cities of the nineteenth century as epitomizing the new economic and social order of industrial capitalism. When studying these cities, they saw places of intense and innovative economic activity, novel social interaction, global interconnection, and massive inequality. Cities, like the world, were in flux as industrial capitalism grew exponentially. While we often imagine Marx and Engels in their later gray-bearded lives, it was a young Engels, only in his mid-20s, who approached London for the first time on a ship travelling up the River Thames in the mid-nineteenth century. As it does for many of us, this first approach to a storied city set his mind racing, his adrenaline pumping, as he tried to comprehend the multitude of sights, sounds, and smells he encountered. London was remarkable for its

> gigantic docks in which are assembled the thousands of ships which always cover the River Thames. I know nothing more imposing than the view one obtains of the river when sailing from the sea up to London Bridge. … The further one goes up the river the thicker becomes the concentration of ships lying at anchor, so that eventually only a narrow shipping lane is left free in midstream. Here hundreds of steamships dart rapidly to and fro. All this is so magnificent and impressive that one is lost in admiration. The traveler has good reason to marvel at England's greatness even before he steps on English soil. (Engels, 1845/1987: 30)

We return to Engels in Chapter 4, but for now we can agree that, whether in the nineteenth century or in the twenty-first century, cities inspire awe as we approach them.

Yet, it would hardly be useful for us as social scientists to simply celebrate the awesome and positively awe-inspiring aspects of cities (Figure 1.1 is an example of such a celebration). Things are never that simple. Indeed, the very next line of Engels' description of London notes, "It is only later that the traveler appreciates the human suffering which has made all this possible," a point he goes on to emphasize in his book through an extended

Figure 1.1 Dubai's iconic architecture on display in an advertisement in a Tokyo train station. The romantic allure of the city is on sale here, invoked through the flowing feminine dress and happy smile. The image also emphasizes the global interconnections among the world's cities. Photo: Eugene McCann.

description of the immiseration of working people in Manchester. Similarly, the purpose of Davis' imaginary descent into spectacular Dubai is to set up his deeply critical analysis of the sources of "Dubai Inc.'s" recent spectacular growth.

Approaching a city, living in one, or studying them necessarily evokes mixed feelings. Cities like society, then and now, are awesome and simultaneously awful. This makes them fascinating and troubling to approach, but it also makes the study of urbanism, in all its various facets, an important task. By studying cities, we are able to shed light not only on *urban* life but also on a vast array of processes, institutions, forces, interests, inequalities, and identities that constitute *society* more generally. This tension is most eloquently expressed by one Marxist scholar, Marshall Berman, speaking of another, Walter Benjamin, who studied the rise of modernity in Paris during the nineteenth century:

> [Benjamin's] heart and his sensibility draw him irresistibly toward the city's bright lights, beautiful women, fashion, luxury, its play of dazzling surfaces and radiant scenes; meanwhile his Marxist conscience wrenches him insistently away from these temptations, instructs him that this whole glittering world is decadent, hollow, vicious, spiritually empty, oppressive to the proletariat, condemned by history … but he cannot resist one last look down the boulevard or under the arcade; he wants to be saved, but not yet. (Berman, 1982: 146)

Urbanists who think critically about cities find that they are sometimes repelled by certain aspects of them, just as they are drawn to others. Box 1.1 contains an exercise that you can perform to think about your relationship to your city or town. So, how do we manage this

---

Box 1.1   Experiencing the City

Many of us inhabit an urban area. We live in its neighborhoods, use its services and infrastructure, participate in its social and cultural activities and experience its various environments. In engaging with your city or town in these various ways, you quickly develop understandings of the place based on your own experience in combination with your understanding of larger forces that shape cities.

Take some time away from this book and: (1) write some field notes on a recent urban experience you have had (i.e., notes written during or immediately after an event that describe and reflect upon it); (2) write a short discussion of the experience, describing it based on your field notes and tying it to larger forces that seem connected to it; (3) use this experience to write a little about your feelings about cities in general and your city or town in particular. Are you in love with the place? Can you hardly wait to leave? Are you ambivalent? No matter your answer, write about why you have these feelings.

For example, if the bus runs past you some morning this week as you are trying to get to campus, or if you have difficulty finding parking when you drive there, this (and its consequences) would be an experience you could discuss. You would also need to link the specific experience to larger issues by identifying possible reasons why the bus ran by you or parking was hard to find (both of which might be related to public investment in transportation infrastructures).

tension between "urbanophila" and "urbanophobia" and use it to aid our understanding of cities? This is where a different connotation of "approaching the city" comes in.

Academic approaches

Travelling toward a place is not all, or even most of, what we mean when we say "approaching the city." An "approach" is also an intellectual stance that we take as we address a process, situation, or problem that we are trying to understand and, perhaps, change. Approaching a city in this intellectual and even political sense involves bringing a specific set of already-existing assumptions, perspectives, theories, categories, frameworks, and analytical methods to bear on the cacophony of sights, structures, and experiences that confront us in the city. Those who define themselves as critical urban geographers adopt numerous approaches to cities. To be critical does not necessarily mean that one must necessarily subscribe to a Marxist approach, for example. Critical urbanists might bring feminist, postcolonial, queer, anarchist, and many other approaches to bear on their studies of cities and, most likely, will combine a number of these intellectual traditions in their analyses.

By the end of the chapter, answers to the following questions will be clear to you:

- What is an intellectual approach to a subject, in this case to cities and urban processes?
- What distinguishes a geographical approach to cities from the various other types of approaches that we might find in other academic disciplines?
- What do the concepts, urbanization and development, urbanism, and planning mean and how do they help us study cities from an geographical perspective?
- What are the key foundations of urban geography and how are they related to each other?

We unpack what it means to be critical in Chapter 2. But first, consider what it means to be an urban geographer.

1.2   Being Geographical, Being Urbanist

"Oh, you're studying geography! So, what's the capital of Mali? Do you know all the capital cities? Do you like maps? Is that about rocks?" You have probably heard versions of these questions, maybe in your dormitory, maybe at a family gathering. The questioner is usually well intentioned and the questions are not surprising since geography is a wide ranging, but often relatively poorly defined, discipline. As a geographer, it is useful to have answers to these basic questions,[1] but it is also worth having a better sense of what defines geography as a discipline. If we focus here only on human or social geographers (those who are most likely to study cities), we must ask what contributions do geographers make to the study of cities and society more generally?

While most social science disciplines can be roughly defined by *what* they study – the economy, culture, society, and so on – geography is defined by *how* we study the world, by our *approach*. Geographers study the economy, society, politics, and culture too, but a

---

[1] We suggest: "Bamako"; "No"; "Yes"; and "Well, some geographers do study rocks, but you might be thinking of Geology. Let me tell you what geographers actually do ..."

> **Space** is a term with many connotations. Most contemporary critical geographers agree that space is both something absolute – the physical, material spaces of the world – and is also socially produced. In this sense, space is a concept that refers to the relationships between society – human practices, representations, institutions, ways of life, and so on – and the spaces that society produces (see **socio-spatial process**). Space then, is very much defined in terms of relationships with other beings and things as well as in relation to power and to change over time.

geographical perspective is one that emphasizes **space** in its approach to any of these subjects.

What this means is that we approach the world's various phenomena in terms of *connections and similarities* across regions or landscapes ranging from the scale of the local to the global (how one can buy the same products in shopping streets in cities in different continents while also buying other goods and engaging in social interactions that are very different from one street to the next, for example). We also pay attention to the way that *divisions and differences* are shaped by, but also shape, various social and environmental processes (how the political jurisdictions of different municipalities in an urban region can make big differences in where industries locate or where housing gets built, for example).

Geographers are very much attuned to the notion that social and environmental processes do not play out in the abstract, but operate *somewhere* – in neighborhoods, across regions, within the unique body of an individual self, and so on. We also see these spaces as active in the production of those social processes – giving them shape, constraining, and enabling them. This is a geographical perspective: an approach that studies the **spatiality** of social and environmental processes by

> **Spatiality** is a term geographers use to indicate that space and society are mutually constitutive (see **space** and **socio-spatial process**).

employing a series of related concepts like **space**, **place**, **scale** (global, local, urban, etc. – but see our definition of this word for more nuance), distance, region, territory, boundary, landscape, environment, clustering, and unevenness.

> **Place** refers to locations imbued with meaning. Place is always being reworked and redefined by the people who live in it and forces stretching beyond it. In this sense, place can be understood as "**scaled**": regions, nations, and even the globe can be understood in some ways to be places, as can localities.

As we will show in the following chapters, this general approach allows geographers to contribute to society's understanding of cities as political and economic spaces, as well as places imbued with meaning and identity that are not only local in character but also defined by their global connections. We are also able to say a lot about the urban built environment, the landscapes of cities, and the physical, environmental processes that shape and are affected by processes of urbanization. This focus on process (geographers are interested in "how" and "why" questions as much as "where" questions) means, too, that we are able to analyze the relationship between places and change – from the ways that migration alters the character of urban populations, to how investment flows reshape city skylines, to how urban growth can both contribute to pollution and also might be able to reduce greenhouse gas emissions. Focusing on how social and environmental processes affect places means that geographers can offer important insights into how planning gets done in cities, regions, and nations (we assume many of you see urban planning, in one of its many facets, as a potential career option in your future). Furthermore, many geographers, including you, perhaps, are politically active in one way or another. In fact, you may have been drawn to geography because you want to dig deeper into the spatial aspects of cities because you find them unjust, problematic, or troublesome in some way or another. Or a geographical perspective may have drawn you into certain types of politics, from electoral campaigning to involvement with community activism or various types of social movements. Geography's diversity, then, is a result of its approach and its openness to influences from other disciplines and from a diverse array of intellectual and political traditions. Geography is a very interdisciplinary discipline in which you can get up to an awful lot of interesting stuff (Gregory, 2009).

Scale is a conceptual arrangement of space. It is commonly thought of in terms of levels – the local, national, global, and so on. And there is some truth to this. Yet, human geographers understand scale as a social product, tied up with power and politics (see **space**). While scales appear natural, fixed, separate, and ahistorical, they are, in fact, produced and often interconnected for certain purposes by particular interests. Think of the European Union, NAFTA, or even the nation-state or the municipality. All have very specific and relatively recent histories (it is not so long ago that none of them existed in their present form). All involve drawing new lines on maps, creating territories, and, thus, assigning certain powers to particular scales and allowing certain activities to take place, while others are disallowed (see **state**). Scales are social and political, and they are performed and produced by social action. Therefore, they are powerful and can be changed ("rescaled"), for better or worse.

Defining "the urban" as an object of study

At the beginning of this chapter, when we described the ways in which one might physically approach a city, we assumed that you would have no problem conjuring up an image of the city you were approaching in your imagination. Yet, the image you have in your head of what a city is, or your definition of what it means to be "urban," are very likely different from ours, from your colleagues in the course you are taking, and from people who are reading this book in other parts of the world. These definitions will not be *entirely* different, of course. We will probably all agree that certain places are cities – New York, London, Shanghai, Mumbai, Tokyo, Johannesburg, Buenos Aires, Sydney, for example – and we will all likely concur that certain phenomena, infrastructures, or experiences – such as being crushed into an overcrowded subway car as it rattles from station to station – are urban in character (Figure 1.2).

Why are we so comfortable with these definitions? We might also want to think about why it matters to put the urban label on certain places and experiences. Furthermore, we should consider the scope of our definitions: where and why do we start to disagree about what a city is and what it means to be urban? Do we simply define a city by its municipal boundary? Or is there a certain population threshold below which places are no longer usefully defined as urban? Does that threshold differ from one country to another? Is the

Figure 1.2   A busy shopping street in the heart of Tokyo. Tokyo is the world's largest urban agglomeration, with a population of 37.2 million in 2011. Photo: Eugene McCann.

world itself now mostly an urbanized place, in terms of population? If so, why and how does that matter?

Certainly, the United Nations reports that more than half of the global population now lives in urban areas. More specifically:

> Between 2011 and 2050, the world population is expected to increase by 2.3 billion, passing from 7.0 billion to 9.3 billion. … At the same time, the population living in urban areas is projected to gain 2.6 billion, passing from 3.6 billion in 2011 to 6.3 billion 2050. Thus, the urban areas of the world are expected to absorb all the population growth expected over the next four decades while at the same time drawing in some of the rural population. … Asia, in particular, is projected to see its urban population increase by 1.4 billion, Africa by 0.9 billion, and Latin America and the Caribbean by 0.2 billion. (United Nations, 2012: 1)

While this is interesting in itself, it is important for social scientists to remember that the real question is: How and why is urbanization important? What does it tell us about the way global society is organized, how the global economy works, and how the environment supports and is exploited, not to mention threatened, by human activity? And, as discussed in Chapter 2, it is important to ask: Who in global society benefits from, and who is exploited, marginalized, and threatened by ongoing urbanization?

Therefore, we do not want to be too enthralled with urbanization statistics simply for their own sake. Nor do we want to become trapped by definitional games about what a city or urban area is, or what it is not. When we attempt to define the city as a *thing* with clear boundaries and coherent, universal characteristics, we quickly find that this game is not as easy as it might have first appeared.

Instead, we quickly question why it matters to reify and categorize cities as concrete things anyway. Clearly, for the purposes of municipal government, it does matter where the boundaries of a city are because these limits define the extent of the rights of citizens to vote in local elections, perhaps, and the responsibilities of a particular government to provide infrastructure and services to its citizens. Yet even this seemingly clear-cut example gets muddied. Should people who own businesses in a city but who live elsewhere be allowed to vote in local elections, given that they have interests there and that they provide jobs locally? Should a municipal government's responsibilities always end at its official boundaries if environmental impacts of industrial activities within its jurisdiction flow downstream to neighboring places, or if its own citizens will benefit from a regional transit system rather than a separate local one? These complexities are, then, exactly why academic urbanists tend to be suspicious of attempts to reify cities, that is, to define them as "things."

Instead, urban geographers tend to approach cities as *processes*. From this perspective, cities are always changing, sometimes quickly, sometimes so slowly that they seem concrete, fixed, and permanent. They are also always connected to wider forces, whether natural or social, cultural, economic, political and so on. Through these connections they both reflect and shape the more general forces, flows, landscapes, and contexts in which they are situated. Cities, then, are social and spatial; they are **socio-spatial processes**. If cities are socio-spatial, then they are always tied up with interests: one need only look at the statues and monuments in cities across the globe to be able to get a sense of who is powerful in each place now and who was powerful in the past. Similarly, the character of contemporary urban built environments gives clues into which interests – economic, political, and cultural; individual, collective, and institutional – influence city building. Cities, like the societies of which they are part, serve people's interests in uneven or stratified ways.

As both Engels and Benjamin understood, the way economic activity, social interaction, and residential landscapes are arranged in cities allows certain groups within society – economic, political, or cultural **elites** – to do very well from them, while the poor, disenfranchised, and even the middle class do less well and tend to wield less influence over the places in which they live (Figure 1.3). As we have

Socio-spatial process A phrase indicating the mutually constitutive relationship between society – the organization of society into groups or classes, the development of cultural mores, and so on – and space – the organization of built environments, landscapes, and so on. How a society operates, understands itself, and is governed is reflected by the spaces (urban and otherwise) that it produces. Furthermore, the legacies of geographies that came before necessarily structure and define the character of contemporary society. The addition of the word "process" indicates that this relationship between society and space is historical and dynamic.

Elites are small groups of people that control large amounts of capital, political power, or social and cultural influence. Their power is often exercised through institutions, such as the **state**, that mediate, facilitate, and occasionally limit their ability to satisfy their interests.

Figure 1.3   This golf course in Jakarta, Indonesia caters to the elite of the city. In the 1970s and 1980s Indonesia and Jakarta specifically engaged in development programs that cleared squatter settlements and prioritized the business elite. Photo courtesy of Sarah Turner.

already suggested, cities are defined in important ways by processes of change, including struggles and negotiations over their present and future character. Thus, cities encapsulate and influence political processes as well as natural, social, and spatial ones.

1.3   Approaching Cities as Processes: Urbanization and Development, Urbanism, and Planning

If we are to define cities in terms of socio-spatial process, we should use concepts and terms that help us focus on the way cities are both fixed, identifiable elements of the landscape while also always being fluid, changing, and connected to the wider world. We should also approach cities by paying close attention to the social practices, interests, identities, and struggles that produce them. Three concepts are particularly helpful in this regard: (1) urbanization and development, (2) urbanism, and (3) planning.

Urbanization and development

In the simplest terms, **urbanization** is the process of becoming urban, or more urban. It has three specific connotations:

i.   It highlights the demographic process in which cities gain more residents, a wider variety of residents, and an increasing density of population.
ii. It speaks to the increasing globalization of urban economic, political, and cultural influence.
iii. It helps us consider the ways in which space is organized and reorganized in tandem with changes in the organization of society and the economy.

> **Urbanization** is a term that refers to the clustering of population in increasingly large, dense, and diverse, cities over time. It also suggests the increasing globalization of cities' and urban processes' influence. Both of these processes indicate the relationship between the (re)organization of space and changes in the character of societies and economies.

Think, for example, of the rise of industrial capitalism in Britain. The development of a system of factory production necessitated large numbers of workers living close to mills and factories. Most of these workers had previously lived in rural areas but, by one method or another, were forced or encouraged to leave those places and to seek employment in a new type of place – the industrial city. This long transition from feudalism to capitalism was reflected in, and facilitated by, urbanization.

More generally, urbanization represents and reinforces a division of labor in society: urbanites generally cannot produce enough food to feed themselves; therefore, they rely on farmers in the countryside around the city and on producers all over the world. Similarly, these farmers need cities as a market for their products. Therefore, urbanization encourages and depends on systems of **commodification**, transportation, trade, marketing, and regulation that have global extent and influence. In turn, as cities grow and people spend more time working in waged employment, other divisions of labor and specializations develop. For example, groups of people are authorized to be bureaucrats and are paid to govern and manage urban social formations and landscapes. As Marx and Engels wrote, "the existence of the town implies ... the necessity of administration, police, taxes, etc.; in short of the municipality, and thus of politics in general" (Marx and Engels, 1845/1987: 69).

Development also suggests socio-spatial change, expressed in the urban built environment. While urbanization refers to the relationship between space and broad structures in society – capitalism, modernity, and so on – urban development can be understood as a more

> **Commodification** is the process by which an object, product, capacity, or even labor, a belief, representation, or piece of land is converted into an element of market exchange by being assigned a price. Once mediated by money, commodities are frequently more able to circulate through markets, being bought and sold.

> **Development** has many meanings, ranging from the global scale (international development), to the scale of the individual (personal development or self-improvement). For our purposes, it refers to the creation, destruction, and recreation of urban built environments over time – land, buildings, and infrastructure – for the purposes of producing and utilizing value of different sorts. It is driven by the interests of specific **elite** groups, often referred to as **growth coalitions** or growth machines.

Figure 1.4 Use value and exchange value in the urban landscape. Photo: Eugene McCann.

specific process; a purposeful one, driven by clearly defined interests. It refers to the creation, destruction, and recreation of urban built environments – land, buildings, and infrastructure – for the purposes of producing and utilizing value of different sorts.

We should think of value in terms of both *use* and *exchange*. If we take a privately
owned family house as an example, we can agree that, on an everyday basis, we value it
because it shelters us and it is a home, with all the meanings, associations, and memories
that that word connotes. Yet at certain times, for better or worse, its exchange value as a
commodity – a product that can be sold on a market – becomes paramount. In this sense,
the house is an asset for its occupant who may own it outright or who might be paying off
a mortgage (i.e., "renting to own" from a bank that holds the mortgage and profits from it
by charging interest). When the house was originally built, it was most likely also seen as
an asset by a developer hoping to sell it for a profit (for a value higher than the price of raw
materials, labor, and other costs necessary to build it). In the future, if it were to become
run-down or seen as obsolete, the land upon which it sits may be regarded by a new owner
as its primary source of value, rather than its use value, leading to its demolition and the
creation of a new house that is more valuable both in terms of use and exchange
(Figure 1.4).

Between these points of creation and destruction, use value and exchange value operate in parallel through the house's history. It becomes more than a building – a home – by being lived in. It becomes the place where relationships blossom, families grow, gatherings are held, food is prepared and shared. It is also a place where illness strikes, divisions occur, violence might unfold, separations are agreed upon, and deaths happen. The house's use value as a shelter is deepened through all these events. It is a place saturated with meanings and memory and a place in reference to which individual and collective identities are forged.

As all this is going on, the homeowner is also hoping that the house's exchange value increases. Furthermore, the house might be drawn upon in other ways for financial necessities. Perhaps a room or a whole floor will be rented out to a tenant to provide the owner with a little extra income or maybe the equity in the house (the portion of its value beyond the amount still owed to the mortgage holder) will be used as collateral to secure a loan to help fund repairs or medical bills. In all these ways, then, development – the building of a house on a piece of land in a neighborhood in a specific city, in a nation with a distinctive set of cultural norms around housing and particular rules around land ownership, and so on – ties use and exchange value together on an ongoing process of change.

We can take the lessons from this one house to think about all the houses in a city and all the other buildings and infrastructures that are valuable both because of how we use them and attach meaning to them (think of sports stadia). We can think similarly about how most buildings in a city can be bought, sold, destroyed, and rebuilt (think of sports stadia!). Using the notion of development to help us approach the city in this way emphasizes that the process of developing a place (of changing it through successive rounds of building, demolition, and rebuilding) as part of a wider process of urbanization, is very much a social one. It is a socio-spatial process both because of how social actors of various types engage in producing the built environment and because it is a process with consequences for how social life is lived.

This approach also raises important questions about who benefits and loses through development. Given that society is unevenly or hierarchically structured, with certain people having more resources and influence to shape decisions about what will be built and where, we can assume that not everyone benefits equally from development and change on the urban landscape. Thus, urban geographers are perfectly equipped to analyze processes of socio-spatial **uneven development** in cities and also to understand the political struggles that so often stem from and revolve around urban development proposals and neighborhood change. We return to this issue in Chapter 2 and throughout the rest of the book.

> **Uneven development** A process and condition that is both the product of and, crucially, the inevitable result of capitalist development. Uneven development can be expressed at all scales, from different levels of development in various parts of the world, to differences in development from neighborhood to neighborhood in a city. This concept (and most evidence) contradicts classical economists' argument that the economy tends toward equilibrium.

Urbanism

A second concept, **urbanism**, is used in two ways. On one hand, it often refers to architecture and design, as when public

> **Urbanism** is often used to refer to urban design (architecture, etc.). In this book, its other meaning is more prominent: ways of life that define cities in specific historical periods. These ways of life, of course, shape and are shaped by the design of urban built environments.

transit infrastructure or green architecture are referred to as examples of sustainable urbanism (Chapter 10 gives definitions of these examples). On the other hand, urbanism is a concept that refers to ways of life and interaction with others that are specific to cities at particular times in history. We will explore this connotation here, but it is worth acknowledging that the two uses of "urbanism" are not entirely separate: as we have already argued, urban built environments are both physical and social, and urban society both produces and is also shaped by urban landscapes.

Thinking of cities in terms of urbanism (ways of living and interacting that define identities and meanings in an urbanized context) helps us think about cities as *social* and *emergent* – lived places, produced and reproduced by people and, therefore, always changing and always reflecting the character of society at a particular time in history and in a particular place on the planet. Sociologists like Georg Simmel (1903/2002) and Louis Wirth (1938) developed the notion of urbanism as a distinct way of life in the early twentieth century. Looking at the rapidly urbanizing cities of Paris and Chicago, these scholars argued that city dwellers seemed to behave and interact differently than their rural or small town counterparts. Urbanites, living in the new type of industrial city that had so awed and disgusted the young Engels in the 1840s, were argued to be more alone than their counterparts elsewhere, even while (paradoxically) being crushed together in larger numbers and in tighter quarters than they might have been in rural villages. This form of urbanism was associated with the rise of industrialism, as we suggested above, and also with modernity. Urbanism as a way of life, according to these sociologists, involved people developing a protective shell around themselves, so as to manage their increasing interactions with larger and larger numbers of strangers.

One classic symptom of urbanism, they argued, was a blasé, individualistic, disinterested, or unconcerned attitude, with little eye contact made with strangers and little concern for the welfare of others, for example. Indeed, their ideas about modern cities resonated with those of Emile Durkheim, a French sociologist who argued that rapid change society, such as those wrought by industrial urbanization, produced "anomie" in people, meaning that they felt disconnected from their community and thus operated in an individualistic or asocial manner, rejecting accepted social norms of behavior (Durkheim, 1893/1997). In turn, this led to a breakdown in society, Durkheim argued, as individuals increasingly felt alienated from it. The individual was in a crowd, but made him/herself alone. Urbanism in rapidly growing industrial cities, Wirth and his colleagues in the Chicago School of urban sociologists (see below) surmised, was a new, often cold and alienating way of life.

Later studies questioned some of these assumptions, however. For example, Herbert Gans (1962) suggested that while urbanites might prefer to stay separate from, or anonymous in, the crowd while travelling to work, shopping in downtowns, and so on, they were also involved in building and maintaining strong community bonds at home in their neighborhoods. These were what Gans called "urban villages," like the Italian–American community of Boston's West End, which he studied in the late 1950s.

More recently, other urbanists have argued that how one lives and experiences urban life is influenced by a whole series of identities and differences, for example, gender, race, sexuality, age, class, and disability. Others have pointed out that Simmel and Wirth's notion of what characterizes urbanism in the modern city might only apply to *their* modern cities (specifically, those of the global North in the industrial age), while examinations of how people cope with urban life in, say, contemporary African cities is very different and perhaps less alienating (Robinson, 2006). We return to this issue in Chapter 2.

Urbanism is a complex and contested concept. It helps us focus on urban places as fundamentally peopled – how they live, how they negotiate processes of change, and how they manage their relationships with each other, with social processes and institutions like the economy and government, and with nature, the landscape, and the wider world.

Planning

The constant change that characterizes cities and their many spaces is not simply the result of individual decisions about how to build and extract value from property, for example. The **state** – the group of institutions that govern society – is also a crucial actor in the process of developing cities. **Planning** is the institution of the state that is primarily responsible for designing and managing how flows of investment circulate in and out of the built environment. Indeed, urban planning is a socio-spatial *process* in itself, since planning is a future-oriented activity in which actors of various types engage so that they can govern how development will take place.

Planning refers to managing and facilitating flows of investment and people as they circulate around urban landscapes. One of the key tools of contemporary planning is **zoning**, in which decisions are made – ideally in a rational, strategic manner that is for the common good – in which different land uses are separated from each other in a manner that is written down in policy documents (plans) and is, therefore, predictable. This system protects vulnerable people or land uses from being polluted or otherwise endangered by other activities. Zoning

State, the A set of institutions, including government and the law, that govern and exercise control over a particular territory. The term usually refers also to the people who work in state institutions – its agents, such as urban planners or police officers. Societies invest rights in the institutions of the state, such as the right to tax and to enforce laws. States are also charged with responsibilities, including providing infrastructure, social services, and so on. States' functions, rights, and responsibilities are divided among different scales. Urban geography deals with both the "local state" – planning, for example – and the ways in which provincial and national state bureaucracies, policies, and actions impact on cities.

Planning has many connotations. This book's focus is on urban and regional planning, which is a set of practices that emerged at the end of the nineteenth century to manage flows of investment into and around urban regions and to address crises (health, sustainability, etc.) that emerge with **development**. **Zoning** is an example of such a planning practice. Historically, planning was the purview of a few visionaries, funded by private donors, and often intent on designing model alternatives to the polluted, crowded industrial city. By the mid-twentieth century, planning had become a professionalized, bureaucratized **state** institution. Increasingly, since the 1980s, the **neoliberalization** of the state has meant that more elements of planning have been made private (e.g., the rise of private consultants contracting with the state). While many worry about the anti-democratic potential of this shift, others see hope in its ability to bring a wider range of voices to the table.

Zoning Cities are often separated into different zones, which then have restrictions attached to them in terms of what kinds of buildings and uses can be placed within them. Common examples include restrictions on the height of buildings, for instance in residential districts seeking to restrict high-rise development. A common use-based example is the restriction on types of businesses that can operate in certain areas, for instance a ban on industry, warehousing, or adult entertainment in residential areas. Zoning is a core feature of urban land-use planning.

regulations are likely to prevent a solid waste incinerator from operating next door to a school, for example. Zoning might also be invoked to prioritize the elite's version of the city, such as when strip clubs are prohibited from operating in certain residential areas identified as middle class but are allowed to operate in lower income areas (Hubbard, 2011). While both of these land uses have use values of one type or another, the problems that would be caused by their proximity make it socially desirable to separate them, at least according to some group's perspective.

Zoning also facilitates economic activity and the extraction of exchange value from the land. For example, the predictability that comes with written, enforceable zoning policies allows the owner of the house discussed earlier to assume that not only will its use value be protected to some extent (no polluting incinerator next door), but also that growth in its exchange value will be facilitated by policies that encourage similar properties to be developed around it and that discourage land uses that would diminish the house's value (that incinerator would also have a negative economic impact, as might a strip club). The company that owns the incinerator might also prefer for it to be located away from houses and schools. Zoning facilitates the agglomeration of similar activities in particular areas of cities and, by doing so, it helps these sorts of land uses to be located near crucial infrastructures and near similar businesses with which they might compete but with which they might also share certain common benefits of location.

As will be discussed in Chapter 2 and later in the book, planning and development are highly political and are often the objects of a great deal of political contestation. In these disputes – over whether new developments should replace farmland on a city's edges, whether social housing should be allowed in wealthy neighborhoods, or whether the gentrification of old working class neighborhoods by shiny new condominiums should proceed unchecked, for example – the state is a group of institutions charged with adjudicating the various private interests who are affected positively or negatively by development. As Chapter 2 will suggest, a critical analysis of planning as a state institution indicates that planning policies, like all other state policies, are not neutral but are the product of, and have an influence on, a society that is economically, socially, and spatially uneven.

Summary

While we often think of cities as epitomizing solidity, permanence, and concreteness (both literal and figurative), thinking of them in terms of urbanization and development, urbanism, and planning reminds us that their solidity and stability is only one part of the story. The city we approach on the plane or train is only fixed, solid, and stable when we think of it as a snapshot in time. If we think of what we see instead as one frame in a long movie, we gain a sense of cities as moments within longer trajectories of change or development. Like any epic movie, the city has numerous actors with various roles of various degrees of prominence. Like many epics, the landscape or setting is more than an inert backdrop but is, in fact, quite active in the narrative – imbued with meaning, identity, and value. Yet, unlike an epic film, cities do not have a single, all-powerful director who calls the shots. A critical perspective insists that they are the product of a wide range of structures, institutions, actors, and relations that operate hyper-locally within individual houses, streets, and neighborhoods, while also stretching far beyond municipal boundaries.

1.4 Urban Geography: Foundational Approaches

While most geographers would probably see some reflection of themselves in our descriptions of urban geographical approach, discussed above, it is important to acknowledge that there are numerous, more specific approaches in the discipline, each with their own particular concepts, characteristics, and objects of study. Geography is not defined by one paradigm or canon of work to which all geographers genuflect. Within the wide range of geographical scholarship, *urban* geographers represent a significant and vibrant subgroup. Like the discipline as a whole, urban geographers are a diverse group who study many things from numerous angles, even if they can be grouped together by their adherence to the sort of spatial perspective described above and by a common interest in cities and urban processes. As geographer Loretta Lees (2009) puts it, urban geography is "[t]he geographical study of urban spaces and urban ways of being." Here we will expand on this definition of urban geography by focusing on key ways in which urban geographers approach the city.

Urban geography, as a subdiscipline, is defined by a series of approaches (each based on a particular combination of concepts and methods and each dominant for a particular period of time), by the insights these approaches bring to our understanding of urbanism, and by the debates and critiques that emerge among the community of scholars over the merits and limits of each approach and of alternative approaches. This is not to suggest that, at some clearly demarcated point, one approach gets debunked, never to be mentioned again, while another gets anointed as the one that will offer newer, truer insights. Rather, the development of an academic subdiscipline is like a long, ongoing conversation in which current topics are always framed in reference to what came before. Defining the key approaches and concerns of contemporary *critical* urban geography, as is done in Chapter 2, needs at least some reference to the approaches of the past because, to a more or less explicit extent, these past approaches are still very much part of the present discussion, even if sometimes only as approaches contemporary urban geographers would like to critique or from which we would like to distance ourselves.

In this regard, it is impossible to ignore the influence of one group of sociologists on the development of urban geography and urban studies in the first half of the twentieth century. This "Chicago School" is discussed in some detail here, including how its work has influenced geographers. We will then briefly discuss how urban geography developed until the early 1970s. Chapter 2 will pick up the story of urban geography's development from that point on, because the early 1970s are usually understood to be the time when critical approaches emerged in the discipline.

Before there was Urban Geography: The Chicago School

Geographers came relatively late to the city as an object, landscape, or process to study. The modern city in the global North had been the object of sustained academic attention since approximately the turn of the twentieth century when sociologists became especially interested in the types of urban-social phenomena, such as inequality, loneliness in crowds, mixing and segregation, and immigration, that Engels and others had identified 50 years previously. From the 1910s onwards, a group of sociologists associated with the University of Chicago developed an approach to the city that remains, even today, foundational to urban studies literature. Inspired by the work of sociologists Georg Simmel and Emile Durkheim, and, especially, by attempts to apply Darwinian theories about natural ecosystems to understandings of new forms of social organization in the industrial age, these sociologists sought to analyze and understand that rapidly changing city developing around them.

We should remember that Chicago, in the nineteenth and early twentieth centuries, was a really new place. A significant part of it had burned to the ground in 1871, but by 1893 it hosted the World's Columbian Exhibition. The Exhibition was a massive world's fair that was intended to present the best of contemporary urbanism (in both the way of life and the design senses of the term) to the world and to advertise Chicago as a new force – a vibrant center of enterprise and innovation. The city certainly was a growing economic powerhouse in the late nineteenth century and in the early decades of the twentieth century. As a result, it attracted huge numbers of European immigrants, domestic rural migrants, and African–American migrants hoping to escape discrimination and poverty in the south of the USA.

Chicago, like London 50 years before, was a roiling landscape of rapid change and startling novelty. It was a place of art and innovation, and a place of segregation and violence. It generated great wealth while many of its residents lived in horrible poverty. It was, then, a modern city of light and shadow. And in all its extremes, contrasts, and innovations, it was a puzzling place – something new on the face of the earth. Perhaps not surprisingly, engaged sociologists were drawn to studying the city.

The Chicago School of sociology approached the city as a biological or ecological system. The Chicago School's approach was defined by its use of metaphors to equate natural processes (like the way species of plants find their best fit within an ecological system) with social ones (like the ethnic geography of a city in which people of the same ethnicity live close to each other). Other key concepts were competition, cooperation, territory, invasion and succession, symbiosis, natural areas, and community. In sum, they regarded the city as an **urban ecology** – the "natural" environment of "man."

Like Engels, the Chicago School placed great emphasis in understanding the city at street level through detailed ethnographic fieldwork, involving observation of and conversations with residents. It also went further by pioneering survey techniques that allowed it to supplement its fine-grained observation with knowledge of large numbers

Urban ecology, an iteration of the Chicago School's human ecology approach, borrows ecological concepts like invasion and succession, in an attempt to explain the organization of society in cities. This approach has been roundly critiqued (Chapter 2) and is no longer a prominent approach in urban geography, although it continues to provide an historical reference point.

of people living in neighborhoods across the city. In turn, it built generalizations, or models, out of all of its data (but see Box 1.2).

Box 1.2   The Hidden History of the Chicago School: Gender and Social Work

If we are to think about cities critically, one thing we must be willing to do is question taken-for-granted understandings of what social science is about, how social scientific knowledge has come about, and how common sense understandings of "valid" or "relevant" forms of research and knowledge have been used. The history of social science, in general, and urban studies more specifically, is full of cases in which certain stories have been hidden or forgotten.

The case of the Chicago School highlights how certain forms of knowledge and particular producers of knowledge can be marginalized and unfairly downgraded because those in power, either in society as a whole or in an academic institution, see what they say or who produced them as a challenge to dominant intellectual, social, and political paradigms. Geographer David Sibley, in his book *Geographies of Exclusion* (1995), recounts how knowledge of Chicago's changing society in the early years of the twentieth century was based in part on the work of women social workers, as well as male sociologists (social work and sociology had their own separate departments at the University of Chicago).

Working in and with Hull House, an institution in Chicago founded in 1889 by Jane Addams and Ellen Gates Starr to provide services and education to the city's largely immigrant working class, the social workers gained and published a great deal of valuable information on the way the city's society was changing. Yet, leaders of the Chicago School of sociology defined their discipline as scientific, while they labeled social work as feminine and less rigorous. Beyond suffering from this sexism, the women of Hull House were seen to have socialist leanings. Thus, they "suffered double exclusion" (Sibley, 1995: 167) and found "their contribution … lost from sight" Sibley, 1995: 170). As is discussed in Chapter 2, Sibley's hidden history is a clear example of how, as critical geographers, we must be willing to think critically about the world and also about the foundation of our academic concepts, debates, and histories.

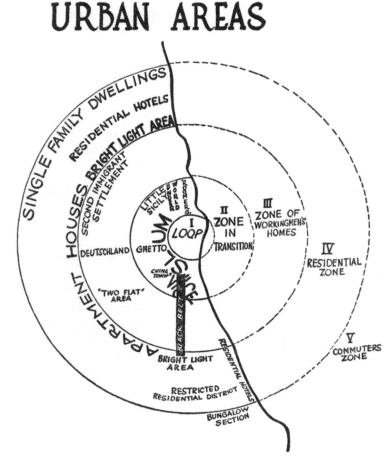

Figure 1.5 Burgess' Concentric Zone Model superimposed on the geography of early twentieth-century Chicago. Source: Park and Burgess (1925/1967: 55). Used with permission, University of Chicago Press.

Most famous of the Chicago School's models was Ernest Burgess' Concentric Zone Model, which every self-respecting urban geographer, even today, has an image of in their head and an opinion of on the tip of their tongue (Figures 1.6 and 1.7). The model reveals how the Chicago School's human ecology approach and its key concepts influenced its arguments about how cities, in general, work. It also epitomizes the limits of its approach that have come to form the basis for more recent critiques, which are briefly outline below and discussed more fully in Chapter 2. Figure 1.5 shows that Burgess's model was very much a product of its time and place. It establishes the term **Central Business District (CBD)** to describe the downtown as the center of the urban region.

Around it are a series of rings, defined roughly by the age of their built environments (oldest to youngest), their quality (least to best), their density (densest to less dense), and their value (least expensive to most). Overlaid on these gradients are references to the

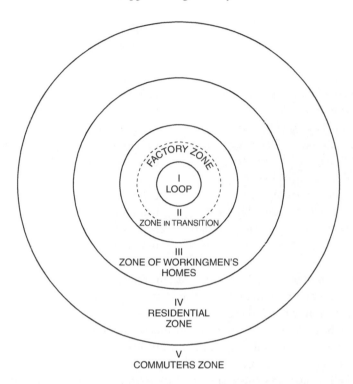

Figure 1.6 The abstract version of Burgess' Concentric Zone Model. Source: Park and Burgess (1925/1967: 51). Used with permission, University of Chicago Press.

class and ethnic character of the city's population, to neighborhood differentiation even within the zones, and allusions to the wider national and global processes that partially produce cities.

Figure 1.5 is the more concrete version, in which the Chicago context is clear. It describes a city of immigration – from Europe ("Deutschland," "Little Sicily"), Asia ("Chinatown"), and elsewhere in the United States (the "Black Belt"). These immigrants were largely poor, as can be seen in the references to apartment dwellings, rooming houses, and residential

Central Business District (CBD) The core of the city, where transport networks converge and land uses are dominated by retail and office functions. Commonly, especially in older global North cities like Chicago, this area has the densest land uses and the highest land prices. Since the mid-twentieth century in the global North, traditional CBDs face competition from suburban office and retail locations, often located at the junctions of major highways.

hotels (single room occupancy establishments for low income people). The city was, then, defined to a great extent by circumstances elsewhere and flows between various other places and Chicago. The model also describes an economically and socially segregated city. This is evident in the ethnic designations mentioned above, but also in its references to ghettos, slums, better residences, and bungalows.

The process of modeling is about abstracting from the concrete context to make generalizations and draw lessons. Figure 1.6 shows how the specifics of Chicago are reflected in a general model. Some of the terms, such as the CBD, and the zones of workers' homes, better residences, and the commuter zone, where people live in bungalows and travel to work in the CBD, are clearly related to the more concrete diagramming of Chicago.

> **Zone in transition** A key term in the Chicago School's ecological diagramming of cities. The zone in transition is the area around the Central Business District of global North industrial cities where a mix of land uses is found and where a general transition from residential uses to retail, office, and light industrial uses was identified by the Chicago sociologists.

Another key term is the **zone in transition**. In Figure 1.5, it can be seen that this zone, like the others, contains a lot of diversity that, in Figure 1.6, gets subsumed under a single label. Yet, while the other labels are relatively understandable, this "zone in transition" needs further explanation. It is the area of the city, surrounding the CBD, in which the Chicago School researchers encountered a mix of building types, qualities, and uses as well as a range of often low income immigrant, ethnic minority communities. They saw it as "in transition" because residential buildings were deteriorating and residential uses in the zone were being replaced by light industry and by the expansion of the CBD.

It would not be too much of a stretch to say that the notion of this transition in this zone did not refer only to the built environment, however. It also has a social connotation because, as discussed more in Chapter 2, the Chicago School's grounding in evolutionary metaphors like invasion and succession, and its tendency to subscribe to a vision of the American Dream in which new immigrants would work hard, succeed, and (naturally) move to new, bigger, houses as their incomes increased, led it to assume that new immigrants lives were in transition. This territory would, over time and as a result of a "natural" process of invasion and succession, see a series of new groups arriving while established ones either lose out in a competition for space or prosper and give up their existing territories as they move onwards, upwards, and outwards.

What this approach to understanding the city and its people means for how we understand cities and what limits it puts on our understanding is discussed critically in the next chapter. For now, what is important is to explore two ways in which the urban ecological approach to the city has progressed since the 1920s: how the model has been modified over time and from place to place and also how urban studies research has developed, based on and extending beyond the Chicago School approach. The first of these is dealt with here and the issue of the legacy of the Chicago School is left to the next section.

The original model prompted a small industry focused on modifying it to account for changes in the character of United States urbanism in the following 90 years. Those who found its abstractness too simplistic (those perfect concentric circles!) proposed taking account of how features such as rivers and railway lines modify the geography of business and residential land uses on a landscape. Homer Hoyt (1939), who we will meet again in Chapter 2, produced a sector model looking more like a sliced-up cake than a series of onion rings. Later, others working on sprawling auto-dependent cities took this logic further, noting that these regions were no longer focused on single CBDs and were, instead, characterized by multiple nuclei, scattered like a galaxy of stars. Beyond the United States context, the Chicago School models have travelled. They are common touchstones in discussions of cities in many places and some scholars have tried to modify them to different contexts. A prominent example of this is the Latin American City Model (Griffin and Ford, 1980), in which the standard rings are cross-cut by sectors defined, among other things, by the elite's tendency to reside closer to the CBD and along a major artery radiating out from it, rather than mainly in a suburban commuter zone.

Urban geography, from the Chicago School to the quantitative revolution

As urban geography emerged as a subdiscipline in the post-Second World War years, the legacy of the Chicago School was strong, as we have suggested above. There is a great deal of value in its approach, after all. It emphasizes the relationship between the character of the urban built environment and the character of contemporary society. Its adherence to a social form of Darwinism, for all its problematic consequences, did emphasize the important of process and change. The Chicago School's city was very much a city that was a *socio-spatial process*. Yet, as attempts to model and remodel cities proceeded through the twentieth century there was a tendency to favor *descriptions* of static, formal models, with their fixed, canonic zones, sectors, and nuclei. Form came to trump process; where questions seemed to take on more salience than how and why questions.

New generations of geographers in the 1950s and 1960s became uncomfortable with the consequences of this idiographic (descriptive) tradition. Indeed, they saw it as a dangerous legacy of the past that threatened to be the death of geography as a discipline because it made geography seem old-fashioned and of little relevance to the world's problems or to the cutting edge trajectories of contemporary social science. This new generation harbored a desire to make geography a scientific discipline; one characterized, not by description, but by a *nomothetic* (law generating) approach that can *explain* the processes going on in cities.

Their worked sparked the discipline's quantitative revolution in the 1960s and 1970s, in which geographers turned to forms of quantitative, locational analysis and **spatial science** in order to both identify economic laws that were common to how cities grew and changed and that, given their law-like character, could be applied to a wide range of different cities. In turn, the laws and the methods used to study cities became the basis for attempts to predict how urban processes might develop in the future. The quantitative revolution promised to make geography relevant to the state and business: planning agencies would call on geographers to consult on land use decisions and businesses would employ geographers to work for them in deciding the optimal location of their new offices, factories, or stores.

Spatial science emerged in geography in the 1960s as many geographers rejected ideographic (descriptive) approaches in favor of nomothetic (law generating) approaches. Major foci are the interactions of objects in space and the diffusion of phenomena across space, which geographers seek to quantify, measure, and model and, thus, explain and predict. While critical urban geography has tended to orientate toward qualitative, rather than quantitative analyses, there is no necessary reason why spatial science approaches cannot contribute to critical analyses of cities.

Yet, as we have already argued, the development of a discipline is not marked by clear breaks between different approaches. Instead, they overlap. In fact, in urban geography, more traditional forms of idiographic analysis continued through the twentieth century, operating in parallel with, or counter to, nomothetic, quantitative approaches. More interestingly, we can identify traces of the Chicago School's models even within the quantitative approach. For example, a prominent focus of quantitative urban economic geography in the 1960s and 1970s was on the factors that caused land uses to be positioned in certain parts of the city and the factors involved in those locations changing over time. While the Chicago School tended toward a mix of social and economic explanations for changes in neighborhood composition, always inflected with its Darwinian metaphors of course, quantitative geographers focused on economic trade-offs that individuals and business make between accessibility of a piece of land and its cost (land rent). This understanding that economic behavior is driven only by cost and use became formalized into **bid rent theory**, which predicted that higher-value land uses (e.g., commercial and retail) tend to gravitate towards the center of the city, outbidding lower rent-generating activities (e.g., housing), which are generally found in outlying suburban areas.

Bid rent theory assumes that the most expensive land is that located closest to the city center. Under bid rent theory, land's value decreases outward. Much like the concentric circles in a bullseye, the best target is at the center. The phrase "bid rent" comes from the idea that businesses or people would offer a price (bid) for prime location (rent), but that they might be outbid by others. This theory is thought to allow us to predict where certain land uses will predominate in a city.

Therefore, there is a location in the city (what planners today still call the "Peak Value Intersection") that is most valuable because it is very accessible. And because of its value and accessibility, it tends to be occupied by businesses that are willing and able to pay the highest rents in the city.

A simplified representation of this understanding of the city involves bid rent curves superimposed on the Chicago School's concentric zone model. In this model, the highest value locations are in the center of the city (the CBD) and, as Figure 1.7 shows, prices for land fall with distance from that location. If we turn the concentric zone model on its side and treat it as the x axis on a graph in which the y axis represents a particular type of economic activity's ability to pay rents in a particular place, then we can see rents curving away from the CBD towards the suburbs. This is, as we said, an admittedly simple version of the model and, clearly, the quantitative geographers who use it are intelligent enough to understand that it is an abstraction that does not take account of variations in the geography of the city or of other factors influencing social and economic decisions around land use. Nonetheless, what the bid rent model did was overlay a quantitative model onto the earlier work of the Chicago School.

1.5   Conclusion: Building on our Foundations

This introductory chapter has introduced a general approach to the city: one that emphasizes the relationship between urban built environments and social life. It, thus, sees the city as a socio-spatial process in which change is manifest on the landscape and continually negotiated and struggled over by individuals, communities, and institutions. The chapter also describes some of the key elements of the history of

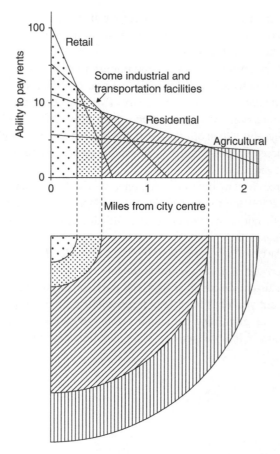

Figure 1.7 The bid rent curve. Source: Pacione (2009), Box 7.3, p.144. Used by permission of Taylor & Francis.

urban geography. These foundational approaches will now form the basis for the remainder of the book.

Outlined in Chapter 2 is the critical approach to urban geography that emerged in the 1970s, grew and flourished in the 1980s and 1990s, and continues to define the discipline today. Only by understanding the foundations of the subdiscipline can we have a good grasp of what the critical approach is being critical *about*. We will see that the notion of "critical" has some different aspects and connotations. Similarly, we will see that, as in earlier periods, legacies of past approaches can still be identified today, often as the basis for new critical approaches. If the city is a social product, continually in a process of change, so is critical urban geography.

1.6 Further Reading

- This book provides a particular approach to urban geography – the critical approach that is outlined in Chapter 2. On the other hand, Pacione's (2009) text, *Urban Geography: A Global Perspective*, is admirably comprehensive it its coverage of every aspect of the history and current diversity of urban geography. If you are interested in that history, or in other approaches, this is a great resource, as are these urban "readers": Fyfe and Kenny (2005) and LeGates and Stout (2011).

- Urban geographers develop their ideas and publish their research in academic journals. These are worth delving into. Journals with a specifically urban focus include: *Environment and Planning A*; *Environment and Planning D: Society and Space*; *Geography Compass* (urban section); the *International Journal of Urban and Regional Research*; *Urban Geography*; and *Urban Studies*. Also, the journal *Progress in Human Geography* is an excellent source of concise reviews of current research in numerous sub-disciplines, including urban geography.
- Excellent resources for any human geographer are the *Dictionary of Human Geography* (Gregory *et al.*, 2009) and the *International Encyclopedia of Human Geography* (Kitchin and Thrift, 2009). With access to these, you will almost never be lost for a definition of a key geographical term.
- Engels' book, *The Condition of the Working Class in England* (1845/1987) is a fascinating and powerful account of life in the industrial city.
- A key figure in urban discussions in many parts of the world (but especially North America) in recent years has been Jane Jacobs. Rather than simply hear or read about what she said about cities, read her classic book, the *Death and Life of Great American Cities* (1961) yourself. It is well written and powerfully argued.

Chapter 2

Cities for Whom?

The Contours and Commitments of Critical Urban Geography

Urban Geography: A Critical Introduction, First Edition. Andrew E.G. Jonas, Eugene McCann, and Mary Thomas.
© 2015 Andrew E.G. Jonas, Eugene McCann, and Mary Thomas. Published 2015 by John Wiley & Sons, Ltd.

2.1   Introduction

In Chapter 1 we outlined a geographical approach to the study of the world and, through the concepts of urbanization and development, urbanism, and planning, we outlined how geographers approach the city as a socio-spatial process. We also sketched some of the foundational approaches to cities that are still relevant to urban geographers, either as understandings to be built upon, or to be critiqued and built beyond. In this chapter, we will detail key themes in contemporary critical urban geography and use them to deepen our understanding of what is distinct about the critical approach. In particular, we ask the question: *Cities for whom?* This question draws attention to who benefits from how cities are unevenly and hierarchically organized. It encourages a focus on how urban spaces operate as unequal and unjust social and spatial processes.

Irrespective of their differences in philosophy and empirical focus, many human geographers feel comfortable describing their research as critical (Painter, 2000; Leitner and Sheppard, 2003; Blomley, 2008a; Best, 2009; Brenner, 2009; Wright, 2010a; Kobayashi, 2013). This is very much a good thing. As we suggested in the Preface, it would be difficult – if not foolhardy – to try to define a consistent view of what critical urban geography ought to be about. These things tend to boil down to personal motivations and experiences as well as being part of collective academic endeavor. And as we suggested in Chapter 1, the development of academic knowledge is a social process, somewhat akin to a long, ongoing conversation among a large and ever-changing group of people.

This book is an invitation to that conversation. So, how might you fit in? In extending the invitation, we assume that you already have a "basic membership." In other words, you are already an urbanist in a general sense because, by taking this course or picking up this book, you have shown an interest in cities, their societies, economies, politics, environments, and geographies. When joining an ongoing conversation, at a party or gathering, for example, it is wise to get a sense of the terms of discussion before wading in with one's own thoughts. What, then, are some of the basic understandings and principles that define the conversation among critical human geographers? What issues might help you define whether you feel comfortable with applying the label critical to your own approach to the city?

We break down the critical aspect of critical urban geography into three components in the following sections. From our perspective, critical urban geography means:

i.   Using urban studies as a way to *propose new concepts* that help shed light on how wider social processes and relationships operate and change. Part of this involves seeing urban space in relation to its constituent local-to-global connections.

ii. Developing research that is *socially relevant and politically engaged*. This includes (but is not limited to) thinking about the different ways in which urban space is a site of grassroots action, progressive intervention, and alternative forms of politics.

iii. Taking seriously the experiences, lives, practices, and words of *ordinary urban residents and marginalized social groups* rather than exclusively those of urban elites. This requires moving beyond a critique of dominant representations of the city to expose its ordinary geographies in all their diverse forms. It also entails moving beyond the traditional centers of urban theory to acknowledge difference in a world of cities.

Figure 2.1 The privatization of space, in this case in an exurban town called Plain City outside of Columbus, OH, has been a central concern for critical urban geographers. An exurb is typically outside of the suburbs and implies long commutes, big houses, and urban expansion into rural areas. This gated community restricts access to those with a magnetic pass, and the sign, "PRIVATE" could not be any clearer about who is welcome in this neighborhood and who is not. In fact, the Darby Lakes gated community is surrounded by farmland, with a trailer park of low income, prefabricated, semi-permanent homes very nearby – perhaps the residents of the trailer park are supposed to be the audience for the "Private" sign? Photo courtesy of Janel Luker.

In this chapter, we also reflect on the key foundational approaches, methods, and assumptions that were discussed in the previous chapter by showing how they have been, and continue to be, built upon or debated by critical geographers. We also highlight the diversity of both the urban world and the multidisciplinary field of urban studies by highlighting different emphases and theorizations that frame approaches to critical urban geography. We conclude by emphasizing that being critical does not mean being negative and we argue that asking *"Cities for whom?"* is a positive questioning of the existing world, looking forward to a better world in the future.

Once you have read this chapter, you should be able to answer the following questions:

- What does it mean to be a *critical* urban geographer?
- How did critical geography develop as a series of approaches?
- What approaches set critical urban geography apart from other approaches, such as liberal ones?
- What are three key aspects of critical urban geography and how are they related to specific case studies of research?
- How do critical geographers engage with activists and communities outside academia?

2.2   Developing Critical Urban Theories and Concepts

David Harvey is an influential urban geographer who was one of the first to consider the city from an explicitly critical perspective. In *Social Justice in the City* (1973/2010), Harvey took aim at the severe limitations of liberal and positivist approaches to understanding urban processes. He argued that to understand and change cities for the better, we must shift the focus away from seeing urban problems solely in terms of their physical, cultural, or environmental characteristics, as the Chicago School did in its analyses (Chapter 1) or in entirely abstract ideal terms, as most dominant forms of economic analysis tend to do. These perspectives are, Harvey argued, "liberal in that they recognize inequity but seek to cure that inequity within an existing set of social mechanisms" (Harvey, 1973/2010: 136). He showed how the workings of the urban land market were inextricably connected to wider social relations and to the way in which capital moves around, or circulates, as he put it, looking for the best locations in which to be invested, or fixed, and to generate profit (Harvey, 1982/2006).

In this and subsequent work, Harvey argues that if the conditions of lower or even middle income people in cities are to be improved, these wider forces and contexts must be dismantled, rather than merely tweaked through zoning regulations, reinvestment, new financing schemes, or service and infrastructure improvements. In practice, he argues, this radical reworking of contemporary urbanization, development, urbanism, and planning must involve a critical analysis of the scarcities and inequalities "in a private market system for land and housing," in which "the value of the housing is not always measured in terms of its use as shelter and residence, but in terms of the amount received in market exchange, which may be affected by external factors such as speculation" (Harvey 1973/2010: 138).

Briefly consider this argument in the light of our discussion of the use and exchange values of the privately owned house in Chapter 1. While it is important to understand a house in terms of its specific use and exchange values, Harvey also emphasizes the wider economic context that allows and encourages some people in society to own property while others cannot or do not. Banks will not lend money to just anyone who wants to buy a house (or, when they do, they may demand interest rates or set terms that are damaging for the borrower, as the 2008 financial crisis showed – a topic that we will return to later in this book). Thus, the private property market reflects, enforces, and often exacerbates existing economic inequality in a capitalist system that is harshly competitive and that operates by exploiting unevenness among workers' wages, nations' taxation and regulatory systems, the evaluation of social groups' races and ethnicities, and among cities' zoning regulations – to name just a few examples.

People with more wealth and social acceptance have a greater command over space in that they have the resources to choose more places to live (Chapter 4). On the other hand, those with less are often forced to rent in places that are not best suited to their well-being and are often vulnerable to the vagaries of the land market (i.e., they might find themselves evicted from their home if their landlord sees an opportunity to raise rents). For Harvey, the social and political goal stemming from his academic analysis is to replace the capitalist urban land market with one in which land is "a social (as opposed to a private) good" (Harvey, 1973/2010: 138).

Gentrification and the "rent gap" as critical concepts

Whether or not one agrees with Harvey's solution to this issue, the pertinent question for us here is how, in critical urban geography, political positions emerge from the creation of critical urban theories and concepts. Take the way neighborhoods change over time as an example. In Chapter 1, we saw how the Chicago School saw neighborhoods as "natural areas" for particular populations, and in line with its ecological approach, it saw change in the social character of those neighborhoods as inevitable and natural. Furthermore, its acceptance of the **myth** of the American Dream, in which impoverished but hard working immigrants are believed to be able move up the socioeconomic hierarchy and concomitantly move out from the inner city to bigger and better housing in other concentric zones, led them to see neighborhood change as desirable.

> **Myth** A narrative about the world that is not necessarily completely untrue, although it tends to resonate with and support particular interests over others. Myths resonate deeply with their audience and provide an agenda and legitimacy for action.

In its more formal, economistic guise – bid rent theory – this approach understands decisions on where to locate to be driven only by individual choices and the cost of land. This is, as Harvey argued, an approach to urban neighborhood change that ignores the ability of different classeses to command space; that highlights individual, supposedly rational choices and preferences ("consumer sovereignty") over larger forces and structures, such as private property and **speculation**; and that suggests that "suburban wealth and growth, juxtaposed with inner city poverty and decline [a]re all natural, logical, and inevitable" (Lees *et al.*, 2008: 46).

> **Speculation** Investing in buildings or land, not primarily to use, but to hold for a period of time, in the hope that their price on the market will increase so that they can then be sold again for a profit.

Through the 1970s, especially in major global North cities such as London and New York, a movement of middle class people was evident, but not out to the suburbs. They moved to particular inner city neighborhoods. At the time, popular descriptions of this shift were not accompanied by useful explanations of how and why it was happening, despite the fact that the process contradicts the standard logics of bid rent theory. Based on his research on gentrifiers in the Society Hill neighborhood of Philadelphia, Harvey's student, Neil Smith (1979), was skeptical of the notion that these people were mostly moving "back to the city" from the suburbs, as opposed to moving from other middle and upper class neighborhoods within the city. For him, what was happening was "a recentralization and reconsolidation of upper and middle class white residences in the city center" (Smith, 1996: 54) and a movement of some capital investment back from the suburbs to the city.

Smith also doubted the idea that the revitalization of places like Society Hill in Philadelphia was an unmitigated good. Instead, he emphasized the way that elite choices about where to live (their relative command over space) constrained the options of lower income people – populations who also tended to be racial minorities. Thus, he sought to

> **Gentrification** is the process by which urban neighborhoods, usually the home of low income residents, become the focus of reinvestment and (re)settlement by middle classes. This process is seen in the redevelopment and upgrading of housing and retail landscapes. Socially, it is frequently represented by displacement of existing residents as rents and property taxes rise. The process is now expressly encouraged by many local states, which hope to gain more amenities and higher tax revenues. While originally associated with the redevelopment of older buildings, the process now also includes "new build" gentrification, where neighborhoods are razed and new buildings are built from scratch.

explain *how* the conditions necessary for **gentrification** were being created in certain neighborhoods and *who* was profiting from the process.

By employing the term gentrification, rather than the more neutral "neighborhood change" or the celebratory "revitalization," Smith put class at the heart of his analysis. He developed a theory of gentrification that spoke back to, and also radically reworked, some of the descriptions of the Chicago School and the bid rent theorists, while extending beyond the idea that this new process was simply the result of the individual preferences of increasing numbers of sovereign consumers. The first step in thinking about gentrification critically, as Smith showed, is to accept that:

the gentrifier as consumer is only one of many actors participating in the process. [Other actors include] builders, developers, landlords, mortgage lenders, government agencies, real estate agents – gentrifiers as producers … [T]he relationship between production and consumption is symbiotic, but it is a symbiosis in which the movement of capital in search of profit predominates. (Smith, 1979, 1996: 57)

> **Sweat equity** is a term used to the increase in value of a building, usually a dwelling, that comes from the labor put into renovations by its owners, rather than paying a contractor to do the work. By sweating to decorate and upgrade their house, these owners hope to see its value in the marketplace increase. The term is commonly associated with gentrifiers who move into older historic buildings (houses, lofts, etc.) early in a neighborhoods' gentrification when even small physical upgrades can translate into significant increases in value.

The second, related, step is to acknowledge that those who invest their money and **sweat equity** to rehabilitate an inner city building do so with the hope that they have made a sound investment that will not result in a loss (see our discussion of why white, gay, middle class men gentrify areas of New Orleans in Chapter 8). The balance between the economic imperative and other, cultural reasons for moving to a particular neighborhood has been hotly debated in the gentrification literature over the subsequent years (Lees *et al.*, 2008), including by feminists who question whether gentrifiers must always be assumed to be heterosexual, married couples (Bondi, 1991). Undoubtedly, however, Smith's key point – that a "theory of gentrification must … explain why some neighborhoods are profitable to redevelop while others are not" (Smith, 1996: 57) – remains crucial to a critical perspective on the changes we see around us in cities in most parts of the world today.

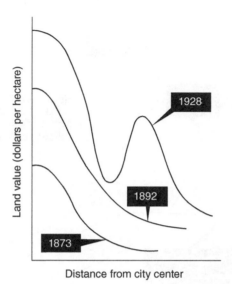

Figure 2.2 Smith's rendition of Hoyt's land value curve (compare with Figure 1.7). Source: After Hoyt 1933. From Smith, Neil. 1979, "Toward a Theory of Gentrification: A Back to the City Movement by Capital, not People," in Journal of the American Planning Association, Vol. 45:4, pp 538–548. Used by permission of Taylor & Francis Ltd.

This geographical question – a question of the uneven development prospects of different neighborhoods – ties Smith's approach back to Harvey's discussion of the circulation of capital and reworks the Chicago School and bid rent models. Drawing specifically on studies of Chicago in the 1920s and 1930s conducted by Homer Hoyt (who is known for, among other things, modifying Burgess' concentric zone model into a sector model of urban ecology [Hoyt, 1939]), Smith noted a longstanding problem with the notion that land values (bid rents) decreased smoothly from the Central Business District to the suburbs. As Smith's rendition of Hoyt's research shows (Figure 2.2), a distinct "valley in the land value curve between the Loop and the outer residential areas … indicat[ing] the location of those sections where the buildings are over forty years old and where the residents rank lowest in rent-paying ability" (Hoyt, 1933, quoted in Smith 1979, 1996: 60) had developed by the early twentieth century.

While Hoyt had merely commented on this as a puzzle, Smith developed an explanation based on the dynamics of capital investment in cities: for a period of time, say 40 or more years, after capital investment is fixed in a neighborhood (i.e., when the neighborhood is built up), it is economically unfeasible to redevelop it by tearing down existing buildings and building newer ones. It is unfeasible because it takes a long time for investors to get their money and profit out of the built environment after they invest in it. For example, they need to use land and buildings for a business or through charging rent in order to gradually recoup their investment. Therefore, they are unlikely to see the economic benefit of destroying or reworking the built environment they have recently invested in, in order to build something new. Furthermore, for capitalists looking to invest in a built environment, the cost of demolishing or reworking a relatively new built environment is prohibitive, compared to finding an empty piece of land on which to build. Thus, other capital circulating around looking for places to be invested is likely to avoid existing built-up neighborhoods in favor of undeveloped ones.

Cities for Whom?

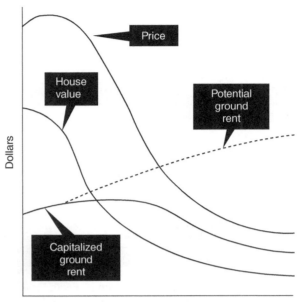

Figure 2.3 Smith's development of Hoyt's diagram to show the evolution of the rent gap. Source: After Hoyt 1933. From Smith, Neil. 1979, "Toward a Theory of Gentrification: A Back to the City Movement by Capital, not People," in Journal of the American Planning Association, Vol. 45:4, pp 538–548. Used by permission of Taylor & Francis Ltd.

The amount of economic return an owner can receive from a piece of land and its building(s) tends to decline over time, unless money is invested in maintenance and renovation. Therefore, the difference between the economic return from existing, older properties in a neighborhood, and the potentially higher returns that might accrue if these old buildings were demolished and replaced, increases over time. At some point, the difference between the income that can be squeezed out of existing buildings through rent and the potential income that might be charged for new or remodeled buildings on the same land becomes great enough that the cost of demolishing or renovating the old buildings is worthwhile. Smith labelled this difference the **rent gap** and argued that it explained a great deal of what was happening in gentrifying neighborhoods (Figure 2.3). The rent gap, then, is a concept with a critical edge. It does not merely describe, it explains. Through its explanation, it connects specific circumstances to wider forces while also identifying the

Rent gap As land and property values in parts of the central city undergo decline, a gap emerges between the actual value of property (ground rent) and its potential value should the property ever be redeveloped to its "highest and best use." Gentrification processes occur when developers and property owners purchase and rehabilitate such property and sell or rent it at a higher value than the cost of initial acquisition, thereby closing the rent gap. The rent gap describes *in theory* what happens to property values in former working class districts the city. In reality, patterns of investment and disinvestment can change dramatically from block-to-block and neighborhood-to-neighborhood in any given city.

Figure 2.4 Graffiti on a storefront in a gentrifying neighborhood of Barcelona, Spain, reads "Stop Speculation." Not only does it indicate the existence of a critical politics around speculation in the city's land market, but the fact that the slogan is written in English ("stop"), as well as in Catalan ("espekulació"), emphasizes that local protestors have a critical geographical awareness that such speculation can flow from places beyond one city or country. Gentrification is, as Neil Smith argued, a global urban strategy. Photo: Eugene McCann.

social conditions and consequences of changes in the urban built environment, rather than focusing on individual consumer preferences.

Gentrification is a particular expression of wider social relationships and the general process of capitalist uneven development, linked in intricate ways to the specificities of particular neighborhoods (including their proximity to downtown business districts, amenities, transit lines, etc.) and to the experiences of individual actors in the land market (Lees *et al.*, 2008). Approaching gentrification critically through the concept of the rent gap allows us to refute the notion that neighborhood change is natural and helps us to identify the agents involved in driving the process – those who tend to benefit from it (the "gentrifiers as producers" in the quote by Smith above; also, see discussions on the growth coalitions in Chapter 7 and artists as gentrifiers in Chapter 11). Crucially, the concept of gentrification also draws our attention to those who tend to lose out as a result of waves of investment in the urban land market – particularly, the low income residents (who are disproportionately minorities and migrants in many cities) of older neighborhoods who are displaced as reinvestment drives rents and property taxes higher.

In turn, this approach facilitates and necessitates a focus on the power dynamics and politics of gentrification. The impacts of gentrification are continually debated and struggled over in cities around the world. And for good reason. It has profound material impacts on many people's lives and is the object of various forms of political activism, from campaigns conducted by urban planners, the real estate industry, and politicians to promote revitalization, to opposing forces that question the benefits of real estate speculation (Figure 2.4).

Being critical by combining the abstract and the concrete

David Harvey writes that the development of the concept of the rent gap emphasizes that to be critical in one's approach to cities involves:

> the self-conscious and aware construction of a new paradigm for social geographic thought through a deep and profound critique of our existing analytical constructs. This is what we are best equipped to do. We are academics, after all, working with the tools of the academic trade. As such, our task is to mobilize our powers of thought to formulate concepts and categories, theories and arguments, which we can apply to the task of bringing about a humanizing social change. These concepts and categories cannot be formulated in abstraction [as the modelers discussed in Chapter 1 did]. They must be forged realistically with respect to the events and actions as they unfold around us. (Harvey, 1973/2010: 145)

Harvey was one of the first urban geographers to make the move from studying the particularities of urban space to making critically engaged statements about society and social relationships.

The analytical move from the particular and local to the general and global was later developed in Doreen Massey's approach to the urban question in the 1980s (Massey, 1984). She was interested in countering the argument that the causes of inner city decline in the United Kingdom were mainly to do with problems intrinsic to the city itself, such as the presence of a supposed culture of unemployment due to people lacking requisite skills. She criticized a tendency in public policy to "blame the victim" (i.e., inner city residents) when the causes of urban decline clearly lie elsewhere in wider society – in, for example, changes in the location and skills requirements of industry associated with the search for more profitable outlets for production and capital accumulation on a global scale. Massey (1991, 2005) went on to outline a way of thinking about space (especially urban space) that focuses on local–global connections and interactions (Chapter 4).

Following Massey's approach, we should not see the city simply as an *expression* or *effect* of wider social relationships. Rather, there is something about urban space (public and private) that *makes a fundamental difference* to how wider social, economic, political, and environmental processes work out in practice. Critical urban geography should likewise inspire us investigate cities as places where global processes, networks, and social relationships come together in uneven and also unique ways. Space is not a closed box within which wider global social processes operate; rather, space makes a difference both in terms of what sorts of global processes come together in the city and the kinds of locally unique outcomes that result from the gathering together of a variety of social relations in urbanized places (see Martin, 2003, on "place-framing").

2.3   Social Relevance and Public Action

If critical urban geography is partly defined by the development of specific types of concepts, it is also shaped by a commitment to urban change and proactive engagement with the different groups of people – publics – who shape and are shaped by urbanization, development, urbanism, and planning. Certainly, most urban geographers are well equipped to demonstrate the public policy relevance of their research. As we have mentioned, many groundbreaking books in urban geography have made questions of public welfare and social justice central motivating themes. When pursuing critical analysis – research that is both intellectually rigorous and politically engaged – it is important to think carefully about how different urban spaces and urban publics offer a variety of opportunities for informed grassroots action and interventions.

Public urban geographies and the right to the city

We might think of these interventions as public geographies, involving geographers both writing books that are read beyond academia and that engage directly with various nonacademic readers and activists (Ward, 2006; Fuller and Askins, 2007, 2010; Fuller, 2008). While this is not necessarily a call for direct political action, it recognizes that most urban geographers are interested in cities because they want to understand and improve the lives of those who live and work there. To do so, many find it necessary to convey their analyses in the public sphere.

For example, and as we suggested above, gentrification is a topic of intense debate. One of the main bones of contention is the notion (or ideal) of different social groups living in proximity to one another (i.e., "social mix"). Proponents of gentrification often argue that low income neighborhoods and low income people will benefit from social mix – that is, when their neighborhoods also house middle class people. This happy talk is, unfortunately, not borne out by the evidence of four decades of detailed urban research, which suggests that, in gentrifying neighborhoods, the classes hardly ever mix in positive ways. The happy talk of social mix is able to be so happy, so idealistic in the face of most available evidence, because it blithely ignores entrenched social and economic divisions in contemporary society. This happy talk is also backed by powerful interests (those profiting from gentrification), which are, unfortunately, also the perspectives most represented in popular media.

There is little point in critical academics sitting in offices complaining that no one reads their (unpopular) journal articles, however! There are other ways to engage in public discussion. A recent debate in Vancouver, British Columbia, Canada, highlights one way in which critical urban geographers engaged in public discourse and brought their analyses to bear on local government decision making. Box 2.1 contains an extract from an editorial in the local newspaper in which the argument that social mix would benefit existing low income residents of Vancouver's gentrifying Downtown Eastside neighborhood was questioned.

Box 2.1 suggests that, if cities and society are to be analyzed critically – if they are to be changed for the better – the fundamental question – the *critical* question – is: *Cities for whom?* The titles of two books by prominent urbanists provide general responses to the "for whom?" question: *Cities for the Many, Not the Few* (Amin *et al.*, 2000) and *Cities for People, Not for Profit* (Brenner *et al.*, 2011). Critical scholars also understand cities to be important *sources* of social change. The title of a recent book by David Harvey (2012) underscores this point: *Rebel Cities: From the Right to the City to the Urban Revolution.*

Box 2.1   Opinion: Mixed Neighborhoods Not Always a Good Idea.
Marginalized Groups Least Likely to Benefit

by Martine August, Lisa Freeman and Nicholas Blomley, Special to the *Vancouver
Sun*, 2 January 2014
(http://www.vancouversun.com/travel/Mixed+neighbourhoods+always+good+
idea/9344177/story.html)

Policy-makers believe that socially mixed communities are healthier, safer, and
more vibrant, and will attract investment, tourism, and economic development. It is
suggested that social mix is beneficial for low-income people, providing employment
and social capital, curbing crime and promoting "better" behaviour and neighbourhood reputation. It also appears intuitively appealing: to oppose "mix" is to foster
"segregation," it seems.

It's not surprising, then, that social mix is often invoked in relation to the
Downtown Eastside. [...] Put simply, the scholarship shows that the supposed beneficiaries of social mix, the poor and marginalized, do not often end up as winners.

While an appealing ideal, the literature points to two big problems with social mix.
First, the benefits promised for low-income groups do not materialize. International
research examining mixed public housing redevelopment, for example, reveals that
improvements in employment, income, educational outcomes, youth delinquency,
and health are not achieved.

Even worse, strong social networks and positive bonds of community – common
features in low-income areas – are often permanently damaged by efforts to "deconcen-
trate" poverty and promote social mix. While social mix is believed to foster a more
inclusive society, the research-based evidence suggests that marginalized groups are the
least likely to benefit from these policies, and may even be worse off as a result of them.

A second problem with social mix involves the ideal of social cohesion. Recent
studies indicate that rather than enhancing community, new residents are much less
likely to engage in neighbourhood social interaction than longtime low and middle-
income residents. When interactions do occur, they are often marked by tensions.

Shattering the "myth of the benevolent middle class," research finds that higher-
income newcomers often use their political know-how and influence to fight against
services for the poor, or to target the activities of marginalized people in public space.
In some communities, tenants are encouraged not to socialize outdoors, hold barbe-
cues, or allow their children to play outdoors, as these activities offend or frighten
wealthier neighbours. Far from fostering social cohesion, these trends speak to unequal power relations and social exclusion.

The problem with social mix is that it assumes an even playing field between people. However, people who have more resources, and stronger property rights, have a
clear advantage. The uncritical adoption of social mix in the Downtown Eastside,
therefore, could lead to the displacement of the many low-income renters who do not
have secure tenancies. Social mix, in other words, could lead to social homogeneity.
Ironically, then, creating forms of inclusionary planning that provide some protection for low-income renters, may be the only way in which downtown Vancouver can
continue to be socially diverse.

The idea of a **right to the city** draws from the work of French urbanist Henri Lefebvre, particularly his book, *Le Droit à la ville* (1968), which was published in English, as part of a larger collection of his work, in the book *Writings on Cities* (1996; see also Harvey, 2003; INURA, 2003). Described by Harvey (2008) as a right to "[t]he freedom to make and remake our cities and ourselves," and as "one of the most precious yet most neglected of our human rights,"

> the right to the city is far more than the individual liberty to access urban resources: it is a right to change ourselves by changing the city. It is, moreover, a common rather than an individual right since this transformation inevitably depends upon the exercise of a collective power to reshape the processes of urbanization. (Harvey, 2008: 23)

Developed and critiqued more recently by many other academics (Dikeç, 2002; Purcell, 2002, 2003; Mitchell, 2003; Fenster, 2005; Marcuse, 2009; Mayer, 2009; Parnell and Pieterse, 2010; Attoh, 2011; Samara *et al.*, 2013), the right to the city is a concept that has been frequently used to critique the **neoliberalism** of contemporary cities. Neoliberalism is an ideology and diverse set of policies and practices based on the idea that the private market and so-called market mechanisms offer the best way to organize and govern society.

Appeals to freedom, choice, and individuality by contemporary politicians tend to be based on neoliberal ideology, as do attempts to downsize government, privatize government functions, and deregulate markets, for example (Brenner and Theodore, 2002; Peck and Tickell, 2002). The right to the city, then, focuses attention on the role of ordinary people in opposing the erosion of the urban public realm by private sector redevelopment

The right to the city is a phrase coined by Henri Lefebvre in 1968 to describe working class struggles for political participation and access to physical space in the city. The right to the city is a central concept in contemporary urban activism and in urban geographical scholarship. It focuses attention on the role of ordinary people in opposing the erosion of the **urban public realm** by private sector redevelopment and in shaping urban political space in a much more democratic and socially inclusive fashion than hitherto possible under mainstream or modernist visions of citizenship and public participation.

Neoliberalism (and neoliberalization) Neoliberalism is an ideology that has become widespread since the 1980s. Its followers, including most contemporary politicians, believe that the competitive free market is the most efficient way of organizing the economy and society in general. It is manifest in government programs to privatize formerly public institutions and economic sectors, from health care to housing, and to deregulate industries like finance. In cities, it is manifest in the outsourcing of state activities to the private sector (e.g., refuse collection) and the reframing of cities as competitive entities and as commodities to be sold (see **urban entrepreneurialism**, Chapter 7). Thus, its rhetoric is that of "smaller government," although, in reality, the process of *neoliberalization* happens through the actions of state institutions that facilitate privatization and deregulation. The process is also highly crisis prone. Therefore, the state is often needed to bail out the worst failures of neoliberalism (as in the recent economic crisis). Needless to say, neoliberalism is a major focus of political debate around the world.

and in shaping urban political space in a much more democratic and socially inclusive fashion than hitherto possible under mainstream visions of citizenship and public participation. This concept is discussed in more detail later in the book.

For now, what is pertinent is the way in which this academic concept has travelled, both beyond university classrooms and also beyond Europe and North America, to become a motivating slogan for many activists pushing for change in cities. A Google image search will quickly reveal the array of places and campaigns in which this idea of a right to the city for ordinary people has taken root (e.g., http://www.righttothecity.org/index.php/about/mission-history). Examples include: opposing the enclosure and privatization of public spaces, housing, and infrastructures in places as diverse as Cape Town and Hamburg; advocacy for these resources to be held in common and available to all in Dublin and Rio de Janeiro; opposing gentrification in Montreal and fighting slum clearance in Chennai; questioning the veracity of government consultation processes and asserting grassroots decision making in The Hague and Santiago; resisting austerity measures in Athens and Madrid; and developing alternative (noncapitalist or hybrid) economic spaces like food cooperatives, credit unions, complementary currencies, local exchange and trading systems, online sales and "freecycling" in cities all over the world (see Chapter 12).

Occupying urban space and urban political discourse

The "Occupy" movement is a recent example that has made the explicit link between struggles to change cities and attempts to promote social justice more generally through its use of the slogan, "Another City is Possible, Another World is Possible" (Figure 2.5).

Doreen Massey is one critical geographer who has engaged with Occupy directly. She lives in London and, in October 2011, she visited the Occupy camp located outside St. Paul's Cathedral, just a few steps from the London Stock Exchange. Occupy activists in various cities around the world attempted to use their camps as spaces of learning and debate. In London, a "Tent University" was organized, and Massey spoke to large audiences there. We discussed some of Massey's key contributions over the years in the previous section. Currently she is most known for her conceptualization of place, space, and the opportunities for counter-hegemonic politics, that is, attempts to think about alternatives to currently **hegemonic** neoliberalism (in which every aspect of social life is subject to the needs of the market), and efforts to move "towards a new political era and new understandings of what constitutes the good society" (Hall *et al.*, 2013: 3; see also Massey, 2011).

In an interview in 2013 (Social Science Bites, 2013), Massey reflected on her time at the camp and its relationship to opportunities for social change. When asked how space and politics are linked, she replied:

> **Hegemony** and "hegemonic" are terms often used in a general sense as synonyms for dominant and widespread. More technically, the concept refers to a variety of coercive and noncoercive strategies used by a ruling class to control and regulate the behavior of other classes. What is crucial, in both senses, is that hegemony is never complete, that is, a class or idea is never completely dominant. It can, and likely will, be questioned, resisted, and perhaps overturned at some point in the future.

Figure 2.5   Possible cities, possible worlds. Occupy's largely urban strategy of taking public spaces emphasizes the importance of cities in promoting more general change and in providing settings for raising questions about what sort of a society most of us would like to live in. Source: Occupy Wall Street, #anothernyc/anothernyc.org.

> There's loads of ways. For instance Occupy, do you remember Occupy London, that group of tents? I got a little bit involved, in fact I gave a couple of lectures in the university tent [see European Revolution (2011)], and what struck me very strongly was how spatial their politics was. For one thing there was a huddle, a very unpretentious low huddle of tents between vast stone edifices of God and Mammon on each side of it. And almost the very unpretentiousness of those tents was an affront to the pretentiousness of Saint Paul's and the London Stock Exchange. … Somehow in its very presence it was asking questions that were too deep to ask.

Emphasizing the importance of engagement and debate among different publics, including academics, Massey continued:

> And what I think they did was to create a new kind of space. One of the things that neoliberalism – if one can use that awful word – has done to our cities, is to privatise a lot of what was public space, and that's one of the things the Occupy people, and lots of other people have complained about. … What I think Occupy did which fascinated me was to create public space in a more meaningful sense because they created a space, and people didn't just pass by

each other on the way to work or shops or whatever; they talked, they conversed, they argued. There was argument going on in the tent, there were people on the steps of Saint Paul's arguing with each other. While I was there people who had nothing to do with the occupation came up to me and asked questions and talked and it seemed to me that what they managed briefly to create there was a really public space, which means it was a place for the creation of a public, of politically engaged subjects if you like, of people who would talk to each other about the wider world. And it seemed to me that that was a real creation of a space of the kind that we need a lot more of. A space that brings us together to talk and to argue about the kind of future world we want.

Occupy and the wider, more established anti-globalization movement have focused their protests and occupations on cities, as have social movements at other times in history. They have literally taken space in places like Seattle, New York, London, and Frankfurt to make their points about social justice (Figure 2.6). Recent movements for democratic change, in places as diverse as Tunis, Cairo, Bangkok, and Kiev have similarly had an urban focus, often claiming significant public spaces in central cities, like Tahrir Square in Cairo, to make claims about how society should change. Critical geographers have had a longstanding interest in urban public space, what it means to different people, how it relates to citizenship, how it is being changed by the state and capital, and how it is being contested and

Figure 2.6   The Occupy camp outside the European Central Bank, Frankfurt, 2012 (Box 2.2). Photo: Eugene McCann.

Figure 2.7 Police kettling Blockupy demonstrators, Frankfurt's Westend neighborhood, 2012. Photo: Eugene McCann.

Box 2.2 The Right to the City and State Control: Occupy and Blockupy in Frankfurt, Germany

The Occupy camp outside the headquarters of the European Central Bank (the central bank of the Euro currency) in Frankfurt-am-Main, Germany, was one of the longest standing camps in Europe, existing from October 2011 until August 2012. It was a visible taking of urban space to make an argument for a different organization of society and the global economy. Yet, the way that it was located meant that, generally, it did not hamper the ability of the local financial industry to operate. The state's tolerance did have its limits, however. When activists from across Europe travelled to the city in May 2012 to support the camp, protest austerity measures, and with the clearly stated goal of stopping workers in the financial sector accessing their offices (the protest was dubbed "Blockupy"), authorities acted to prevent them from reaching the city at all, temporarily broke up the camp, and vigorously policed the protest (while advising workers to work from home if possible). In Figure 2.7 a group of Occupy supporters is being "kettled" (constrained or corralled) by police in a residential neighborhood adjacent to the city's downtown after they broke away from a larger protest march.

appropriated by ordinary people and activists. The general insight from this work is that the "publicness" of public spaces like squares, sidewalks, and parks cannot be taken for granted – it must be seen in historical, cultural, and geographical context and must be understood as developing and changing in complex ways.

This is borne out by the way state institutions in different parts of the world have reacted to Occupy and recent democratic change movements. Reactions have ranged from limited acceptance (as long as protestors stay in particular areas, for example), to the enforcement of bylaws (prohibitions on sleeping in parks, for example, and the many arrests made when protestors refused to disperse), to outright violence (like the various shootings, beatings, pepper-sprayings, and disappearances that have been meted out to protestors in cities around the world in recent years). These reactions further emphasize the symbolic and practical importance of urban places to the operation and legitimacy of contemporary social and economic systems and to movements' intent on changing them.

The purpose of this book is not to answer the "cities for whom?" question definitively (although "the many" and "for people" are better answers than "the few" and "for profit"). The purpose of this book is to introduce you to a critical, geographical approach to cities that identifies how they shape and are shaped by contemporary society. After all, without analyzing the city, we cannot hope to change it. Like the Occupy movement, critical scholars can raise questions, create opportunities for argument, provide concepts (like "gentrification" and "the right to the city"), analyze social processes in ways that offer opportunities for thought and action, and join alliances with activists and community members.

2.4   Ordinary Urbanism in a World of Cities

Being critical means being willing to question even the most apparently concrete orthodoxies in our thinking. The way the concept of the rent gap has been poked, prodded, and debated since Neil Smith introduced it (Lees *et al.*, 2008) is a good example of how critical geographers tend to productively question concepts that are themselves fundamentally critical. And in the spirit of openness to continual critique, we certainly hope that you will think critically about the arguments we present in this and subsequent chapters and that you will explore them by questioning them. In this section, using the idea of ordinary urbanism, we will outline how critical urban geography continues to develop through theory development and critique while, at the same time, we explain how a focus on the experiences, lives, practices, and words of ordinary urban residents and marginalized social groups is a third distinctive element of a critical approach to cities.

Critical geographies beyond the academy

There is a long tradition of urban geographical investigation concerned with the lives of ordinary people and how they make use of urban space. Early work in this vein sought to challenge mainstream views that the urban spaces we use and encounter on a daily basis, such as parks, playgrounds, residential neighborhoods, and so on, are uninteresting because they are not exceptional or particularly important. By looking at ordinary urban lives and spaces, humanistic geographers such as David Ley (1983) were able to demonstrate that the mundane use of urban spaces is a worthwhile topic of inquiry precisely because of what it reveals about how people themselves experience and impose meaning on those spaces.

This is important because it is another form of analysis that links the abstract with the lived or concrete. Analyses that are overly abstract tend to lend themselves to policies that are justified by appeals to some (usually elite) definition of the common good. For example, **urban renewal** programs associated with powerful bureaucrats like New York's Robert Moses in the mid-twentieth century justified the destruction of entire neighborhoods and the displacement of their residents by arguing that a freeway or a public housing development was a better land use for the city as a whole and that the experiences and fears of those who protested were invalid in the grand scheme of things. By turning the narrative of what makes a good city on its head, by making the experience of ordinary people and neighborhoods central to their analyses, opponents of urban renewal, like Jane Jacobs, were eventually able to change dominant ideas of how to redevelop cities (Jacobs, 1961; Flint, 2011).

It has generally been the case that the best critical urban geography involves direct engagement with people and communities by researchers who also maintain a focus on the wider structures and forces to which those communities are connected (Elwood, 2006). A pioneer of this method of inquiry was the radical geographer Bill Bunge, who led the Detroit Geographic Expedition in the late 1960s (Bunge, 1969). The goal of the Expedition was to encourage encounters between academic urban geographers and "folk geographers" (ordinary people without formal training as geographers) including members of the city's African–American community. The Expedition created maps of Detroit that showed how things were at the time and how they ought to be: so-called "oughtness maps." Bunge envisioned urban geography as a people's project that required mapping the city with a view to achieving alternative geographies of social and racial justice. Paraphrasing a famous statement by Marx about the role of philosophers, Bunge argued in one of the Expedition's publications that "it is not the function of geographers to merely map the earth, but to change it" (Bunge, 1969, quoted in Kanarinka, 2013).

> **Urban renewal** generally refers to extensive state-led redevelopment in mid-twentieth century Europe and in North America. It frequently razed established neighborhoods and replaced them with new retail districts, housing projects, and highways. State bureaucrats wielded their urban renewal powers not only to address self-evident urban problems but also to define certain neighborhoods and people (especially racial minorities and low income people) as problems to be remedied or banished. The term is less used today, largely due to its negative connotations, but the state's fondness for erasure of the old in favor of the newly built is still evident. Urban renewal has long been an object of political struggle, often related to anti-gentrification politics.

Critical geographies beyond the global North: Ordinariness, difference, and decentering urban theory

So far in this chapter and in Chapter 1 we have discussed examples from cities in the **global North**. We have shown how important concepts recognized by urban geographers all over the world, like concentric zones and the rent gap, emerged in reference to cities

Global North /global South Over the years, the uneven development of the world and its cultural differences have been defined by general terms, including First World, Third World, West, Non-West, Developed, Less Developed, Core, and Periphery. Global North and global South are the commonly accepted general terms in contemporary critical geography largely because they do not necessarily connote a hierarchy in the ways that most of the others do.

like Chicago. Does this mean that all useful theories of how cities work emerge from scholars in the global North? Does it mean that all cities in the world can be understood through the experiences of a few cities like Chicago, New York, London, or Paris? Sometimes, reading urban geography literatures, it might appear that scholars would answer "yes" to these questions! But this would be far from true. In fact, the geography of urban geographical knowledge – where influential theorists and theories come from and which cities are the common referents for discussions among urbanists – does not reflect some natural order of the most important or most informative cities and theories. Rather, this geography of knowledge is very much an uneven geography of **power**.

Power (A) is commonly thought of as being something that some people or institutions, such as elites like the members of growth coalitions, possess and wield. Others, in this view, tend to be powerless. There is much truth to this view, yet power can also be usefully understood to be widely distributed in society and always productive of capacities to make change, even among those who might normally be seen to be powerless. Critical geographers, as a group, use the concept in both these ways. Fundamentally, power is the result of social interactions in the present, in the past, and always in places. It is a key concept when studying urban politics, broadly defined, where coalitions of like-minded people come together to enhance their capacities and, thus, their interests.

Scholarship and research also contain a legacy of uneven development across the world – one where certain languages (English) have become dominant, through colonialism, for example, where certain wealthier countries' academics (those in the United States and the United Kingdom, for example) have been better paid and better funded to conduct research, to attend academic conferences, and to publish findings, and where the most respected academic publications are based in only a few countries. Given this legacy, the stories we tell and are told about the urban world can become very narrow. Should Chicago still be such a major reference point for our understanding of the urban world when very different places – in China, India, Brazil, or South Africa, for example – have long

being experiencing significant urbanization and have been developing their own technologies for managing it (Figure 2.8)?

This question leads us back to our argument that thinking critically entails both studying urbanization, development, urbanism, and planning in the world but also being willing to critique our own assumptions, reference points, and approaches as part of our academic discussions. An important debate among urban geographers in the last decade has been about this very issue. A key figure in this debate is Jennifer Robinson. A South African who was educated and is working at universities in and around London, Robinson is both an

Figure 2.8 Urban transit in Johannesburg, South Africa: Thokoza Park Rea Vaya Terminus. The main route of Johannesburg's Rea Vaya Bus Rapid Transit (BRT) system began operating in August 2009 as the first full-feature BRT on the African continent and carries an average of 40 000 riders daily. This steel, glass and concrete station at Thokoza Park enables pre-boarding fare collection and fare integration between routes (on BRT, see Wood 2014a and 2014b). Photo courtesy of Astrid Wood.

urbanist and an Africanist. Studying African urbanism in a discipline heavily influenced by theories developed in reference to North American and European cities and by discussions of only a few cities considered as the most globally important and influential in terms of economic control and social change (Chapter 4 provides a full discussion), Robinson (2002) lamented all the people and places that were quite literally left off of the map of contemporary urban studies research.

Developing the theme further in her book, *Ordinary Cities* (Robinson, 2006), she notes how the Chicago School, global cities researchers (Chapter 4), and many other academic urbanists tend to put the experiences, priorities, and concepts of the global North, or the West, at the center of their world view in a way reminiscent of colonial mind-sets. While these powerful theories often claim or are assumed to possess near-universal resonance, Robinson and others take a **postcolonial** stance to suggest that they are actually quite parochial visions of the urban world – ones that, through their deep associations with certain places, institutions, and intellectual traditions only tell a limited story. They only offer a limited degree of analytical insight into the wide diversity of contemporary global urbanization, development, urbanism, and planning.

Nonetheless, theories and case studies from the global North are frequently represented in the literature as universal and, therefore, central to global understandings of cities.

Postcolonialism In one sense, the term refers to an epoch: the present period after most formal colonialism has ended (although it is important to note that former colonizers still maintain many economic advantages rooted in their former colonial adventures). More pertinent is the definition of postcolonialism as a set of related critical approaches. Postcolonial analytical and political approaches: take seriously the power of naming, categorizing, and language (see **global North/global South**); critique dualistic thinking like East/West and the ways that dualism stigmatizes certain people and places outside of Europe and North America; emphasize the importance of acknowledging researchers' identity and social position in analyses; question "Development" when understood as a singular trajectory toward some ideal form of advancement; and seek to locate dominant theories in particular places so that they cannot be assumed to be universally true or real beyond the very specific contexts of their origin (thus "provincializing" or "decentering" them).

The task Robinson and others have set themselves is to parochialize and decenter urban theory by offering new approaches based on studies of different contexts that disrupt or question dominant understandings of how cities operate and that show how our theories *come from* particular places, with all the specificities that their provenance entails. This brings us back to how critical geographers must develop new concepts in order to develop their analyses, since new concepts change our perspective and allow us to see the same urban processes from a different angle – to avoid "privileging the experiences of only certain types of cities in our analyses" (Robinson, 2006: 108).

Concepts like "ordinariness," "cityness," "periphery," and "worlding" have been central to attempts by scholars working in the **global South** to decenter urban geographical understandings. Robinson argues that to think differently about cities we must explore different forms of urbanism in different cities (Figure 2.9), do so in reference to the wider flows that shape cities, and strive to "appreciate the potential creativity and dynamism of all cities" (Robinson, 2006: 108), rather than seeing some cities as more modern, developed, dynamic, and more worthy of attention than others. We should, in other words, pay attention to the apparently mundane cities and forms of urbanism that exist around the world as much as we should pay attention to apparently cutting-edge and paradigmatic places and ways of life.

A focus on ordinary cities leads to examples of urbanism that contradict standard, hegemonic stories about how cities and urban life work. For instance, Robinson questions the notion – developed, again, by some Chicago School scholars – that people who live in modern, crowded cities tend to be guarded or blasé in their interactions with those around them (Chapter 1). While there is some truth to this argument, Robinson uses a discussion of the building of community among people living in Zambian cities to suggest that we cannot assume that a loss of community will always necessarily happen with the rise of modern cities. The Zambian case, where "urbanites have generated fictive kin, eagerly sought to make connections where none really existed, carefully nurtured neighbors and family, built communities and defended difference" (Robinson, 2006: 9), might at least raise critical questions about how we know, and what we know, about cities.

Making community in this way involves many minor acts, like sharing food, taking care of others' children, or engaging in longer conversations with neighbors. While these need

Figure 2.9 An ordinary school day in Kochi, India. Many scholars examining children's urban geographies focus on everyday activities for kids, and what they tell us about kids' abilities to play freely, be healthy, and have education opportunities. Photo: Mary Thomas.

not always necessarily create community across lines of difference (Valentine, 2014 gives a strong argument to this effect), they very often can and do. As such, many critical scholars argue that these small interactions not only make community, but make the city. Indeed, "cityness" is a concept developed by another critical urbanist, Abdoumaliq Simone, a sociologist who engages closely with geographers and shares Robinson's concern for postcolonializing urban studies. For him, "[c]ityness refers to the city as a thing in the making" (Simone, 2010: 3). Based on his research on everyday life, informal economies, and livelihood strategies in a range of African cities, such as Dakar, Pretoria, Kinshasa, and Abidjan, as well as in Jakarta, Indonesia, he argues that cityness "may only be identifiable in the hundreds upon hundreds of small initiatives that affect, even unwittingly, some kind of articulation" (Simone, 2010: 16), rather than in the grand schemes of the state to make certain cities globally prominent or economically viable, in a formal sense. "Still," he notes:

> cityness remains at the periphery of our attention. … the periphery can be "brought back in" to our considerations of urban life … [by considering] cities that have been at the periphery of urban analysis or which embody urban processes and realities that have largely been left out when these cities are taken into consideration. (Simone, 2010: 14)

How, then, are critical urbanists seeking to position supposedly ordinary and peripheral places and ways of life – particularly those in the global South – closer to the center

Figure 2.10   A woman carries goods through a market in Hanoi, Vietnam. Photo courtesy of Sarah Turner.

of contemporary urban research and analysis? Simone, for example, seeks to rework the concept of periphery itself. Traditionally in discussions of global economic development, the periphery was the hinterland where not much was going on – a place that should be made more developed, more modern, more like the core, developed world. Simone identifies elements of the periphery that highlight not its backwardness, but its vibrancy; he emphasizes what can be learned from the periphery, not what needs to be fixed.

Living a peripheral life in the periphery of a peripheral city does not mean that one is abject, meek, or helpless (Figure 2.10). Rather, Simone provides vibrant examples of the ways in which people, as individuals and as part of networks and communities, invent ways of making a living and making a life through legal and illegal means in cities that are off the radar screen of most urbanists. Scaling his argument up to the level of urban policy, he argues, in a vein similar to Robinson, that "cities can effectively operate in the world without having to adhere to a uniform set of prescriptions [of how to be economically successful]…

Instead cities must find their own particular way to … make themselves something more than eligible sites of inward investment … [and] be active players in making new kinds of economic relationships across different scales and spaces" (Simone, 2010: 15).

Worlding is another concept that has been proposed recently as a way of reorienting urbanists' perspectives on cities, thus opening our vision to alternative aspects of urbanization, development, urbanism, and planning. The notion of worlding has been explored by Ananya Roy, who writes about Asian cities like Calcutta, Mumbai, and Shenzhen in her work. A planning professor who, again, works closely with geographers, Roy notes, first of all, that global South cities and people are positioned within a global regime of material and symbolic power through which they tend to be "worlded," or understood to be part of the world, only through reference to dominant global North perspectives. They are positioned in certain ways on the periphery of the presumed global North center and then are understood narrowly in relation to that positioning. This, she argues, is worlding in the domain of states and corporate actors, something that she hopes critical urbanists can question "by highlighting the remaking of core-periphery geographies and thereby urban claims to the global future" (Roy, 2011: 312; McCann *et al.*, 2013).

Indeed, her related argument is that global South cities are more than merely peripheral in a formal economic sense: "worlding is much more than the control of global economic functions; it is also the transactions of those "most marginal from these new economic capacities" (Roy, 2011a: 313, quoting Simone 2001: 16). The concept also highlights how ordinary people engage in worlding themselves and their cities by migrating, trading, working in resource extraction, engaging with tourists, or with extended cultural communities. Thus, worlding is always an incomplete and emergent process. Its contours are continually changing and changeable as people find ways to world themselves and their cities through various types of social practices.

2.5 Positively Different, Positively Critical

As critical urban geographers, we must take difference seriously and position it centrally in our understanding of cities. Difference connotes who has resources to live well or to live at all; who is allowed to live without being persecuted, stigmatized, or assaulted. Who is able to command space in their cities and in the world makes a difference to people's everyday lives. Difference also influences whose theories of the city are elevated, read, engaged, and built upon…and whose are not. We want to emphasize that debates over concepts and key terms are not just esoteric academic gymnastics. Our language and concepts *matter*: they put frames around our thinking and our vision. They help us focus on certain elements of the world while letting us ignore other places, people, and processes that, for one reason or another, have been defined as less relevant. The danger, of course, in a complex and interconnected world, is that what is beyond the frame is, in fact, often very relevant. Reframing – questioning, debating, adjusting, or changing our concepts and terms – allows us to focus differently on the world and see elements of city life that have previously been outside of our vision. Using new or reframed concepts allows us to be open to think critically about and act in the urban world in all its diversity.

This chapter suggests that thinking critically and engaging in critique (of the urban world and of urban studies) are productive activities. The term "critical" does have a negative connotation in common language, however. Being critical might be understood to involve tearing people or things to shreds and leaving the parts scattered on the ground. Therefore, we want to conclude our discussion of the contours and commitments of critical urban geography by emphasizing the positive elements and outcomes of approaching cities critically. We have argued that the crucial critical question for urban geographers is: *Cities for Whom?* This is not a negative question. Quite the opposite, it is a question that looks to identify the subjects of a better, more socially just city.

As suggested above, critical geographers should not necessarily expect to define the characteristics of how such a city will be organized. Indeed, in many ways, critical academics draw their understandings from the innovative practices and visions of urban residents and urban social movements. As Massey noted in the case of Occupy, and as we continue to see in various uprisings from the Arab Spring to Ukraine to Thailand, ordinary people are perfectly capable of envisioning and struggling over possible (urban) worlds. The way in which the notion of the Right to the City has travelled from academic urbanists into social movements across the world exemplifies that there is a great deal of value in critical academics' ability to analyze cities and to offer ways of thinking about – and thinking differently about – urbanization, development, urbanism, and planning. This, after all, is what we are trained to do.

As a critical urban geographer in training, you have the ability ask critical questions and question dominant wisdoms about cities. We hope that the following chapters will provide you with ways to pose those questions – to critique what (and who!) is wrong with cities as well as to discover potential and existing alternatives. If your urban geography classes involve research projects, you might be able to research a topic that is of interest not only to you but that has been identified by a community group, activist organization, or politically engaged student club as something they would like to learn more about. In doing so, you will be able to both learn and act at the same time.

2.6   Further Reading

- Many of the books and articles we cite in this chapter offer useful insights into the subarea of critical urban geography. The journals we mentioned in the Further Readings section of Chapter 1 are excellent sources for cutting edge critical work on cities. Furthermore, the journal *City* presents urban issues from a broadly critical perspective, while the journal *Antipode* does the same for all of human geography.
- As we have argued, to be a critical urban geographer is to be engaged with the world. This means making a habit of consuming news and opinion from local, national, and global sources on a daily basis. Ask your instructor which sources from your city and country she or he would recommend.
- In this chapter, we have mentioned some web sites of activist organizations. Find the web sites of activist organizations whose causes motivate or excite you and follow them.

Chapter 3

Production, Economy, and the City

Urban Geography: A Critical Introduction, First Edition. Andrew E.G. Jonas, Eugene McCann, and Mary Thomas.
© 2015 Andrew E.G. Jonas, Eugene McCann, and Mary Thomas. Published 2015 by John Wiley & Sons, Ltd.

3.1   Introduction

You can get a bird's eye view of the economic geography of Chicago by visiting the Observatory in the John Hancock Center, one of the tallest buildings in the downtown area known as the Loop (you can also go to Google Earth and rotate the view to scan the area online; see the screenshot in Figure 3.1). Surrounded by government office buildings and corporate skyscrapers, your first impression might be that wealth and economic power is spatially concentrated in the center of Chicago. From the Hancock Center, you can spot the headquarters of companies like United Airlines in the Willis Tower or the Boeing Corporation to the west across the Chicago River at 100 North Riverside Plaza. You can also see how the density of high-rise office buildings decreases sharply once you get beyond the river.

As you look toward the southwest you might just be able to pick out the site of the old Union Stockyards, where for more than a century cattle were slaughtered and processed into canned meat in a prototypical form of mass production. The site of the stockyards is now occupied by new housing developments. Further in the distance you can see signs of abandoned buildings and aging infrastructure where the steel mills and auto shops of the South Side once operated. To the northwest you see a very different kind of urban landscape. You catch glimpses of planes landing and taking off at O'Hare, one of the busiest airports in the world with its own concentration of high-rise offices and hotels. You might

Figure 3.1   Screenshot of Chicago's Loop facing west. Source: Landsat, Google Earth.

wonder if this is a separate downtown, competing with the Loop to attract investment and employment.

From your vantage point, you start to get the impression that economic activity in Chicago is not all that spatially concentrated, after all; instead it is dispersed across a wide region. Like an archipelago in a sea of sprawl, the city's economic sphere of influence seems to follow major freeways and industrial corridors into a vast suburban hinterland comprised of islands of low-rise industrial units, office parks, downtown areas, and sprawling housing developments. Some of the largest corporations in the world are headquartered in suburban Chicago, far from the Loop's impressive verticality. These include Walgreens (a retail pharmacy chain), McDonalds Corporation (billions and billions of hamburgers served), Abbott Laboratories (a pharmaceutical and health care products company), and the Allstate Corporation (an insurance company), to name just a few examples.

Chicago's pattern of land uses and the distribution of economic activities across the metropolitan region has fascinated several generations of urban scholars. As the home of the Chicago School of urban ecology in the early twentieth century, Chicago became famous for inspiring concentric zone urban models (Chapter 1). Once upon a time, scholars and students attributed land use patterns in such models to competition for the highest and best use of space in the central city (see the discussion of **bid rent theory** in Chapter 1).

Today, however, critical urban geographers question whether a model like that of the Chicago School or a theory like bid rent accurately predicts the richly textured and complex spatial patterns that have a global economic impact, and can be observed from the Observatory in the Hancock Center. For example, industrial land uses between the Loop and the working class inner suburbs have been displaced by new housing developments, suggesting that upscale housing now commands higher rents and taxes in the city than traditional manufacturing industry. Today, you are just as likely to encounter abandoned factories and crumbling infrastructure in the suburbs as in the inner city, and some parts of downtown Chicago have even managed to retain traditional industrial activity as well as to attract newer high technology industry.

Urban development is not static and fixed – as was once suggested by the classical models of urban structure like the Chicago School's – but is instead, to borrow a term used by Karl Marx to describe capitalism, restless. Critical urban geographers are intensely interested in how the underlying logic of capitalism can be read into the restless urban landscape (Knox, 1993). However, urban scholars now look to sprawling cities like Los Angeles rather than just Chicago for their critical inspiration. There the geography of urban development seems to have flipped. Urbanization no longer gradually spreads *outwards* from the central city towards the suburbs like the ripples created after a single stone is dropped into the middle of a pond. Instead urban development seems to spreads *inwards* simultaneously from several suburban and exurban centers like multiple ripples emanating from stones scattered throughout a pond.

Viewing urbanization from a regional and global perspective contrasts with the earlier emphasis on the city as a distinctive socio-ecological terrain. Throughout the history of urban geography as a discipline there has been a tendency to separate the urban as a social space from the region or the globe as an economic space. This separation was even reflected in early Marxist accounts of the city, which defined the urban as the space of collective consumption and the region as the space of production (Saunders, 1981). Your focus in this chapter should instead be on exploring the connections between urbanization and regional development processes in global capitalism. You will consider how the spatial circulation of capital through the built environment leads to a differentiation of metropolitan space into distinct spaces of economic activity.

By the end of the chapter, you should be able to answer the following questions:

- What is meant by planetary urbanization and how is it reshaping urban economic space?
- What is the relationship between urbanization and the regional dynamics of the production system in capitalism?
- How do changes in the geography of production and the division of labor at a global scale map onto metropolitan space?
- What is the relationship between finance capital and the ethnic, racial, and social geography of the city?
- How is the economy of the inner city being reshaped by gentrification?

3.2   Urbanization and the Regional Dynamics of the Production System

We now live in a world where more people live in cities than in rural areas. The United Nations predicts that by 2050 cities will house almost 70% of the world's population (United Nations, 2012). Given that many advanced capitalist countries such as the USA already have urbanization levels well above 80%, it might be assumed that "percentage urban" is a good measure of economic development in a particular country. Aggregated national statistics tend to conceal vast differences in wealth and poverty within and between cities, however. In many of the world's great cities, from Rio de Janeiro and Mumbai to Los Angeles and Seoul, spaces of conspicuous wealth and consumption exist alongside areas of extreme poverty and destitution (Davis, 2006b).

Accumulation. The drive to accumulate capital is definitive of capitalism. Capitalism is a system that exploits social relationships, so that wealthier classes can profit from the labor power of poorer classes. Excess capital comes from the difference between the labor power of the working classes plus the cost of production, and the money paid for the goods they produce. Thus, the ability to accumulate capital under capitalism involves the production process as well as the social relations of waged labor. When labor and production costs are kept low, then accumulation is higher. The drive to accumulate means that capital is always searching for ways to maximize accumulation.

National indicators of economic development are becoming less meaningful in a world where urbanization occurs on a planetary scale (Brenner, 2013). Urbanization is so extensive, in other words, that it has become increasingly difficult to distinguish urban economies from "national" ones. The phrase planetary emphasizes the centrality of urban economies across space at the global scale. This section considers how urban economies became planetary over time and how urban development now drives global economic growth rather than the other way round. It encourages you to consider how critical urban geographers approach the relationship between **accumulation**, urbanization, and capitalist development.

Accumulation, urbanization, and capitalist development

The origins of capitalism in Feudal Europe are often attributed to changes in the countryside, including the enclosure of common land, the dispossession of the peasantry, and the emergence of a new class of agricultural wage laborers. However, the conditions for urbanization were established well before the development of capitalist modes of industrial production in Europe and North America. In fact, cities predate the rise of industrial capitalism by several centuries, if not millennia. In *Cities and the Wealth of Nations*, Jane Jacobs (1984) offered a persuasive analysis of the historical role of cities in the development of global trade. She argued that the basic architecture of the modern world economy was based not on nation-states (which appeared around the sixteenth century) but instead on much older city-regional economies, each specializing in the exchange and trade of commodities and services over long distances. Well before the rise of the modern nation-state and the world economy, cities provided focal points for the accumulation of wealth and power under modes of production ranging from slavery to mercantilism.

For example, in late-Medieval and Renaissance Europe (the Golden Age of mercantile production) proto-global cities fostered networks of trade and commerce throughout the Mediterranean, eventually extending their influence to the New World and the Far East. In this early phase of globalization, new urban institutions, such as guilds, stock exchanges, and courts of justice, enabled city-based merchant elites to dictate the terms of international trade. Elites in cities such as Genoa, Constantinople (Istanbul), Barcelona, Amsterdam, Paris, Venice, and London laid the foundations for a later phase of economic globalization in the eighteenth and nineteenth centuries, which took the form of colonialism and the spread of wage labor to the periphery, eventually creating an **international division of labor** based on the exportation of manufactured products and the importation of raw materials.

As places began to specialize in producing manufactured products, so different cities grew, prospered, or declined during different periods of capitalist development. Indeed, historical patterns of urbanization can say quite a lot about the wider dynamics of production and regional development in capitalism. You

International division of labor. Labor is unevenly valued across space. In the past, colonial or imperial states, and now, transnational corporations, can take advantage of this unevenness by locating to places where labor is cheap and plentiful. Under colonialism, labor was often coerced by the power of the gun and then by the introduction of capitalist economies that required people to have wages to pay for basic needs. The international division of labor refers to the global asymmetry of labor value and connotes the power of capital to exploit labor by moving between places. It is vital to remember that the regulation of labor by states affects the international division of labor. For example, state policies that protect labor by supporting fair labor practices, unionization, and worksite safety might deter transnational corporations from hiring in that place. Thus, the international division of labor also becomes uneven through state policy, and the lack of policy encourages transnational, capitalist investment in places where labor is not only cheap, but less regulated and protected by the state.

Table 3.1 Ranking by population of the top 10 urban places in the USA, 1800, 1900, 1950, 2010.

	1800			1900	
1.	New York City, NY	60 515	1.	New York, NY	3 437 202
2.	Philadelphia, PA	41 220	2.	Chicago, IL	1 698 575
3.	Baltimore, MD	26 514	3.	Philadelphia, PA	1 293 697
4.	Boston, MA	24 937	4.	St. Louis, MO	575 238
5.	Charleston, SC	18 824	5.	Boston, MA	560 892
6.	Northern Liberties township, PA	10 718	6.	Baltimore, MD	508 957
7.	Southwark District, PA	9621	7.	Cleveland, OH	381 768
8.	Salem, MA	9457	8.	Buffalo, NY	352 387
9.	Providence, RI	7614	9.	San Francisco, CA	342 782
10.	Norfolk Borough, VA	6926	10.	Cincinnati, OH	325 902

	1950			2010	
1.	New York, NY	7 891 957	1.	New York, NY	8 175 133
2.	Chicago, IL	3 620 962	2.	Los Angeles, CA	3 792 621
3.	Philadelphia, PA	2 071 605	3.	Chicago, IL	2 695 598
4.	Los Angeles, CA	1 970 358	4.	Houston, TX	2 099 451
5.	Detroit, MI	1 849 568	5.	Philadelphia, PA	1 526 006
6.	Baltimore, MD	949 708	6.	Phoenix, AZ	1 445 632
7.	Cleveland, OH	914 808	7.	San Antonio, TX	1 327 407
8.	St. Louis, MO	856 796	8.	San Diego, CA	1 307 402
9.	Washington, DC	802 178	9.	Dallas, TX	1 197 816
10.	Boston, MA	801 444	10.	San Jose, CA	945 942

Source: U.S. Census Bureau.

can get some sense of these dynamics by examining the population ranking of the 10 largest urban places in the United States in four different time periods from 1800 to 2010 (Table 3.1).

In 1800, the pattern of urbanization in the US captures the initial settlement of the eastern coastal states (i.e., the former colonies) and the emergence of entrepôts (port cities) having trade links to Europe and the slave economies of the American South, the Caribbean, and the west coast of Africa. Cities such as Baltimore, Boston, Philadelphia, and Charleston prospered in this period as did rural townships in Pennsylvania and Virginia (although not all residents prospered; for example, about half of Charleston's population at this time was enslaved). By 1900, you can see a very different geography of urban development. While New York retained its dominance of the US urban system (having just absorbed the surrounding cities and communities of Brooklyn, Queens, the Bronx, and Staten Island), new industrial centers such as Chicago, Cleveland, and Pittsburgh had ascended the urban hierarchy. At this point, the regional structure of urban development began to shift towards the US Midwest. After World War II, it shifted once again but this time towards the west and south with the rise of new metropolitan agglomerations (or collections of cities) around the cities of San Francisco and Los Angeles (Houston and Dallas reached the top ten in the next two decades). Yet the major industrial centers of the Midwest continued to grow. Detroit ranked sixth in the urban hierarchy in 1950, albeit this marked its zenith prior to the collapse of the auto industry and manufacturing in the city. By 2010 it had fallen off of the top ten list.

By 2010, most established US cities had been absorbed into much larger metropolitan regions and in some case population growth in the central city had stagnated if not started to decline, as with Chicago and Philadelphia. Meanwhile, by 2010 six of the ten were south-western cities like Houston, San Diego, Phoenix, and San Antonio. This growth occurred largely on the back of employment growth in defense industries, government, and services, and an influx of migrants from the Midwest and northeastern USA, plus immigrants from Mexico and Central America. Almost 40 per cent of the resident population of Los Angeles in 2010 was born outside the USA (39.1% in Los Angeles compared to 12.9% of the US as a whole).

Recent urbanization trends across the USA have continued to reflect regional differences and divergence. A study conducted for the Brookings Institution shows that the fastest growing metropolitan areas between 2000 and 2010 were in the states of Nevada, Florida, California, Texas, North Carolina, and Idaho; in comparison, metropolitan areas with the highest rates of population decline were located in Ohio, Michigan, Pennsylvania, New York, and Rhode Island (Frey, 2012). Metropolitan New Orleans in Louisiana also lost population over that period but that can be largely explained by the lasting impact of Hurricane Katrina.

Urban development under mass production

You are probably familiar with the idea that industrial cities owed their economic success to the fact that they were able to specialize in producing certain products and by deploying efficient production methods and labor processes. For example, in early nineteenth-century England, cities like Manchester, Leeds, and Birmingham grew around metal workshops and textile factories deploying new machine-driven production processes and employing vast workforces, including women and children recruited from the surrounding towns and rural villages. As the industrial workforce expanded, however, much larger factories were required. New manufacturing facilities (and housing for the workforce) had to be built in specialized industrial districts located on **greenfield sites** outside the ancient walls of the older mercantile city. For instance, towards the latter part of the nineteenth century, Barcelona (soon dubbed the "Manchester of Catalunya") became a major center for textile manufacturing in Spain. In order to house the city's expanding industrial workforce, new industrial districts were constructed outside the Cuitat Vella (i.e., old city) in the suburbs of Sants and Poble Nou, which were soon annexed to the City of Barcelona.

> **Greenfield sites.** Greenfield sites are areas of undeveloped land targeted for capitalist development. The opposite of a greenfield site is a brownfield site, which is an industrial area of land that has been abandoned. Many brownfield sites are environmentally polluted.

The markets for the products of these new urban industrial districts were, by the standards of the day, global. Industrial machinery, armaments, steam trains, ships, and textiles manufactured in the British cities of Manchester, Birmingham, Glasgow, Newcastle, and

Sheffield found their way to the furthest corners of the British Empire, where there was a growing captive market for manufactured commodities. Many Indians, for example, found that they had to buy cotton cloth from Manchester's looms, rather than their own (resistance to British cloth was a core target by Indian nationalists like Gandhi, who was often seated at his loom in protest of British imperial domination). Toward the end of the nineteenth century, the working class in cities like Manchester and London began to see a material connection between their livelihoods and economic globalization in the form of colonial domination, often leading to inter- and intra-class tensions in the city (Stedman Jones, 1984). In contrast, the new industrial bourgeoisie in Europe and the United States flagrantly displayed the urban spoils of global capital accumulation. In the 1880s, major international exhibitions were hosted in Chicago, Glasgow, and Barcelona inviting visitors and residents representing all the different social classes of the city to enjoy the new urban spectacle of industrialism and modernity.

New machine-based mass production processes were likewise being developed and refined in new industrial districts growing up around fast-growing US cities such as Chicago (meatpacking), Pittsburgh (steel), Philadelphia (pharmaceuticals), and Detroit (automobiles). In the first decade of the twentieth century, a new system of mass production was perfected at Henry Ford's massive new River Rouge plant in suburban Detroit, which combined automobile manufacturing with steel production in a continuous horizontally integrated process. The Fordist system of mass production, known as **Fordism**, tied rates of labor remuneration based on an eight-hour workday to worker productivity and factory output. In doing so, this system unleashed the productive potential of capital accumulation based on mass consumption of standardized products, such as the automobile, domestic appliances, and, eventually, even single-family housing (Checkoway, 1984). Fordism left its imprint on the geography of the twentieth-century metropolis in the form of inter-urban freeways (known as the interstate highway system in the United States), suburban housing developments, large suburban retail outlets, shopping malls, auto dealerships, fast-food restaurants, drive-in movie theatres, and theme parks (Chapter 6 discusses suburbanization and the sexual division of labor at this time).

Fordism. Fordism describes the system of mass production adopted by the Ford Company during the early years of the twentieth century. This system of production and its ability to be very profitable at large scales became generalized across the US political economy within decades. Fordism shaped urban development by linking mass production to mass consumption. The working class could afford to buy the products (cars, domestic appliances) it was producing. Thus, both production (the assembly line) and social relationships (of wage labor and consumers simultaneously) are implied in the term Fordism.

The Fordist centers of mass production in the United States, such as Chicago and Detroit, continued to expand well into the middle of the twentieth century. But their inner cities had already started to lose manufacturing employment to the surrounding suburbs; this was due to the growing ability of employers to separate geographically capital-intensive production functions from labor-intensive operations (Scott, 1982). Growing problems within the Fordist system (e.g., declining productivity, labor disputes and strikes, and lack of technological innovation and investment in existing infrastructure) prompted major US corporations seeking to increase their profit margins to relocate assembly functions to new industrial zones in peripheral urban regions outside the old manufacturing "Rustbelt," often in the southern and western "Sunbelt" regions where labor and land were cheap and unions were weak or nonexistent. New forms of capital investment fueled by massive amounts of Cold War defense and military spending also tended to go to Sunbelt locations, too.

By the 1970s and 1980s the forces of spatial decentralization of manufacturing led to the establishment of off-shore assembly in urban regions such as Tijuana or Cuidad Juárez on the United States–Mexico border, and export processing zones around the world in places like the Dominican Republic, Hong Kong, Singapore, South Korea, India, and China. Cheap transport, easier global communications, and **structural adjustment programs** opened up new locations for capital investment worldwide.

In short, the new geography of production after Fordism – often called post-Fordism – began to generate new global patterns of regional and urban development. Under post-Fordism, there is considerably more competition between states and cities as they try to lure direct investment to their locales (Chapter 4). A firm like Nike can easily place a shoe assembly factory in Indonesia, China, or Bangladesh, and can exploit the competition between these places to its advantage given its relative mobility and the wide range of options it has when deciding where to place an assembly line around the globe. In Fordism, the regional economy was important – a car assembly plant in Detroit was likely using tires from nearby Akron, OH, and steel from Pittsburgh, PA. But the shoes assembled in a plant in Vietnam might be using component parts from ten or more different countries. Under post-Fordism, regional urban economies are vastly dispersed. What does this mean for urban agglomerations in the global North that once relied on manufacturing?

> **Structural adjustment programs.** Structural adjustment programs, or SAPs, result from the policies of the International Monetary Fund (IMF) and the World Bank. In order for countries to access loans from the IMF, or development funds from the World Bank, they must agree to conditions that require a range of changes to national fiscal policy, social spending, and privatization. SAPs encourage foreign investment by insisting on the reduction of trade barriers, through an emphasis on direct export and the extraction of resources for the global market. SAPs also require states to deregulate labor and privatize land and industry.

3.3 Patterns and Processes of Urban and Regional Development after Fordism

The decline of mass production has ushered in new regional patterns of urban development within North America and Europe (Storper and Scott, 1989). Urban centers of mass production in the old Fordist heartlands – notably cities like Detroit and Cleveland in the United States or cities like Sheffield in the United Kingdom – experienced a catastrophic loss of manufacturing jobs. Yet, the process of industrial restructuring did not map uniformly onto urban space. Different cities experienced different rates of deindustrialization depending on the types of industries involved, flows of capital investment, rates of deskilling, and levels of unionization. Doreen Massey has high-lighted how industrial restructuring in the United Kingdom in the 1970s and 1980s often had uneven urban and regional impacts:

> The loss of manufacturing jobs in the cities has not, for the most part, been because they had a high proportion of jobs in industries which were declining fastest nationally. It was not, in other words, as a result of the cities' industrial structure. ... The cities suffered most because, *within* particular industries, they tended to have the oldest factories and the oldest production techniques. Most of all they had the lowest levels of labor productivity. ... It was also the case that workers in the cities had won the higher wages and, in manufacturing industries, were better organized than those in out-of-town locations. Whether explicitly motivated or not, the decline of manufacturing activity in the cities has taken with it some of the old bastions of trade union strength. (Massey, 1994: 73)

In those urbanized regions most severely threatened with industrial decline, such as the US Midwest, individual cities have struggled to compete and retain or attract decentral-izing industries. A recent case in point is the competition between cities in the US Midwest to attract the Chrysler Corporation's Jeep manufacturing facility (Box 3.1). The Chrysler Corporation's relocation decision took into account the existence of a regional skills base, a condition which was used to exact various tax concessions from local urban jurisdictions. This example of intra-regional urban competition can be compared and contrasted with the decision made by the Boeing Corporation in 2001 to relocate its headquarters from the City of Seattle to downtown Chicago. In this case, the range of services – including access to O'Hare Airport and its ability to connect executives to cities worldwide through direct flights – and agglomeration economies of a global urban center located in the US Midwest appeared to outweigh the locational advantages for Boeing to remain in a city otherwise well-positioned to trade and compete with the emergent Pacific Rim economies.

Regional patterns of urbanization in post-Fordism are associated with the rise of new industrial districts. In the Third Italy (an industrial region in northern Italy), the success of clothing, footwear, and a range of other design-focused products appears to signal the revival of artisanal production based around specialized industrial districts, which bear certain similarities in terms of their labor processes and organizational structures to those that prospered in the nineteenth century (Amin and Thrift, 1992). In other European cities, industrial districts once dominated by textile manufacturing, such as Poble Nou in Barcelona, have seen a renaissance around a new generation of high technology, media, and cultural industries. New regional industrialization processes have likewise been observed in regions like the Silicon Valley in California, the South East of England, the Paris region in France, southwest Finland, the Stockholm region in Sweden, and the regions of Baden-Württemberg and Bavaria in Germany.

In seeking to explain these new regional patterns of urban development, urban scholars have been critical of commonsensical explanations which often privilege factors such as the locational preferences of firms and consumers or the changing attitudes of the workforce. In his recent book, *Keys to The City*, Michael Storper (2013) points to a more complex

Box 3.1 Regional Development and Urban Competition: The Case of Toledo Jeep

In 1996, Chrysler announced that it needed to replace its Toledo, OH, operations with a new state-of-the-art factory on a bigger site. In such instances, automobile manufacturers often relocate to areas of lower-cost production, such as a southern US state or Mexico. The unusual aspect about the Toledo relocation was that Chrysler favored locating the new plant within 50 miles of the existing facility to retain established advantages, such as its highly productive workers. The northwest Ohio/southeast Michigan regional economy would not lose the new plant's jobs, tax base, and other benefits. Nevertheless, a number of government jurisdictions within this region were prepared to compete with incentives for the new plant. In 1997, Chrysler announced that it would relocate to a site within Toledo. The City's *Keep Jeep in Toledo* public–private partnership efforts secured the company's $1.2 billion investment, but at significant public expense – over $300 million alone in local and state incentives, including tax credits, loans, and grants.

Chrysler's desire to relocate near its existing facilities demonstrates the relationship between regional economic development and inter-urban competition. Individual cities were presented with an opportunity to consider alternatives to the usual cut-throat contest that occurs when a transnational corporation solicits concessions from cities throughout the USA and abroad. However, rather than engage in regional cooperation, the Jeep plant represented the retention of a high profile company for Toledo – not the attraction of new investment to the region. For starters, the United Auto Workers union had to agree to concessions at the new plant *before* Chrysler solicited incentive offers. The City also razed a neighborhood of 83 homes and 18 businesses to provide parking for the plant.

Total tax breaks cut over $92 million from the local rolls, while the City agreed to over $75 million in out-of-pocket expenses, such as environmental cleanup and resident relocation, and $26 million to cover loans. Concerns have been raised that the tax breaks have impacted public expenditures. The schools have been operating with reduced tax revenues; residential property owners may be shouldering higher relative taxes.

Moreover, the long-term future of the plant is not guaranteed. In 2007, Cerebus purchased 80% of Chrysler, whose future now depends on the investment strategies of a private equity firm. The actual jobs – about 4000 – are less than the 5600 in Chrysler's pre-existing Toledo operations, or the 4900 originally "anticipated" by the company, or even the 4200 "estimated" in the Development Agreement between the City of Toledo and Chrysler.

Source: Adapted from Jonas and McCarthy (2010: 54–56). Used by permission of Taylor and Francis Group LLC Books.

sequence of events underlying the rise of new industrial spaces in US Sunbelt cities. These include:

> institutional changes in the 1940s (right-to-work laws; local economic development policies in the South; and a decline in farming opportunities for abundant labor in some southern states) [which]... interacted with industries that were maturing technologically and less dependent on labor skills than before. Then there were important innovations: improvements in infrastructure, notably the construction of the interstate highway system, radically reducing transport costs to markets. And there were massive federal expenditures for regional development in certain politically influential southern metropolitan regions. (Storper, 2013: 27)

Storper argues that precisely which of the above factors – and in what sequence – actually triggered the urbanization of the Sunbelt cannot be established with any great deal of precision.

Explanations for urbanization have to take into account both the general dynamics of the capitalist production system (e.g., the search for profit, competition, technological change, processes of deskilling, etc.) and contingent place-specific conditions (e.g., public subsidies for infrastructure, local laws governing employment and trades union activity, etc.). Nevertheless, once a particular sequence of events is set in motion, urbanization appears to be path dependent. **Path-dependent urban development** means that patterns of urban development typically adopt certain characteristics salient to the locational needs of the wider production system. Table 3.2 represents this idea of path dependency by contrasting urban forms typical of Fordism with those of the post-Fordist city.

> **Path-dependent urban development.** Urban development often follows spatial patterns that reflect the built environment needs and infrastructural requirements of the wider production system and supporting social and political institutions. For example, urban scholars sometimes distinguish between Fordist and post-Fordist patterns and pathways of urban development in order to highlight their different urban development trajectories.

Table 3.2   Some general features of urban structure under Fordism and post-Fordism.

Fordism	Post-Fordism
• Financial/corporate central business district	• Knowledge/creative/finance industries in the downtown
• Declining industrial activity in the inner city	
• Growth of regional branch plant economies	• Selectively revitalized inner city districts
• Cities specialized in making standardized manufactured products	• Global clusters of new economic activity
	• New industrial districts based around flexible products and processes
• Spatial concentrations of unionized labor	
• Strong functional ties between city and suburbs	• Urban reserves of nonunion and contingent labor
	• Weak ties between central city and suburbs
• Emerging suburban retail centers and office parks	• Edge cities and suburban downtowns with back offices
• Specialized industrial and residential suburbs	• Mixed industrial and residential suburbs
• Auto-dependent urban development	• Transit-oriented urban development
• Metropolitan planning to achieve economies of scale	• Regional collaboration to achieve economies of scope

3.4 Globalization as regional urbanization

After years of infighting between Denver and its surrounding suburbs, in 1990 the President of the Greater Denver Chamber of Commerce was quoted as saying:

> The world sees Denver as you see it from an airplane – without artificial boundaries. We should treat it that way and deal together on common problems of air pollution, economic development, transportation, and water. We need to market Denver as a five-county metropolis and let prospects see all the alternatives. That's a lot better than having each county try to build itself up by running down the others. (cited in Leonard and Noel, 1990: 473)

The Denver Chamber of Commerce President is not alone amongst corporate executives and economic development practitioners in the USA (as well as other advanced industrial countries) in touting the economic benefits of the region. In Denver, for example, regional collaboration has enabled the city to support economic development initiatives around creative industries such as the arts (Figure 3.2). Moreover, it resonates with a

Figure 3.2 Denver, once dubbed America's "cowtown" due to its historical role in the settlement of the frontier cattle industry, has become a new frontier in the development of the creative economy, attracting artists and designers to gentrifying neighborhoods on Santa Fe Drive shown above. Artists and designers potentially contribute to the revitalization of the urban economy by stimulating new forms of employment, generating sales and exports, enhancing the design and marketing of products and services in other sectors, and inducing innovation on the part of suppliers and customers (Markusen and Gadwa, 2010). Photo: Andy Jonas.

Regional urbanization. Today's mega-urban agglomerations appear to grow not so much outwards from a single urban core but rather inwards from multiple centers often located at the metropolitan periphery. In doing so, they spread across many local jurisdictions, coalescing into larger regional territories which, in some cases, generate more economic activity than entire countries. Examples include the Yangtze River Delta (Greater Shanghai) region in China, Greater Tokyo in Japan, and Malaysia's Multimedia Super Corridor around Kuala Lumpur.

growing belief that when it comes to competing for investment in a global economy, larger economic regions (including cross-border regions) are far more effective and efficient spatial-economic units than a single city or suburb competing alone for investment. It also resonates with what urban scholars, including Jane Jacobs, have been arguing for many years: in a capitalist system city–regional agglomerations are the basic units of creativity and wealth creation and, consequently, nation-states are becoming powerless to regulate global economic activity (such as through trade and currency regulation).

Some critical urban scholars have even argued that the increasingly fluid and financially unstable nature of the global economy *requires* a new global regulatory order. Global regulation would necessitate coordination between global and national institutions and the corresponding institutions at the urban and regional scales (Peck and Tickell, 1994). One example is the case of environmental protections and pollution. While some countries have protections in place, they might be unevenly enforced over space and scale – perhaps there is a national institution to make policy but no local or city-based regulators to inspect plants. The unruly nature of neoliberal urbanization has created regionally extensive urban agglomerations whose very existence threatens to undermine the authority of the national state.

Harking back to Jean Gottmann's idea of the megalopolis, which described a continuous urban agglomeration along the eastern seaboard of the USA, stretching from Boston to New York and Washington, DC (Gottmann, 1961), scholars like Edward Soja (2000a) refer to this era as the age of the postmetropolis. It is no longer the case that cities naturally grow outwards by adding new residential and commercial developments to the existing urban fringe. Instead, **regional urbanization** defies the old territorial divisions existing between city, suburb, region, and nation by fostering new urban forms that seem to have no defining center or core territory (Soja, 2011).

For Ananya Roy (2009), these new urban forms are "extra-territorial" because they challenge the political and economic order of the mid-twentieth-century metropolis. A case in point is Malaysia's Multimedia Super Corridor, which connects the center of Kuala Lumpur – its gleaming skyline dominated by the Petronas Towers (which, for Roy, are symbolic of the new wealth of the postcolonial state) – to the new satellite suburbs of Putrajaya (the capital city) and Cyberjaya (a burgeoning center for technology-based industries) (Figures 3.3 and 3.4):

Kuala Lumpur's Multimedia Super Corridor … stretches 38 miles from Kuala Lumpur International Airport to the Petronas Towers and city center. This spatial plan is a shorthand for transnational ambitions, a "Cyberjaya" metropolis that can harness the benefits of informational capitalism and stretch the Kuala Lumpur metropolitan region to meet up with the development boom in neighboring Singapore. But it is also anchored by a deeply nationalistic set of aspirations, including the new town capital "Putrajaya" complete with an architectural

Figure 3.3 Kuala Lumpur and the Petronas Towers. Photo: Andy Jonas.

Figure 3.4 Malaysia's Multimedia Super Corridor at Cyberjaya. Photo: Andy Jonas.

aesthetics that conveys the image of a globalized, and yet distinctively Malaysian, modernity. Malaysia's cultural slogan after all is "Malaysia, Truly Asia," a modernity of multicultural intermingling and a postcolonial harmony of colonial landmarks and hypermodern spatialities. (Roy, 2009: 827)

Regional urbanization is not an expression of economic globalization unmediated by culture, meaning, and politics. Instead, for critical urban scholars like Ananya Roy it represents a curious blend of transnationalism and nationalism (also see Chapter 11 on the Petronas Towers and national culture embodied in architectural design).

Uneven regional development in the United Kingdom

Until the 1980s, the United Kingdom state supported regional development through **Keynesian spatial policies**, such as public assistance for urban areas with high levels of poverty or subsidies to local areas for regional infrastructure projects. Since then, regional development assistance has been drastically reduced. State spending on infrastructure is more likely these days to be justified in terms of promoting global competitiveness rather than on addressing regional economic decline. In turn, aid to the poor has also diminished.

Keynesian spatial policies. Keynesian spatial policies are geographically targeted measures implemented by the state in order to bolster aggregate demand in the economy. During the Great Depression of the 1930s, the British economist John Maynard Keynes argued that state monetary and fiscal policies were necessary in order to correct market inefficiencies and offset the effects of downturns in the business cycle. After World War II, many countries implemented Keynesian economic policy measures in order to ensure that the productivity gains achieved with Fordism were realized by corresponding increase in aggregate (national) demand. Such measures were often targeted at regions and cities where economic activity and demand lagged behind the national average. In this way, Keynesian policies often had an explicitly spatial component.

On a global scale, regional urbanization has further reinforced the dominance of international centers of finance. Places like London, New York, Los Angeles, Frankfurt, and Sydney continue to attract the headquarters of major banking and finance corporations as well as strategic divisions and functions thereof. However, the growth these so-called "global cities" can also reinforce uneven regional development. For example, the continuing attractiveness of London and the South East region to foreign direct investment appears to be at the expense of investment in cities located in other regions of the United Kingdom.

A case in point concerns an ongoing national political debate about whether to continue to focus investment in new infrastructure around London or, instead, spread such investment to cities in the provincial northern regions, such as Manchester, Sheffield, Leeds, and Newcastle – in other words, places that suffered during earlier rounds of deindustrialization. In the wake of the recent global financial crisis (which resulted in the state bailing out major banks based in the City of London), there are concerns that London could lose its

Table 3.3 National political discourse on urban competitiveness and high-speed rail investment in the United Kingdom.

UK Prime Minister David Cameron on HS2 (28 January 2013)	UK Deputy Prime Minister Nick Clegg on HS2 (6 September 2013):
"Linking communities and businesses across the country and shrinking the distances between our greatest cities, high-speed rail is an engine for growth that will help to drive regional regeneration and invigorate our regional economies."	"Our capital's long-term status as an economic global superpower is threatened if we do not constantly upgrade the housing and transport infrastructure inside London and the links to and from the city."

Source: http://www.theguardian.com/uk/2013/jan/28/hs2-ministers-sceptical-nation; http://www.transport-network.co.uk/Clegg-London-needs-HS2-to-compete-with-worlds-magacities/9388

status as a global center of finance, especially if multinational banks and investment companies were to establish their operations in rival urban centers in order to exploit emerging markets. This issue (of how to balance global urban competition with uneven regional development) has recently played out in proposals to build a new high speed rail network (HS2), linking London to Birmingham, Leeds, and Manchester. The HS2 project represents a substantial public investment and national politicians in the United Kingdom have struggled to legitimize such a vast public expenditure at a time of national austerity.

One approach has been to talk up the role of London as a global financial center, and thereby justify further expenditure in the capital city (e.g., on a major rail infrastructure project known as Crossrail, linking the western and eastern suburbs of London to the City of London). Another is to recognize the need to balance further investment in London with promoting regional development around the peripheral cities. These arguments are not entirely incompatible insofar as projects like HS2 could be viewed as achieving both goals by linking regional cities more closely to London. You should compare and contrast the two quotes about the HS2 project shown in Table 3.3 by, respectively, the Prime Minister, David Cameron, and Deputy Prime Minister, Nick Clegg (who represents a district in the City of Sheffield). These quotes reveal how the uneven regional geography of urban development within the United Kingdom not only feeds into the national debate about the HS2 project but also plays into the consciousness of national politicians, who clearly are struggling to coordinate an unruly global financial order around future urban and regional developments within their national territory.

Racism and uneven urban development: the case of redlining

Critical urban scholars recognize that the process of financial globalization has transformed the social geography of cities (Box 3.2), and that social movements like civil rights movements can affect the practices and regulation of mighty financial institutions. One example of this is the case of race and home ownership in the United States. Prior to the 1930s, home ownership was very difficult for lower and middle class families because access to credit in

Box 3.2   Ethnobanking and the New Global *Social*
Economies of Finance

In Greater Los Angeles, one sign of the new urban social geography of finance is
the rapid growth of Chinese ethnic banking. This growth has been fuelled by Chinese
banking capital looking for new investment outlets, international migration, and the
growth of cross-border monetary transfers. "Ethnobanks" are owned and operated by
minorities in the United States, and there are dozens that tap into local social networks within the Chinese–American community of Greater Los Angeles. In 2001,
one fifth of all branches of major banking corporations in Los Angeles County were
operated by minority-owned banks, and half of these were branches of Chinese banks
(Li *et al.*, 2001). The rise of "ethnobanking" signifies the complex and evolving relationships between regional urbanization and the new cultural economy of the city. As
Li *et al.* put it, Chinese ethnobanks have "the ability to tap into community-specific
business networks extending across national borders. These banks thus benefit from
the globalization of industry and trade, which has gone hand in hand with growing
cross-border population and money flows" (Li *et al.*, 2001: 1925). Ethnobanks also
provide social aid to immigrant communities ill-served by mainstream banking while
simultaneously capitalizing on these immigrants' particular transnational financial
needs. Finally, ethnobanks are located in the communities they serve – hence,
Chinese–American ethnobanks are more likely to be in the eastern Los Angeles suburbs where concentrations of Chinese–Americans live, for example, San Marino,
Alhambra, and Monterey Park (Table 3.4).

the form of mortgages was very restricted. One hundred years ago, 40% down payment was
necessary, followed by extremely brief periods for mortgage repayment on the rest (perhaps
as short as only 3 years!). New Deal legislation introduced the 30-year mortgage, which
opened up credit opportunities for home ownership. New Deal legislation also inaugurated
new federal government policies such as mortgage insurance, which protected banks and
lenders should borrowers default on their loans (there was no private mortgage insurance
in the United States until the 1950s).

In 1935 the Home Owners Loan Corporation (HOLC) – a government-funded entity
meant to slow default during the Great Depression by offering refinancing terms – was
charged by the Federal Home Loan Bank Board to create maps for 239 US cities indicating which neighborhoods could be trusted with financing. Existing conditions of
racism affected the rating of certain urban neighborhoods. African–Americans were
often prohibited from home ownership through the widespread use of contracts called
covenants; white homeowners signed these covenants upon purchase, agreeing not to
sell their homes to minorities (the practices also often extended to restrictions on
potential Jewish and Hispanic buyers, too). The use of restrictive covenants enforced
racial segregation over time, not to mention the everyday, vicious racist sentiment that
African–Americans had to face when attempting to access credit. It is no surprise, then,

Table 3.4 Locations for headquarters of the largest Chinese American Banks in Los Angeles County (ranked by total value of assets in 2000).

Bank	Headquarters location
East West Bank	San Marino
Cathay Bank	Los Angeles
General Bank	Los Angeles
Chinatrust Bank (USA)	Torrance
Far East National Bank	Los Angeles
Standard Savings Bank	Monterey Park
Preferred Bank	Los Angeles
United National Bank	San Marino
Universal Bank West	Covina
First Continental Bank	Rosemead
American International Bank	City of Industry
Omni Bank	Alhambra
Trust Bank, FSB.	Monterey Park
Pacific Business Bank	Santa Fe Springs
United Pacific Bank	City of Industry
Grand National Bank	Alhambra
International Bank of California	Los Angeles
FCB Taiwan California Bank	Alhambra
Evertrust Bank	City of Industry
Guaranty Bank of California	Los Angeles
Golden Security Bank	Alhambra
Eastern International Bank	Los Angeles
Asian Pacific National Bank	San Gabriel

Source: Adapted from Table 1 in Li *et al.* (2001: 1932). Used with permission of Pion, Ltd, London.

that their communities were marked as "no-go" zones for financial investment in the form of mortgages.

On the HOLC maps, such communities were marked in red – and, hence, the term redlining has come to indicate the denial of credit or other financial services based on racial exclusion (Figure 3.5). The racialized hierarchy of credit meant that black communities could not invest in homes and infrastructure for many years, could not participate in banking in the same ways that middle class white Americans could, and experienced urban disinvestment and decay in their inner city neighborhoods. Redlining practices remained widespread even after being abolished by law by the Fair Housing Act of 1968 after years of successful civil rights struggles.

Over time, communities of color in the United States have dealt with financial services deserts in their communities by overpaying for financial services such as payday lenders and rent-to-own businesses, and by having to settle to accept subprime terms for lending even when their credit deserved the best rates (Rogers, 2013). With financial deregulation in the 1980s and 1990s, banks and finance capital began to market new services to minorities like African–Americans who have large rates of "unbanking" – that is, not using banks for financial needs. There was great opportunity for profit in these underserved

Figure 3.5 The HOLC map of St. Louis, Missouri, from 1937. The "Residential Security Map" shows the grades each area received from the Appraisal Department of the Home Owners' Loan Corporation: green was "A First Grade", blue "B Second Grade", yellow "C Third Grand", and red, "D Fourth Grade". Note the placement of red areas next to the Business and Industrial areas marked with the gray cross marks, along the Mississippi River. Source: LaDale Winling and www.urbanoasis.org.

communities (Box 3.2). Reverse redlining is when minority customers are particularly sought after for expensive financial services – the reverse of redlining which cut them off from finance and credit. **Subprime lending** is one recent example of reverse redlining.

Christy Rogers writes in *Where Credit is Due: Bringing Equity to Credit and Housing after the Market Meltdown* that widespread targeting of African–Americans for subprime lending in the 2000s places them at greater risk for foreclosure. Many qualified for the best rates on loans but were not informed of their credit options when they applied for mortgages; many African–Americans were also aggressively targeted for second mortgages as financial institutions sought

> **Subprime lending.** Banks and brokers offer subprime loans to people who have poor credit histories or who are at higher risk of being unable to pay back loans. Subprime loans carry higher interest rates and, therefore, this form of credit is more costly to borrowers than prime loans – and, correspondingly, they are more profitable for lenders. Legacies of racism in American financial institutions affect the ability of minority people to access prime lending, even when their credit histories were rated very highly. Brokers and banks can, therefore, potentially profit from structural racism by selling subprime loans to racial minorities in the United States.

new lending markets. Because most "household wealth in the United States is (or was) in home equity", the foreclosure crisis which is overrepresented in communities of color in the United States will continue to have effects on the racial wealth hierarchy long into the future (Rogers, 2013: 20). Inner cities and neighborhoods of color will continue to confront the effects of racist uneven development, too.

3.5 Gentrification: The Economic Revival of the Inner City?

With the decline of labor-intensive manufacturing in the inner city, and the growing attraction of downtown areas to postindustrial economic activities such as banking, insurance, and retail, a new professional urban service class has moved back in the city. These residents, often young and family-less, colonize former working class and often minority or immigrant neighborhoods through a process known as gentrification. The term gentrification was first coined by Ruth Glass in 1964, when she observed the rehabilitation of old Victorian lodging houses in various residential areas of inner London (Glass, 1964, cited in Slater, 2011). She argued that the return of property-owning gentry to the city was accompanied by changes in tenure and class: working class renters were being displaced by upper and upper-middle class property owners. These gentrifiers channeled their labor or **sweat equity** into purchasing and restoring rundown and abandoned houses in former working class districts of the inner city. Since the 1960s and 1970s, gentrification has relentlessly transformed inner city neighborhoods and districts in places as diverse as Notting Hill in London, Harlem in New York, Society Hill in Philadelphia, and False Creek in Vancouver (Smith and Williams, 1986).

Neil Smith (1979) argued that gentrification is driven by the switching of capital investment from the suburbs back into the inner city. Capital, he showed, seeks to exploit the emergence of a **rent gap** between the actual and potential value of urban property. Rent

gaps tend to appear in older working class districts where capital flight has allowed properties to become run down and where a lack of re-investment in infrastructure and services
has encouraged urban authorities to declare these districts "blighted" and, therefore, in
need of redevelopment.

Gentrification processes tend to be most developed in global cities having highly inflated
property markets, or, in other words, in places where professional, managerial, and knowledge workers possess sufficient surplus capital to invest speculatively in residential property. Gentrification can also be prevalent in cities where new zoning regulations have
opened up opportunities selectively to redevelop former manufacturing districts or historic
markets. In Chicago, for instance, abandoned factories and industrial warehouses in the
Clybourn Corridor district on the North Side have been rezoned and converted into condominiums and townhouses for urban professionals. Likewise, following the rezoning of
New York City's former meatpacking district in the west Chelsea district, gentrification has
occurred around the newly redeveloped High Line (an abandoned elevated railway which
has been converted into a linear park) (See Figure 3.6).

Neil Smith (1996) argues that capitalist cities like New York have become "revanchist"
cities. The term "revanchist" comes from the French word *revanche*, which means revenge.

Figure 3.6   Tourists and residents enjoy the winter sunshine in the High Line park, Manhattan.
Note the contrasting ages, styles, and uses of the buildings bordering the former rail line. Photo:
Eugene McCann.

Smith suggests that aggressive gentrification processes are accompanied by zealous actions on the part of urban authorities to drive out the poor, minorities, homeless, and gay people. Such policies include those, for instance, which increase the policing of public space and privatize public space to restrict access by poor, homeless, and, often, people of color. These revanchist policies "reclaim" city streets and neighborhoods for the wealthy and the white. The backlash against marginalized populations in the city, Smith argues, occurred because the white middle and upper classes blamed poor people of color for the economic recession of the late 1980s and early 1990s. Revanchist cities and their outcomes illustrate the social dimensions of uneven economic development, and how capitalist priorities infiltrate state policy and apparatus in ways that benefit the most privileged residents of cities.

3.6   Summary and Conclusions

The focus of this chapter has been on understanding urbanization in relation to the accumulation process in capitalism. It has paid particular attention to how the changing geographical requirements of production in different time periods produce quite distinctive patterns and trajectories of urban development at the global, regional and intra-urban scales. We have compared and contrasted patterns of metropolitan agglomeration, suburban growth, and inner city decline in the Fordist era with the corresponding patterns of industrial clustering, regional urbanization, and inner city redevelopment after Fordism. We have also examined the role of class, race and ethnicity in influencing how capital (investment) flows into some parts of the city but not others.

Furthermore, the chapter has highlighted how the globalization of production and the emergence of an **international division of labor** have intensified inter-urban competition and reinforced inequality between cities. Territorial competition can work to the advantage of those cities that are capable of attracting the headquarters of major banking and finance corporations. At the same time, the growth of these so-called "global cities" intensifies problems of uneven regional development, prompting spatial interventions by the state in the form of **structural adjustment programs**, urban assistance, or spending on major infrastructure projects.

These urbanization processes, many of which began in the industrial heartlands of Western Europe and North America during the nineteenth and early twentieth centuries, are today spreading to many other parts of world, especially the **global South**. In the process, cities in countries as diverse as China, India, Malaysia, and Brazil are becoming much more interconnected through global flows of finance, capital and labor. It used to be the case that urban geographers examined urbanization in these different parts of the world separately through the lens of categories such as the "Socialist City" or the "Third World City". The aim was to show how patterns of urban development occurring outside the confines of North America and Western Europe deviated from models of urban structure based on the "First World City". Today, however, such categories are being challenged by new patterns of urbanization unfolding in the global South and their growing influence on cities in the **global North** (Roy, 2009). The next chapter invites you to examine more closely some critical concepts arising from this "worlding" of cities.

3.7   Further Reading

- For definitive perspectives on urbanization and the accumulation process in capitalism, consult the two-volume collection of essays by David Harvey (1985a, 1985b). The latter book includes a detailed examination of class struggle around the built environment of Paris between 1850 and 1870. Harvey has written extensively on capitalist urbanization and there are other more up-to-date examples of his writings, but few match the depth and scope of critical insights offered in these two volumes.
- A useful collection of essays about the development of the US urban system from around 1800 to the late twentieth century (written from the vantage of urban political economy) can be found in Tabb and Sawers (1984). To get a sense of how Los Angeles has shaped contemporary critical thinking about urbanization, the collection of essays edited by Scott and Soja (1996) is worth consulting as is the book by Mike Davis, *City of Quartz* (Davis, 1991/2006).
- *Metropolis: From the Division of Labor to Urban Form* by Allen Scott (1988) looks at changes in metropolitan form from the vantage point of production and the division of labor. Storper and Scott (1989) is a useful survey of production and urbanization trends after Fordism. Storper (2013) is more up-to-date but less geared toward a critical audience. Amin and Thrift (1992) is a widely cited analysis of the role of industrial districts in urban development.
- The literature on gentrification is vast but good starting points are the collection of chapters in Smith and Williams (1986) and the study of New York by Smith (1996). Slater (2011) provides an-up-to-date review of the literature. For an entertaining critical discussion of the role of the creative class in inner-city redevelopment, consult Peck (2005).

Chapter 4

A World of Cities

Urban Geography: A Critical Introduction, First Edition. Andrew E.G. Jonas, Eugene McCann, and Mary Thomas.
© 2015 Andrew E.G. Jonas, Eugene McCann, and Mary Thomas. Published 2015 by John Wiley & Sons, Ltd.

4.1   Introduction

"Imagine for a moment that you are on a satellite, further out and beyond all actual satel-
lites." This is what English geographer, Doreen Massey, asked her readers to do in her classic
essay from the early 1990s, "A global sense of place." "You can see 'planet earth' from a distance," she continues,

> and, unusually for someone with only peaceful intentions, you are equipped with the kind of
> technology which allows you to see the colours of people's eyes and the numbers on their num-
> berplates. You can see all the movement and tune in to all the communication that is going on.
> Furthest out are the satellites, then aeroplanes, the long haul between London and Tokyo and
> the hop from San Salvador to Guatemala City. Some of this is people moving, some of it is physical
> trade, some is media broadcasting. There are faxes, e-mail, film-distribution networks, financial
> flows and transactions. Look in closer and there are ships and trains, steam trains slogging labori-
> ously up hills somewhere in Asia. Look in closer still and there are lorries and cars and buses, and
> on down further, somewhere in sub-Saharan Africa, there's a woman – amongst many women –
> on foot, who still spends hours a day collecting water. (Massey, 1994, 154)

A striking feature of the essay is Massey's stroll down Kilburn High Road, her local shopping street in London. While there are few places in a city that are more ordinary and
"local" than those in which we do our everyday shopping, Massey points out all the ways in
which this "local" place is also global. Over there is a shop selling Irish newspapers while
the traffic in the street waits to join the motorway to northern England and Scotland. Down the street, shops sell saris to the local Indian population while a shopkeeper from the Middle East frets about ongoing conflict there. Up above, international flights to and from Heathrow airport connect London to Delhi, Dubai, and elsewhere. Her point is that we can-not think of cities, or neighborhoods, as enclosed, coherent, or introverted enti-ties, defined by their "**community**" (as if there is only *one* community in any place) or by their boundaries or borders. Rather, she says, it "is (or ought to be) impossible even to begin thinking about Kilburn High Road without bringing into play half the world and a considerable amount of British imperialist history."

> **Community.** A group of people who share commonalities of culture, values, or interests. While often thought of in terms of local territories or neighborhoods (a view stemming at least in part from the Chicago School's use of the term), communities are often scaled (stretched across the world, especially in the context of advances in communication technologies), and neighborhoods are almost always defined by numerous, overlapping and intersecting communities. Community is not pre-given or natural. It is a social product that is continually being produced and reproduced through social practices.

Massey's essay has had a profound impact on how urban geographers study cities. The
essay and her other work shed light on how we can think of the local as global and vice
versa. We can jump forward 17 years, for example, and watch Danish geographer Anders
Lund Hansen's short film, "Space wars" (http://liminalities.net/4-1/spacewars.htm), in
which he walks through some of New York City's neighborhoods. (You have our permission

to stop reading for a few minutes and watch it, as long as you promise to come back to our book afterwards!) The streets you see in the film are also global places and it is a thoroughly *lived* globality – a tangible, visceral, ordinary everyday localness that is clearly also global. As he argues,

> Flows of capital and people in the built environment generate urban change. ... The city, however, is more than these abstract rhythms. People inhabit the city; they are not passive bodies. ... Here space wars are expressed through class, ethnic, and gender tensions, revealing how urban space is constituted by many different kinds of boundaries, mobilities, and transnational flows of capital, people, and information. The city's streets offer opportunities to explore and feel a variety of idiosyncratic urban transformations. (Lund Hansen, 2008)

Understanding the globalness of cities involves not only the satellite view but also the intensely local view from the street and the neighborhood.

The point is that an understanding of global cities and urban globalness is only achievable through an approach that takes seriously the mutually constitutive relationships between everyday life and that abstract "thing" (which is actually a set of socio-spatial processes) that we tend to call "the global." Massey asks us to "get back in your mind's eye on a satellite; go right out again, and look back at the globe."

> This time, however, imagine not just all the physical movement, nor even all the often invisible communications, but also and especially all the social relations, all the links between people. ... [T]he geography of social relations is changing. In many cases such relations are increasingly stretched out over space. Economic, political and cultural social relations, each full of power and with internal structures of domination and subordination, stretched out over the planet at every different level, from the household to the local area to the international.
>
> It is from that perspective that it is possible to envisage an alternative interpretation of place. In this interpretation, what gives a place its specificity is not some long internalized history but the fact that it is constructed out of a particular constellation of social relations, meeting and weaving together at a particular locus. If one moves in from the satellite towards the globe, holding all those networks of social relations and movements and communications in one's head, then each "place" can be seen as a particular, unique, point of their intersection. It is, indeed, a *meeting* place. ... And this [view] allows a sense of place which is extroverted, which includes a consciousness of its links with the wider world, which integrates in a positive way the global and the local. (Massey, 1994: 154–155, her emphasis)

All cities are global, then, from this perspective. They are all assemblages of parts of nearby and far away. The point is to identify and analyze their most salient and important characteristics and connections and to ask whose interests are served, and whose interest are hurt, by their particular global character.

This, however, is where it gets tricky. In this chapter we will outline contemporary debates around the relationship between urbanism and globalization. Our key reference point will be the large and longstanding literature on global cities that emerged in the 1980s. This approach has had a great influence on how geographers and urbanists understand the urbanization/globalization nexus. It has also been influential beyond academia as policy makers and others have taken on board some of the lessons and certainly the language of the "global city." The literature's influence is also clear in the way that it has become an object of sustained criticism and a foil for debate over how to best understand cities in the world. We will consider these critiques and discuss contemporary approaches to urban globalness that build upon but also extend these debates.

In this chapter, we will address these questions:

- How do critical geographers think about the (mutually constitutive) relationships between urbanization and globalization?
- What is the world cities/global cities approach and what does it tell us about how the world works?
- What roles do contemporary cities and their residents play in the organization of the global economy?
- What ways are there to think about how cities are global beyond the world/global cities approach?
- What are "mobilities" and "policy mobilities" and on which practices and politics of urban–global connection do these concepts shed light?

4.2   There is Nothing New About Global Cities

Before plunging into the contemporary discussion, it is important to acknowledge that there is nothing new, or even recent, about urban globalness. "Cities as nodes in networks are not a new phenomenon," argues one prominent urbanist. "Indeed, the fact that cities lie at the center of complex networks constitutes their *essential* feature" (Abu-Lughod, 1999: 401, her emphasis). Throughout history, to different degrees, people in cities have engaged with, and been shaped by, the world around them. Places like Timbuktu (in present-day Mali), Tenochtitlán (now Mexico City), and Samarkand (now in Uzbekistan) were defined and enriched by their position along trading routes that spanned known worlds at certain points in history. It is impossible to think about Venice, for example, without understanding it in relation to the Silk Road that stretched all the way to China and, via connecting routes, to India.

More recently, of course, it is impossible to understand the built environments of cities in Latin America, with their monumental architecture, and central plazas dominated by state and religious buildings, without acknowledging the imprint of Spanish and Portuguese colonialism. Later, mercantile capitalism was based on a system of wealthy trading cities and, even today, in cities that are no longer wealthy and prominent like Bremen in Northern Germany, the prosperity and global connections of the past are evident in the iconography and opulence of certain prominent buildings (Figure 4.1). In turn, industrial capitalism was also a global system that shaped cities and could not exist without them. This system worked with the colonial enterprises of countries like Britain to draw wealth into the core of what became a truly world economy. Perceptive observers saw this connection through the lens of the built environment even as it was still early in its development. Look back at the first section of Chapter 1 and remind yourself of how Friedrich Engels saw mid-nineteenth Century London with his own global sense of place.

We could fill this chapter with more examples of the ways in which cities have long been global. We hope, however, that this is enough to make our point: there is nothing new about cities acting globally and being defined by their global connections. Yet, what we would also

Figure 4.1 A mural in Bremen, Germany's main train station celebrates the city's history of trade. Photo: Eugene McCann.

argue is that today, the specific character of urban globalness and how it is expressed in cities is worth studying, not as some predictable echo of the past, but as a significantly different combination of longstanding forces. Today's urban globalness is, in other words, both built upon but also somewhat different from its predecessors.

4.3 Cities in the Contemporary World:
The Global Cities Literature

What contemporary cities might we define as "global"? Perhaps the largest cities? In a world where more than half the population is urban, surely the largest of these urban areas, cities like Tokyo, Guangzhou, Jakarta, Mexico City, Sao Paulo, and Mumbai, must be profoundly global? Or can we think of certain cities as having global cultural significance – centers of religion such as Rome, Jerusalem, or Mecca, for example? Or is political influence the most crucial measure of a city's globalness? If so, Washington, DC, Beijing, Geneva, and Brussels might be prominent in our mental maps. Alternatively, cities associated with oppositional struggle, such as Seattle, Cairo, or the many "Occupy cities" might be foremost in our minds (Chapter 2). These are all perfectly valid metrics around which to construct a definition of global influence. Each addresses a certain form of significance and, once the categorization is agreed upon, research and analysis focuses

Global cities literature. A literature in geography and urban studies that emerged in the 1980s around the term "world cities" before adopting the term "global cities" in the 1990s. Still, the terms are used in combination and sometimes interchangeably. The literature is focused on understanding the ways in which cities are related to the organization of the contemporary global economy. A key argument is that certain cities are "global" because they are locations of intense bundles of "command and control" functions which allow firms to maintain their global operations.

on refining methods and definitions (How exactly do we measure what a city is demographically, for example?) and on assessing these cities' role in the world.

Nonetheless, for the majority of urbanists, the term "global cities" refers to a specific way of thinking about urban globalness – one associated with an extensive body of work conducted by geographers, sociologists, planners, and others that has come to be known as the **"global cities literature."** This literature does not exemplify the *only* approach to understanding the relationships between cities and global processes, but it has been very influential and very useful. Therefore, it is a good starting point for a wider discussion of the variety of ways in which critical urbanists analyze urban globalness.

Economic command, control, and connection, post-1970

The primary criteria for defining a city's globalness in the global cities literature is economic "command and control." Therefore, when urban geographers refer to global cities, they tend to be talking about London, New York (Figure 4.2), Tokyo and about 50 others that host certain activities that allow transnational corporations to manage their global operations efficiently. Contemporary work on global cities has, then, been spurred by a desire to understand how cities have influenced the global economic system, especially in the period after 1970 when a series of crises shook up the way that the global economy was organized.

The "New International Division of Labor" that emerged after 1970 is characterized by the growing industrialization of parts of the world beyond the traditional capitalist core countries and by the rise of transnational corporations, rather than national economies, as the key organizing units in the global capitalist system. As these developments occurred, questions arose about how transnational corporations could manage their increasingly far-flung production networks. The answer from urbanists was that transnational capital relied on certain cities as "basing points" and "command and control centers" for their widespread operations. Thus, with the rise of globalization, geography, place, proximity, physical human interaction, and so on did not become *less* important. Rather, the need for key services and decision makers to be clustered in certain places in order to manage and finance globally extensive production networks in an efficient way made some cities increasingly *more* crucial to the operation of the global economy.

So, what exactly is the new, powerful role of certain cites in the contemporary global economy and how does a city's specific role affect its society and built environment? For John Friedmann and Goetz Wolff (1982; see also Friedmann, 1986), originators of what was at that time called the "World Cities" approach, the character of urbanization varies among

Figure 4.2 The financial district in Lower Manhattan, New York. A preeminent "command and control" center for global capital. Photo: Eugene McCann.

cities but is defined by the different ways in which they are integrated into the global economy. They argue that this difference in economic roles among cities – where some are important sites of power to organize the global economy, others' power is limited to regional and national economies, while others have little influence over wider economic relations or their place within them – "gives rise to an urban hierarchy of influence and control. At the apex of this hierarchy are found a small number of … urban regions. … Tightly interconnected with each other through *decision making and finance*, they constitute a worldwide system of control over production and market expansion" (Friedmann and Wolf, 1982: 310, our emphasis). The world cities Friedmann and Wolff saw emerging at the top of the command and control hierarchy included, "Tokyo, Los Angeles, San Francisco, Miami, New York, London, Paris, Randstadt [the region comprised the four largest Dutch cities], Frankfurt, Zurich, Cairo, Bangkok, Singapore, Hong Kong, Mexico City and São Paulo" (Friedmann and Wolf, 1982). As we will see, this list has been modified in the intervening years.

Friedmann and Wolff hypothesized that these world cities share characteristic production sectors and "employment clusters" that defined their role in the new global economy: a cluster of transnational elite professionals offering high-level business services and making decisions about how global investments will be channeled and managed are served by local services, from construction and real estate, to hotels and restaurants. Yet, world cities involve more than transnational and local elites benefiting mutually from the city's influential role in global economic decision making. Friedmann and Wolff emphasized these cities are also marked by distinct divisions and inequalities – a point not dissimilar to Engels' argument about nineteenth Century London. They argue that world cities are also characterized by: declining manufacturing employment as global office functions tend to push up land prices, thus making it difficult for manufacturers to operate; a significant cluster of precarious, informal, and sometimes illegal employment, often involving immigrants, women, and children (Box 4.1); and employment in government services. Whether their typology rings true outside of the Europe and North America is a point of ongoing debate.

In summary, this is the vision upon which the global cities approach has been built over the subsequent three decades: certain cities have clusters of key decision makers and service providers whose close proximity and intense interactions produce a capacity to command

---

Box 4.1   Seeing the Bifurcated Global City in the World Trade Center Tragedy

Illegal Immigrants: The "Hidden" Victims of World Trade Center Attacks
Voice of America Radio

Source: http://www.voanews.com/content/a-13-a-2001-10-09-35-illegal-66410257/ 549542.html

Scores of legal and undocumented immigrants were among the victims of the September 11 attacks on the World Trade Center. But many of their identities remain unknown. They worked on all floors of the Twin Towers as deliverymen, busboys, janitors and construction workers. One Mexican organization is trying to locate the families of the immigrants, while assisting the survivors in crisis. [...]

Now, [...] many undocumented immigrants who worked in or near the World Trade Center, face a unique array of problems, since they do not have visas and most speak little English.

Four Mexican immigrants who used to work in the Twin Towers as deliverymen are filling out paper work, applying for aid from Tepeyac [an immigrant services organization] and the International Red Cross. They are the lucky ones. They are also filling out a form for their friend, Juan Ortega, another deliveryman, who did not make it out of the towers.

For years in the United States, it is friends who make up the support system for many migrants, who send money home to their families. Sometimes, it was the victims' friends who put up signs, reporting the missing.

[... Estimates suggest] that there were at least 400 undocumented immigrants from all over the world working in the service industry in the World Trade Center. [...]

The Immigration and Naturalization Service has announced that immigrants who survived the attacks, and relatives of those who died, should identify themselves as part of the rescue effort. The INS assures, they will not be arrested or detained.

[Worries persist that] many immigrants, who face difficult challenges in the best of times, do not even know it is safe to come forward.

and control globally extensive networks of economic activity, yet this elite cluster is both reliant on and in conflict with other groups and institutions within the city whose fortunes are often in sharp contrast to those of the transnational elite (Brenner and Keil, 2006). From this perspective, the global city is a divided and tense place, a condition manifest in the built environment where, Friedmann and Wolff argued, the landscape is separated between citadels and ghettos – small, luxurious, and defensive "upper cities" of power and privilege on the one hand and the poorly serviced, repressed "lower cities" of the poor, on the other. Furthermore, this landscape is also defined by race and ethnicity, with certain ethnicities and the majority of new immigrants consigned to the ghetto and to poorly paying, often precarious employment on the periphery of the global city's power and wealth.

The attack on New York's World Trade Centre highlighted the separate but related lives of workers in the city's financial district. It was an attack on a symbol of the United States' economic power via its primary global city, but those who worked and died in the towers were by no means only members of the command and control elite. As the news article excerpted in Box 4.1 shows, many immigrants, often illegally in the United States, were among the dead. Their labor was essential to the smooth running of the firms who occupied the towers.

Specifying "globalness": Advanced producer services and the command and control of the global economy

Friedmann and Wolff's hypothesis about the global role of certain cities after 1970 quickly became the basis for a great deal of scholarship and debate (Brenner, 1998; Brenner and Keil, 2006). Sociologist Saskia Sassen's work was one of the swiftest and most influential elaborations on their initial ideas. Sassen employed the term "global city" rather than Friedmann's "world city." One reason for doing this was to emphasize that these cities are not separate but are, instead, networked together in a single *system* (Sassen, 2001: 171, 2012/1994). This is a fine distinction from Friedmann's conceptualization and it can be argued that Friedman did see the key basing points as linked (Friedmann, 1986). As a result, it is common in the literature to see "global city" and "world city" used interchangeably.

This definitional issue aside, Sassen's contribution is in her analysis of the global command and control functions of New York, London, and Tokyo – cities that she defines as being at the apex of the global urban hierarchy because of the power held within them through their financial markets and through companies located in them that provide advanced services to transnational corporations, services known as "**advanced producer services**" (APS).

Advanced Producer Services (APS). Services that transnational corporations need if they are to operate effectively in many different contexts across the world. They include: insurance, banking, financial, real estate, legal, accounting, and advertising services, business consulting, and professional organizations. They are offered by APS firms who contract with corporations. These firms tend to cluster in certain major cities, like New York, London, Hong Kong, and Tokyo. Thus, their presence has a great deal to do with those cities being defined as global cities.

For Sassen, these "highly specialized services and financial goods" (Sassen, 2001: 6) support and enhance the control capacities of transnational firms and, by extension, the cities in which these capacities are clustered. Significantly, Sassen is interested not only in which cities have major clusters of these activities and capacities but in precisely *how* such capacities are generated in these places. She is interested in global cities as places where important *work* gets done, including the work of workers beyond the transnational elite (Chapter 5). As she puts it, her focus is on the everyday "practice of global control" (Sassen, 2001: 6) as it is manifested in global cities.

It is the work done in the complex of interrelated APS firms in a given city – or neighborhood within a city, such as the financial district in London, or in Lower Manhattan – that interests Sassen. Her argument is that these firms and their services are more crucial – if perhaps less visible – than corporate headquarters to the command and control of global economic activity. Indeed, she sees "today's global cities and high-technology districts as partly denationalized strategic territorializations with considerable regulatory autonomy" (Sassen, 2006: 54–55). This is a fundamentally geographical argument and one that contradicts the mainstream popular story of globalization that suggests it (i) provides the freedom for economic activity to happen almost anywhere in a functionally place-less, free-flowing, hypermobile world and (ii) that this new freedom and global reach benefits everyone in society and every place in the world.

Sassen points out that the first of these myths – the myth of the ongoing erosion of the significance of place and distance – is belied by the plain fact that APS activity is clustered in certain cities, not spread evenly or randomly across the globe. She argues that the reason for this colocation is that it benefits both the APS firms and their clients, the transnational corporations, by allowing a lot of face-to-face contact, informal as well as formal interactions, and, in time, *trust* among key players who otherwise are involved in investment activities that involve a great degree of uncertainty, risk, and *distance*, of both the physical and social kind. Thus, the combination of location, communications, labor, and so on that are necessary to produce goods or other forms of value – such as command and control – cannot be so easily moved to or found elsewhere. APS activities are, then, embedded in certain places precisely *because* the economy is globalized, not despite of that process, as the popular myth might suggest.

So, the point is to analyze how this global economy is produced; how and by whom various dispersed capacities, embedded in various localities, are linked up together to create "the global" (think back here to how Massey understands "the global" as produced by relations and connections among simultaneously local and global places). This work of command, control, and connection is done to a great extent, Sassen argues, by APS firms (Table 4.1). Why are these firms so crucial? "Finance and advanced corporate services are," she contends, "industries producing the organizational commodities necessary for the implementation and management of global economic systems." These include, "all the top-level legal, accounting, managerial, executive and planning functions necessary to run a corporate organization operating in … several countries" since these "handle the complexities of operating in more than one national legal system, national accounting system, advertising culture, and so on, and to do so under conditions of rapid innovation in all these fields" (Sassen, 2002: 17). In turn, as we will see below, these APS firms themselves tend to be global, with offices in many cities around the world.

Table 4.1   Key activities in the Advanced Producer Services Sector.

• Insurance	• Accounting
• Banking	• Advertising
• Financial services	• Consulting
• Real estate	• Professional associations
• Legal services	

The second mainstream (i.e., uncritical) myth about globalization involves claims about its universal benefit. In fact, global capitalism thrives on uneven development – inequalities and uneven levels of pay or environmental regulation in different countries around the world – and Sassen is interested in emphasizing this point by deepening Friedmann and Wolff's focus on the inequalities that seem to be inherent within global cities. Sassen thus pursues the question of labor markets, or "employment clusters," and urban inequality. Picking up from her argument about the importance of high-level corporate service indus-tries in global cities, she argues that the rise of global cities has meant the rise of "new eco-nomic regimes" of "denationalized elites" making "super-profits" and very high wages who are able to impose their will on the larger economy. For example, these "waged rich" (Beaverstock *et al.*, 2000) have been argued to be drivers in the hyper-gentrification of many neighborhoods in cities such as New York and London. Their presence in cities makes manufacturing less important to the local economy, drives up the price of land and housing while distorting the local labor market, and, therefore, displaces people making reasonable incomes and firms with moderate profit-making potential. She also echoes Friedmann's argument about the parallel "informalization" of many economic sectors in global cities and the growing "reserve army" of immigrant workers that underpin many of the more valued economic activities in these cities, including, for example, the provision of food, security, and janitorial services to the corporate sector (Box 4.1).

The global cities literature has grown massively and in many different directions since these early statements by Friedmann and Sassen. Not surprisingly, this growth has entailed a number of attempts to expand, specify, and correct the key assumptions that underpin research into global cities. One important addition to the original approach has been to emphasize that global cities might be better understood as global city–regions. The argu-ment is that while certain central areas of cities have become command and control "Citadels" through the concentration of financial and advanced corporate service activities within them, cities' capacities to accommodate these functions and, therefore, to exert global control are based on a wider, complex of offices that are often spread across an urban region. Therefore, Los Angeles' globalness is not only radiated from its central core but is, instead, built on an integrated system of offices and other activities across Southern California. Similarly, Amsterdam's globalness is a function of its place within the wider Randstad region, as Friedmann and Wolff originally acknowledged (for an interesting com-parison of LA and Amsterdam and their regions, see Soja, 2000).

A second prominent attempt to expand the global cities literature has involved efforts to identify evidence of globalness of, or aspirations to globalness, in other cities as diverse as Delhi, Mexico City, Mumbai, and Accra (Grant and Nijman, 2002; Dupont, 2011; Parnreiter, 2012). For example, Simon (1995) argues that Nairobi is a global city, given the concentra-tion of United Nations and NGO agencies located there. He argues that the criteria used to

> **Globalizing cities.** A term used to indicate that being a global city is, for some cities, a goal that their elites strive towards, while, for others, it is a status that is always in process and must be maintained and developed. In either case, the point is that globalization and urbanization are socio-spatial processes that never find an end state.

define urban globalness must be loosened to allow more types of city (more types of globalness) to be part of the category. A third modification of the approach has been the use of the term "**globalizing cities**," rather than global cities to indicate that globalization is a process rather than an end-state and that it affects all cities, not just the "chosen few" (Marcuse and van Kempen, 2000).

Measuring and mapping command, control, and connections

A fourth addition to the global cities approach takes a different approach to Simon. Instead of broadening the definition of command and control, this work, by the Globalization and World Cities (GaWC) research group at Loughborough University in England, led by geographer Peter Taylor, seeks to take the economic definition of command and control seriously and to use various quantitative methods to define it very specifically. This approach has been extremely prominent in urban studies and, through its maps, diagrams, and tables, not to mention its prolific output of detailed and innovative analyses, has come to define what the global cities approach is for many urban geographers (recent summaries and reviews: Derudder *et al.*, 2012; Taylor *et al.*, 2012).

The GaWC approach scopes back out from the streets and workplaces of global cities, back up to Massey's satellite view, high above the earth. From this vantage point, it picks up on Sassen's argument that global cities must be understood as an *interconnected system*, not primarily as individual entities set within their national "containers." The group's argument, since they began their work in the 1990s, has been that in order to understand how global cities operate as an interconnected *system* of command and control, we must look at data that shows those connections or relations. Unfortunately, most data available, with the exception of statistics on airline traffic, deal with individual nation-states. Therefore, they argued, a great deal of early work on global cities, while agreeing with Sassen on the importance of inter city relations and connections as central to global command and control, was in fact using data that were not relational at all. The GaWC group has spent the last couple of decades overcoming this problem by developing its own data that can be used as a proxy measure of global city status.

There are various aspects to their work, too numerous to detail here (but we encourage you to explore their web site: http://www.lboro.ac.uk/gawc/). We will conclude our discussion of the global cities literature by focusing on one early output of GaWC's work that has become a lightning rod for criticism of this whole approach to understanding cities' role in the world. Its map, published in 1999 and somewhat dramatically referred to on their web site as, "The World According to GaWC" (Figure 4.3), is striking in its simplicity. Fifty-five circles, representing cities grouped into three levels of "globalness" are presented in a borderless, continent-less, featureless space. These are what GaWC regarded at the time as the 55 most important global cities (the list has subsequently changed over time, see Taylor *et al.*, 2012, and also: http://www.lboro.ac.uk/gawc/gawcworlds.html). These cities – especially

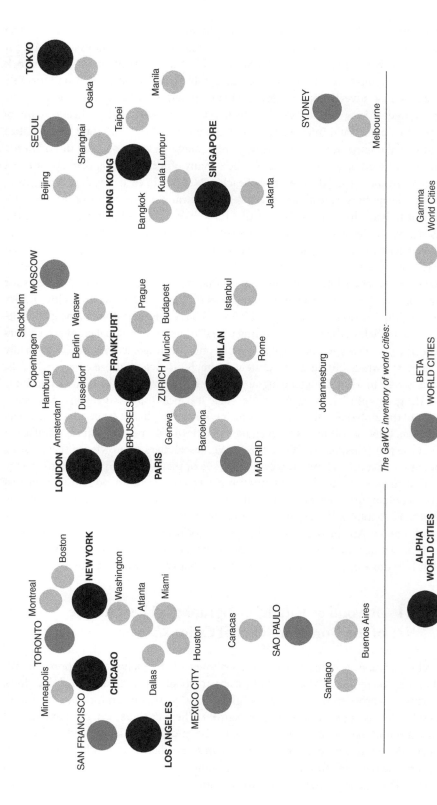

Figure 4.3 The world according to GaWC. Source: adapted from Beaverstock *et al.* (1999). Used by permission of Elsevier.

the 10 Alpha cities – are at the apex of the hierarchy first envisioned by Friedmann. The map's simplicity belies the hard work of analysis that underlies it: the authors started from Sassen's argument that a city is "global" if it has a concentration of APS firms (Beaverstock *et al.*, 1999). To develop their ranking of the most global cities, they focused on four APS sectors: accountancy, advertising, banking, and law operating in 122 of the world's cities. They then scoured various data sources – trade directories, professional publications, internal company documents, and Internet resources – to measure how important certain cities were to individual companies' operations (e.g., how many partners of a big international accountancy firms work in a particular city or how many offices does that firm operate in a particular city). By measuring the presence of each APS sector in each city, then aggregating the scores, the researchers were able to give every city a ranking from 1 to 12, where a city with a score of 12 had a high concentration of APS activity across all sectors. These are the Alpha cities, global cities with the highest level of global command and control. The map they produced from this ranking has become one of the most recognizable images in urban studies in recent years and one of the most controversial.

The GaWC researchers have subsequently produced other, more nuanced, metrics for measuring world citiness. These again seek to focus on the relations between cities rather than their individual attributes; the map in Figure 4.3 has come to epitomize the global cities approach. Nonetheless, the world according to GaWC and other global cities researchers is a *very* specific one. It is a world of elite financial and corporate activity, based not really in global cities as a whole but, more accurately, in small districts of those cities – Citadels. Therefore, it is very much a "Citadel geography" at the scale of the individual city and it is also a "Citadel geography" at the global scale, since it concentrates largely on a few privileged centers of the **global North**. Furthermore, it is an approach that emphasizes hierarchy and competition. Implicit within it is an imaginary of cities as competitive entities vying to get to the top of the pile (Chapter 9). While the GaWC researchers acknowledge these issues, they do not argue that this is how the world *should* be or that we should not seek to change it. Rather, they are seeking to show the uneven geography of command and control that characterizes contemporary economic globalization. Thus, they are engaging, very much, in critical urban geography. We cannot wish away the role of elites and hierarchies in shaping the world, after all. And before we can change the world, we must analyze it. Nonetheless, there have been strong and valid critiques of the global cities literature and how it analyzes the world. It is to those critiques from other critical urbanists that we now turn.

4.4   Beyond a "Citadel Geography": The Critique of the Dominant Global Cities Approach

In the previous section, we mentioned some critiques of the global cities approach. We discussed the argument that it is better to think about global city–regions than global cities, and the attempts to broaden the category of "global city" so that it can include other cities exhibiting other forms of globalness, such as Nairobi. These critiques can be characterized as *internal* critiques. They remain convinced of the basic categories and analytical benefits of the global cities approach but try to "tweak" them somewhat. On the other hand, recent years have seen the rise of a number of *external* critiques of the global cities approach from other critical urban geographers. These are critiques that question the validity of the categories and criteria used to create the notion of the global city in the first place and that also worry about the conceptual and political consequences of placing this particular definition of globalness (defined by economic command and control and represented in starkly hierarchical terms) at the heart of our discussions of cities in the world.

Jennifer Robinson, who we met in Chapter 2, has articulated the strongest and most cogent external critique of the global cities approach. Reacting to GaWC's iconic map and to the wider literature's tendency to associate the urban global with a small number of mostly global North cities, Robinson critiques the fundamental assumptions, methods, and categories of global cities research. She argues that the literature has been dominated by conceptually and politically dangerous attempts to slot cities into rigid categories in a pre-assumed, necessarily competitive, hierarchy. "From the dizzy heights of the diagrammer," she argues,

> certain significant cities are identified, labeled, processed, and placed in a hierarchy, with very little attentiveness to the diverse experiences of that city, or even to extant literature about that place. … In [these sorts of] economistic approach[es] to identifying world cities, a view of the world of cities emerges where millions of people and hundreds of cities are dropped off the map of much research in urban studies to service one particular and very restricted view. (Robinson, 2002: 534–535)

For her, this particular approach to global cities, one which makes broad claims about globalness on the basis of narrow data sets and very specific interests, categories, and assumptions "can limit imaginations about the futures of cities."

Specifically, Robinson's critique has three parts.

i. First, she worries that the global cities literature (and a great deal of contemporary urban studies research) suffers from an underlying developmentalism – the promotion, or unquestioning acceptance, of a specific Western notion of development as the path to improving the lives of people in poor countries. This, she sees exhibited in the tendency for theories and case studies from global North cities to be assumed to have global applicability, relevance, or importance.

ii. Second, there is the issue of **episte-mology** and **methodology**: how we identify and define the "things" or processes that we study and how we then study them. For Robinson, global cities researchers are too reliant on problematic categories, such as the category of "globalness" defined

Epistemology. How we know the world. It highlights the ways in which the knowledge we develop about the world is conditioned by our approaches to it and beliefs about it. An approach like the Chicago School's, with its ecological metaphors, brings one particular knowledge of the world to the fore, as do the positivist approaches of bid-rent theorists, and the postcolonial approaches of Robinson and others.

Methodology is the process of combining approaches (theories, concepts, etc.) with specific methods (surveys, interviews, observation) and analyses in order to produce a research project. Methodology is always closely related to one's research questions and is not merely about the practicalities of methods.

by economic command and control, on the acceptance of hierarchy, with all its competitive connotations, as the defining feature of the global urban system, and on problematic data, which she argues is skewed toward Western firms. Robinson suggests that the researchers should refer not to "global cities" but to "new industrial districts of transnational management and control." That does not roll off the tongue so easily but, in a way, that is her point: the activities being analyzed are too particular to be talked about in simple, universal terms (see the discussion in Chapter 2 of attempts to "decenter" urban studies).

iii.   The third element of Robinson's critique deals with the potential political and policy implications of the global cities approach. When academic categories and concepts gain popularity in business and government circles, their meaning or intention is often modified. The terms "world city" and "global city" have also circulated beyond the bounds and control of the academic literature. As shown in Box 4.2, the terms are often combined with the boosterist notion of "world class" (see also Chapter 9) to justify certain forms of urban development. Thus, for Robinson, the global city hypothesis has become a "regulating fiction" in urban governance across the world: an "authorized" story of how the world works and a definition of city success that identifies a clear goal toward which to strive by creating policies that seem to aid in achieving that goal. Echoing many other authors, she argues that if a city, particularly a poor city, puts its limited resources into becoming a global city in the narrow sense, then those resources are not being used to fund other services and forms of development that benefit the many in city but are, instead, focused on the needs and aspirations of the few.

In sum, Robinson's critique of the global cities literature centers on what she argues is its use of a number of representational strategies that "frame" the world in a particular way. A few types of economic activity are its focus and, by extension, so are a small number of cities. Yet, "global" claims are made on the basis of this very particular research focus. In turn, these ideas leak out beyond academia and can have real and harmful consequences on cities.

4.5   Toward Critical Geographies of Ordinary Urbanism: Researching a World of Cities

How might we construct an understanding of the urban world that builds on the useful insights of the global cities literature, avoids its pitfalls, includes and learns from all cities, and highlights the sort of complex cross-scale relationality that Massey, Robinson and others discuss? This cannot be an easy task and there is no single or simple answer to the question. From a critical perspective, the point is not so much that we should define *one* answer. Instead, we should continually try to adjust our categories and conceptualizations in order to better analyze the always changing processes and connections that shape the urban world. And, importantly, we should develop ideas from, and in the service of people who are working every day to change the world for the better and for the many (Chapter 2).

Robinson proposes a postcolonial and cosmopolitan notion of "ordinary cities," instead of global cities. The idea here is that all cities – the New Yorks and the Lusakas – are global

Box 4.2   Global Seattle

How is your city global? This was a question geographer Matthew Sparke addressed in 2010 when he was asked to write an introduction to Seattle for his colleagues who would soon be visiting the city for a conference. "Seattle," Sparke (2010: 10) notes, "is frequently called a "global city," but the question geographers should be asking ... is: what sort of global city is it? This means coming to terms with its development as a so-called World Class City." He identifies three visions of how Seattle might be "a world class global city:"

"From the competitive global business city of the skyscrapers and Pacific Rim trade, to the collaborative global justice city of anti-WTO protesting [in 1999], to the curative global philanthropy city of the Bill and Melinda Gates foundation [which sponsors health campaigns around the world], these variations in vision are important because they reflect ongoing struggles over the political and economic geography of globalization. They are also intertwined in the life and landscape of the city [including the gentrification of the South Lake Union neighborhood]. As such, they have helped produce an urban geography that literally embodies controversy over market led development and neoliberalism" (Sparke, 2010).

In his article, Sparke shows the complexities and contradictions that characterize his city, and all cities' relationships with globalization. These manifestations are both "big" and "small" but they are profound in their own ways. They certainly beg our crucial, critical question: (global) cities for whom? (Chapter 2). "By ... complicating the simple sorts of competitive economic calculations that usually put big financial centers such as London and New York at the top of global city rankings," he argues, "Seattle invites us as geographers to explore what it really means to be 'world class'" (Sparke, 2010).

Source: Sparke, M. 2010. *Association of American Geographers Newsletter*, **45**(11): 1 and 10–11. Used by permission of the AAG.

and "*ordinary*" because the flows and processes of urbanization, development, urbanism, and planning that constitute them are *common* to all cities (Chapter 2). Each city is, at the same time, unique (extraordinary) because the particular combination of those processes and flows is different in each place (see Massey's "global sense of place" above). Therefore, there is difference across the urban system (who could argue that New York and Lusaka are the same, after all?), but Robinson argues that we should not try to define that difference using rigid categories or think of it in hierarchical terms, with certain cities as more different in more important ways positioned at the top. Difference is, as she puts it, "distributed promiscuously across cities, rather than neatly allocated according to pre-given categories" (109).

Furthermore, her point is not only that the global urban system is multiple, complex, and differentiated, but that individual cities are too. Remember that the global cities literature has, from its inception, relied on a notion of these cities as markedly polarized or dualistic – the city of the Citadel and ghetto. Robinson, objects to this vision and argues that, "[t]hese two extremes by no means capture the range of employment opportunities or social circumstances in these cities" (Robinson, 2006: 110). This is a point that many global cities researchers would agree with and have identified in their work, but nonetheless is an important one to bear in mind in the face of sometimes simplistic, if nonetheless powerful, representations of the social, landscape, and political character of cities (including, for example, the Occupy movement's use of "99% versus 1%" imagery).

Focusing on the diversity and ordinariness of all cities leads Robinson to two more points. First, she argues that the ordinary complexity of all cities offers numerous opportunities for innovation and inventiveness in economic as well as in social, cultural, and political realms. This innovative potential, which she emphasizes is always constrained to some extent by uneven power relations, provides the opportunity for cities "to imagine … their own futures and distinctive forms of cityness" (Robinson, 2006: 110). Second, she notes that urban geographers and other academics would do well to open themselves up to the diversity of the urban world and not only focus their analysis on cities in one category (whether that be "global" or "nonglobal," "global North" or "global South.") "[I]deas about what cities are and what they might become need to draw their inspiration from a much wider range of urban contexts" (Robinson, 2006: 112).

This approach to the world of cities is paralleled by others, from studies of immigration into cities (Ley, 2004), to the notion of "transnational urbanism" (Smith, 2000), to the use of the term "worlding" by scholars focusing on African and Asian cities (Roy, 2011a; Simone 2001, 2010) as a way of emphasizing the ongoing *practice* of living and making urban globalness. For Robinson herself, her discomfort with the global cities approach and her argument about the ordinary globalness and creative potential of cities has led her to explore the phenomenon of city-wide strategic planning exercises. These are exercises in which large numbers of residents in cities are brought together to create a vision for that place's future. In the poorer cities she studies – places like Dar es Salaam and Johannesburg – these efforts frequently involve connections to cities in other parts of the world, including some of the wealthiest, like London. She is optimistic about these connections and that colearning opportunities offer potential for innovative future development in cities on both sides of the connections (Robinson, 2008, 2011a).

Policy mobilities. A recent approach to the study of how policy is made in global context. It focuses on the socially produced and circulated forms of knowledge that address how cities are governed. The fundamental part of this approach is the argument that policies are not "merely" local. Instead, it is argued that they develop in, are conditioned by, travel through, connect, and shape various places, spatial scales, networks, policy communities, and institutional contexts. Studies of policy mobilities are, therefore, studies of the practices, contexts, and politics of making (urban) policy in a global context.

Ordinary urbanism on the move

Robinson's point about cities engaging with and learning from each other deserves some further elaboration, as it points to an emerging approach to urban globalness that asks how specific actors in cities act globally in the realm of policy making. This approach is focused on the related notions of **policy mobilities**, assemblages, and mutations. It builds on the idea that urban policies are not just local "things" but are constituted by global interconnections and "**mobilities**" in a way somewhat similar to Massey's notion of place (Box 4.3). Models of good policy or "best practice" can be seen to be mobilized from place to place by experts and advocates who believe that a particular way of governing one city – a method for encouraging more sustainable development, for example – could be of use in other places too. Policies and the cities they govern are, then, not local things but assemblages or gatherings of expertise, practices, example, models, and resources from here, there, and elsewhere. Yet, as these various elements are brought together through the sorts of learning and engagement that Robinson says defines the ordinary globalness of cities, they change or mutate: once they are adopted in a new location, they must be molded to the specific local contingencies of that place.

The policy mobilities approach is, then, interested in the globalness of cities, just like the global cities literature. But its approach differs from, even as it builds on, some of that literature's insights. It

Mobilities defines a particular, relatively recent, "turn" among social science researchers, especially sociologists, geographers, and anthropologists. Their central argument is that the social sciences have tended to focus on the world as if it is not in constant motion or have tended to "freeze" the mobile world in order to study it. Instead mobilities scholars seek to understand and explain the world by starting from the assumption that movement is fundamental to how it works and to people's lives. This leads to the study of a range of topics from the experiences and infrastructures of urban transportation to the character of international migration. Yet, mobilities scholars are careful not to suggest that the world is nothing but flows. They note, as Harvey and Massey both do in their own ways, that the world operates through tensions between fixities and mobilities and between local embeddings and global interconnections.

tends to involve "following" particular policy models as they circulate through various localities and analyzing the practices and politics that develop in those global–local places (Peck and Theodore, 2010; McCann, 2011a; McCann and Ward, 2011; Cochrane and Ward, 2012; Temenos and McCann, 2013). How, then, might we see alternative and oppositional politics using similar circuits and pathways of policy knowledge as those being used by more dominant models and how might this form of mobilities help question and disrupt hegemonic urban policies?

Take the example of people who inject drugs (PWIDs), particularly those who are low income, endure addiction and other concurrent health issues including mental health challenges, are at high risk of contracting blood-borne diseases such as HIV/AIDS and Hepatitis C, and who are homeless or marginally housed. This population is one of the most marginalized and stigmatized in cities across the world. PWIDs are the object of policies at various levels: the substances they are dependent on – heroin, cocaine, methamphetamine, and others – are illegal as a result of international treaties and prohibitory national laws and their presence in public space is often the subject of repressive local regulations and enforcement tactics. Their access to jobs and to social and legal services is often hampered by their precarious lives, health conditions, and need to constantly search for money and their next fix. While their lives are very local in some ways, as they are often confined to small areas of cities, they are also governed by policies defined and implemented at wider scales. Yet, it might be hard to imagine that these people or those who provide services and support to

Box 4.3   The "Mobilities Approach" in the Social Sciences

A "mobilities approach" has emerged in the social sciences since the early 2000s. It focuses on how humans are mobile, how people mobilize various objects, how technologies facilitate movement, and on socioeconomic hierarchies of mobility, where some people have more command over space (Chapter 2) than others, thus emphasizing the relationship between mobility and social exclusion/inclusion. The notion of mobility/mobilities has been applied to a wide range of topics, especially automobile travel and its associated infrastructures and cultures, air travel and airports, tourism, convention, business, and spiritual travel, migration and transnational lives (for examples of work on all of these, see the journal, *Mobilities*).

Mobilities scholars, some of whom are geographers, accuse much social science research of being "relatively 'a-mobile'" (Hannam *et al.*, 2006: 5) in its approach (i.e., of not focusing on the importance of circulations, relationships, etc. in the way that critical geographers like Harvey and Massey certainly have done). In their research, they want to avoid treating "place, stability, and dwelling as a natural steady-state" (Hannam *et al.*, 2006). By the same token, they do not want to go too far in the other direction by suggesting that "mobility, fluidity or liquidity [define] a pervasive condition of postmodernity or globalization" (Hannam *et al.*, 2006). Instead, inspired by geographers who emphasize the need to understand the production of place in terms of fixity and mobility, place identities and wider interrelations, they have proposed a "broader theoretical project aimed at going beyond the imagery of 'terrains' as spatially fixed geographical containers for social processes, and calling into question scalar logics such as local/global as descriptors of regional extent …" (Hannam *et al.*, 2006).

Thus, the mobilities approach has had at least two impacts: (i) it has provided a new language and, therefore, a new conceptual frame through which to view the role a range of mobilities, from local transportation to international migration, and their inequalities play in shaping urban, regional, and global geographies; and (ii) the mobilities approach provides an opportunity to think about the transfer, translation, or transformation of policy knowledge among various actors and interests in localities around the world. We use mobilities – policy mobilities – in this second sense in the remainder of this chapter because it provides a way of thinking about the practices and politics of global-urban connection (McCann, 2011a).

them and advocate for their rights would have much opportunity to range across these wider geographical fields to influence policy and gain the attention or sympathy of other members of society.

Indeed, PWIDs often find it hard to bring their combined concerns with poverty, marginalization, and addiction to those in power. Yet, examples exist of how global connections have affected local change in drug policy – allowing PWIDs to assert their rights to the city and to health care. In the mid-1990s, Vancouver, Canada suffered a health crisis with extremely high rates of HIV infection and overdose deaths among PWIDs in the city's poorest neighborhood, the Downtown Eastside. In response, a remarkable political coalition arose to question the status quo. A relatively conservative mayor was convinced by activists and some of his own staff to address the issue, and activists working with PWIDs set up a drug user advocacy organization. By 1998, the Vancouver Area Network of Drug Users (VANDU) had secured some funding from the local health authority and had begun advocating for changes drug policy. The mayor and VANDU were soon joined by a group of residents from one of Vancouver's wealthier neighborhoods who were motivated by the fear that members of their families who injected drugs might also succumb to infection if something was not done.

While these local political actions were powerful, to affect change the coalition could not merely criticize the status quo. An alternative way of dealing with urban drug use had to be found. For that, they had to think globally and look elsewhere. Rumors and anecdotal stories of an alternative European model of drug policy were soon confirmed by searches on the (at that time still relatively new and limited) World Wide Web. Soon, the mayor dispatched one of his staff on a fact-finding trip to a conference of the International Harm Reduction Association in Geneva and to facilities there and in Frankfurt, where PWIDs had a very different interaction with the public health system and legal authorities. His report back to Vancouver city council detailed an approach to dealing with PWIDs that combined four "columns," as the Swiss put it: the standard prevention, treatment, and law enforcement approaches, coupled with "harm reduction," a public health approach to the problematic of illicit drugs that understands use and addiction as health, rather than criminal, issues. Harm reduction advocates argue for public health policies, facilities, and practices that reduce the harms of drug use, including infection and overdose death, costs to the health care system, drug-related litter and "disorder" in public spaces. Examples of harm reduction programs include needle exchanges and methadone prescription and, often more controversially, the establishment of legalized, supervised injection sites or drug consumption rooms where users bring their street-bought drugs and inject them using sterile equipment in a supervised environment with appropriate emergency facilities and counseling opportunities at hand.

Soon, city staff proposed to Vancouver's council that the city should break away from the traditional North American criminalization model of drug policy and adopt a "four pillar" approach, including a supervised injection site. This proposal was backed by the mayor but looked upon with skepticism, if not horror, by many of his political allies on council. It set off an intense period of public debate in the city. Again, this "local" politics was marked by its global reach. Other supporters travelled to Frankfurt and other European cities to gain firsthand knowledge and video footage of the system there with the intention of returning to Vancouver with evidence of its merits. Soon opponents followed the path of the harm reduction supporters but returned with less glowing stories of how things worked in places like Amsterdam. In turn, supporters gathered funds to fly experts from Europe – mainly from Swiss and German cities – to Vancouver to speak firsthand about harm reduction (for further discussion, see McCann, 2008, 2011b).

Eventually, in 2001, Vancouver's policy changed and harm reduction became part of its new "four pillar" approach. In 2003, Insite, the supervised injection site, opened and in 2011 it was granted legal sanction from the Canadian Supreme Court to continue operating permanently. In 2012, over 9000 people used the facility, which averaged of 529 injection room visits per day. A great deal of research has been conducted on the effectiveness of the facility and it suggests that it is successful in mitigating many of the harms associated with illicit drug use. In 2012, there were almost 500 overdoses at Insite (the drugs being used are still unregulated and untested, after all) but there have been no deaths since the site opened. 2012 also saw over 4500 referrals to social and health services from the facility (Vancouver Coastal Health, n.d.). In recent years, Insite has become a place visited by many people from elsewhere, keen to learn about the harm reduction models and how it works in an urban context (Figure 4.4).

While we are not suggesting that the interwoven problems of poverty, health, and social stigmatization have been solved for Vancouver PWIDs, some progress has been made and this case does resonate with Robinson's arguments that cities are multiply global, that their various interconnections offer the potential to make real change, and that opening our eyes and our categories to these different urban globalisms enriches our analyses, not to mention our political perspectives. It is worth acknowledging, for example, that while Robinson is arguing for Western academics to pay attention to and acknowledge the lessons to be learned from global South cities, among others, our example above is, yet again, about connections across the North Atlantic! Nonetheless, we believe, that it shows the benefit of defining urban globalness in terms of different objects of study (policy making, political activism), connecting different cities in different ways.

Figure 4.4   Global Insite. German geography students and their professor learn about Vancouver's Supervised Injection Site from its manager after a tour of the facility. Photo: Eugene McCann.

4.6   Conclusion

All cities are global and the critical point is to identify how they are global, in whose interests their various forms of globalness operate, and against whose interests particular practices and representations of global urbanism work. In this chapter, we have taken a clear
position on these questions and have, in the core of the chapter, presented an account of a
key debate in urban studies over the last 30 years. This debate about the usefulness of and
limits to the global cities concept brings to light a number of key issues for the critical study
of cities: how we define our object of study, how we research our topic, and how we represent our results. It also very clearly raises the question of the politics of research: What are
the consequences of our research in the "real world"?

The global cities approach has brought, and continues to bring, numerous important
insights to the study of the world of cities. Yet, it is only one way of framing that world and
frames are tricky things. They have two, often related, functions. Think of a picture frame.
Interior designers will often say – only half jokingly – that any picture looks better when it
is framed. This is because a frame focuses the eye on the object and sets it in an attractive
context. Yet frames, by definition, also exclude other objects and contexts. They set a specific object or image *apart* from its surroundings, allowing the eye to focus, undistracted,
upon it. So, a frame helps us focus on the framed object by helping us ignore what is around
it. While this may be a good thing for a piece of art (although some artists would argue that
it isn't), it has problematic consequences for the study of complex interconnected cities.
Robinson's notion of "ordinary cities" is intended to reframe and, therefore, refocus the
study of urban globalness in a way that acknowledges a greater diversity of cities, processes,
and potentialities.

4.7   Further Reading

- Brenner and Keil's (2006) *Global Cities Reader* is an excellent starting point for reading
  key works in the world/global cities literature.
- Robinson's (2006) book, *Ordinary Cities*, is an essential source for an alternative vision
  of the world of cities.
- The essays collected in McCann and Ward's (2011) volume, *Mobile Urbanism*, represent
  a number of "takes" on how to think about the urban world's relationship to circulations
  of policies.
- More on Harm Reduction can be found at http://www.ihra.net/.

Chapter 5

Labor and the City

Urban Geography: A Critical Introduction, First Edition. Andrew E.G. Jonas, Eugene McCann, and Mary Thomas.
© 2015 Andrew E.G. Jonas, Eugene McCann, and Mary Thomas. Published 2015 by John Wiley & Sons, Ltd.

5.1   Introduction

Cities are not just places where people live; they are also places where people work and try to make a living. Places like Mexico City, Tokyo, Mumbai (Figure 5.1), or London, offer an impressive spectacle in terms of the size and density of office buildings, factories, infrastructure, and residential neighborhoods; but, equally, you cannot help but notice the sheer numbers of people going about the ordinary everyday business of making a living. One sign of this incessant flow of labor is the volume of people commuting into the city by foot, bike, rickshaw, motorbike, car, subway, tube, metro, bus, tram, or railway. Standing outside downtown offices at lunchtime, the street view offers a range of workers – some in suits and company attire, others wearing uniforms, dungarees, and hard hats – making their ways to nearby sandwich shops, street vendors, or wine bars. They are the visible signs of the urban labor force, which increasingly pivots around those employed in construction, various professional occupations, services, retail, cultural industries, routine office work, street vending, and the like.

Then there are the areas of the city where it is more difficult to see workers and the kinds of work being performed. By their nature, sweatshops, back offices, domestic workplaces,

Figure 5.1   Men's workshops are the street itself in this example from Mumbai, India: a barber cuts hair, mechanics work on cars and motorbikes. Photo: Mary Thomas.

adult entertainment clubs, and so forth tend to be less visible features in the landscape of the laboring urban economy. In yet other parts of the city (e.g., the sites of abandoned factories, closed-up retail outlets, and homeless shelters) it seems as if there is no work going on at all: capital and labor have long since fled elsewhere (e.g., to the suburbs, rural areas, or other far-off cities in emerging economies). Finally, there are those parts of the city where those who are actively looking for gainful employment congregate, namely, job centers, day labor sites, and street corners. In each of these respects, cities can be thought of as dense agglomerations of work and employment as much as they are often thought of as places of residence and consumption (Scott, 1988).

Until quite recently, urban geography concentrated its efforts on analyzing and mapping residential social conditions (e.g., housing types, social class, income, and residential status) rather than understanding patterns of occupational segmentation and the types of paid (and unpaid) work found in the city. Despite the central importance of work to the functioning of urban life, urban geographers made only passing reference to the role of **labor geographies** in shaping spatial patterns of the city. While the Chicago School's classic zonal model of urban structure captured a snapshot of social life in industrial cities such as Chicago in the early twentieth century, the model of the city curiously made no mention of the work occurring in zones like "working class suburbs," or "immigrant ghettos." Nor, indeed, did the model reference workers.

> **Labor geographies** is a reference to the variety of ways in which workers are organized across space and how, in turn, space shapes workers' organizations (e.g., trades unions). For example, the membership of national trades unions representing the service sector might be made up of workers mainly based in major cities where service industries are concentrated. As a result, trade union practices and policies can reflect urban service workers' interests, such as their demands for a **living wage**.

The Chicago School's silence on the role of labor in the city was all the more surprising given that at least one contemporary novel, written by Upton Sinclair in 1906, *The Jungle*, conveyed a powerful and poignant message about the linkages between working conditions in the stockyards and life in immigrant communities on Chicago's South Side (Sinclair, 1906). With a few exceptions, notably David Ward's classic study of *Cities and Immigrants* (1971), you will find little critical reflection in the mainstream geography literature on the relationship between occupation, work, and social life in working class immigrant neighborhoods at the turn of the twentieth century.

This chapter considers how workers shape urban social geographies and, in turn, how the geography of the city makes a difference to patterns of work and employment. It begins with some observations about changing spatial patterns of work and employment – spatial divisions of labor – in the industrial, Fordist city and the postindustrial, post-Fordist city. It proceeds to examine processes of labor market segmentation and the **dynamic dependencies** existing between employers' recruitment practices, labor markets, and the social geography of the city (Hanson and Pratt, 1992). The chapter also considers the gendering of the urban labor market and how feminist urban scholars in particular have examined differences in the working practices, commuting behavior, and social experiences of men and women. An important issue here is whether women, due to child care issues or the recruitment and hiring practices of employers, are in effect "spatially entrapped" within the city. Later sections of the chapter examine workers as agents of urban change, focusing upon labor-community coalitions and campaigns for a living wage in the city.

By the end of the chapter, you should be able to answer the following questions:

Dynamic dependencies refers to the complex, intimate, and evolving relationships between employers, employees, and the social geography of the city. It used to be the case that the labor requirements of local employers were studied separately from the patterns of social life in the city. However, urban geographers now recognize that employers are very dependent on exploiting the social dynamics linking the workplace to the living place. These dynamic dependencies strongly influence how and why employers recruit their labor force from different areas in the city.

- How has economic restructuring impacted cities and urban labor markets in the **global North**?
- Why do certain cities and districts within them attract particular types of work and employment?
- Do employers' labor recruitment practices shape the social geography of the city – or vice versa?
- What are some differences between men and women in terms of occupations, income, and patterns of commuting across the city?
- How does the geography of the city influence and shape workers' resistance to economic and social change?
- For whom and why is it becoming more difficult to make a living in the city?

5.2   Why your Labor Matters: Making a Living in the City

In their classic study of Middletown (based on Muncie, Indiana) in the 1920s, Robert S. and Helen Merrell Lynd (1929/1957) devoted an entire chapter to the "dominance of getting a living" in the city. Noting the preoccupation on the part of Middletowners in making money, the Lynds reflected on the increasing segmentation of work in the city. They attempted to capture this labor segmentation by drawing a distinction between "those who make things with their hands" (the "working class") and "those who sell or promote things" (the "business class"). They argued:

> If the Federal Census distribution of those gainfully employed in Middletown in 1920 is reclassified according to this grouping we find that there are two and one-half times as many in the working class as in the business class – seventy-one in each 100 as against twenty-nine. (Lynd and Lynd, 1929/1957: 23)

The Lynds then proceeded to question whether it was appropriate to divide working life in Middletown into two classes:

> No such classification is entirely satisfactory. The aerial photographer inevitably sacrifices minor contours as he [sic] ascends high enough to view a total terrain. Within these two major

groups there is an infinite number of gradations all the way from the roughest day laborer to the foreman, the foundry molder, and the linotype operator in the one group, and from the retail clerk and cashier to the factory owner and professional man [sic] in the other. There is naturally, too, a twilight belt in which some members of the two groups overlap or merge. (Lynd and Lynd, 1929/1957: 23)

This snapshot of working life in Middletown in the early years of the twentieth century is revealing for several reasons. First, it points to some significant changes in the types of work undertaken in cities over the past 100 years. Places like Middletown in the 1920s were very much involved in making things rather than selling and marketing services. This was reflected in the preponderance of working class people involved in manual work. Today, instead of manufacturing and manual labor, one would imagine that a majority of workers in a place like Middletown would be employed in service industries and a raft of newer occupations related to information and communications technologies and the creative economy. The social division of labor within Middletown today is also closely interconnected with working practices in other cities in the USA as well as those in other parts of the world.

Second, reading *Middletown* nearly a century after its first publication one gets a glimpse of a gradual yet relentless process of change involving the separation, segmentation, and routinization of work tasks. For the Lynds, this made for a certain degree of fuzziness in terms of how to classify the types of work undertaken across the city; nevertheless, they persisted with a fairly crude taxonomy that divided the labor force into two class categories. Third, reflecting the language and attitudes of the times there was a taken-for-granted assumption that both manual labor and professional positions were performed by men. However, an increasing proportion of paid (as well as unpaid) work undertaken in cities is now performed by women – and indeed, many women, especially minority women in US cities like "Middletown," have worked outside the home in the twentieth century, as cleaners, teachers, caregivers, secretaries, retail salespeople, nurses, and so on (Box 5.1). Moreover, there are substantial differences in levels of pay and income between men and women across most urban occupations, suggesting that the experience of "making a living" in the city today is very different for women as compared to men. Race, age, and migration status are also just as important as gender in understanding wage discrepancies.

The Lynds were reluctant to map patterns of labor segmentation across Middletown in any great detail. Nowadays, however, critical urban geographers are keen to engage in such a mapping, not least in order to tease out the "multitude of overlapping groupings" observable within contemporary urban labor markets. Some of this work seeks to understand the relationship between labor market segmentation and the clustering of certain types of economic activities in different districts of the city. Other studies consider how gender, race, ethnicity, and nationality shape the restructuring of urban and suburban labor markets, seeking to highlight social differences in terms of occupations, patterns of work, and commuting behavior. Finally, there is growing attention to the challenges of "making a living" in the modern city and how workers, along with community organizations and trades unions, have sought to shape urban geographies in order to protect their livelihoods. Together, these themes all point to the importance of seeing labor as an active agent of social and economic change in the city.

Box 5.1 The Feminization of the Global Labor Force

Although many women have always worked outside of the home, in recent decades there has been a massive growth in the numbers of women participating in labor markets across the world. The rate of women's labor force participation in 2008, the International Labor Organization (ILO, 2010: 3) reports, is now over 51%. That means that just over half of all women in the world engage in the labor market; in comparison, men's labor force participation is just over 77%. However, these numbers mask huge discrepancies within regions of the world, and within cities. For some women in the poorer regions of the world, low numbers of participation in the formal labor market stems from the fact that women cannot find jobs. It is likely that "women would opt to work" if they could – for social-cultural or economic reasons, they may be discouraged from working.

It is also crucial to keep in mind that the quality of women's work options and conditions are poor relative to men's. As the ILO states, " the circumstances of female employment – the sectors where women work, the types of work they do, the relationship of women to their jobs, the wages they receive – bring fewer gains (monetarily, socially and structurally)" (ILO, 2010: xi). Women are often segregated into occupations with the lowest pay, the longest hours, and the least regulation. Women, the ILO states, also rarely hold upper managerial jobs (ILO, 2010: 5). One example the ILO provides is from Sri Lanka. Women make up over 90% of factory workers there, but are less than 40% of senior government officials, managers, and technicians (ILO, 2010: 44).

5.3 The Control and Segmentation of Labor in the Industrial City

During the nineteenth century, cities in the **global North** became major centers of manufacturing employment. The presence of a vast industrial workforce often provoked fears on the part of employers that workers would become organized and militant. In the 1870s and 1880s, industrial strikes indeed occurred throughout many cities in the Northeastern region of the United States. In Chicago, the Haymarket "riots" of 4 May 1886 began as a peaceful demonstration for an eight-hour working day. But when several demonstrators were killed by a bomb set off by an unknown assailant, the police moved in, leading to the arrest, trial, and conviction of labor activists. The anniversary of the Haymarket incident came to be celebrated as International Workers' Day, which coincides with May Day.

Other industrial cities soon featured prominently in the spread of the international labor movement, especially in the early decades of the twentieth century. In 1909, industrial strikes swept through Barcelona, the capital of the Spanish textile industry, resulting in the deaths of many people, including Catholic priests and nuns, in an event now known as Tragic Week. Turin, the capital of the Italian automobile industry, became a center of workers' industrial action in the 1910s and 1920s, eventually leading to the founding of the Italian Communist Party. Its leader, the radical scholar Antonio Gramsci, was imprisoned and wrote the famous *Prison Notebooks* whilst incarcerated in a Rome jail (Gramsci, 1971).

Critical scholars have speculated as to why growing urban resistance to mass production often failed to translate into national political parties representing workers' collective interests, such as was the eventual fate of the Socialist Party in the USA (Davis, 1986). Social conditions in industrial cities like Chicago were indicative; a key factor was that immigrant workers did not always self-identify on the basis of class and occupation. Instead, language, ethnicity, and race were more likely to afford urban industrial workers the social basis for solidarity. A further factor is that in many cities the authorities clamped down hard on strikers, and employers adopted measures of their own in order to control workers and resist the intrusion of radical trades unions. Some employers thoroughly insinuated themselves into the urban social fabric by building model communities and company towns, such as Pullman in Chicago and Bourneville in Birmingham, England. Others set up schools, charities, and foundations or encouraged their workers to engage in company-sanctioned social and community activities, thereby discouraging them from joining trades unions. Far from enhancing labor solidarity, the process of urban industrialization often fostered ideas and practices of community, identity, and solidarity that, over time, became less threatening to the interests of capitalist class.

Flexible work. The demise of mass production has been linked to the emergence of more flexible forms of work. Flexible work covers a range of practices such as nonstandard working hours, job sharing, working from home, and part-time work. It is increasingly seen as a solution to the challenges of managing the work–life balance in the city. From a geographical perspective, flexible labor systems have tended to flourish well away from the traditional urban heartlands of mass production and, especially, in locations where workers are less unionized (e.g., suburbs and rural towns). However, feminist urban geographers question whether labor flexibility is an inevitable spatial outcome of the demise of Fordism. Instead, it has encouraged the rise of new gender divisions in the workplace as more and more women enter the urban labor market. Notably, flexible work allows employers to pay women lower wages than their male counterparts.

Under mass production in the **global North** the very identity of the city and its constituent neighborhoods was strongly determined by the local mix of industries, working practices, and labor control regimes (Jonas, 1992). The journey-to-work, the daily rhythm of working and social life, and the consequent division of the city into different spaces catering to the respective needs of employers, workers, and residents were, to a greater or lesser degree, shaped by mass production methods. However, the close relationship that existed between work and home in the old industrial city was soon disrupted by the spatial separation of capital-intensive production processes from labor-intensive activities (Scott, 1988), suburbanization (Gordon, 1984), and, eventually, the rise of new urban centers of flexible production (Storper and Scott, 1989). Across most cities today one finds far more fluid, complex and overlapping geographies of labor, employment, and social life than once seemed the norm in the industrial city (Figure 5.2; also see Chapter 6 on social reproduction and urban form).

The rise of more **flexible work** has prompted research on whether industries and employers continue to depend on the city for labor. No longer simply a question of a particular industry's ties to a city (e.g., the automobile industry in Detroit), it seems that certain employers are very dependent on particular neighborhoods and districts *within* the city for

Figure 5.2   "Hammering Man" sculpture of an industrial (male) laborer in a post-industrial landscape in Frankfurt, Germany. The kinetic sculpture was designed by Jonathan Borofsky and sits in front of the Frankfurt Trade Fair. On the artist's website, he writes: "The Hammering Man is a symbol for the worker in all of us" (http://www.borofsky.com/pastwork/public/hammeringman%5 Bgermany%5D/index.html). Source: Eugene McCann.

their labor. Allen Scott (1998) has conducted a study of local labor-market geographies for different sectors across Los Angeles, CA. He notes that previous work on the role of the "friction of distance" in delimiting the spatial extent of the urban labor market failed to appreciate the complex patterning of *local labor market geographies* within the city. After mapping the emerging local labor markets of the digital media and special effects industries (Figure 5.3) in Greater Los Angeles, Scott (1998: 32) concludes that a "tight spatial relationship between employment places and residences is a persistent feature of local labor markets in all metropolitan areas, even Los Angeles which is often (mistakenly) seen to be a more-or-less fluid commuting field across its entire extent."

Indeed, segmented labor markets have a very clear spatial expression (Storper and Walker, 1989): employers in different sectors having different labor requirements tend to search out particular districts for their labor. Accordingly, these districts become specialized in certain types of occupations and skills. Perhaps more importantly, the spatial characteristics of occupation and skill within the urban labor market influences when and why employers chose to remain *in situ* rather than relocate to other cities, regions, or countries.

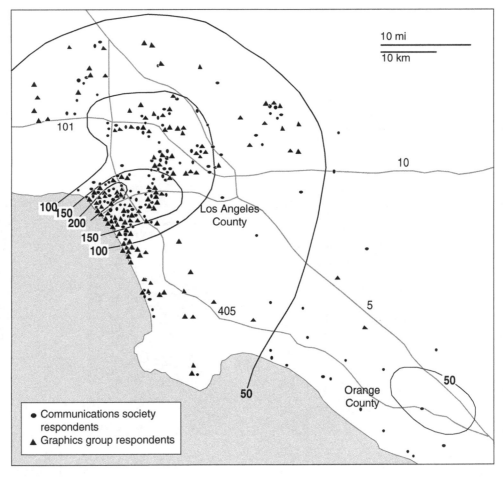

Figure 5.3   The emerging local labor market geographies of the digital media and special effects industries in Greater Los Angeles, CA. Source: US Bureau of Labor Statistics.

The control and segregation of labor in the new international division of labor

Transnational employers increasingly search for low-cost labor in less developed economies in the **global South** (Figure 5.4). Labor-cost differentials are substantial; for most workers in the burgeoning cities of Asia, Africa, or South America levels of pay are a fraction of the wages found in equivalent occupations in many European and North American cities. A manufacturing employee in China or the Philippines, for example, only receives a small fraction of what European or American workers make. In China in 2009, the hourly compensation for an average Chinese worker in the manufacturing section made US$1.74; in the Philippines it was $1.70 (Banister, 2013). An urban worker in China, on the other hand, makes over twice what a rural Chinese manufacturing employee makes: $2.85 versus $1.15 (BLS, 2013).

Figure 5.4 Construction workers in Dubai are migrants largely from Africa and South Asia seeking higher wages and more steady work than is available in their home countries. Migrant laborers like these men and other foreigners make up 90% of the entire population of Dubai (Buckley, 2013; also ITUC, 2011). See also Box 5.2. Photo: Eugene McCann.

In order to exploit these labor cost differences, an enormous amount of time and investment is involved in creating suitable labor market environments for transnational corporations wanting to invest or expand in the cities of developing economies. Philip Kelly (2001) has examined the dynamics of the local **labor control regime** emerging around in the burgeoning garment, textile, and electronic goods industries in Manila in the Philippines. Kelly notes that the growth of strong urban–rural linkages build around, on the one hand, the employment practices of multinational corporations based in the major cities and, on the other hand, the activities of labor market intermediaries, including local recruitment agencies, which draw labor (mainly young women) from surrounding rural towns and villages.

Labor control regime refers to a social need in capitalism for employers to develop social mechanisms for integrating workers into the production system (e.g., assembly-line mass production). This need arises because workers, in theory, can sell their labor power (i.e., capacity to work) to any employer, and, moreover, they tend to resist exploitative work practices. It also reflects that fact that workers usually require appropriate supervision by employers, not just within the immediate workplace but also in terms of fostering good relations with the wider community. The *local* labor control regime means the place-specific labor control practices through which workers are integrated into the workplace.

Box 5.2   Migrant Labor in Dubai

International labor union and human rights organizations point to the indentured nature of many migrant construction workers' lives in the United Arab Emirates. The International Trade Union Confederation (ITUC, 2011) reports on the horrible conditions of work and residence that migrants must endure. Workers live stacked in slum housing, work very long hours with little rest time, often stay in the emirate of Dubai for years on end without visits home, and laws ban them from organizing into unions. The ITUC also explains that the "migrants have few chances of escaping from abusive employers. A system known as Kafala binds foreign workers to the local companies that sponsored their travel to the Gulf nations. The workers need their employers' authorization to switch jobs, and companies frequently hold migrants' passports to ensure they do not leave the country before the end of their contracts" (ITUC, 2011: 2–3).

While the government has recently implemented new regulations to protect migrant workers, these are only enforced sporadically. Nonetheless, as geographer Michelle Buckley (2013) shows, migrant workers are finding ways to resist and are organizing for better conditions. She writes that "in the mid-2000s, dozens of highly public strikes by migrant construction workers swept across Dubai… The factors motivating the strikes were diverse" (Buckley, 2013: 265), including nonpayment of wages, squalid dormitories, and poor transportation. The largest strike occurred in November 2007, when 30 000–40 000 workers refused to work for two weeks, including those working on "iconic mega-projects, such as the Burj Khalifa" (Buckley, 2013: 267, see Chapter 11 for more on this skyscraper).

While the autocratic state of Dubai has a tight control over labor and the gains of the strike were limited, Buckley states that the workers' collective agency illustrates how their actions also had "a real and tangible effect on the conditions for many lower-waged builders in specific companies and on particular projects. In a number of cases, labor actions enabled workers to successfully negotiate a pay raise, receive unpaid back wages, and, in some cases, win other concessions such as bi-annual plane tickets back home to visit family" (Buckley, 2013: 271).

For those who do end up working in the city, their lives are divided between the long hours on the factory shop floor and remaining time spent in cramped living conditions, either in dormitories provided by their employers or temporary structures in shanty towns (Figure 5.5). These urban living places are notorious for power cuts, lack of supporting services, and poor sanitation. As Melissa Wright (2006) also explains in her book, *Disposable Women and Other Myths of Global Capitalism*, there is a notion that the abundance of workers in the developing world equates to an attitude that they are disposable, easily used up and replaced by others. She shows how this notion plays out in the border maquila zones between the United States and Mexico. On the one hand, Wright says that the myth of the disposable woman explains a "wasting process" of a woman laborer in a third world factory because "within a relatively short period of time and at a young age, [she] loses the physical and mental faculties for which she was initially employed, and she is worth no more than the cost

Figure 5.5 Service sector worker at home in the Duaripara district of Dhaka, the capital city of Bangladesh. Throughout the global South millions of workers operate in cramped conditions, either at home or in overcrowded and often unsafe factories; many are doing piecework for the international garment industry. In April, 2013, the Rana Plaza garment factory building collapsed in the capital of Bangladesh, Dhaka, resulting in the deaths of more than 1130 employees (see also Box 5.3). Photo courtesy of Maksudur Rahman.

Box 5.3 Is Your College Campus Sweatshop Free?

In the 2000s, university students in the United States, Canada, and United Kingdom began to question the labor conditions that went into making their college apparel. Groups such as United Students Against Sweatshops formed to pressure universities to license college logos and sportswear only through factories that support workers' rights to unionize and that pass inspections evaluating the conditions of work. Hundreds of universities in the United Kingdom, United States, and Canada have by now committed to buying garments made only in sweatshop-free conditions.

One large student group, United Students Against Sweatshops (USAS, www.usas. org) illustrates the pressure that thousands of students can exert. By the threat and actuality of boycott, students forced their universities to disclose where all the T-shirts, sweatshirts, and uniforms were being manufactured. They then insisted – by occupying administrative offices, boycotting garments, and even marching through campuses naked – that their schools recognize the right of manufacturing workers to unionize, work in sweatshop-free environments, and earn living wages.

More recently, the USAS launched the "End Deathtraps" campaign in response to the collapse of a large sweatshop building called Rana Plaza in Dhaka, Bangladesh in April, 2013. Over 1000 garment workers were killed when the eight-story building collapsed, with another 2500 injured. Most of the families of those killed, and those workers who were injured and left jobless after the collapse, still have not received compensation from the transnational corporations subcontracting through Rana Plaza companies.

of her dismissal and substitute" (Wright, 2006: 2). The draining, repetitive, and taxing work of assembly lines causes horrible damage to bodies and minds, and keep in mind that many of the woman workers who assemble goods for first world markets are extremely young.

On the other hand, Wright argues, "even as this [worker] turns into a living form of human waste" in the eyes of corporate hirers and first world consumers, "global firms go out of their way to employ her whenever possible because the things that she makes generate value even as she depreciates in value" (Wright, 2006: 2). Wright's book encourages consumers far removed from the factories where all of their belongings are made to confront the ways that they also perpetuate the myth of the disposable worker. There is no "truth" to the myth of disposability, and there is a steep human cost to the gross inequities structured into the new international division of labor.

5.4   The Urban Labor Market: Dynamic Dependencies Between Employers and Workers

Across the world, given the gross disparities of wages and working condition, why do urban employers tap into *certain* local labor markets and not others? This might seem a strange question to ask given how much emphasis today is often placed on the global mobility of capital in relation to the immobility of workers and cities. There is plenty of evidence that manual industrial work has relocated on a massive scale to major cities in the developing economies of China, India, and other regions within Asia and the Pacific Rim, and that much of this shift has to do with the search for a cheaper and more malleable urban workforce. How else does one account for the collapse of manufacturing in once dynamic industrial–urban centers like Detroit and Chicago in the USA, or Sheffield and Manchester in the United Kingdom, and the corresponding rise of new industrial spaces in cities like Mumbai, Manila, or Bangalore? Yet it is not the case that when faced with rising costs or intense competition every employer will necessarily seek out cheap and unskilled labor elsewhere; irrespective of skills or remuneration levels employers tend to locate in order to tap into labor pools of different qualities and quantities within the city.

Some evidence of the local labor-market dependence of employers comes from detailed studies undertaken in Worcester, MA. Worcester has a rich industrial labor history extending back to the mid-nineteenth century, when the city developed into a regional center of the metal working, ceramics and garment industries. As industries in these sectors expanded, employers adopted labor control practices that contributed to strong ties between their workers and the wider community (Jonas, 1992). In the meantime, Worcester has lost many skilled manufacturing jobs and gained new jobs in services, computing and other forms of high-technology industry. While some inner city districts in Worcester have retained manufacturing employment, services and other new forms of employment have been attracted to the surrounding suburbs and townships.

In the late 1980s and early 1990s, Susan Hanson and Geraldine Pratt undertook detailed analyses of local labor market dynamics in Worcester (Hanson and Pratt, 1992, 1995). Their studies were based on surveys and interviews with local employers and employees in four districts in the Worcester Metropolitan Statistical Area. Two of these areas were central city locations with a mixture of manufacturing and producer services industries: Main South, which is an ethnically diverse inner urban neighborhood containing a mixture of low-rent

Table 5.1   Percentage of employers sharing each type of labor with other employers in the Worcester study area. Source: Table 6.5 in Hanson and Pratt, 1995: 177. Used with permission of Routledge Publishing.

	Main South	Upper Burncoat	Blackstone Valley	Westborough
General/unskilled (e.g., janitors)	10.8	0	18.5	15.0
Routine production	67.7	50.0	70.4	27.5
Skilled production	54.1	25.0	51.9	25.0
Engineers	0	25.0	0	27.5
Clerical/office	5.4	16.7	11.1	32.5
Sales/marketing	5.4	16.7	7.4	12.5
Professional/managerial	2.7	8.3	0	12.5

apartments and established single-family homes; and Upper Burncoat, which includes relatively prosperous predominantly white middle class residential areas. The other two case study areas were outside the Worcester city limits: the Blackstone Valley, which was once the center of the region's textile industry but has retained a blue collar, albeit nonunion, workforce; and Westborough, which is a more prosperous edge city with good regional transport links and is attractive to computer software and hardware companies.

Several important factors governing how local labor markets operate came out of the Worcester study as follows (see Chapters 6 and 7 in Hanson and Pratt, 1995):

- Access to labor is a crucial variable in the initial decision to locate in one part of Worcester but it also influences the decision to remain in the local area even when pressure to close facilities and relocate intensifies. When local employers do consider relocating or expanding facilities, they tend to do so within the same area of the city.
- Employers draw their labor from within well-defined commuting zones. Irrespective of the type of industry, most employers prefer their employees to live close to the workplace. At times, differences in commuting patterns reflect gender differences, with women working much closer to home than men, especially in Main South and Blackstone Valley.
- Labor recruitment practices are highly localized. Advertising for jobs is usually done through local newspapers and trade magazines; in some cases it involves word of mouth.
- Employers operating in the same districts within the Worcester metropolitan area tend to recruit from the same local labor markets; in other words, local labor markets for different sectors overlap spatially. This is demonstrated in Table 5.1 which shows especially high levels of spatial overlap around routine production and, to a lesser extent, skilled production in the Main South, Blackstone and Upper Burncoat districts. In the case of Westborough, shared pools of labor occur around clerical/office work.

One finding from the Worcester study is worth considering in greater depth: the relationship between the urban labor market, commuting patterns, and changing gender roles and relations. The classic spatial pattern of employment in the immediate post-World War II period might be characterized as follows: corporate control service functions and some labor-intensive manufacturing jobs would typically be found in the central city; routine mass production and retail functions would locate in the suburbs. This occupational geography was further premised upon the prevailing gender stereotypes, such that men were, in the main, prepared to commute longer distances for well-paid jobs in the city and women – especially married women – remained at home and raised the children. This stereotypical pattern began to break down as the more routine elements of production and services began to move the suburbs, and, as the Worcester study demonstrated, women began to participate in the urban labor market, both in traditional manufacturing and the newer service sector jobs (Nelson, 1986).

As more women enter urban and suburban labor markets, new pressures and trade-offs occur around work and social life, which have further spatial ramifications. Consider the rise of new employment opportunities for women in the suburbs. Since many women have not been habituated into the routines and (pay) demands of male-dominated production jobs in the city, it has been assumed that they are prepared to accept lower-paid, routine service sector occupations in the suburbs, especially if the hours are more flexible. On the face of it, it seems that the *suburban relocation of office work* has indeed been motivated by the opportunity to tap into pools of readily available female labor. A question then arises as to whether women are, in effect, spatially entrapped: due to their domestic responsibilities (e.g., child rearing), women are restricted in their job search area and choice of career paths, and so are forced to accept low-wage service sector jobs because this is the only type of employment available in close spatial proximity to their suburban places of residence. The suburbs, so it seems, have been transformed into "pink-collar ghettos" (England, 1993).

> **Spatial entrapment hypothesis.** Many women are spatially restricted in their job search area and choice of career paths due to various domestic responsibilities. The spatial entrapment hypothesis proposes that the *only* forms of employment available to women are low wage, service sector jobs, which are typically located in close spatial proximity to their suburban places of residence. Consequently, women are trapped in suburban labor markets dominated by low wage, service sector employment.

Research shows that the labor market dynamics associated with suburban office location are far more complicated than the **spatial entrapment hypothesis** suggests. Kim England conducted a detailed study of suburban office employment and women's commuting behavior in Columbus, OH, which revealed the complex issues at play (England, 1993). First, England showed that, in general terms, women do have shorter commutes than men; however, the travel time differences are not as great as might be predicted by the spatial entrapment hypothesis. Indeed, married women with dependent children tend to have longer and more varied commutes than those without children or who have never married. Second, England argued that journey-to-work distances seem to depend on whether women are in single-parent households or whether they still live with their partners. This is demonstrated in Table 5.2, which shows that women in two-adult households tend to have much longer and more varied commutes than those in one-adult households. There are also differences due to current marital status. Third, the Columbus study highlights several factors that could contribute to the 'spatial entrapment' of women, such as:

- whether affordable child care is provided by employers or, instead, close to one's place of residence;
- one's ability to match work schedules with school pick-up and drop-off times;

Table 5.2 Commuting distances (in miles) of women and men in different household categories.

	One-adult household		Two-adult household	
	Never Married	*Divorced*	*Women*	*Men*
Mean	7.87	11.12	14.03	14.90
s.d.	6.65	8.01	12.13	22.40
N*	18	17	65	55
Relative frequency (4-mile intervals in percentages)				
0–3.9	28	17	4	25
4–7.9	33	23	29	5
8–11.9	28	23	23	25
12–15.9	0	12	11	9
16–19.9	5	12	14	18
20–23.9	0	6	4	7
24–27.9	0	0	7	2
28–31.9	5	0	4	2
32 plus	0	6	4	5

Source: Table 2 in England, 1993: 232, used with permission of Taylor and Francis Publishing.
*N for partners is lower than N for women they live with because no information was provided regarding three of the partners' place of work. Seven were either retired or had jobs that involved multiple workplaces. Source: survey questionnaire by author.

- whether it is possible to sell one's home to be nearer to work should an employer decide to relocate to another part of the city;
- the availability of other family support networks, such as nonworking grandparents able to look after children.

Cities and suburbs vary considerably in the characteristics of the local labor market and much of this has to do with the changing locational needs of employers. Perhaps more importantly, spatial variations in labor-market dynamics occur not just between cities but, crucially, also within them. The result is highly localized urban geographies of work, employment, and labor recruitment, which have three additional spatial consequences. First, employers are generally attracted to, and remain located in, specific areas of the city depending on their local labor and recruitment needs. Second, distinctive patterns of social life and commuting behavior tend to develop around each district and neighborhood in the city once these become dominated by particular types of employment and livelihoods. Third, and finally, such dynamic dependencies within the city are mediated by spatial differences in gender roles and relations. We now address some recent restructurings around the urban labor market.

5.5 Welfare-to-Work and the Rise of Contingent Labor in the City

Much of the discussion so far in this chapter has been about the restructuring of the geography of formal (i.e., regulated) work and employment across the city. Particular emphasis went on identifying the strong ties between work and residence in the city as reflected in the

Contingent labor covers a range of developments in how labor is regulated and recruited, such as the growth of casual employment and short-term (e.g., zero hour) labor contracts, along with the replacement of welfare with workfare as a system of state support for the unemployed. The rise of contingent labor suggests that for many the work–life balance has become more precarious, since employers have much more freedom to lay off workers, and the state can impose stringent conditions on how the unemployed receive public assistance.

emergence of highly localized labor market geographies. All of this assumes, of course, that it is possible to find stable employment and that the skill sets of workers corresponds more or less to the recruitment needs of local employers. Yet a particular feature of working life in the city today is the decline of long-term apprentice schemes and stable employment prospects and the corresponding rise of what is known as the **contingent labor** market. This term covers a range of developments, including the growth of informal, part-time, and casual employment, short-term labor contracts, and deregulated labor markets. In some circles, these developments are embraced by the term labor flexibility, which is assumed to have positive ramifications, such as making for a better work–life balance and giving employers more flexibility to hire (or fire) labor. However, contingent labor also points to new and less subtle forms of labor control and regulation in the city.

In many cities, the support structures that enabled men and women to transition from the home and community to the factory and full-time employment have disappeared. In their place, the state has stepped in, variously, to encourage, steer, or cajole workers to enter into the new urban labor market and, potentially, acquire new skills and jobs. For critical urban scholars like Jamie Peck (1996, 2001), the last 20 years is one of regulatory instability and experimentation with a new labor control regime in the city, one based less on welfare and more on finding work. National-scale forms of welfare provision have been dismantled to be replaced by devolved and local scale institutional arrangements, especially in cities where the emphasis is on getting people into work. These city-based *workfare states* usually consist of some or all of the following elements:

- An overarching emphasis on reducing dependence on welfare by putting emphasis on work.
- Funding or incentivizing labor market intermediaries (usually private sector firms) to act as recruitment and selection agencies rather than relying employers and state.
- Shifting the costs (and risks) of labor recruitment from employers and the state onto unemployed individuals, temporary workers, and labor-market intermediaries.
- Less reliance on skills development and long-term apprenticeships and growing dependence on short-term job placement schemes.
- Creating a raft of new regulations and policies that focus on employability rather than welfare provision.
- A reduction of employee benefits, including reduction or loss of pension plans, health benefits, and retirement savings schemes.
- Widespread use of zero hour employment contracts, which do not guarantee workers fixed hours even as they require workers to be always on call for work.

The new geography of workfare is having a profound disciplining effect on those at the margins the formal labor market: labor is not just being regulated but also is, in effect, "put in its place" by a harsh urban labor control regime.

Such signs of labor market restructuring are especially well developed in older industrial cities where new jobs are hard to come by. Sheffield, in the North of England, is a case in point. Famed for its steel industry, the city experienced deindustrialization in the 1970s and 1980s as major steel mills and supporting industries closed throughout the city. The fate of the city's male industrial workforce was amusingly yet poignantly captured in the hit movie *The Full Monty* (dir. Peter Cattaneo), which followed the fate of a small band of unemployed steel workers as they found a new outlet for their respective talents as male strippers. While the movie celebrated the entrepreneurial spirit and agency of the working class, it also hinted at another side of labor market restructuring: the rise of reserves of contingent labor in the city.

One sign of this is the proliferation of temporary labor agencies across the city. The main purpose of these agencies is to recruit labor in response to the immediate workaday needs of local employers. Usually this involves imposing strict conditions on recruits, including extensive profiling and multiple interviews. Agencies transport day labor by coach or van to different places across the city where jobs are in demand; increasingly this involves transporting day-labor recruits from the inner city to the suburbs. Wages are based on time spent at the workplace and costs of transport may be deducted from pay. In some cities, such as Chicago, large hiring halls have flourished in response to the growth of contingent day labor (Peck and Theodore, 2001). Such workfare labor control regimes tend to flourish in city-regions having dynamic economies capable of generating plenty of part-time employment rather than in established industrial cities, where the labor market tends to be more rigid and local welfare support structures remain in place (Etherington and Jones, 2009).

5.6 Resisting Urban Economic Change: Labor and Community Coalitions

As already indicated, cities are places where large industrial workforces have been assembled. Workers have often developed strong community ties based around work and residence; in some cases, these ties have fostered labor solidarity. The dominant political culture of community reflected the daily rhythms of work and production, albeit workers were never totally subjected to capitalist methods of labor control. Indeed, the city and its constituent spaces afforded many opportunities and distractions in the form of family, leisure, food, drink, music, and entertainment, thereby enabling workers to cope with the monotony and brutality of factory production. Family and community support networks provided the means of coping with difficult economic times, especially when plants were shut down and workers were laid off. Charities, clubs and societies would often step in when employers and local welfare systems failed. In these respects, the city not only created spaces of social and community support for workers in good times but also afforded various means for workers to survive under even more challenging conditions.

A growing body of critical urban scholarship is interested in evidence of workers' resistance to urban economic and social change. A particular focus is on coalitions between workers and community organizations, where these coalitions form, and how they can successfully challenge various economic threats and injustices, such as the closure of otherwise profitable industrial plants, the imposition of regressive employment regulations, differences in levels of pay between sexes, or low wage levels in general (Figure 5.6). We now consider two quite different examples of how labor and community resistance has been shaped by the geography of the city.

Living wage. A living wage is the amount of salary a worker should receive to cover the cost of a standard of living that is deemed decent, normal, and acceptable to the majority of the population. A living wage is, therefore, well above minimum wages set by law in most countries, since minimum wages often only allow people to live at or below the poverty line. A living wage would increase costs of business, but is more just because the distribution of income is spread more equally in society.

The first example concerns an attempt to retain manufacturing jobs in Chicago in the context of deindustrialization and rampant processes of gentrification in the city's North Side. The second considers new worker and community coalitions in the city, focussing on a **living wage** campaign in London. Both examples serve to emphasize the importance of mapping in greater detail the connections between the changing nature of the city as a place of work and its function as a place of social reproduction; in other words, to explore in a geographical respect what constitutes "making a living" in the city.

Figure 5.6   A living wage campaign in London. Photo courtesy of Jane Wills.

Contesting deindustrialization in Chicago

Until the 1980s, labor and trade union involvement in community-based economic development initiatives in Chicago had been very piecemeal. Community organizations had devoted their efforts to eliminating housing segregation and promoting integrated schools. But when industrial displacement began to threat entire neighborhoods and districts, especially on the North Side, workers and community groups began to mobilize around the goal of preventing further manufacturing displacement through gentrification. Community organizers put forward the idea of Planned Manufacturing Districts (PMDs) in which certain tax abatements and other incentives would be made available for industrial firms willing to remain in Chicago. However, the PMD proposal brought community organizations into conflict with real estate interests and city planners, who wanted the city's "obsolete" manufacturing districts converted into new residential and commercial developments. Nevertheless, with support from Mayor Harold Washington, the concept of PMDs was formally incorporated into the City of Chicago's economic development policies in the late 1980s (Jonas, 1998).

One of the first PMDs created was in the Goose Island/Clybourn Corridor area, which in 1990 included 350 manufacturers and 20 000 workers. Parts of the proposed area for the PMD were undergoing conversion to residential and commercial uses, putting pressure on remaining manufacturers (e.g., local steel producers, auto suppliers, etc.) to sell up and relocate elsewhere. This was the fate of the Stewart-Warner Corporation, which closed down its production in Chicago despite a strong campaign of union–community resistance (Jonas, 1998). When the PMD was eventually approved by the Chicago City Council it covered a much smaller area than originally proposed with less than 200 manufacturers protected. The reasons for this related to ongoing pressures to redevelop and gentrify Diversey Avenue, a major thoroughfare linking the Clybourn Corridor to the Lake Michigan Waterfront. Today, however, the Goose Island/Clybourn Corridor PMD has retained some manufacturing, including a major specialist brewery.

Living wage campaigns in London

The economies of many of the so-called global cities discussed in Chapter 4 would not survive without the toil of low paid and informal economy workers along with an army of unpaid and voluntary labor (Sassen, 1991). Low-wage workers have especially suffered under neoliberal welfare-to-work regimes, yet attempts to press for higher wages often price these workers out of the local labor market. Nonetheless, workers in some cities have started to fight back, finding new networks of support in local community institutions, including churches, charities, and social service organizations.

Jane Wills and her colleagues at Queen Mary University of London have conducted a detailed analysis of living wage campaigns in London (Wills et al., 2009). Living wage campaigns are devoted to securing earning levels sufficient to ensure workers and their families meet the essentials of life. Such campaigns have been forged around new alliances between low paid workers, religious groups, charities, trades unions, and local authorities. They led to the creation of London Citizens, which is a broad-based umbrella alliance of some 120 different organizations. This alliance grew out of a campaign to target health and public sector organizations in the East End of London. Later on, the campaign broadened its scope to embrace the financial services industries, higher education, cultural industries and contractors involved in the developments for the 2012 Summer Olympics.

The experiences of labor and community coalitions in Chicago and London suggest that cities afford a number of opportunities for workers' collective action against both deindustrialization and exploitative conditions of work and pay. Workers, the low paid, and the unemployed, become empowered by developing stronger ties with community organizations across the city. In some cases, labor and community coalitions have been able to marshal resources and foster networks, which eventually feed into wider social and political movements, such as reunionization initiatives and national and international living wage campaigns. In contrast to claims that labor is becoming more localized or spatially entrapped, cities seem to afford new ways of building labor solidarity and challenging exploitative tendencies in capitalism. As our knowledge of the changing nature of work and employment in the city improves, it could help further to demystify some of the local-global tensions and paradoxes of contemporary processes of economic restructuring.

5.7   Summary and Conclusion

This chapter has examined the complex and evolving relationship between employers, employees, and workers' organizations in the city. Until quite recently, urban geography was solely interested in the spatial patterning of urban social life. This emphasis on urban social conditions afforded very little scope for understanding corresponding changes in the spaces of work and employment across the city. Some of the earliest work in critical urban geography addressed this gap by examining the uneven impact of deindustrialization in terms of changes in class structure and gender relations, the rise of unemployment, and gentrification processes. Work on deindustrialization and uneven urban development later inspired detailed studies of the dynamics of local labor markets, helping to highlight the reciprocities between the locational strategies of firms and the presence of locally differentiated and segmented labor markets across the city. It further revealed evidence of new spatial patterns of work and commuting across the city, especially as new high technology and service sector jobs have located in the suburbs and women increasingly participate in urban and suburban labor markets. Urban geographical research has started to reveal the dynamic dependencies between employment, labor recruitment, and household behavior in the city.

Overall, this chapter has identified a shift in the focus of urban geography away from seeing the location of work and employment as completely separate from the social geography of the city. Today, the city is viewed less as a place of residence and more as a *work place* where strong ties have developed between employers, labor markets, workers, and communities in different parts of the city. Nevertheless, the kinds of labor control and recruitment practices that once produced strong community bonds in the industrial city are fast disappearing. In their place, cities have become strategic sites in the growth of contingent labor markets and new welfare-to-work regimes. These regimes seek to capitalize on the massive growth of informal, part-time, and casual labor in the city.

In the face of these profound changes in the nature of urban work and employment, labor has found new ways to engage in struggle and resistance to socially undesirable forces of social, technological, and cultural change. Here there is plenty of scope in critical urban geography for exploring growing tensions around the work–life balance. By putting labor at the center of the picture our understanding of the detailed geography of the city has been profoundly altered.

5.8 Further Reading

- Samers (1998) is an excellent analysis of the relationship between immigrant communities and labor recruitment in the automobile industry in the suburbs of Paris.
- For a discussion of the work–life balance in the contemporary city, see Jarvis (2005).
- Gordon (1984) offers an interesting interpretation of the relationship between Fordist labor control practices and suburbanization of industry. On post-Fordist modes of labor control and regulation in the city, the following are well worth consulting: Chapter 5 in Castree *et al.* (2004); Pollard (1995); Peck (1996, 2001); and Peck and Theodore (2001).
- For useful examples of labor and community coalitions in the city, see Chapter 6 in Castree *et al.* (2004) and Jonas (1998). Jane Wills has published widely on living wage campaigns in London (see, in particular, Wills *et al.*, 2009 and Wills and Linneker, 2013). Walsh (2000) offers an excellent case study of a living wage campaign in Baltimore, MD, USA.

Chapter 6

The City and Social Reproduction

Urban Geography: A Critical Introduction, First Edition. Andrew E.G. Jonas, Eugene McCann, and Mary Thomas.
© 2015 Andrew E.G. Jonas, Eugene McCann, and Mary Thomas. Published 2015 by John Wiley & Sons, Ltd.

6.1   Introduction

How is life maintained in the city? You might think that the only truly basic needs humans have are clothing, food, and shelter, but this short list of material goods deceptively masks just how complicated it is to keep people alive, not to mention healthy. If you think about where and from whom you receive the so-called basic needs of life, you will find that it represents a vast and complicated scenario. Caregivers and parents would be foremost in your mind, especially during childhood; but remember all of the economic and political infrastructures, institutions, and workers, and their global reach, that set up transportation networks, educate youth and workers, bring food to market, build housing of all sorts, sell potable water and process sewerage, and provide incomes to allow for the purchase of basic needs in the first place – that is, if there are regular incomes to be had.

While Cindi Katz (2001) explains **social reproduction** as "the fleshy, messy, and indeterminate stuff of everyday life," she also warns us to remember that everyday life exceeds the basic needs of biological life:

> According to Marxist theory, social reproduction is much more than this; it also encompasses the reproduction of the labor force at a certain and fluid level of differentiation and expertise. This differentiated and skilled labor force is socially constituted. Not only are the material social practices associated with its production historically and geographically specific, but its contours and requirements are the outcome of ongoing struggle. Apart from the means to secure the means of existence, the production and reproduction of the labor force calls forth a range of cultural forms and practices. (Katz, 2001: 711)

It would, therefore, be grossly mistaken for us to separate work and nonwork, given that the capitalist production of goods and services is wholly dependent on the so called "nonwork" spaces of social reproduction (Mitchell *et al.*, 2004).

Gender is one of the core processes that frame social reproduction, since the sexual division of labor is present worldwide, and overwhelmingly women remain the central caregivers of infants, youth, and the elderly. This work is often unpaid in families, or hired out mostly to other women to do household chores for pitiful wages. Generational and national differences are also important when thinking about the sexual division of labor, as are class and income. For example, aging populations in many European cities demand everyday care, and their relative wealth (on a global scale) allows them to hire caregivers; this is increasingly done by migrant labor in many cities. Therefore, when thinking about social reproduction, gender and the sexual division of labor must be thought of in tandem with wealth, nationality, generation, and ethnicity/race (Box 6.1).

> **Social reproduction** refers to the myriad of ways that the workforce is sustained and replenished under capitalism. These include childbirth and child rearing and regenerating the body through food, sleep, pleasure, and daily care. Without reproduction, production would cease, and capitalism would therefore collapse.

There are myriad other ways that money ensures social reproduction and allows it to flourish. Money insulates the wealthy from spikes in food prices, provides a wider "choice" of where one can live and raise a family, and allows excellent educational opportunities. And finally, geography and mobility clearly matter when thinking about social

Box 6.1   Caring Labor: Who Benefits Where?

According to the Philippines 2009 Survey on Overseas Filipinos (Census of Philippines, 2010), almost one million Filipino women left their homes to work abroad in 2009, almost all in cities. Nearly 400 000 of these Filipino women went to cities in the Middle East like Abu Dhabi, Doha, and Riyadh, or to cities in Asia like Hong Kong, Singapore, and Tokyo. In Middle Eastern cities where domestic worker protection is scant or even nonexistent, they work long hours often with no days off for months at very low pay, in order to pay for their children's school fees, housing, food, and other basic needs at home in the Philippines. They usually go years without seeing family, friends, lovers, partners, or their own children, given strict labor contracts and no money to pay for international flights.

These migrant women do the bulk of what is called *caring labor*, the work of caring for young and old bodies, sick bodies, and hungry bodies, and they maintain the household by washing clothes, preparing meals, cleaning toilets, and caring for pets. Their labor provides the support needed to keep life going, although their migration for waged labor often leaves their own children and parents in the care of others. Their caring labor is thus matched by a care drain in their home countries (Hochschild, 2002), as the reproductive work they would provide as mothers to their young children, or as daughters to their elderly parents, must be hired out or made up by extended family networks. Reproductive, waged labor is a primary export of the Philippines, and the children of those migrant bear the emotional brunt of the loss of their parents.

Much of the wages earned by exported laborers is sent home as remittances in order to pay for the gap in caring labor that they leave behind when they migrate. New demands for reproductive labor are created by migration, so that domestic workers are hired, or extended family members take up the responsibility of caring for the children staying at home. This demand exacerbates existing inequalities in countries like the Philippines, so that workers who cannot afford the expensive fees and travel costs to work abroad instead work for very low wages as domestic workers at home. Cindi Katz insists that "the social reproduction of the migrant workforce is carried out in its members' countries of origins" and represents a "direct transfer of wealth from generally poorer to richer countries" (Katz, 2001: 710). The question of who benefits where is indeed complicated, and trailing the intricate global geographies of social reproduction shows not only the financial flows of capital and worth, but also the emotional flows of pain, loss, and love (Pratt, 2012).

reproduction, since the migration of millions of people into cities, or to cities with excess wealth to spend on the salaries of household workers, provides the backbone to ensure social reproduction in many cities. Nannies, maids, sex workers, and more, often travel far from their own families to fill the demand for cheap, social reproductive labor.

This chapter begins to unravel the complex processes that underlie the reproduction of urban life. It starts by delineating the ways that global capitalism, state policy, and social

Figure 6.1 Domestic workers at a 2010 protest in Hong Kong hold up a sign demanding a wage increase. Photo courtesy of Nicole Constable.

reproduction are inherently intertwined. Social reproduction also shapes urban life through contemporary contexts of neoliberalism and economic restructuring. We shall see that the assumption of separate spheres of "work" and "nonwork" devalues women and racial and national minorities, to the effect that their labors are more easily manipulated and exploited. While much life is sustained under capitalism and informal economies, the chapter shows that not all lives are equally valued and, indeed, many are lost because of capitalism's cruelties and unjust social, political, and economic systems. Urban privilege also means that the rural poor have increasingly been forced to migrate to cities to find waged labor, setting up rural-to-urban migration patterns that leave rural places dependent on wages sent home from cities.

The chapter's purpose is to answer the following questions, so that you will understand the vital role that social reproduction plays in historical and contemporary urban geographies:

- How did social reproduction come to be associated with women's work?
- How has social reproduction shaped urban form over time and space?
- How do critical urban geographers delineate the spaces and activities of social reproduction?
- What are the connections between social reproduction and production?

Figure 6.2   Foreign domestic workers protested in Hong Kong in 2011 demanding the right to abode, that is, the right to choose where they may live while working in Hong Kong. Photo courtesy of Nicole Constable.

6.2   Defining the Gendered Spaces of Social Reproduction

Before the Industrial Revolution, the separation of home and work did not exist for the vast majority of the world's population. Agriculture, cottage industry, and even education were largely carried out at home and by family units, including by children. It was only with the advent of industry and the mass migration of labor to cities in nineteenth-century Europe and North America that the separation of work and home began in earnest, especially first in the newly industrializing regions. As work became separated from home in the West, women, always the primary caretakers of children, were equated with home spaces, so that private space became defined as separate from the public work world of men. The home became idealized as a retreat from the grueling, masculine shop floor, and "work" conceptually became divided through a gendered division of labor: between the productive, masculine wage work of industry, and the reproductive, feminine unpaid work of home (Box 6.2).

Central to this gendered division of space and labor was a heterosexual and class imperative for women to marry and be proper, domestic wives and mothers. The "public" woman was a threat to the image of women's purity, since women were supposed to remain home, care for the next generation, and stay off of public streets where the threat of their unrestrained sexuality could disrupt the ideology of the separate spheres of domesticity and

Box 6.2   The Gender Relations of Post-Fordism

Post-Fordism is a term used to reflect the changes in Western capitalism in the late twentieth and early twenty-first centuries (see also Chapter 3). In contrast to the Fordist factory line, which represented men doing assembly work that was often relatively well paid and union organized, post-Fordism reflects an era of disempowered workers in the global North and the shift of industrial work to the global South, where the mobility of capital can use up a workforce and move on to the next location for fresh bodies leaving underemployment in its wake (Wright, 2006). The Western ideal of Father going to work and bringing home the paycheck to his housewife and his children's mother exists only on television shows from the 1950s and 1960s when the ideology of the separate sphere was in full media force.

Linda McDowell, in a 1991 article titled, "Life without father and Ford: the new gender order of post-Fordism," examined the gender relations of this economic shift. She argued that geographers and economists needed to drop their reliance on a gender binary that insinuated that all men profit, and correspondingly that all women lose, with shifting forms of capitalism. Instead, in post-Fordism class differences between women intensify (for example, think about the class and race differences between wealthy women and their nannies) which makes a primary classification between women and men difficult to sustain.

Rather, she wrote, post-Fordism has "opened up opportunities for some women to join the core occupations and so increased class divisions *between* women. But what it has also succeeded in doing is turning upside down the gender divisions between large numbers of men and women. Increasing numbers of men are employed in the peripheral labour market too, on terms and conditions that traditionally were regarded as 'female'" (McDowell, 1991). McDowell offers an important rejoinder to the idea that women entering the workforce achieve greater liberation because they make their own money. In fact, as women entered into the workforce in large numbers through the 1970s and 1980s, what is called the feminization of the workforce (Chapter 5), they did so by placing social reproductive responsibility onto structurally disadvantaged workers.

work (Domosh and Seager, 2001). The "domestic" woman became an idealized caregiver and her proper place was the home.

Ideas like these about gender and work reflect a geographically specific group's or class's position or priorities. Of course, many women worked outside of their own homes, and even engaged in revenue-producing work at home, throughout the nineteenth and twentieth centuries. The idea that women did not engage in public and waged work in this timeframe was that of a particular class, race, and location, and of heterosexuality and **patriarchy**. The separation of women and their domestic work to the homeplace served the interests of white, Western, bourgeois patriarchy, since women's work in the home was unpaid – essentially free to those receiving the fruits of feminine labor. The capitalist and patriarchal state in the industrialized world of the nineteenth and early twentieth centuries

Patriarchy is the systematic domination of men over women. Patriarchy is sustained by the everyday exploitation of women, the practices that prioritize men's work and needs over women's, and also by social structures such as heteronormative marriage that place men in positions of authority and power over women. Patriarchy is not universal, since the domination and exploitation of women take very different forms throughout the world and affect women to greater and lesser extents.

ensured that women's wealth and work, as well as the work of racialized minorities not deemed to be equal citizens of the Western nation, accrued to white men's property holdings and lineage. In many countries like the United Kingdom, the United States, and Australia, married women did not have the right to own or inherit property, to gain custody of their children if divorced, to have the exclusive right to their own money, and more, until the twentieth century.

The separation of domestic work was, therefore, a powerful check on women's political, economic, and personal power, as women were scrutinized against racial, sexual, social, and cultural requirements to be proper wives and mothers, at home. Even today, after huge gains through the women's rights movements of the twentieth century, women do far more reproductive work than their male counterparts in almost all countries, spending more hours per week on domestic chores and child rearing. According to Bridgman *et al.* of the US Bureau of Economic Analysis, in 2010 women worked 26 hours a week on home production, while men only spent 17 (Bridgman *et al.*, 2012: 23). In many ways, the home remains a feminized workplace, with the unpaid labor of women reproducing the lives of new generations.

Of course, as the earlier example of migrant labor attests, gender is only part of the story of the how domestic work gets naturalized through the distinction of private space. Slave and indentured labor was also free labor in many places for hundreds of years and shockingly continues to be found worldwide through child slave labor in domestic situations and through the human trafficking of domestic and sex workers. Slave labor relied on a racial hierarchy that established another central system of reproductive work, first forced and then through the devalued work of black servants, particularly in the United States, the Caribbean, and in parts of South America. Furthermore, the exploitation of labor during colonialism set into motion the racial, ethnic, and geographic hierarchies of a global workforce that we see even today in the streams of migrant labor that flow to urban centers and core Western economies.

Women's work, love, and the social reproduction of capitalism

Mitchell *et al.* write that,

> in order to really understand how labor-power is constituted as a class and capitalism is reproduced as an economic system and a set of social relations, we must understand how these particular groups are constituted as workers – waged and unwaged – within this system. Further, we must problematize the very categories of production and social reproduction, which determine the nature and value of "work" in far too limited ways. (Mitchell *et al.*, 2004: 11)

"Women's work" is one such category that escapes easy distinction, as seen not only in the great range of people who do this work but also in the values given to it. The value of "women's work" has been defined in part by naturalizing all of that reproductive labor that mothers do for children, and wives do for husbands, as loving or **caring labor** (England and Folbre, 1999). The labor of love thus maintains some women's desire to work for free in the interests of others like children and partners. Just thinking of labor as propelled by love neglects the ways that the family is the core of productive labor, and not just reproduction (England and Folbre, 1999); love might flourish in many families, but it has also an economic function within capitalism.

> **Caring labor** is paid and unpaid work that involves the care of others who are typically in close proximity to the worker. Examples include day care workers, nurses, teachers, wait staff, and therapists. Feminists like Paula England and Nancy Folbre have argued that aid care workers experience a disadvantage in the wage labor market because care work is associated with love, or the requirement that such care be done for emotional reasons and not economic ones.

The phrase "women's work" also implies that maids, housekeepers, and other forms of privatized household workers do so in part for the emotional investments they have in their caregiving – and not just for the wages they earn. For example, the image of the "mammy" figure in the United States still impacts the working lives of thousands of nannies who are racial and national minorities in American cities. The mammy is a racist figure which depicts a slave woman holding the interests of white children above herself or her own children (just think about Scarlet O'Hara's mammy from *Gone with the Wind*). The mammy figure has been a powerful force in shaping expectations of children's caregivers of color. When the story is told that nannies do their work because they love those for whom they care, then their labor is devalued: they are supposed to work for love and not (enough) money. Whether or not nannies and other caring laborers do in fact love the families for whom they work is beside the point. They should be paid a living wage and be allowed to parent their own children, which is often impossible for caregivers who work very long days for pitiful wages, often far from home.

Hiring domestic workers in turn transforms the family home into a capitalist space, where the relationship between worker and boss is marked by an exchange of money. Domestic labor has become commodified in this way in every city across the world (Figures 6.3 and 6.4). Reproductive waged work in the home workplace is often not regulated by the state, since home is deemed a "private space." The idea of the home as a private space, untouched by the state or the commodity exchange of labor, is a legacy of the naturalization of "women's work" done for love, not money. This leads to gross injustice, including the nonpayment of wages, the physical, sexual, and mental abuse of domestic workers. "Many domestic workers are not covered by provisions regulating their working time. As can be seen in Figure 6.3, there is no applicable limitation of the normal weekly hours of work for 29.7 million domestic workers (or 56.6% of the total). The average is weakest in Asia and the Middle East, where more than 95% of domestic workers are not entitled to such a limit" (quoted and adapted from Luebker *et al.*, 2011).

Few states have policies setting the hours of a domestic worker's day and providing for days off to rest. Domestic workers earn pittances but are often devalued as laborers because work in the home has been defined historically and spatially as "nonwork." The division of

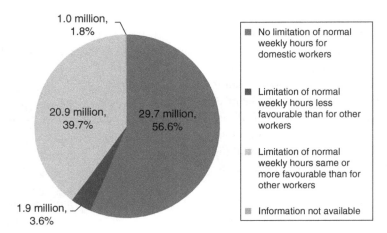

Figure 6.3   Limitation of normal weekly hours of work for domestic workers under national law. (Luebker *et al.*, 2011. Used with permission of the International Labour Office.)

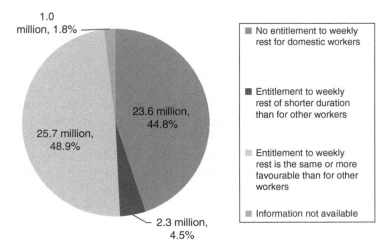

Figure 6.4   Entitlement to weekly rest (at least 24 consecutive hours) for domestic workers under national law. (Luebker *et al.*, 2011. Used with permission of the International Labour Office.)

work and home space means that reproductive workers are literally hidden from public view. The irony is that their work is the very backbone of global capitalism, as the production of goods and services would collapse without social reproduction.

6.3   Social Reproduction and Urban Form

Critical urban and feminist geographers ask how the separate spheres of "work" and "home" contribute to urban spatial form. Kim England explains that:

[T]he location of residential areas, work places, transportation networks, and the overall layout of cities in general reflect a patriarchal capitalist society's expectations of what types of activities take place where, when, and by whom. In turn, the city supports and perpetuates the beliefs about gender that generated it. Thus society is involved at the deepest level in determining the very nature and form of the city and, as such, cities contain important visual symbols of social attitudes. (England, 1991: 136)

One of her examples is the suburb, its historical geography, and its development as a domestic, living space in contradistinction to the urban core's emphasis on male work and business.

The **suburb** in post-World War II America depended on the separate spheres to maintain the segregation between women "at home" and men who commuted "to work." The model of the white nuclear family in the suburbs also highlights a heterosexual binary of marriage, traditional gender roles, and the reflection of the separate sphere in material spatial form. Poor transportation options beyond the individual car, limited child care centers given the force of normative messages about the values of "stay-at-home moms," and housing types that emphasize middle class consumption, all illustrate the material geographies that fuel gender relations and white privilege in North American urban spaces (England 1991, 1996) (Figure 6.5).

A **suburb** is an area outside of a town or city and is considered to be primarily a residential area. Suburbanization includes, however, the spread of not just people's housing outside the core city but also industry, businesses, and commercialized leisure. Suburbs are often represented as North American inventions and require mobility, as they are often ill-served by poor public transport networks. Therefore, suburbs especially developed around automobility and highway infrastructures.

By the 1980s with the growing presence of women in the workforce and the Western feminist movement's growing political emphasis on women's access to wealth and formal employment, the suburb's force as an ideal American community was fading. Of course, the suburb was only that: an ideal. The reality is that suburbs were and are never free from crime, domestic violence, child abuse, homelessness, hunger, poverty, and other harsh realities. Yet the ideal exerts force on the form of urban geographies.

One example that illustrates the making of an idealized suburban community is from Orange County, CA. In this case Karen Till (1993) shows that new suburban developments like to draw on "traditional" American values when planning housing types and neighborhoods. She argues that no such tradition actually ever existed, but rather these planners created the vision of an idyllic suburban past to sell new homes in Rancho Santa Margarita in the 1980s and 1990s. These are called *neotraditional towns*. In her example of Rancho Santa Margarita in Orange County, planners sold Californian Spanish colonial architecture styles to evoke "the feeling of a European, traditional model of community" (Till, 1993: 717). Such images are romantic investments in a past that never existed.

The developers of neotraditional towns like Rancho Santa Margarita are also banking on wealthy whites' fear of the city itself – in this case, Los Angeles. In short, suburban development fabricates identities of homeowners based on the ideology of separate spheres, and in the United States this ideology is writ through with white privilege. Nowadays, Orange County as a whole is a minority white place, which means that there are more people living

Figure 6.5   Levittown, Pennsylvania, was a planned suburb in the 1950s. Close to both Trenton, NJ, and Philadelphia, PA, the suburb amassed individual family homes on what was previously farmland. Pete Seeger, an American folk singer, described the suburb in a song written by Malvina Reynolds in 1962 called Little Boxes: "They're all made out of ticky-tacky, and they all look just the same." See Kushner (2009) for the history of civil rights struggles in the suburb.

there who are Asian, Latino, and Black, than who are whites. However, within Orange County the town of Rancho Santa Margarita remains a majority white community. The nonwhite population over time was not reflected in surburban developments like Rancho Santa Margarita, and thus nonwhite presence was quieted by the developers' representations of places as populated only by middle class, white, male-headed households.

Social reproduction and urban form in Kolkata, India

Social reproduction is far from uniform in the way it shapes urban form, such as housing patterns and availability in different cities. If we turn, for example, to megacities in the global South that have grown very rapidly in a short period of time, we must consider the shantytowns, slums, and informal housing that spring up to house the millions who have migrated to the city from rural locations in search of work. The metropolitan area of Kolkata, India, for example, went from a city of under eight million in 1975 to 15 million in just 30 years; by 2025 it will have over 20 million residents. Kolkata has extremely wide disparities in housing. Its rapid growth has exacerbated those inequalities, but so have the processes of globalization.

For instance, nonresident Indians (NRIs), like those working in the highly skilled service sectors of United States, Middle Eastern, and European cities (think computing, banking, finance, and engineering), are able to send money home to buy expensive condominiums for family members and for themselves. High-rise development backed by the international capital of NRIs has displaced millions of Kolkata's residents whose homes were torn down to make way for new construction. Pablo Bose (2008) describes these developments as displacements:

> Hand in hand with these developments have come the wholesale displacement of the former populations that used to live there, agrarians, horticulturalists, landless labourers, migrant workers and others. The more fortunate have found jobs as drivers, domestics and the ubiquitous security guards for the new housing estates and their affluent denizens; others have been pushed out into city slums and rural villages and into conflicts with the working poor and marginalised in those spaces. In some of these situations those evicted are directly making way for the living spaces of the transnational elites; in others the dislocation is in service of the lifestyles supposedly embodied in such figures and expressed through the building of golf courses, country clubs, movie theatres, luxury condominiums and other amenities. (Bose 2008: 125)

Seeing high rises or golf courses in cities like Kolkata – or in any city – should immediately raise the question: What was there before this development? Whose capital was invested in this new urban form, and who lost their own investments in homes and businesses, when this displacement occurred? Urban geographers like Bose show that, increasingly, we must answer these questions with a global lens, since capital flows internationally to affect urban form and to reshape the social reproduction capacities of urban poor who are pushed away from homes, work, and community networks.

City politics and governance needs to be examined for their roles in the development of new high-rise condominiums, too. The urban scholar Ananya Roy shifts the locus of urban scholarship and planning on megacities like Kolkata away from "its population density or its shortage of resources" (Roy, 2011b: 107). She instead implores analysis on the spatial processes of "eminent domain, special economic zones, land acquisition, displacement" (Roy, 2011b: 104). In other words, examining a city's land use and urban form requires a look at both the economic *and* political processes that lead to them.

In the case of Kolkata, Roy describes the city's Operation Sunshine in 1996 that sought to remove informal economic activities through a series of sweeps that destroyed informal vendors' stalls and thus livelihoods. The Operation was also meant to sanitize the city. Roy writes, "In many ways, this 'sweep' was the municipality's first high-profile effort to render informal, even criminal, the very structures of vending and hawking that had long been established features of the city's commercial landscape. But the sweep was also an attempt to recuperate a city of air and light, governed by values of hygiene, order, and beauty" (Roy, 2011b: 95). In short, the city's and metropolitan area's planners wanted to return Kolkata to the colonial ideal of a "gentleman's city," and Roy argues that this was both a physical and a symbolic attempt to remake the city (Roy, 2011b: 95).

Examining megacities like Kolkata with just a view on the demographic shifts of population growth and urbanization, or the power of wealthy elites to invest in new housing, therefore neglects a consideration of a city's planning responses to rapid change. Social reproduction is not just reflected in urban form, urban form also impacts social reproduction and offers an insightful lens for exploring differing values placed on particular lives and on city planning and policy making.

6.4   Changing Spaces of Social Reproduction

The shift to workfare described in Chapter 5 entails the realignment of responsibility for the poor away from the nation-state onto the poor themselves. This has had a dramatic impact on the abilities of poor urban residents to maintain livelihoods. As states began the steady pace of defunding social programs, cities, in particular, felt the brunt of the effects of the abandonment of the nation-state's attention to social reproduction (see Box 6.3 on structural adjustment's impact on social reproduction in Jamaica).

The case of public housing in the United States

In the United States, the example of housing provision for the poor illustrates how neoliberalism and privatization have fed on a disregard for the struggles of lower income groups to attain adequate housing. In the United States, large public housing projects have largely disappeared. First imagined as a solution to the inability of the poor, especially minorities, the elderly, and the disabled, to access housing markets – in part because

---

Box 6.3   Health Care Disparities

While urban populations generally have access to a greater range of health services than those in rural or remote locations, the disparity between those who can afford them and those who cannot leads directly to the question of who lives and who dies. Within Glasgow, Scotland, according to the World Health Organization (WHO), "there is a 28-year difference in the life expectancy of people living in different neighborhoods" (http://www.who.int/world-health-day/2010/media/whd2010faq.pdf; see also Box 6.4). While infectious diseases like diarrhea or malaria might be more of a concern in global South slums than in urban Glasgow, violence, crime, physical inactivity, stress, and traffic accidents impact poor neighborhoods with more deadly outcomes than in wealthier neighborhoods.

Poor health increases the demands on caring labor, to be sure, but public health crises and challenges can affect political systems, labor supplies, and the urban infrastructure. Better urban planning processes that include participation from the most disadvantaged can illuminate the burden that social reproduction places on the poor, especially women, and national, racial, and ethnic minorities. Critical urban geographers insist that social and economic inequality cannot be addressed until political inequality is challenged. The struggle to stay alive, and to live happy and healthy lives, is a social, economic, and political struggle.

of exclusion and segregation in renting and lending markets described in Chapter 3 – housing projects by the 1990s had become symbols of failed housing policies. Early that decade, the US Department of Housing and Urban Development (HUD) implemented the Congress-approved **HOPE VI program**, meant to clear inner cities of blighted, domineering housing projects. Residents of "the projects," it was argued, would be better off in areas without such high degrees of concentrated poverty. In the wake of demolitions, neighborhood

> **HOPE VI** is a US federal program that provides funding to revitalize public housing areas, largely in inner city locations. The funding aims to redevelop large scale public housing projects that are in disrepair into mixed-use developments. This process encourages privatization of public housing. In many cities, developers can pay fines instead of fulfilling affordable housing requirements, so the loss of public housing is not replaced with different options for the poor.

design emphasized the creation of mixed income housing, smaller building construction, and mixed use, pedestrian-friendly streets reflecting new urbanism ideals.

Figure 6.6   Compare Chicago's Cabrini-Green housing tower in the background to the new construction of "Parkside of Old Town" in the foreground. The tower was demolished in 2011 and has been replaced by some new housing and new retail, although empty land in the area remains. Too few "affordable" units exist for low income residents interested in moving back to the neighborhood, however (Vale 2013). Residents must pass credit checks to gain apartments, and as discussed in Chapter 3, credit has a problematically racialized history in American cities. Mandates for developers to include affordable units often translate into the inclusion of small units interspersed with larger ones. Small units are "affordable," since they have less square footage and rent for less money, but poorly serve families with children. Social reproduction of poor families is therefore maligned in the interests of "redevelopment". Photo: Lawrence J. Vale.

But did the residents of the former housing projects benefit from new construction? Critical scholars argue that the large scaling back of public housing in fact led to its rampant privatization, with construction companies and landlords profiting from new financing opportunities, tax breaks, and contracts (Figure 6.6). The very poor lost their homes and were forced to enter new housing markets – but overwhelmingly in areas of similar concentrations of poverty. They did not necessarily "move to opportunity" as the federal government hoped they would.

In fact, Susan Popkin of the Urban Institute, in an assessment presented to the US Congress, finds that "there have been no overall changes in employment" of HOPE VI program participants (Popkin, 2007: 11). The reason is not that surprising: the geographies of home did not necessary determine those of work. Job markets in less poverty-concentrated areas did not match the job skills of the poorly educated laborers of HOPE VI, namely single mothers, many of whom are women of color. Nor could single mothers travel far for work when they had to consider child care constraints and duties alongside poor transportation networks. Caring for extended families in the old neighborhood also required geographic proximity, and few had private means of transportation (Rogers, 2011). Social reproduction duties and caring labor, compounded by the racial and gender marginalization present in many job markets, trumped public policy.

The case of undocumented migrant life in the United States

Particularly in North America, the national state shifted many previous social reproduction supports to lower territorial levels of government (Mitchell *et al.*, 2004: 17). This includes the regulation of labor and not just the procurement of basic needs such as housing, food, and education. Increasingly in the United States, for example, local sheriffs and police are given primary responsibility for policing undocumented migration (Coleman, 2009). Local police and deputies go into neighborhoods and communities of migrant laborers, collect them in sweeps or through traffic stops, and start deportation proceedings. Mathew Coleman (2012) found that from June 2008 until December 2009 in Wake County, NC, home to the city of Raleigh, 50% of all immigrant detainees placed in the Wake County jail originated from traffic enforcement (Coleman, 2012: 174).

The social reproduction of the unskilled workforce – the workers who keep the city and suburbs looking manicured through landscaping services, who build new housing in construction services, who work is a wide array of manufacturing jobs, and who care for young children as nannies – is impossible to maintain under the constant threat of arrest simply from getting in one's car. This is occurring in many cities across the United States. In fact, since 9/11 the United States has removed more people than it did the previous century (Box 6.4). Families are torn apart, education and the workplace are disrupted, and migrants avoid health and educational services in attempts to avoid police.

As Chapter 9 illustrates, cities work hard to market images of themselves as open for business. But clearly the marketing or "branding" of cities emphasizes certain types of labor over others – that is, skilled labor bringing in big corporate investment in service economies. It is important to question whose lives in cities are rendered more precarious in the process (McCann, 2007). Nina Martin (2010) argues that many undocumented Mexican migrant

Box 6.4 The "Facts" about Urban Health according to the World Health Organization

The World Health Organization's web portal on urban health lists "facts" to consider when thinking about the social determinants of health. Some of them are listed here.

- Fact: Of the three billion people who live in urban settings, an estimated one billion live in slums.
- Fact: An estimated 130 000 premature deaths and 50–70 million incidents of respiratory illness occur each year due to episodes of urban air pollutions in developing countries, half of them in East Asia.
- Fact: In spite of nightmarish congestion, motor vehicle use in developing cities is soaring. In 1980, the third world accounted for only 18% of global vehicle ownership; by 2020 about half of the world's projected 1.3 billion cars, trucks and buses will clog the streets and alleys of poorer countries.
- Fact: The WHO considers traffic to be one of the worst health hazards facing the urban poor, and predicts that road accidents by 2020 will be the third leading cause of death.
- Fact: Breathing Mumbai's air is the equivalent of smoking two-and-a-half packs of cigarettes per day.
- Fact: In Quito, Ecuador, infant mortality is 30 times higher in the slums than in wealthier neighborhoods.

(See http://www.who.int/social_determinants/publications/urbanization/factfile/en/index.html for the other four facts). Used with permission of the World Health Organization.

workers in the United States engage in **informal labor** unregulated by markets. This means that they cannot find regular or steady work, are often paid wages below the legal minimum wage, and cannot fight against unfair labor practices. She writes that "the conditions workers face mean that the number of hours they work will never result in economic security. Rather, they find themselves facing a crisis of social reproduction, where they need help with housing, food, child care, and transportation in order to survive on their wages" (Martin, 2010: 131).

Martin's research in Chicago shows

Informal labor refers to work in the informal sector. The informal sector is typically economic activity that is unregulated, untaxed, and may even include examples of criminal or illegal activity. Examples can range from street hawkers to cash-only workers mowing the lawn, from prostitutes and drug sellers to agricultural day-laborers or maids. Migrants, women, and children form the bulk of the informal sector's laborers, as they have less access to formal and legal sector employment.

that nonprofit groups aid migrants' daily struggles. The combined work of community organizations, nongovernmental organizations (NGOs), and social movements – what

Martin refers to as migrant civil society – impact labor markets in significant and unlikely ways. This is another example through which we can see that interrelationships between production and social production. These organizations make up for poor wages by offering free services to migrants in the neighborhoods where they live, such as health clinics, impromptu child care, and food pantries. In turn, these services act like a form of subsidy to the substandard labor markets in which migrants must work.

Ironically, Martin suggests, the good work of migrant civil society actually *enables* the continuation of poor working conditions, since it ensures the reproduction of the migrant workforce. Migrant civil society cushions the crisis of social reproduction, in effect (if not in intention) in the interests of capital. At the same time, of course, Martin also insists that these organizations agitate for better futures for migrant workers: "Through policy advocacy, community organizing, protests, partnerships with unions, and popular education they have the potential to translate the alienating experiences of exploitative workplaces into a broader demand for worker rights, for migrant rights, and ultimately for human rights" (Martin, 2010: 148). Her research in Chicago illustrates the impossibility of separating work and nonwork spheres and spaces, and the important role that charity organizations, religious groups and institutions, and NGOs play in supporting everyday life.

The case of structural adjustment in Kingston, Jamaica

The privatization of social reproduction began decades ago in global South cities with restructuring programs. Geographer Beverley Mullings reports that in postcolonial Jamaica through the 1970s income inequality fell as the state focused on economic development for all. However, with rising oil prices and falling commodity export prices, Jamaica was forced to enter structural adjustment when the access to credit by the International Monetary Fund (IMF) came with conditions. The conditions of borrowing money from the IMF included the introduction of user fees for health care and education; thus, many social reproduction costs shifted from the government to the individual household.

> **Spatial fix** is a phrase indebted to the work of Marxist geographer David Harvey. He argues that capitalism attempts geographical expansion and restructuring to address its inability to grow indefinitely. In general terms, a spatial fix is a geographic solution or attempted solution to problems of accumulation, control, and stasis.

Yet in the 1990s under the era of structural adjustment in Jamaica, poverty rates fell even as domestic wages fell and the costs of everyday life increased dramatically. Why? Mullings reports that households became ever more reliant on remittances, money sent to Jamaica from relatives living abroad in places like Toronto, London, and New York City. She refers to this process as the "**spatial fix** of social reproduction," as the space of households became transnational. Mullings writes of the 1980s and 1990s, "By stretching the spaces of social reproduction across international borders, Jamaican migrants filled the void created by the retreat of the state and private sector from social reproduction" (Mullings, 2009: 179).

The second spatial fix Mullings describes is gang welfare, particularly in the slums around Kingston. Gang leaders, or "dons," negotiated access to work, housing, and government contracts (for things like housing construction) and increasingly invested their lucrative profits from these activities in the illicit transnational drug trade. Of course, government contracts began to dry up when state funds were directed away from social reproduction projects through structural adjustment. Gang leaders solidified their influence through "garrison communities." Mullings explains: "garrison communities became the spatial expression of Jamaica's clientelistic political culture, as self-appointed area leaders increasingly assume control over the flows of labour and capital that crossed the community's boundaries" (Mullings, 2009: 179). Accompanying the growth of gang welfare, however, was violence.

Mullings argues that the loss of caring labor at home through migration, and the sustained levels of violence through garrison spatiality, present a long-term challenge to social reproduction even as they offer short-term spatial fixes to social reproduction. Disorder and violence inhibit capitalism. While some might laud the challenge to capitalist systems that crisis presents, Mullings fears that "Jamaica is teetering towards social collapse because the fear and cost of violence is slowly grinding its system of economic production to a halt" (Mullings, 2009: 185). Her arguments show that the blame for disorder and violence must begin with neoliberal development strategies and their abandonment of social reproduction priorities (Box 6.3).

6.5 Summary

A critical approach to urban geography places social reproduction at the center of political, economic, *and* social processes in the city. This chapter has defined social reproduction as the myriad ways that the workforce is sustained and replenished under capitalism. The relations of capitalism, however, extend beyond the confines of money and class. The chapter has insisted that social differences including gender, sexuality, nationality, age, and race/ethnicity are integral to the question of whose reproductive labor is valued, rewarded, and remunerated, and whose is exploited, disposable, and undervalued. We cannot separate out the actual lives and bodies of those workers who fulfill the need for labor, since the ways they themselves are actually valued leads to their ability to exert influence in the workplace, in political process and planning, and in transnational labor flows.

Reproductive labor is often highly gendered, since "women's work" has been defined by a long history and geography of assigning caring work to mothers and wives. Urban form reflects the segregation of women's work over time in different places. Yet it is vital to remember that focusing merely on gender erases the divisions between women, and the ways that race, sexuality, generation, and location have always been a part of social reproduction. The chapter therefore insisted that reproductive labor is shaped by international flows of migrants, by capitalism, by race and ethnicity, and by age. The erasure of these differences can result in a myopic focus on "women's work" as only a gendered phenomenon.

Thus, the spatial and gendered separation of "home" and "work" continue to have impact on the lives of many social reproductive laborers. This supposed separation of home and work includes impacts on domestic workers, whose devalued, poorly paid labor exposes the low values placed on traditional "women's work" even today. The example of domestic work also illustrates the ways that home has become a space of capitalism and wage relationships. A critical analysis of the devaluation of social reproduction helps to identify the exploitation of waged workers doing all sorts of reproductive labor but, just as importantly, it insists that there is little to gain in distinguishing reproductive from productive labor under capitalism. When they are separated, a critical response to ongoing inequality is curtailed.

6.6 Further Reading

- The introduction to the book, *Life's Work: Geographies of Social Reproduction*, edited by Mitchell *et al.* (2004), is a useful starting place to understand the Marxist theory underlying feminist commitments to thinking though social reproduction.
- Children bear the brunt of the devaluation of social reproduction under capitalism (Katz, 1998, 2004). The pain of separation from migrant mothers is explored in *Families Apart: Migrant Mothers and the Conflicts of Labor and Love* by Pratt (2012). While migrant mothers do provide the means for better education and potentially richer futures for their children, the cost is painfully high for both.
- In some cases, migrant woman face extreme consequences if they become pregnant; see Constable's (2014) *Born Out of Place: Migrant Mothers and the Politics of International Labor*, where she asks: Are migrants just laborers, or are they allowed to be people with sexualities, relationships, and a right to decide the conditions of their lives?
- See Hubbard's (2011) *Cities and Sexualities* to get a range of examples and arguments about the ways sexual reproductive labor undergirds urban form, politics, and erotic work. Sex work is also a caring labor, as argued in Ehrenreich and Hochschild (2002); also see Kempadoo and Doezema (1998) and Dewey (2011).
- Oswin (2010, 2012) shows how heterosexual norms operate to exclude migrant labor integration in Singapore, particularly through the cases of housing, immigration policy, and marriage and natal restrictions.

Chapter 7

Governing the City
The State, Urban Planning, and Politics

Urban Geography: A Critical Introduction, First Edition. Andrew E.G. Jonas, Eugene McCann, and Mary Thomas.
© 2015 Andrew E.G. Jonas, Eugene McCann, and Mary Thomas. Published 2015 by John Wiley & Sons, Ltd.

7.1   Introduction

In the spring and summer of 2005 a series of street protests involving housing activists, social planners, local residents, and recent immigrants occurred in the Raval district in the old quarter of central Barcelona, Spain (Figure 7.1). The protests sought to draw attention to the displacement of local residents resulting from the gentrification and redevelopment of the district. Once associated with vice, crime, and prostitution, El Raval first became a target of the city's urban redevelopment policies in the late 1980s. Several blocks of low income housing were razed in order to make way for the creation of a new *ramblas*, or pedestrian street, along with up-scale hotels and cultural facilities. With the build-up to the 1992 Summer Olympic Games, the scale of development in Barcelona expanded ambitiously. El Raval occupied a prime location in the city, and developers, the government, and business interests sought to reimagine the neighborhood in their interests. The prostitutes, drug users, and low income residents have been replaced with tourist shops catering to an international clientele, fancy bars, and art galleries – and a not insignificant immigrant population.

The conflict over the redevelopment of the Raval has come to represent a struggle over a new vision for the City of Barcelona, notably its transformation from the industrial capital of the Spanish region of Catalunya into a European cultural center with global aspirations. At its heart was the attempt to reposition of Barcelona nationally and internationally as the economic and cultural capital of an imagined urban axis stretching from Barcelona to Milan and London. As the experiences of cities like Barcelona suggest, contemporary urban

Figure 7.1   Graffiti from a Barcelona, Spain, wall protesting tourism in the city. Photo: Eugene McCann.

political struggles revolve around a complex set of global and local processes, which often combine to focus our attention on the planning and governance of the neoliberal city (Rossi and Vanolo, 2012).

As urbanization has proceeded apace it has become that much more difficult to pin down the boundaries of the "urban." The urban is being stretched out and up-scaled so as to incorporate the regional, national, and global scales. Moreover, the capacity of the state to regulate and inter-vene in urban development has drastically changed. A new era of **urban entrepre-neurialism** has flourished with the growth of public–private partnerships, the private financing of urban development and infrastructure, and the contracting out of urban services formerly funded and delivered by the state (Hall and Hubbard, 1998).

> **Urban entrepreneurialism** refers to the investment-friendly strategies used by urban authorities to entice companies and entrepreneurs to their jurisdictions. One sign of urban entrepreneurialism is the proliferation of public–private partner-ships around the redevelopment of the city. Entrepreneurialism is one manifestation of **neoliberalism** and **neoliberalization**.

How we think critically about the city is inseparable from wider – regional, national and international – political-economic transformations; processes originating outside the city increasingly shape what goes on within it. In an interconnected world urban authorities can learn from each other, often drawing upon on urban policies and institutions assembled else-where. However, there still seems to be something distinctive about the urban political realm insofar as it looks, feels and works differently to, say, the "suburban", the "rural" or the "national" (these categories likewise should not to be taken for granted). As you reflect on the changing role of urban politics, planning and governance it is important for you to remain focused the wider context. In this chapter, we invite you to consider the following questions:

- What is the role of the state in urban planning, housing provision and governance?
- What are urban growth coalitions and how do they influence planning and politics in the city?
- Why and how do cities compete for economic activity?
- In what ways are urban political institutions becoming neoliberal?
- Are suburban spaces becoming more private and exclusive?
- In a regional urban world, where are the territorial limits of the city?

7.2 Capitalist Urbanization: Planning, Social Provision, and the Housing Question

Chapter 3 examined the relationship between the development of capitalism and urbaniza-tion. In that chapter we argued that the value (social wealth) created in capitalism often depends on the creative synergies generated in cities, not to mention the daily toil of ordinary people working in cramped sweatshops and menial service jobs (also Chapters 5 and 6). While all cities represent particular assemblages of capital and labor, specific economic sectors are involved in developing urban land, producing housing for the workforce, and providing infrastructure. These include developers, transportation companies, architects, builders, insurance companies, utilities, and the like. The fact that urban development plays such a crucial role in regulating patterns and processes of economic growth and social redistribution in capitalism is not lost on those critical geographers interested in such issues as housing, urban planning, land use conflict, redevelopment, and urban politics (Scott, 1980).

Writing in the latter half of the nineteenth century, Friedrich Engels (1872/1935) famously argued that the housing question in capitalism is not about the slum and overcrowded conditions of the cities but rather is an enduring effect of the class relations of capitalist production. As spaces of collective consumption (Cox and Jonas, 1993), cities help to sustain capitalism by providing housing and basic serves for workers, their families, and dependents. Urban authorities play a crucial role in supporting collective consumption and social provision through, for example, the delivery of supporting physical and social infrastructures, connecting homes and workplaces through public transportation, providing essential services like water and electricity, operating local school systems and child care facilities, and training the workforce. The failure of the prevailing system of production to provide such services and internalize the externalities of urban growth often leads to tensions and conflicts, such as:

- struggles around the provision of basic infrastructure and services;
- tensions around land use planning, housing provision, and urban growth;
- conflicts around urban renewal and redevelopment;
- competition between cities and suburbs for investment and jobs.

The City of Cambridge in the East of England, offers an example to illustrate how one city managed to provide services and how it sought to ameliorate tension and conflict.

Cambridge represents an urban growth hotspot in the UK economy. Notably, as a national center of innovation and learning, Cambridge attracts clusters of high-technology industries and supporting infrastructure and services, which collectively have come to be known as the "Cambridge Phenomenon." In the early 1990s, Cambridge business leaders became concerned that the economic demands being placed on the city were outstripping the capacities of local authorities to deliver affordable housing, road improvements, and rail infrastructure. With house prices in Cambridge up to six times that of the national average, Cambridge and its surrounding communities were becoming unaffordable for professional workers, trainees, and young families. Another set of problems was insufficient investment in infrastructure and supporting urban facilities (While *et al.*, 2004a). Urban growth pressures reached a point where they were perceived to threaten the continued success of the Cambridge Phenomenon. Without further social investment in Cambridge and the wider region, then the wider UK economy might even begin to suffer as a whole.

The newspapers and prominent local business leaders began to talk up a "growth crisis" in Cambridge, proclaiming that without public intervention the city's growth bubble would burst (Figure 7.2). Their main objective was to reform urban planning and, specifically, the policy of urban growth restraint associated with the green belt. Originating in the post-war era, greenbelt policy was designed to protect the special character and setting of cities like Cambridge by using development restrictions on rural land and open space to define clearly the limits of urban growth (see also Chapter 11). Local business and political leaders – the Cambridge **"growth coalition"** – argued that this planning policy had restricted the potential for major new housing developments in the city and surrounding areas.

Government
University
Housing
Shoppers
Business
Tourists
Traffic
People

Figure 7.2 The political ingredients of urban growth in Cambridge, UK, as imagined by a local entrepreneur. Source: Dawe and Martin (2001). Used with permission of P. Dawe Consulting Ltd.

The growth coalition began to talk of the need to "invest in success" or risk losing investment to rival urban growth centers in Europe. Pressure was put on the ruling UK Labour government to increase its regional allocation of housing to the Cambridge area and to find new mechanisms to invest in infrastructure. These demands continued after the election of a new national Conservative–Liberal Coalition government in 2010. The UK state responded by promising to relax restrictions on housing development and streamlining planning processes, including abolishing housing targets established by the previous Labour government in its regional spatial strategies. In addition, there has been a commitment to investing in new road infrastructure and improved public transportation (bus and rail).

> The urban **growth coalition** is an alliance of business organizations and local government actors, whose interest is in the further expansion of the local (city) or regional economy. It unites and mobilizes around the shaping of land use policies and other instruments of urban development with a view to enticing further investment and growth to the locality. The term "growth coalition" is derived from the writings of the sociologists Harvey Molotch and John Logan (Logan and Molotch, 1987) and has been widely used in critical urban geography (see Jonas and Wilson, 1999 and the discussion of **rentiers** in Chapter 9).

The Cambridge story demonstrates how in a capitalist economy state intervention can result from political pressure from below by organized urban growth coalitions. Such coalitions represent the spatial interests of sectors, firms, and entrepreneurs locally dependent on the urban economy, loosely defined, as well as local public services (schools, roads, transport, water, etc.). As Cox and Mair (1988) argue, firms are locally dependent when it is difficult for them to move to, or operate in, other urban localities; they do what they can to ensure that growth and investment continues to occur in the cities where they have already invested or where a market exists for their products and services. When local businesses face expansion problems due to, for example, a shortage of affordable housing for new employees, planning restrictions, or inadequate infrastructure, they entrust the growth coalition to lobby city authorities, regional government, or the state at large. The aim is to influence local zoning decisions, reform local planning regulations, improve services, or find ways of funding infrastructure, among other possibilities.

Typical participants in urban growth coalitions are developers, private utilities, builders, retailers, local industrial firms, local politicians, and, in some cases, even local colleges and universities (Logan and Molotch, 1987). Most cities have some sort of organized growth lobby, be it a chamber of commerce, an economic development organization, or an infrastructure development committee. Take, for example, Columbus, OH, in the USA. Metropolitan economic development organizations have worked with city and county authorities to ensure that economic development and infrastructure are delivered throughout Columbus and the surrounding areas of Franklin County. The City of Columbus provides water and sewer services to outlying suburban areas under contractual arrangements which limit the amount of land that can be annexed to the suburbs, thereby allowing Columbus to generate economies of scale in service provision, protect its tax base, and lower the cost of issuing municipal bonds. In addition, Columbus sets aside 25% of its income tax revenues for a fund to improve capital spending on public services, a policy which the metropolitan growth lobby was instrumental in creating (Jonas, 1991).

Usually the focus of growth coalition activity is on attracting investment and jobs to the city. But the Columbus example demonstrates how it might be necessary to work with county, regional, state, or even national authorities in order to draw down new powers for urban development and infrastructure provision. This demonstrates an important idea in critical approaches to urban governance: how territories and scales stretching beyond those of the urban can be enrolled. Business and political elites in urban areas frequently resort to higher territorial structures of the state to attract new powers, resources, and expenditures to their cities. In the Cambridge case above, there was recourse to the national level because local fiscal structures and planning mechanisms depend on the actions of UK government ministries rather than local authorities.

In India, however, regional government has played quite a crucial role in urban growth tensions. In Bangalore, India's so-called "Silicon Valley," locally based information and communication technology firms have turned to the regional government, the State of Karnataka, to address the city's crippling infrastructure problems. The issue in this case is finding sufficient leverage over urban authorities to fund basic infrastructure and, thereby, to prevent multinational firms from leaving Bangalore for other cities. One solution in this case could be the introduction of mechanisms to tax wealthy property owners and use the revenue to fund road improvements and other infrastructure regarded as suitable for a high-technology economy. Bangalore entrepreneurs have therefore tried to encourage non-governmental organizations (NGOs) working with the urban poor to put political pressure on the authorities to tax the city's wealthier residents (Box 7.1). Such an urban politics might be more feasible in a country like India where the urban poor have at least, in numerical terms, greater political heft in urban politics.

Box 7.1 India's Silicon City Booms to Busting: As IT Firms Pour into Bangalore, the City's Infrastructure is Struggling to Keep Up

The following extract is from an article by Randeep Ramesh published under the above headline in *The Guardian* on Friday, 24 September 2004:

More than 100 firms from outside India, including Microsoft, Google and Reuters, set up offices in Bangalore last year. Hundreds more have farmed out white-collar work such as call centres to Indian companies in the city. Drawn by a booming economy and a temperate climate, a large slice of middle-class India is setting up home in this high-technology hub. The result is that Bangalore is Asia's fastest growing city, albeit one that is unable to cope with the speed of its own progress.

Behind the facade of gleaming steel towers, shopping malls and industrial parks, lies a conurbation groaning under traffic jams, power cuts and spiralling property prices.

City administrators say that Bangalore is a victim of its own success. MK Shankarlinge Gowda, the senior civil servant in the information technology ministry, points out that a decade ago Bangalore was a city of 2 million people with a million vehicles, whereas today it has a population of 6 million and 3 million vehicles. "These are the problems of being perhaps too successful. But we are doing what we can for all the people in the city. IT companies could themselves help by building housing for their workers near their offices."

Campaigners however say that the problem lies not with industry or government but with the state's citizens.

Ramesh Ramanathan is a former Wall Street banker who returned to Bangalore and set up a civic movement, Janaagraha, with £500 000 of his own money three years ago, to encourage voters to demand greater accountability and effectiveness from their government.

"The problem here is that there is no civic responsibility for the garbage collection, bad roads, water supply. There are 1 million properties in Bangalore, but fewer than half pay taxes. The result is that we collect only 2 billion rupees (£24 million) in revenue rather than 6 billion (£72 million)."

Source: http://www.theguardian.com/world/2004/sep/24/india.randeepramesh. Copyright Guardian News & Media Ltd 2004. Used by permission.

The provision of housing

Housing affordability – and for that matter also daily urban living – is a major challenge in most cities, especially expensive global cities like London, New York, or Tokyo. These cities attract highly paid workers in finance and professional services, workers who can pay a premium for housing near the center of the city. The result is upward pressure on the cost of housing and rents, which in turn attracts property speculators and fuels further house price inflation and gentrification. This demand for housing exacerbates the problem of affordability for middle and low income groups. In response, lenders may resort to new mortgage instruments as a way of encouraging people to purchase private single-family housing.

Adjustable rate mortgage. An adjustable rate mortgage (ARM) is a way to borrow money to buy property. In this type of mortgage, the interest rate fluctuates with the market, rather than being a fixed rate. If the interest rate rises, so does the mortgage payment. Thus, the risk of the rising costs of credit is passed to the consumer rather than being held primarily by the financial institution offering the mortgage.

One example of this sort of mortgage instrument is the **adjustable rate mortgage**.

This approach to the housing problem contributed to the global housing market crash of 2008; many people were stretched too thin and could not afford balloon payments or inflated interest rates on mortgages. Cities like Las Vegas experienced a sharp decline in home values as homeowners defaulted on properties and hundreds of houses went unsold and sat vacant. In suburban Los Angeles, occurrences of West Nile Virus, a mosquito-borne illness, spiked as swimming pools sat untreated and stagnant water allowed mosquito populations to explode. Some cities, on the other hand, bucked the housing market crash; property values in major cities like London and Toronto

Figure 7.3   A poster illustrating the housing affordability problem in the suburbs of Boston, MA. Photo by Andy Jonas. Used with permission of the Citizens Housing and Planning Association (CHAPA).

remained stable or even continued to grow, fuelling yet more property speculation. The consequences are evident to see: people living in major cities but working in low paid and menial jobs often cannot afford the cost of housing. For these people, homelessness or resorting to precarious and temporary housing can be a serious threat. For people experiencing foreclosure, the effect on their credit histories may preclude home ownership for decades.

One solution to housing shortages for a variety of people might be to supply more subsidized housing – either public (council) housing or social housing delivered by the private sector or not-for-profit organizations. However, there is often resistance to this from local authorities. In London, the UK state has had to mediate between obstructionist local boroughs, on the one hand, and employers, including schools, universities, hospitals, and financial services firms, concerned about the lack of affordable workforce housing, on the other (Ancien, 2011). This problem is replicated in many cities ranging from Boston (Figure 7.3) and Seattle in the United States to Sydney and Melbourne in Australia, places that remain attractive to new economic sectors.

These cities and their surrounding suburbs have placed a premium on zoning land for low density, single-family housing units rather than multiple or shared occupancy units, social housing, and work–live spaces. Nonetheless, new demands for affordable work and living spaces in the city put pressure on urban authorities to modify zoning designations and deliver more low income and subsidized housing, even those that are most strongly wedded to neoliberalism and noninterventionist approaches to the housing problem. In many respects, Engels' views on the housing question in capitalism continue to resonate through to this day.

7.3   Urban Entrepreneurialism and the New Urban Politics

The examples discussed above point to an important new dimension of entrepreneurial urban politics, namely, a competition between cities to attract investment, create jobs, and grow the local economy (see also Chapter 9). One of the first to comment on this trend from a critical perspective was David Harvey (1989). He noted that the managerial style or redistributive urban governments that emerged in the post-war period in North America and Western Europe were undergoing major transformations as they become more entrepreneurial and risk taking.

Most city governments are now involved in competing for flagship projects (e.g., attracting a major corporation), prestigious public events (e.g., the Olympics), cultural activities (e.g., a new museum or exhibition), or new economy industries (e.g., medical research clusters, creative industries, etc.). It is generally believed that inter-urban competition helps to raise the national and international profile of cities, bringing huge commercial and fiscal rewards to those places that can land mega-urban projects and investments, such as the Olympic Games. It is usually local businesses and political leaders – members of the urban growth coalition – rather than residents and workers who are most likely to benefit. These members include developers involved in property transactions, banks looking to lend money, realtors (estate agents) selling homes, media companies offering advertising space, speculators wanting to capitalize on inflated property values, utilities looking to attract new customers, local governments struggling to garner new sources of tax revenue, and mayors seeking re-election.

Nowadays, much of the business of urban competition involves attracting so-called creative workers. It has been suggested that high wage earners in new economy businesses are increasingly sensitive to the quality-of-life package offered by different cities (Nevarez, 2003). However, this says little about the distributional impacts of creative-city policies on other sectors of the population, including the poor, the unemployed, and those dependent on general city services (McCann, 2007). Moreover, just because there is competition between cities for creative industries, this does not mean that it is uncontested.

As the Barcelona example at the beginning of this chapter shows, urban redevelopment imposes additional costs on local residents, disrupts the normal flow of the city, displaces households, destroys historic landmarks, and changes the character of neighborhoods as places to work and live in the city. Facing public political backlash, urban renewal authorities and redevelopment agencies often enlist support from neighborhood organizations and community groups, thereby giving a semblance of grassroots political participation to what are, in many other respects, quite regressive urban transformation processes.

The rise of competition between cities for investment, jobs, and fiscal resources is symptomatic of what some critical urban geographers have called the New Urban Politics (NUP) (Cox, 1993). The term NUP refers to the new urban leadership styles and institutional structures associated with attracting mobile capital to cities and, correspondingly, the decline of a more redistributive form of urban politics. It is not that urban competition did not exist before – after all, in the fourteenth and fifteenth centuries European city states often battled for mercantile trade and in the nineteenth century US cities competed vigorously to attract canals, railroads, and manufacturing– but rather that its nature has changed.

Entrepreneurial urban policies

In a study of more than 170 US cities, Clarke and Gaile (1998) observed a shift from cost-cutting strategies typical of urban competition in the 1970s (e.g., tax breaks and zoning to attract manufacturing branch plants) to today's entrepreneurial urban policies, of which the following are typical (see also Jonas and McCarthy, 2009):

Eminent domain involves the taking (i.e., acquisition or regulation) of private property by government agencies in situations where there is deemed to be an overriding public interest. Typically in the United States, it involves a municipal government exercising its police power to assemble land and acquire property prior to undertaking a program of urban renewal or redevelopment. Eminent domain is controversial because it removes the control of the redevelopment process out of the hands of local residents and property owners. Moreover, the affected residents and property owners do not always receive just compensation for any losses incurred following the compulsory purchase of their homes and properties.

- *Public–private partnerships:* Public–private partnerships (PPPs) facilitate flagship urban redevelopment projects or major infrastructure programs. PPPs operate like private corporations but are authorized to use public funds to leverage private investment. Despite claims that they induce economic development, PPPs often have limited benefits for surrounding neighborhoods: tax breaks cut into municipal revenues and use of the power of **eminent domain** often generates public opposition.

- *Special purpose districts:* Many urban redevelopment projects involve the establishment of a regional or metropolitan district having special powers separate from the daily functions of municipal government. Special districts usually raise capital by selling revenue bonds dedicated to a particular income stream, such as sales taxes and user fees. The ability to pay back money borrowed depends on the creditworthiness of the district. Credit rating agencies such as Moody's and Standard and Poor's have become powerful players when it comes to determining which cities and their districts attract investment (Hackworth, 2007).
- *Business improvement districts (BIDs) and other special zoning districts:* BIDS are amendments to a city's overall zoning ordinance that set aside an area of a city for a special zoning designation. The case for setting up BIDs usually comes from downtown businesses and city governments worried about the loss of retail in competition with the suburbs. Downtown retailers and landowners agree to self-levy taxes to pay for local business improvements such as street maintenance, security patrols, and marketing. BIDs are signs of the increasing intrusion of private interests into the urban public realm (Ward, 2010).
- *Tax increment financing (TIF) of redevelopment:* Under enabling legislation, a tax increment district (TID) is set up for a specified period (often it is at least 20 years) to conduct the redevelopment process, typically raising money by selling bonds. As redevelopment occurs, property values theoretically should rise. The "tax increment" (the property tax income over and above the pre-redevelopment rate) is used to pay off the bonds. Unless they

Business Improvement Districts (BIDs). This is the most common term for a number of similar organizations operating around the world, sometimes with other designations, like Business Improvement Associations (BIAs). They are areas of cities with clear boundaries within which businesses pay a special levy on top of their regular taxes. The board of the BID, comprising largely of local business representatives, is then permitted to take that extra revenue and decide how to use it within the district. Often, its uses include advertising for the District, extra street cleaning, private security, or special events. Critics accuse BIDs of being undemocratic because the decision to set one up and the control of how to use the extra revenue are not subject to a full democratic vote among the whole population of the area.

Tax increment financing (TIF) is a mechanism for financing urban redevelopment that is widely used by cities in the United States and, to a lesser extent, also in other countries like the United Kingdom. In the United States, redevelopment legislation allows local governments to establish a public-private redevelopment agency which has powers to set up a designated a tax increment district (TID) for any part of a city deemed in need of redevelopment due to low property values or "blight." Working with private developers, the agency raises money by selling bonds in order to fund infrastructure and improve the development prospects of the TID. As redevelopment occurs, property tax revenues rise and, in theory, the increment (i.e., the tax above the pre-redevelopment amount) is used to pay off the bonds. However, TIF is controversial because other public entities such as school districts, which also rely on property tax revenues, do not always receive their share of the tax increment. Despite requirements to spend TIF revenue on affordable housing, this designated revenue is often not spent on such housing. Finally, there is a lack of public accountability because TIF bonds do not require voter approval.

can negotiate a favorable deal, other public entities that normally receive property tax revenues, such as school districts and library districts, do not receive TIF revenue. Moreover, even if TIF income is set aside for public housing projects, most redevelopment agencies do not spend their share, leading to criticism that the use of TIFs channels resources away from general urban social provision such as local education (Weber, 2003).

As cities become more entrepreneurial, they tend to undertake similar regeneration activities and produce almost identical urban forms: waterfront developments; shopping centers; business districts; tourist attractions; cultural quarters; and suchlike. Globalization is generating a certain degree of uniformity in the look and feel of cities, which might be variously described as "Manhattanization" or the "Barcelona model" (Box 7.2 and Figure 7.4). Such global uniformity also reflects a tendency for city policymakers to draw selectively on urban policy instruments such as TIFs and BIDs which have seemed to work well in other cities.

Figure 7.4   An early stage view of the redevelopment of the Poble Nou district of Barcelona, Spain. The redevelopment of Poble Nou is known as the 22@ project, as it is based on an old planning area (zone 22) identified in the first metropolitan plan for Barcelona in the 1920s (Casellas and Pallares-Barbera, 2009). In districts like Poble Nou, new public spaces have been created not just for local residents but also to encourage private investment. Photo: Andy Jonas.

Box 7.2 Barcelona: A Model of Urban Entrepreneurialism?

For many urban leaders and politicians around the world, Barcelona in North East Spain has become a model of urban transformation. So what is the "Barcelona model"? The first thing to note is the important role of urban politics. The trigger for Barcelona's urban transformation is usually attributed to changes in the governance of the city following the death of General Francisco Franco in 1974, and with it the end of Fascism and dictatorship in Spain. It led to democratic elections throughout the country, including major cities like Barcelona, where a progressive-left city council was elected headed by Pasqual Maragall, who served as mayor from 1982 to 1997 (McNeill, 1999). Maragall was the urban politician who is widely credited for bringing the Olympic Games to the city in 1992. However, this was just one part of a much larger story.

Prior to the Olympics, the city administration undertook major political and governance reforms, removing many of the centralized planning structures of the Franco era. These included the abolition of the old metropolitan corporation, which was responsible for metropolitan services, and the decentralization of urban administration around ten neighborhood districts. Neighborhood organizations had flourished in the 1960s and 1970s as demands increased for services in the city's public housing projects, shanty towns, and informal settlements (Calavita and Ferrer, 2004). The intention then was to privatize public services and formally incorporate grassroots citizen organizations movements into the apparatus of urban government.

Since the Olympics in 1992, the language of urban democratization has been used to legitimize wider interventions into public urban space, with a view to making Barcelona attractive to new private investment. Working in partnership with regional government in Catalunya and the European Union, the city authorities have put into effect major urban transformations. These have included the demolition of older housing stock such as in the Raval district mentioned at the start of this chapter, the removal of shanty housing on the Mediterranean waterfront, the construction of a hotel–office–marina complex, and the redevelopment of the old textile districts of Sants and Poble Nou around new economy industries (Figure 7.4). Not surprisingly struggles around the redevelopment of parts of the inner city have been quite bitter, often led by housing activists, local residents including the elderly, recent immigrants, radical planners and architects, and even anarchists, all of whom feel threatened by these changes. One conclusion that can be drawn is that although Barcelona is often viewed as a model of progressive urban entrepreneurialism it is also a symbol of urban conflict and public protest in an age of austerity.

In the UK, the Conservative Government led by Prime Minister Margaret Thatcher famously copied the American approach to urban renewal by setting up Urban Development Corporations tasked with clearing older industrial sites and redeveloping these into new office and commercial centers, such as Canary Wharf in London. Critics on the left saw this as a political maneuver to take key planning and land use decisions out of the hands of urban authorities and refocus them around redevelopment authorities, which were beyond public control and local accountability. In a recent continuation of this trend, some British cities are now looking to tools like TIF as a solution to problems of financing urban redevelopment in an age of public austerity.

7.4   Suburban Development and Metropolitan Political Fragmentation

For mainstream economists, urban competition represents rational economic decision making in the face of global competition and capital mobility; for them state intervention in urban policy is an anathema. In countries like the United States and United Kingdom the state is indeed far less directly involved today in urban welfare and social provision as compared to, say, the height of spatial Keynesianism in the 1950s and 1960s (Chapter 3). Differences between urban places increasingly reflect national economic priorities rather than local political decisions (Jessop *et al.*, 1999). However, national urban policy differences between countries matter. The territorial structure of the state (like the allocation of powers and functions between different levels and units of local government) sets the context for national differences and disparities in urban political outcomes.

A case in point is suburban development in the United States and, in particular, local land use planning. Municipalities use zoning to influence the pattern and mix of land uses, including housing and industry, and the local tax base. Local land use policies can serve in effect to keep out or exclude unwanted land uses (chemical factories, landfills, low income housing) and keep in or include the desirable (good schools, access to services, lower property taxes). The capacity to exercise **exclusionary zoning** often contributes to fiscal disparities and social differences, which are exacerbated by the fragmentation of metropolitan areas into separate cities, suburbs, and special districts. For economists, fragmentation (or fiscal localism) is often seen as a good thing, as it encourages urban competition and lowers local

Exclusionary zoning involves the exercise of local land use authority to keep out locally undesirable land uses from the city. In the United States, it has contributed to metropolitan disparities in levels of fiscal effort and service provision.

tax rates. However, suburban officials and planners are often confronted with demands from commercial and residential developers for additional investments in infrastructure and services even as suburban voters remain notoriously conservative on issues like land use policy and taxation. As a result, many municipalities struggle to fund basic services such as policing, snow removal, lighting, and libraries. Despite holding the promise of a better quality of life, the suburbs are not necessarily devoid of "urban" problems such as fiscal austerity, inadequate service levels, crime, discrimination, and social unrest.

For those of a more liberal persuasion, local exclusionary politics is the prime cause of urban inequality; it reinforces existing class and racial divisions within the urban populace. It has given rise to an alternative politics of metropolitan integration. This alternative politics originates in the US civil rights movement of the 1960s. A key issue here was the harnessing of federal powers to override local zoning and open up the suburbs to people previously denied access to affordable housing, especially Black and Hispanic families. Another goal was to integrate public school systems engaged in practices of racial segregation.

A case in point is Columbus, OH, where due to infrastructure and land use policies mentioned above, some fringe neighborhoods in the City are educationally served by suburban school districts (Cox and Jonas, 1993). Housing developers often shunned the opportunity of building homes in the Columbus School District in the past because of a legal requirement imposed on the District in the 1970s to bus students of different races to different schools throughout the city. In the face of a massive public backlash in the 1980s, busing for racial balance was discontinued in most major US cities including Columbus (the result is an unfortunate return of severe racial segregation in American public schools).

Edge cities and postsuburban space

While social and racial disparities between cities and suburbs have framed many discussions of urban politics in the United States, there are signs that urbanization is throwing up new settlement forms that challenge such a framing. One important trend is the emergence of new developments on the outermost edges of metropolitan areas, which seem to have an economic and political life of their own. These have various been described as **edge cities** (Garreau, 1991) and **boomburbs**

> **Edge cities and boomburbs.** Edge cities are places at the outer reaches of major metropolitan areas that have attracted new office developments and retail activities but not necessarily housing. Boomburbs are residential suburbs comprised of master-planned estates that have grown exceptionally quickly and, consequently, tend to be lacking in supporting employment and infrastructure.

(Lang and LeFurgy, 2007). These outer-edge developments are evidence of a world wherein urbanization is no longer driven by growth around a core urban center (Phelps and Wu, 2011). Another notable feature of these postsuburban spaces is the proliferation of special purpose districts, which have been set up exclusively to service new development. Here the private sector has scope to negotiate favorable financing for infrastructure without formal recourse to the urban electorate.

Along with these privatized forms of development, new patterns of consumption are being fostered across the city. Developers can exploit these new arrangements and generate class-monopoly rents (Harvey, 1985a: chapter 3). This refers to the ways in which housing developers and landlords are able to sell or rent homes catering exclusively to certain categories of consumer, especially middle and upper income households, on a sufficient scale that it is possible to appropriate extra income for little additional per-unit cost in terms of outlays on land, services, infrastructure, and repairs.

Urban political geography plays a crucial role in how class-monopoly rents are structured across the metropolis. One sign of this is the premium some households are prepared to pay for a good education for their children by moving to suburban school districts. This is a well-known feature of metropolitan development in the United States, where the differences in property values and rents between urban and suburban public school districts can be quite pronounced (often suburban real estate taxes are the equivalent or more to a year of private education tuition in the city). The quality of local education provision is also a contentious issue in the United Kingdom, where league tables comparing local schools in terms of educational performance mean that the location of school catchment-area boundaries can influence residential choice and, hence, housing costs. While realtors (estate agent) do not necessarily refer to school league tables when marketing properties, nonetheless subtle messages can be used to convey a sense of social exclusivity to potential buyers having children. One response by inner city authorities has been to invest in privately funded and managed school academies to improve local educational outcomes in the city and, indirectly, to re-energize the market for private single-family accommodation. The privatization of inner city education exemplifies just how deeply urban entrepreneurialism permeates into contemporary urban living. Yet it also throws into sharp perspective the central role of affordable public services and basic infrastructure to everyday life in the city (Jarvis, 2005).

Gated communities

Another example of the trend toward the privatization of the urban living place is the proliferation of gated communities, especially in outer suburban areas. These are master-planned communities where entrance to the community is controlled by a security gate and special rules apply to how the community is managed (Box 7.3 and Figure 7.5). Research by Pauline McGuirk and Robyn Dowling has documented the kinds of political identities being produced in these self-governing communities. Their focus is on Master Planned Residential Estates (MPREs) in Sydney, Australia, and they argue that "MPREs can be understood as an expression of the contemporary politics of social reproduction … in

Figure 7.5   Entrance to a gated community in Las Vegas, NV. Photo: Andy Jonas.

Box 7.3　The Governance of Gated Communities in the
United States

Across many American cities and suburbs, new residential gated communities have been built. These provide their residents (homeowners and, occasionally, renters) with exclusive access to a community's amenities, private security, and control over how the community functions. Most of these gated developments are designed with amenities suitable for particular lifestyles, such as championship golf courses, tennis courts, health clubs, swimming pools, or equestrian facilities. They are often located on high-value land having access to good views, beaches, resorts, and suchlike. Access to the gated community is usually monitored by private security firms operating out of controlled access points, that is, the gate (Figure 7.5).

One of the defining characteristics these communities is the existence of the Homeowner's Association (HOA). Membership of the HOA is restricted to local residents, who pay an annual fee. Depending on the exclusivity of the community and the range of its services, these fees can vary from as little as a few hundred dollars to several thousand dollars. The HOA is responsible for collection of the association's fees and enforcing community rules and regulations. Some HOAs are also responsible for maintaining streets, security, parks, golf courses, and community buildings, and for enforcing housing design and architectural standards: "[t]ypically, there are rules pertaining to upkeep and appearance of the homes within the development, specifying the colors of paint on outside walls, types of fencing, size and types of pets, rental restrictions, guidelines for landscaping, and storage of boats or recreational vehicles" (source: Gulf Coast Associates, Realtors, http://www.findsouthwestfloridahomes.com/gated-communities. php. Used with permission of findsouthwestfloridahomes.com).

Heightened levels of security and surveillance, along with a certain degree of self-regulation irrespective of prevailing municipal or state laws, are central features of any gated community. Accordingly, anyone perceived to be a visitor, outsider, or otherwise not a *bona fide* member of the community is usually treated with a certain degree of suspicion. This can have tragic consequences, as illustrated by the case of Trayvon Martin, a black teenager who was visiting a gated community in Sanford, FL.

On 26 February 2012, Trayvon was shot and killed while walking to a family member's home from a local convenience store where he had just bought some candy (sweets). George Zimmerman, the community's self-appointed neighborhood watch coordinator, admitted to police that he shot Trayvon in the chest after calling to report a suspicious person walking in the community. One can infer that this suspicion was aroused because Trayvon, an African–American young man, looked "different" than other residents of the community.

which traditional public goods and services have been commodified, privatised and contractualised … as responsibility for the means of social reproduction is absorbed by households and individuals in a wider political-economic context of restructuring social investment" (McGuirk and Dowling, 2011: 2615).

One political effect of gated communities is that they reduce levels of social and cultural mixing and political integration. So in Sydney the rise of a "global city" political discourse alongside that of private neighborhood governance has, if anything, intensified demands for greater suburban political autonomy; outer suburban spaces are becoming further detached politically and discursively from "global" Sydney. In the meantime, inner working class suburbs and other poorer districts of the city tend to get excluded from wider political decisions influencing the allocation of infrastructure and services; these can be called the "in-between" spaces of established urban centers (Keil, 2011).

7.5   *De Facto* Urban Policy and the Rise of City-Regionalism

Much of what we have suggested so far presumes there is such a thing as "urban" politics and, moreover, that what is "urban" is fundamentally different than, say, "suburban" or "national" politics. However, there is a view that suburban development is itself a product of national urban policy. Suburbanization was not an expression of individual consumer choice but rather a by-product of capitalist urbanization and the Keynesian demand management policies (Harvey, 1985a: 202–211). An integral aspect of this in the United States was the central role played by the federal government after World War II to encourage economic growth via fiscal and regulatory incentives that stimulated private housing development and supported the provision of urban infrastructure such as freeways (Florida and Jonas, 1991). Cheap land and good quality housing suddenly became available on a mass scale, encouraging many households to escape the overcrowding, taxes, and deteriorating services of traditional manufacturing urban centers. The availability of cheap oil was central to this movement to the suburbs, too, illustrating the importance of the American state to ensure ongoing access to petroleum once automobility was the norm (Huber, 2013). The suburbs therefore played a dual economic and political role: providing an outlet for effective demand in the economy and legitimizing the American dream of upward mobility, affordable housing, job security, and freedom from extreme price spikes for things like oil.

This somewhat cozy situation has been challenged by the rise of neoliberal urbanism signified by state withdrawal from urban policy, the turn to free-market urban entrepreneurialism and fiscal austerity. All of this is evident in Southern California, a region once emblematic of Fordist–Keynesian urbanization but now deeply marked by neoliberal suburbanism in the form of:

- widespread competition between suburban municipalities for tax revenue from new commercial and industrial land development to make up for shortfalls in federal funds and local property taxes;
- the ongoing fragmentation and privatization of local government as a result of the creation of newly incorporated municipalities, gated residential communities, and special purpose districts;
- financial deregulation and speculative private residential and commercial development at the urban fringe; Southern California has been at the forefront of successive housing market crises triggered by financial deregulation, mortgage foreclosures and loss of jobs in defense industries;

- a growing reliance upon direct rather than representative democracy in the form of local voter initiatives and reliance on instruments like TIF to fund urban services and deliver new growth (Note, however, that the State of California abolished TIF in 2013).

There can be no doubt that major city-regions like Southern California are vast and difficult to manage even under formal governmental arrangements. Such city-regions might span several counties, metropolitan areas, provinces and even (if we include places like Tijuana in northern Mexico) national borders.

The growth of mega-urban regions like Southern California is prompting changes in urban governance, planning, and state policy. A premium is being placed less on self-contained metropolitan government and more on looser confederations of city-regional governance having strong external linkages and networks. This is the basis of what is known as the **new regionalism**, a movement to promote greater collaboration between what might formerly have been rival urban and suburban centers.

Take, for instance, Detroit, MI; there the Metropolitan Organizing Strategy Enabling Strength (MOSES) was set up in 1997 to bring together businesses, religious leaders, and civic activists involved in low income communities around a campaign to establish a regional transportation authority and to increase regional public transit funds. Or consider Denver, CO, where tensions in the metropolitan area have been a serious impediment to regional economic development over the years. These conflicts date back in the early 1970s when a major referendum was held in which the public voted against Denver's plans to host the Winter Olympics in 1976. In 2004, however, a major turnaround occurred when an impressive coalition of business, mayors, environmentalists, and the public was forged and voted for an increase in the regional sales tax for Denver's new light and commuter rail project known as FasTracks. In uniting formerly divided urban and suburban political constituencies, the coalition has profoundly reshaped the economic, cultural, and political development of a major US city-region which, until recently, was notable for suburban sprawl, chronic infrastructure problems, and a fiscally conservative electorate.

New regionalism. The belief that government should operate at larger territorial scales than the neighborhood, city, or county levels. New regionalism suggests that metropolitan-wide planning and economic development does a better job than disconnected local governments, and that economies operate beyond local jurisdictions and, therefore, so too should planning. In the main, it has led to the creation of new regional collaborative arrangements between local governments, civic groups, and business organizations across metropolitan areas.

Some urban scholars believe that the power and authority of the nation-state is potentially being undermined by the rise of city-regions (Scott, 2001), a view anticipated by Jacobs (1984) who claimed that city-regions are first-and-foremost wealth creators and distributors whereas nation-states tend to engage in "transactions of decline." Jacobs felt it was important to unleash the creative energies of cities by freeing them from government regulation. Nonetheless, most major city-regions still benefit from state social investment (Ward and Jonas, 2004) and city-regionalism, in turn, is often central to how states compete globally for investment and infrastructure (McGuirk, 2004). For example, the Finnish state has identified Helsinki and the southwest region as the economic growth engine for Finland, thereby channeling resources away from its other regions and cities that hitherto relied on state-redistributive policies.

For Brenner (2002), the fact that national states are turning to city-regionalism reflects a deeper structural crisis of capitalism and the failure of earlier neoliberal urban reforms. But what is also in question is the idea that the urban political arena represents a fixed territory. Not only has the practice of urban politics become stretched out to encapsulate city-regions and globalization but also nation-states, in turn, rely on city-regions to deliver harder edged neoliberal policies on infrastructure, welfare reform, and economic development.

7.6   Summary and Conclusions

For a long time it was felt that there was something distinctively "urban" about urban politics. The politics of cities were different to, say, national politics or the politics of suburbia. This was partly because the substance of urban conflict seemed to be about planning, collective consumption, and the provision of services to urban residents. As we have seen in this chapter, it is a perspective that has been challenged by those who suggest that the city is also an arena of economic development; hence, the recent interest in the entrepreneurial activities of urban authorities. However, this might also be called into question as various distributional struggles continue to permeate the urban political arena. At the same time, it is becoming quite difficult to contain urban politics; struggles around urban redevelopment cannot be explained simply in respect of processes operating inside city limits – at least limits defined in a jurisdictional sense. Accordingly, there has been a shift of emphasis in approaches to urban politics from what goes on inside cities to processes beyond city limits, be these flows of investment into or out of the city, state intervention, urban policy transfers, and so forth.

In this chapter we considered several ways in which the governance and politics of cities and suburbs have been re-imagined by critical urban geographers. One important theme is that the geography of the city and its supporting governance structures are being rescaled upwards, with the appearance of new metropolitan and city-regional structures, and downwards as cities become more fragmented and privatized. Of course it is difficult to say that what eventually emerges is something other than an urban-scaled politics as traditionally understood; but there is clearly a sense in which some powerful economic interests – the growth coalitions – now think and act regionally (and globally) these days while others (e.g., community developers) are attracted to smaller-scale political spaces and imaginaries.

At the same time, there are signs of a revival of urban politics, one which offers some sort of buttress against the intrusion of neoliberal ideas and market-based reforms into the public urban realm. Several additional themes fall out of this, such as the need to examine the changing meaning of citizenship, new forms of democratic participation, and the right to the city. Each in its turn is premised on the idea that urban entrepreneurialism, privatization, and reduced state intervention have drastically eroded and undermined the urban public realm – the traditional space where people can voice their dissatisfaction with urban authorities, capitalism and, for that matter, the state at large. In the future we might see further evidence of urban geographers looking at how the public urban realm is being claimed back.

7.7   Further Reading

- On the urbanization process in capitalism and urban politics, Castells (1977) and Harvey (1985a) are important sources.
- Useful critical re-assessments of themes in the New Urban Politics literature can be found in Lauria (1997), Jonas and Wilson (1999) MacLeod and Jones (2011) and the accompanying special issue of *Urban Studies* (2011) **48**(12).
- The topic of neoliberal urbanism is widely featured in the critical urban geography literature and the following treatments are especially helpful: Brenner and Theodore (2002), Hackworth (2007), and Rossi and Vanolo (2012).
- Engels (1872/1935) on the housing question is worth reviewing. An excellent critical analysis of housing affordability and the work–life balance in the contemporary city can be found in Jarvis (2005).
- Useful critical discussions of city-regionalism and the rescaling of urban politics can be found in Cox and Jonas (1993), Brenner (2002), Ward and Jonas (2004) and a special debates issue of the *International Journal of Urban and Regional Research* (2007) 31:1.

Chapter 8

Experiencing Cities

Urban Geography: A Critical Introduction, First Edition. Andrew E.G. Jonas, Eugene McCann,
and Mary Thomas.
© 2015 Andrew E.G. Jonas, Eugene McCann, and Mary Thomas. Published 2015 by John Wiley & Sons, Ltd.

8.1 Introduction

You may be surprised to know that for hundreds of millions of city dwellers globally, the biggest problem they face waking in the morning is where to use the toilet. Perhaps in your house or apartment you have one or more toilets for every person; in countries like the United States and the United Kingdom, 100% of the urban population has access to sanitary toilets. In contrast, India, the second most populous country on earth, provides access to only half of its urban residents to a sanitation facility. That is 170 million people with no access to a clean toilet – or in most cases even to a dirty toilet – including at home, work, and school. Daily in India's cities, over twice the population of the United Kingdom must figure out where to perform the most basic of bodily functions (Box 8.1).

Box 8.1   Mumbai Toilet Construction and Women

According to the World Health Organization, 2.4 billion people globally do not have access to any type of improved sanitation facility. That is over 30% of the world's total population. Mumbai, India, is one of the world's largest cities with 13 million inhabitants, and over half of these people live in slums with little or no sanitation infrastructure. In some areas many hundreds of people share one public toilet – an unfeasible statistic resulting in thousands of tons of public excreta *per day*.

Often girls cannot attend school for the lack of toilets, especially as they grow older and being to menstruate, plus girls and women suffer illnesses such as bladder and urinary tract infections when they must "hold" their toileting. For those women who have a shared toilet in their neighborhood, they must "queue to pee," and their queuing times are much longer than men's, often prohibitively so. In the documentary film, *Q2P*, filmmaker Paromita Vohra (2007) suggests that providing clean public toilets allows more girls to stay in school as they grow, helps women avoid daily shame for natural bodily needs, and works to end sexism through building the urban infrastructure. Through their political struggles around toilet access, women also become public citizens, whose experiences and bodies are publically present, articulated, and addressed.

In response, public works projects in Mumbai (in large part funded through international finance from The World Bank) have begun the monumental task of constructing adequate community toilets in many poor areas, although access remains heavily gendered (Figure 8.1). In Vohra's film, viewers are shown the difficulties of having gender difference taken seriously in the construction program. Who, after all, designs such projects? Men, and more specifically, men from more privileged class and caste backgrounds than the poor for whom they design. Thus, poor women's experiences continue to be devalued, ignored, unsolicited, or brushed aside. But women continue to fight back. They demanded participation in planning for women's and children's needs, and hundreds of projects building thousands of toilets have developed from these community approaches (Chinai, 2002: 684). While community-based projects, they require an annual or monthly usage fee. For the very poor, this can still be prohibitive; it also privatizes what many argue should be a basic right to clean toilets and water (McFarlane, 2008a).

Figure 8.1   Try not to imagine *Slumdog Millionaire*! This is what a new public toilet block looks like, in Khotwadi, Mumbai, India, built by the Slum Sanitation Project (SSP). Photo courtesy of Colin McFarlane.

When 1 in 20 people in India's cities must relieve themselves in public space – in the open – the question of where to use the toilet also becomes a gendered problem. Because girls and women face strong social stigmas, shame, and even potential violence for relieving themselves in public, they must try to go before daylight breaks or after the sun sets. This affects their health over time, with increased risk for urinary and bladder infections, among many other sanitation and disease risks. The daily experience of living in the city for girls and women with no access to a toilet – or to a toilet shared by hundreds of people – becomes an exhausting, demeaning, and physically degrading experience. The problem of access to toilets is, therefore, not just a question of uneven development globally or an issue of providing public funds to urban sanitation projects. It also comes down to who you are, in other words your social and economic position in society. This example illustrates all too easily that city life is an **embodied experience**.

> **Embodied experience.** Embodied experience denotes that the body of the human is a context and space of all experience. Humans never have an experience that is not embodied, as even thoughts depend on a body to happen. Every body, too, is specific in terms of its size, shape, color, age, ability, gender, and so on. Therefore, embodied experiences are also racial, gender, sexual experiences (to name just a few).

Before you conclude that poverty, lack of sanitation, and embodied experience only have a combined effect in poorer countries, think again. A guarantee that 100% of United States and United Kingdom urbanites have toilet access falsely assumes that 100% of city dwellers are adequately housed. Obviously, the homeless do not always have consistent access to a toilet, nor do the very poor whose housing stock is abhorrently maintained. The ability to find a toilet when you have to go relies on whether you have power and money, and therefore access to the excellent existing sanitation infrastructure. Middle class urban residents can always find a restroom away from home somewhere, even if they have to pay for access; for instance, purchasing a coffee in the local Starbucks or something from a fast food restaurant grants access to the locked restroom in a big city. Because you are clean you might even be given the key or have the ability to walk into a store to use the toilet with no pressure to purchase, with no one even raising an eyebrow at you. Class and race, appearance, and the ability to pay, all allow pressing needs easier relief. The public disgust often levied at the homeless for urinating or defecating in public combines with a dominant class privilege of never having to urinate or defecate outside. A **norm** is created that defines public urban space through the middle class, white, consumer ideal of behaving properly and having clean, odorless bodies. There may even be laws against urinating or defecating in public, so the state sanctions that norm and helps to produce – and police – the city's sanitized, consumerist public spaces.

> **Norms.** Norms are idealized and enforced representations of social hierarchies of power that gain everyday, mainstream acceptance over long periods of time and through complex workings of power. Norms are impersonal social forces that shape how subjects experience life and how spatial exclusion forms over time (Sibley, 1995).

This chapter considers the social differences, such as gender, class, age, race, location, dis/ability, that people inhabit and embody, and the multiple ways these shape everyday life and space in the city. Critical urban geographers focus on urban experience to illuminate the struggles of all people and to bring minority or disadvantaged groups' experiences to bear on urban theory. After reading this chapter, you should be able to answer the following questions, and offer examples illustrating their importance:

- How do scholars theorize experience? Why does thinking about experience matter for our understandings of urban power relations?
- What social differences affect people's experiences of daily life in cities?
- Is there such a thing as *an* urban identity?
- In what ways have experiences and identities mattered in the shaping of urban spaces and the resistance strategies of nondominant groups?
- How do emotions provide critical insight for urban geographers?

8.2   What is "Experience"?

While it is easy to see that poverty, sexism, and caste work to undermine women's abilities to demand a radical reprioritization of Mumbai's urban elite and their resources, as in the case of public toilets, it is more complicated to understand how the lack of sanitation contributes to the continued vilification of lower caste and poor women. Through what

> **Social difference.** The ways that people are divided into categories are socially determined. Social difference is a phrase that insists that the categories used to separate and segregate people are constructed and enforced over time and space. For example, "race" is a category that comes from a colonial past and through which "whiteness" was valued over "blackness," leading to the justification of slavery and colonial conquest. Critical scholars therefore insist that social differences are never just reflections of our identities but also derive from inequality.

processes are urban poor women disenfranchised, their bodies deemed shameful (or in case of the **global North**, the urban homeless disgusting)? Their "experiences" as women must be framed by a careful analysis of gender and caste hierarchies, politics and economic change in Mumbai and India, rapid urbanization and globalization, and theories of embodiment. Experiences of shame or ill health develop within complex geographies of **social difference** that extend dramatically beyond any individual's own history, locality, or body. Yet, experience is always embodied, personal, particular, and shifting, since experiences vary dramatically from place to place, day to day, minute to minute – not to mention the ambivalence that any person can feel about any one experience.

It is vital for urban theorists to remember that no individual is either a predetermined outcome of the social relations that contextualize their life, or a fully autonomous subject not affected by social relations like location, gender, sexuality, age, race, dis/ability, and class. Everyone's "experiences" are their own, but they are densely embedded in social and spatial relations. Given this complexity – what then *is* "experience"? The seeming simplicity of this question, as critical feminist and urban geographers have discovered, masks the complicated processes underlying everyday life and identity.

On the face of it, experience relates to all of the activities of life, which include the accounts of one's life (or stories) given with hindsight over time to indicate learning, memory, and bias. Identities directly impinge on everyday and remembered experiences, both in terms of subjective interpretations for what happens in daily life and in terms of what the range of possibilities for everyday life are in the first place. Therefore, experience is deeply subjective and particular, so that the meanings and values accorded to life's activities are richly influenced by the ways individuals understand the world.

The challenge when considering "experience," according to historian Joan W. Scott, is to avoid treating it as "evidence for the fact of difference, rather than a way of exploring how difference is established, how it operates, how and in what ways it constitutes subjects" (Scott, 1991: 779). Merely telling stories about diverse lives, or evidencing the great range of experiences that happen in urban space, is insufficient. We all know there is a huge variety

> **Power** (B) can also mean ability to act or the capacity to influence others. Power relations means that some groups have historically and geographically been able to do both of these more than others.

of people and places, but this tells us nothing about how social difference happens within relations of **power**, how it is evaluated according to different perspectives, how it produces urban space, how it constitutes us. Most importantly, there is no "difference" without power because, if there were, there would be no inequality, injustice, or suffering. Therefore, critical geographers start with the idea that varied experiences are evidence that social difference structures urban life and space in uneven ways (Fincher and Jacobs, 1998), and in unique ways to each person, given that identification with social differences like gender, race, class, age, and location, is a deeply personal – yet fully social and spatial – process.

Social difference and power

Critical scholars suggest that identity, experience, and difference are not useful concepts without also theorizing power relations. Theoretical thinking about power helps determine why certain identities become predominant over time and space, and what social differences become articulated through particular places and spaces at the expense of others. Theories on power relations allow geographers to ask: How can we have critical understandings of the many ways that "experiences" constitute subjects? How do individuals learn about and reproduce difference through normative urban spaces? Given the imperative to articulate oneself through social differences (being gendered, racialized, etc.), do people also have an ability to act or resist normative power relations, spaces, and structures?

Power never just acts *on* a person, determining them in cookie cutter patterns of exact social sameness. Power acts through us, enabling people to contest normative social meaning at the same time as it effectively constrains each individual's ability to break completely free of social and spatial context. Thus, while we might remember that social categories like gender, sexuality, or race are not optional (everyone must be gendered and sexualized and raced, or risk social **abjection**), these very differences are often the grounds for agency and political action. Think about feminism, LGBTQ (lesbian, gay, bi-, trans, and queer) politics, and anti-racism. Each of these social movements began in the West with an identity politics that claimed exclusion from mainstream (i.e., male, white, straight) society because of prejudice and bias against that category of difference. Simultaneously, each also used that same identity as a source of strength (e.g., "Black is Beautiful," "Gay Power," or even today's "Girl Power"). Each also was at heart a struggle for spatial, as well as social, belonging, often fought for in the everyday spaces of the city. For example, the civil rights movement in the United States in the 1950s and 1960s used particular urban strategies in their quests to claim equal rights, like peaceful marches or sit-ins at lunch counters. These resistant strategies occupied urban spaces and demanded that they be redefined from their dominant representation as white space. Thus, civil rights movements also fought in order to gain acceptance, visibility, and spatial inclusion in cities, including equal access to housing, public space, and workplaces, and the benefits that these spaces give to people, like access to health care, leisure, livable wages, and so on.

> **Abjection.** A process of casting away those who are different than the self because the different, other person represents a threat to the self. Abjection often involves disgust, fear, and repulsion.

Media coverage across the world brought intense spotlight onto these cities in the US South, which were more likely to be smaller, "ordinary" cities, like Birmingham, AL, and Greensboro, NC. Movements like these were highly successful and resulted in very real, changed lived experiences everywhere: the end of legalized segregation in the case of anti-racist struggles in the United States, huge shifts in the gendered labor market and women's

inclusion into political and social spheres in feminist movements in the West, and a growing public acceptance of homosexuality and even the legalization of gay marriage in many
places (although all of these "gains" are very place specific and many struggles remain). But
identity politics also forced an emphasis on categories of social differentiation, realigning
gender, race, and sexuality in these examples, rather than transcending difference altogether. Social difference in a sense is emphasized in these identity political movements,
rather than resisted *per se*. While social movements such as feminism or civil rights work to
include women and minorities, they do not necessarily tackle the differentiation of people
into categories of social difference. Thus, the question of whether one's social differences
can be transcended in an unequal world remains. In the next section, we consider how
theories of social difference and power combine with a geographic sense of space and place
in the work of urban critical geographers.

8.3   Social Space, City Space

Critical geographers studying urban experience focus on how social differences affect individual subjects in daily urban life. Think, for example, about **heteronormativity**: the social
force of it implies a so-called "natural" sexual pairing of "properly" gendered men and women (Butler, 1993). It has a social force that shapes nonnormatively gendered and sexual subjects, such as transgendered people, gays and lesbians, and those identified as queer. Gill Valentine (1996) documents the force of heteronormativity in urban space by showing how lesbians "hide" their identi-ties and sexual desire by refusing to kiss or touch in public. She argues that a lot of

> **Heteronormativity.** The idea that men and women fall into distinct categories and that a corresponding sexual pairing between them is the only correct way to express desire. Heteronormativity denotes a binary relationship between femininity/masculinity, so that feminine men are not "normal," nor are masculine women. Thus, heterosexuality requires gendered norms, not just sexual ones.

social energy – including violence and harassment – goes into maintaining the hegemony
of the heterosexual street. "Heterosexual looks of disapproval, whispers, and stares are used
to spread discomfort and make lesbians feel 'out of place' in everyday spaces. These in turn
pressurize many women into policing their own desires and hence reinforce the appearance
that 'normal' space is straight space" (Valentine, 1996: 149). In turn, heterosexuals do not
have to question their own public behaviors; given the force of heteronormativity, "they can
take the street for granted as a 'commonsense' heterosexual space" (Valentine, 1996: 149).
Gay and lesbian, queer and other nonnormative sexualities offer many resistances to this
spatial and social force, as seen in Pride festivals and parades, public rallies, and everyday
acts of resistance like kissing or holding hands in public (Browne, 2007).

   However, while gay pride marches, among many other public political protests and
activities, have increased the visibility and acceptance of LGBTQ people in many cities, the
effects of these politics are not always merely progressive. As Natalie Oswin (2008) reminds
us, resisting straight space and claiming it as queer often results through the direct neglect
of other social differences and oppressions. Thus, queer space "is implicitly white space"
(Oswin, 2008: 93). The problem in her view is "the fact that all 'queers' are always and

everywhere sexualized *and raced* is rendered illegible. … [T]he need for an analysis of race and racism is considered necessary only when queers are non-white" (Oswin, 2008: 94, emphasis added). Resistant experiences and identities do not necessarily result in purely progressive politics, and may indeed end up reinscribing other oppressions, such as racial exclusion or class privilege in the case of some GLBTQ politics. Thus, resistance in one way might not be resistance in other ways. A few more examples will help to illustrate these arguments.

Gentrification

It is not uncommon to hear gentrification posited as a polemical issue of property and economic value in the classroom: "If poor people do not take care of their neighborhoods, why shouldn't another group restore dilapidated properties? Isn't it better that old houses be restored, than destroyed from neglect?" This question comes from an interest in seeing city housing renovated and utilized. However, in particular, poor communities depicted as neglecting property are often nonwhite and are always poor, including new immigrants, racial and ethnic minorities, indigenous groups, and also working class, underemployed whites. Note incidentally, there is often overrepresentation of single parent, woman-headed households in many poor and minority neighborhoods.

Thus, the question of property value and the "restoration" of housing stock becomes one that prioritizes ownership and economics but disregards the experiences of poverty, racism, sexism, and how these relate to the de/valuation of central city neighborhoods. Often, social differences get subsumed by economistic rationale, and the perspective most valued by economistic rationale is monetary value and profit. On the other hand, the poorer residents experience eviction, displacement, and dispersal into other neighborhoods. Their experiences of forced mobility are painful losses of home and neighborhood that often are invisible under economistic norms emphasizing property values (also see Lees *et al.*, 2008).

As one Hispanic interviewee from Lower Park Slope, Brooklyn, New York, put it to geographer Tom Slater:

> It was much more of a neighborhood [in the 1980s] than it is now. You saw many more familiar faces, and people tended to look out for each other. There were some places where you would have to watch your back, like near the crack house, but my street, Union, was a place where you didn't have to worry because if someone gave you any trouble about 10 people were always out on their stoops watching what was going on. Another thing is that when a new family moved in, it was a major event and everybody knew about it. These days you can't tell who is new and who isn't, as everyone moves around so much more. (Luis, interview, 6 November 2001, quoted in Slater, 2004: 1204)

In the case of Lower Park Slope, gentrification was a process of more whites moving in, while Hispanics were displaced. Slater's interviewees referred to this as a "whiting out" of the neighborhood (Slater, 2004: 1205).

Gentrification stories offer a chance to analyze how social difference is established through the very process of gentrification itself. Manuel Castells' (1983) groundbreaking work on urban social movements argues that in San Francisco, CA, gay male gentrification around the Castro neighborhood established gay politics as an urban force. Creating "territories" in cities, in Castells' mind, expanded "the increasing capacity of gay people to define themselves and to build up a series of autonomous institutions" (Castells, 1983: 139). Space is, therefore, "a fundamental dimension for the gay community" (Castells, 1983: 145), in terms of meeting other homosexuals and for feeling and being safe in intolerant, heter-onormative cities and spaces.

But Castells also showed that creating gay-dominated neighborhoods like the Castro was more than social: it was politically advantageous because concentration also brought voting power, visibility, and proximity for political activity. However, Castells reminds us that this history and activity paid a price: it excluded lesbians and feminists, displaced racial/ethnic minorities, and its political project was defined narrowly by voting (Castells, 1983: 172). In sum, the gay gentrifiers oppressed other groups in order to struggle for and win their own urban inclusion in San Francisco.

Geographer Lawrence Knopp (1990, 1995) responds to Castells' arguments by insisting that gay gentrification is fundamentally also a class issue, always gendered, and in many cases, also racialized (Figures 8.2 and 8.3). In his study of the Marigny neighborhood of New Orleans, LA, Knopp found a surprising dynamic at play in gentrification: gay identity was not the primary force fueling changes in the land market. Rather, single, white, middle class gay men used their relative wealth as single men, and white racial and class privileges, to form alliances that solidified their land ownership and community control. Thus, the accumulation of property and wealth motivated their gentrification, not identity politics as Castells would have it. Knopp writes that in New Orleans, "The issue is therefore not so much one of overcoming discrimination as it is one of overcoming institutional obstacles to investment in certain parts of the city. Gay speculators and developers in Marigny saw an opportunity first for themselves and only secondarily for the gay community as a whole" (Knopp, 1990: 347). There was also a stated resistance to being seen primarily as "gay." As one interviewee told Knopp, "How do we want our city to see us? … [As] responsible busi-nesspeople who have money, or fags coming out of the streets with makeup?" (Knopp, 1990: 344). The men saw the advantages of identifying themselves as moneyed, rather than as gay.

In fact, as Knopp shows, having money means having an ability to gentrify, so class is as critical to consider in this case as sexuality. So is gender. Men have more economic power than woman as a whole, and gay gentrifiers are more commonly men, not lesbians: "The perpetuation of male economic privilege within the context of a gay community's influence on a land market is thus a testament to the resilience of male social dominance generally" (Knopp, 1990: 349; Lauria and Knopp, 1985). Knopp's study is a fascinating look at the idiosyncrasies of gentrification and the importance of looking at its motivations, effects, and experiences in a case by case basis.

Is the "ghetto" your home?

Because "ghetto" is a disparaged word, it sits uneasily next to "home." The US-American use of the term ghetto, after all, describes an urban area defined by its divergence from so-called mainstream society (Wacquant, 1997: 345; Klodawsky and Blomley, 2010). Inordinate attention focuses on its so-called pathologies, from rampant teenage pregnancy to violent crime, drugs, unemployment, and welfare (Wacquant, 1997: 348). Analyzing "ghetto" through the problematic of identity, difference, and experience, however, raises the

Figures 8.2 and 8.3 The home in Figure 8.2 has a rainbow flag on its porch denoting the sexual identity of its owners. The house is in a predominantly African–American neighborhood called Olde Towne East in Columbus, OH. It faces the Kwanzaa Playground directly across the street, as seen in Figure 8.3. The documentary film *Flag Wars* (2003; dir. Linda Goode Bryant and Laura Poitras) examines the conflict over gentrification in this neighborhood between gay and African–American residents. Photos: Mary Thomas.

question of whose perspective such a term represents. Let us face it: the ghetto is black. The social problems that point to issues like crime and "decay" are loaded with racist bias. The putative ghetto is no place to live from a normative middle class perspective.

Loic Wacquant, an urban sociologist, suggests that the word's use "thwarts" an analysis of how exclusion operates, and "it obscures the fact that blacks are the only group ever to have experienced ghettoization in American society, i.e., involuntary, permanent, and total residential separation premised on caste as basis for the development of a *parallel (and inferior) social structure*" (Waquant, 1997: 343, emphasis in original). Ghetto is a **trope** that prevents a rendering of life within its terms; ghetto life is unlivable life. The trope provides a circularity of justification for the inferior treatment it receives from powerful, normative urban society, leading to further vilification and experiences of spatial segregation.

> **Trope.** A representation with an overwhelming image and message not likely to be read in alternative ways. They are often "taken for granted" and thus are difficult to question.

In *Vancouver's Chinatown: Racial Discourse in Canada, 1875–1980*, Kay Anderson (1991) provided an important step in understanding how racialized tropes become established through urban space and place – and the implications for their naturalization over time and space. She turned the question of racial/ethnic neighborhoods on its head. Instead of assuming that groups came together "naturally" and formed urban neighborhoods because they shared a culture (for instance, that Chinese migrants built Chinatowns because they had an affinity for each other given their ethnicity and nationality), Anderson argued that Chinatown was a Western invention. Through law making and zoning, racist discourse and segregation, economic exclusion, and, finally, the celebration of multiculturalism, Chinatown "belongs as much to the society with the power to define and shape it as it does to its residents" (Anderson, 1991: 10).

Far from being neighborhoods primarily built from self-segregating ethnic–cultural affinity, Chinatown is a result of divisions made by the Europeans from the Chinese. This forced division erased the definitions that the Chinese themselves had about their own diversity (language, surname, generation, gender, class, ethnicity, origin location, etc.) (Anderson, 1991: 30). Anderson's book was pivotal in showing that urban form and sociality have a long history of effective and diffuse power relations. Differences like race are constructed over time and space through Eurocentric knowledge, urban politics, and economics, but these also have provided identities of diversity for Canadians to celebrate in the present. By illustrating the layers that built "Chinatown" over many decades, Anderson argued that no social difference or space can be taken as a fact or essence in the present; difference is complexly, spatially and historically, constructed and paradoxical.

Wendy Shaw, in her book *Cities of Whiteness*, takes a more recent look at urban racial segregation and identity, in this case Sydney, Australia. She argues that "ghetto" was imported from the United States for use in Sydney to mark the racialized process of exclusion in the city. For one Aboriginal housing settlement in Sydney known as The Block, the term showed up in pejorative media coverage of crime, urban state responsibility, and residents' suffering, among others. "While Sydney embraces its emergent global status," Shaw writes, "the Indigenous community of The Block has become the city's 'black ghetto' in contemporary understandings" (Shaw, 2007: 137). This is a way for whiteness to shrug off systemic racism and abjection of Aboriginals, as "ghetto" implies a recurrent urban form.

As Shaw explains this perspective, "after all, big international cities have (racialized) ghettos" (Shaw, 2007: 138). The ghetto, in other words, becomes a price to pay for an internationally recognized, global city, so that privileged whites can justify exclusionary urban politics and policies. The "ghetto" then becomes sectioned off socially and spatially over time, a "no-go zone," where subjects fail to live up to normative expectations of "proper" lives – that is, white, middle and upper class lives. Shaw even argues that by using the American term "ghetto," such dominant forces deem the Indigenous neighborhood a "foreign" space (Shaw, 2007: 139) not properly making use of Australian democracy – a democracy supposedly promising inclusion and equality for all.

On the other hand, in this Australian "city of whiteness," Shaw quotes a white resident as saying, "as much as I love the Aboriginal culture, once you bring these people away from their culture ... you put them in the city, they are really up against it. I believe The Block must be razed, it's a failed human experiment" (Shaw, 2007: 70). Aboriginal bodies in this quote cannot be in urban space, and must literally be de-spatialized by losing their home, since Aboriginals in this racist view only belong in the "outback." The white can, therefore, justify gentrification, because their subjectivity is determined as more properly urban, as properly a "modern" Australian. Nonwhite, poor Aboriginals, or "these people," are reduced to an "experiment" without claim to their own homes. Shaw's book effectively illustrates the workings of whiteness in urban representations of race, ethnicity, poverty, and property, and how Aboriginal experiences of home and urban life become disqualified for urban belonging according to this privileged and elitist logic.

Homelessness

Critical urban geographers insist that homelessness cannot be evaluated primarily or solely as a result of individual failings. Thousands of people do not end up living on a city's streets as a result of individual actions; millions of people are homeless in the world's cities, which points to a very large scale, structural issue of poverty and lack of affordable housing, mental health provision, and adequate work (Tipple and Speak, 2009). Perhaps placing individualized blame as the reason for homelessness might work if there were many, many fewer unhoused people, but the horrifying scale of homelessness across the world's cities evidences a much broader and more insidious problem: widespread **social exclusion** (Klodawsky and Blomley, 2009). Whole areas can be marked as exclusion zones, such as the case of "ghettos" seen above. Those experiencing social exclusion worldwide include racial, ethnic and national minorities, indigenous groups, the poor, the disabled or chronically ill, sexual minorities, and, of course, the homeless. In some critical geographers' views, the city has become a mean place, punitive against the poor, leading to increased policing and privatization of public space and outright criminalization of homeless existence (Smith, 1996; Duneier, 1999; Mitchell, 2003; DeVerteuil, 2006). The homeless are some of the most powerless of urban people, so why do they evoke such strong resentment, fear, disgust, and anger?

> **Social exclusion.** The process of stigmatizing and marginalizing certain groups and identities in society. This tends to have economic as well as social and cultural dimensions.
>
> Social exclusion involves the definition of groups as nonnormal, and it has a spatial process: people being cast out of and prohibited entry into "normal" urban spaces defined by mainstream categories of race, health, national status, class privilege, sexuality, and so on (Sibley, 1995).

David Sibley, in his important early exploration of *Outsiders in Urban Societies* (1981), asks, "in relation to what social model are people judged to be deviant or deprived?" (Sibley, 1981: 24). In this book, as in his subsequent work on exclusion (Sibley, 1995), Sibley unpacks the "norms" of a dominant society and shows that they reflect bias, stereotyping, moralizing, unconscious disgust, and fear of contamination. These powerful emotions lead to combined material, social, economic, and legal outcomes including everyday hardship. He writes, "Portrayals of minorities as defiling and threatening have for long been used to order society internally and to demarcate the boundaries of society, beyond which lie those who do not belong" (Sibley, 1995: 49). Deeming people "dirty," "dangerous," and as "outsiders," Sibley argues, translates into exclusionary practices over time and space.

The homeless certainly contend with exclusion personally; it affects how some experience their own bodies. As one New York city unhoused street vendor, Ron, explains in Mitchell Duneier's *Sidewalk* (1999: 177): "Sometimes you can't help but pee in the street. Because when a person is dirty or stinkin' he don't want to go to a bathroom with decent people in there. You don't feel good about yourself." But as Duneier also points out, if Ron were to leave his vending table to use the toilet, he would lose the ability to make any money that day, since sidewalk tables must be manned or New York's city police discard them. He writes, "Whether a man comes to see the bathroom as *the* natural or best way to do his bodily functions is conditioned by access to the bathroom resource itself and the fear of having his table and belongings seized by the police when he leaves it. These conditions lead to a resocialization of the individual" (Duneier, 1999: 185). Ron's economic livelihood directly interacts with his bodily needs and to the city's regulations about vending. His embodied experiences are compounded by social, political, and economic norms about who "proper" bodies are, or as Ron puts it, "decent" people. This is Ron's way of showing "respect," but public urination further stigmatizes him as dirty, improper, and dangerous to the mainstream public – and maybe even to himself.

These social and spatial norms are reinforced through urban policing of the homeless. As Don Mitchell (2003: 163) insists, "Survival itself is criminalized." Mitchell ties the criminalization of the homeless in American cities to the contemporary selling of urban image (Chapter 9). Capitalist cities seek to "cleanse" their streets of poor, minority, mentally ill, and alcoholic people so that they can urge investment monies to relocate given their "extravagant convention centers, downtown tourist amusement, up-market, gentrified restaurant and bar districts, new baseball and football stadiums" and even occasionally museums and theaters (Mitchell, 2003: 166). Cities "annihilate" the homeless by annihilating the spaces they call home; public space itself is also annihilated in the process.

In many developed countries, the archetypical homeless figure is the single man, but the idea that homelessness is only a problem for poor, racial minority men, erases the experiences of women and children who live and work on the street. This idea often leads to gender-blind policies that do little to address their different needs and problems. Women and children are the most vulnerable of the unhoused. In developing countries, most women "still rely on marriage as their only route to a home independent from their birth families" (Tipple and Speak, 2009: 8); women are at disproportionate risk of being very poor, with children the poorest of all; and women's and family issues often fail to garner widespread political support or advocacy.

Children, however, might also present families with extra workers to earn money that makes a real difference to households. Kate Swanson, in her book, *Begging as a Path to Progress* (2010), shows that migration to the cities of Ecuador provide indigenous households with money for food, education, and improved shelter. The children migrate from their rural highland homes for short periods of time with adults to work selling gum or begging on the streets of Quito or Guayaquil (Figure 8.4). While most are not homeless, since they return to shared (and often very crowded) rented rooms while in the city, their lives are lived largely on the streets amidst cars, trolley buses, pedestrians, exhaust, and other working children, under the hot sun and in dangerous traffic for hours at a time.

The children's experiences working on the streets are marked strongly by their racial difference as indigenous, and they must confront racist sentiments that deem their presence on the street as "lazy." In fact, the children work very hard and are loath to be called "beggar." One 14 year old girl, Malena, said to Swanson, "We work like donkeys but we don't make any money" (Swanson, 2010: 111). The little money they do make, however, can be the difference that allows them to seek better futures. Swanson reports that for those in school, 60% report that they work on the streets so that they can continue education (Swanson, 2010: 56). Ecuador's cities actively seek to remove beggars like Malena, to "clean up" their streets (itself a racialized metaphor and an exclusionary process according to Swanson), but the city streets provide opportunities to make a little money that goes a long way for those living in deep poverty.

Youth geographies and consumption spaces

Whether it is for basic sustenance or for guilty pleasure, shopping is one of those regular activities that just about everyone in the world must do. In the contemporary United States, shopping is also a primary experience through which many youth strive to be unique and

Figure 8.4 Children sell gum and beg on the streets of Quito, Ecuador. Photo courtesy of Kate Swanson.

to show their individualism. But the idea that *what* you buy illustrates *who* you are, is deeply problematic. Instead, critical geographers argue that shopping is a fraught practice that intimately ties subjects to systems of inequality and oppression (for example, think about sweatshop labor and the "pleasures" of urban elites buying clothing made under such miserable working conditions). Therefore, shopping and consumption have become an important focus of research and an interesting way to think about youth social activity in the city (Vanderbeck and Johnson, 2000; Jayne *et al.*, 2006).

In the United States, many teenaged youth must shop in order to have a place to "hang out," since their relatively older bodies are seen as "out of place" in public playgrounds designed for younger kids – especially at night when such public spaces are closed and surveilled for "dangerous" activity. Because teenagers are considered to be inappropriate and potentially disruptive to parks at night (and often during the day), the question becomes: Where *can* teens hang out? Often, only in places that require money, like fast food restaurants and shopping malls. While these places may seem like public places (Figures 8.5 and 8.6), they are heavily policed for so-called proper behavior, and many restrict youth from hanging out in groups or being there entirely in evening hours. For example, many shopping malls have curfews, disallowing youth under age 16 or 17 after early evening hours. They also often have posted rules and behavioral restrictions that can be cited when removing youth from the premises. For example, in one shopping center in Columbus, OH, posted signs indicate that people can be evicted for "Discourteous Behavior: This can be described as rude behavior, behavior which may cause an inconvenience to others, or anything that is ill-mannered or disrespectful such as loitering, blocking walkways, running, yelling, and skateboarding." This rule is clearly targeted at youth audiences, since adults are not likely to be skateboarding or running.

Figures 8.5 and 8.6   An upscale outdoor shopping space in Columbus, OH. While the design of the shopping mall evokes symbols of public space, it is entirely privately owned. It even has its own police force. Photos: Mary Thomas.

The exclusion of youth from consumption spaces is a racialized process, in two ways. First, as Maureen O'Dougherty (2006) found in her study of the Mall of America in the suburbs of Minneapolis–St. Paul, MN, black youth in the mall are more heavily policed than white youth. They are more likely to be followed by security, especially after curfew. White youth, who at the mall typically have more money to spend, are rarely as hyper-targeted as black, Asian, and Latino youth. Thus, as O'Dougherty suggests, "a mall [is] not devoid of diversity, but [is] a space where diversity is managed" by a collusion of private security, public police, and the mall's public relations department (O'Dougherty, 2006:150).

Second, minority youth in the United States learn to understand the qualities of being nonwhite in racist cities that fear or abhor their presence in public spaces – in other words, these urban spaces of experience shape and affect their racial identifications. Mary Thomas (2005) asked one African–American teen why she thought that the city police (in Charleston, SC) force black youth to move on when they arre hanging out in the city's public parks – or worse, they are arrested for loitering. The girl replied, "Cuz they think that when we [black youth] get together, we [are] plotting something. … They lock you up in a heartbeat" (Thomas, 2005: 600–601). She understood this as specifically racially driven, and this confrontation with police leads her to articulate her own racialized, oppositional identity as a black youth in a racist city. The white, middle class kids in Thomas's study had no trouble hanging out in bowling alleys, parks, and shopping centers, and had no understanding that their race and parents' incomes allowed them such luxuries. Instead, these were just "normal" hang out places to them.

8.4   Is there an Urban Identity?

Given the dramatic differences that distinguish city residents, is there something we can call a specifically *urban* identity in the contemporary world? Cities are so divergent from each other, and everyday life takes such different forms, can there possibly be shared experiences of urban life? The basis for claiming an urban identity is perhaps more usefully sought in the city's differences than in an assumption of sameness. For that reason, urban theorists of contemporary identity look to the ways that globalization has sharply altered city life and space, demographics and diversity, and yes, experience.

Globalization results in more people living in cities, regions, and countries that are not their birth places. Increased mobility and migration in the late twentieth and twenty-first centuries, in particular, mean that significant numbers of people have unique city identities that are made as much in rela-
tion to where they come from, than where they currently live. The "cosmopolitan city" typically invokes a new global urban identity that transcends the urban or national scale. The term **cosmopolitanism** has a long history in philosophy, but critical urban scholars use it primarily in two ways (Binnie *et al.*, 2006a).

> **Cosmopolitanism.** Defined in terms of elite groups having the ability to traverse space and manage difference in their trav-els. A second definition refers to more of us: people who may not be cosmopolitan elites but now accept difference as a basis for constructing unity.

First, it conveys a sense of the world as being more intimate and shared, since globaliza-
tion has contributed to more knowledge about other places, communications that bring people "closer together" that previously were experienced as prohibitively expensive or slow, and, relatedly, technologies that allow incredible interconnectedness both in body (e.g., air travel) or in person (e.g., Skype, e-mail, social networking). With a more intimately experienced world, cosmopolitans have a sense of responsibility to others beyond those whom they might identify with in terms of nationalism, ethnicity, or place (Ley, 2004). In short, cosmopolitans seek a unified, peaceful world. Thus, this first use of cosmopolitanism relates to a sense of global citizenship and connection despite difference. This raises several problems, not least of which is the question of who specifically has the ability to know about others, to travel globally, and to set the terms of a global coming together.

The second use of cosmopolitanism follows from the hope that diversity brings cities strength, not division. The idea rests on an assumption that city dwellers will value dif-
ference based on their knowledge about groups, practices, and places divergent from their own. As Jon Binnie *et al.* summarize, "The cosmopolite therefore becomes skilled in navigating and negotiating difference" (Binnie *et al.*, 2006a: 8; see also Jeffrey and McFarlane, 2008). Here you can see that Binnie *et al.* relate cosmopolitans with the "skill" of understanding difference. Who can have such a skill? Those with education, travel experience, a desire for worldliness – in short, those with money. Who gets to decide what differences are "valuable" in city space and practice? Often, those "differences" that are consumed by the middle and upper classes: think about value placed on the range of diverse and "authentic" food, entertainment, multicultural shopping, arts, and so on in larger cities (Hage, 2000; Shaw, 2007). These consumables are the differences lauded, not necessarily by the working poor and the nonnative migrants who staff the urban service economy. Thus, the critique of urban cosmopolitanism rests, again, on its elitist under-
pinnings that value mobility, middle and upper class priorities, and consumption. Racial and ethnic minorities are seen to have value to the cosmopolitan city insofar as they are deemed consumable as exotics from a white perspective; as Wendy Shaw shows in the case of Sydney, Australia, this is just a step along the slippery slope of redevelopment, as "cultural centers" promoted as sites of urban diversity (in this case, Aboriginal theater is a prime example) often lead to gentrification (Shaw, 2007).

Given these critiques, from a critical urban perspective is there any redeeming value to cosmopolitanism as an urban identity? The resounding reply is, well, perhaps. Cosmopolitans are urbanites, with an experience of city life in all its complex diversity and transnationalism. Most cities, especially global cities, are less nationally, ethnically, or racially uniform, than they are brought together by a *lack* of commonality. Cosmopolitanism, therefore, can be a claim of difference as unity, and does not need to fundamentally signify an elitist stance on globe-hopping, consumption, or arrogant universalism. As urban planner Leonie Sandercock puts it in her book, *Towards Cosmopolis* (1998: 218), the cosmopolitan city ideal works toward "a society in which difference can flourish – difference in all its multiplicity – as we continue to struggle for economic and environmental justice, for human community, and for the survival of the spirit in the face of the onslaught of a global consumer culture." She argues that cosmopolitan urbanism can provide a way to keep open the urban identity. Thus, the identity is continuously challenged, debated, political: in sum, dynamic. Conflict over identity need not be necessarily problematic, in other words, but can be a basis for democratic exchange and shared claims to all urban spaces (see also Sandercock, 2003).

Finally, there are also advocates of utilizing references to cosmopolitanism through emphasis on migrants, nonelites, and non-Western contexts (Nagel, 2002; Leitner and Ehrkamp, 2006; Jeffrey and McFarlane, 2008). These scholars show that even those with little political or economic power can strategically utilize mobilities of difference (Jeffrey and McFarlane 2008: 420). For example, Colin McFarlane (2008b) examines "solidarities" of anti-poverty and women's rights advocacy groups in Mumbai, India. Despite "living in different contexts, [the groups] share a perceived common space on the socioeconomic and political peripheries of the city" (McFarlane, 2008b: 493). He argues that these solidarities are cosmopolitan because they utilize strategies of shared learning, work across difference rather than in top-down modes, and seek to refashion urban life from local networks, thus nonelite and non-Western norms of diversity. Not all of the new cosmopolitanisms in Mumbai that he documents have progressive outcomes, however, which is a reminder that cosmopolitan hopes carry with them the risk of being coopted by corporate and urban elites and capitalism, wherever in the world they are put into practice (see also McFarlane, 2008a).

8.5   Emotions and City Life

Critical geographers, including those working to counter racism and homophobia, have sought to undermine claims about "naturalness" or "inevitability" of social categories and spatial divisions. Exploring the relationality of emotion offers a promising avenue through which to advance understandings of dynamic geographies of difference, exclusion and oppression. But it is important also to attend to – and denaturalize – emotional geographies of connection, pleasure, desire, love and attachment. (Bondi *et al.*, 2005: 8)

Life in the city, no matter who you are, is a messy combination of a great range of experiences and emotions (Box 8.2). In many ways, this whole chapter has been about **emotion**, since it would be impossible to decouple it from experience. Ending the chapter with an explicit consideration of emotion reminds us of that fact but also highlights the importance of thinking about urban experiences as both subjective and individual, *and* social and collective. After all, we feel deeply as individuals, but feelings are informed by social processes that are unequal, prejudicial, and violently differentiating. Bondi *et al.* (2005) therefore rightly claim that emotions provide critical geographers insight into the geographies of "difference, exclusion and oppression" (also Fincher and Jacobs, 1998: 2–3). As Anderson and Smith tell us (2001: 7), "Emotions are an intensely political issue."

> **Emotions.** Visceral feelings that are brought on by our understandings of how cities are and should be, and by encounters with difference. They shape our normative positions about how cities should be.

Of course, cities are a lot of fun, too (Figure 8.7). But consider how even "fun" experiences can offer a critical lens into urban geographies. One of the first questions to ask when thinking about enjoyment and urban living is whose pleasure is prioritized in the design, regulation, and leisure planning in cities? Why is the city fun, in what particular places, and for whom exactly?

Figure 8.7 A temporary artificial beach by the River Seine; part of the annual "*Paris Plages*" program. Each summer since 2002, the municipal government has provided these beaches to residents and tourists. This fun space highlights how regulations about appropriate behavior in public spaces are socially and spatially contextual. While middle class people sleeping in this public space may be advertised as evidence of a city's attractiveness, a homeless person doing the same thing in the same space may well be woken up and moved along. Photo: Eugene McCann.

Figure 8.8   The 1990 American with Disabilities Act guarantees equal opportunities for those with disabilities, including access to transportation. Many United States, European, and Canadian cities now provide "accessibility" maps for those with mobility impairments, like in this case for Seattle, WA. Source: http://metro.kingcounty.gov/maps/pdf/seattle-accessible-map.pdf. Map provided courtesy of King County Metro Transit.

For example, our previous discussion about shopping and privatized space provide some clues about the workings of many urban leisure spaces: the pleasure of middle class, adult consumers tend to win out over the open public spaces that threaten social disorder and that undermine capital's interests. The emotional undertones of many consumerist spaces

Box 8.2   Dis/ability

Experiences and cities are sometimes delusional, even if they are altogether too real. Geographies of disability highlight the battles that the mentally ill face every day, especially in cities that have severely reduced public funding for health care, supportive institutional care, and homeless services (Knowles, 2000; Parr, 1997; 1999). Parr and Butler (1999: 9) challenge geography to "interrogate the unacknowledged imaginings of shared communities or ablebodied/ableminded people which results in an othering of people whose bodies and minds do not meet with a mythical norm (ableism)." In other words, "normal" people and cities can only be defined as such by excluding those whose experiences are abjected, or cast aside (Parr and Butler, 1999:14). Many experience dislocation as a result of their "psychic disruption in the city" (Parr and Davidson, 2011): "Most of the time, I can be walking down the street and hear thousands of voices and I feel terrible, like I'm not really there" (Parr 1999: 683; cited in Parr and Davidson, 2011).

For the physically disabled, barriers to those whose mobility is impaired prohibitively restricts their range of possible urban experiences. Consider, again, the case of public toilets. Kitchen and Law (2001: 289) claim that access to a toilet "is not just about spatial configuration and design, but is a political and social issue: it is about the ability to take part in public life" (their study considered Newbridge, Ireland). As a woman Aine put it to them: "Because when, as I say, you go outside your door if you're going someplace – if you're going to a shopping centre, going to a pub, going to a hotel; if you are going to a cinema, or any type of entertainment, or if you're going to a class in a school or college, you have to check to see if there is a toilet there. Otherwise, you can't spend longer than three hours away from the house."

Urban worlds framed primarily by toileting needs: this is an overwhelming indication that critical urban geographers' work on experience has a vital role to play in understanding the everyday challenges of all bodies – and in advocating for justice for those bodies and people who have been degraded and deemed second class urban citizens (Kitchen and Law, 2001: 297) (Figures 8.8 and 8.9).

include fear, anxiety, and racism; consider, for example, the recent "sanitization" of Times Square, New York, in order to entice tourists eager to experience urban life but without the threat of cross-class contact with homeless, hustlers, beggars, or any evidence of public sexual or drug practice (Delany, 1999).

Being afraid of the city has typically been represented as a feminine experience. The image of the threatened, innocent woman walking down the dark street is an easy one to conjure (unless of course the woman is marked as an improperly public, sexual deviant – and therefore not innocent and undeserving of violence). However, as Bondi and Rose (2003: 233) point out:

> First, the demographic groups displaying the highest levels of fear (typically elderly women) are at lower risk of experiencing urban violence than any others (notably racialised young men). Secondly, while women tend to be most fearful of violence perpetrated by strangers in urban public space, they are statistically most at risk from acts of violence perpetrated in domestic spaces by men they know.

Figure 8.9   A disabled man crosses the street in a wheelchair. This city street offers accessible crosswalks but many in the world are much harder, if not impossible, to navigate with ease. Photo: Mary Thomas.

Rachel Pain (1991; cited in Bondi and Rose, 2003) asks whether this fear – far from being just "irrational" women acting against reality – relates to women's experiences of being harassed in public space. In the documentary *War Zone* (1998), filmmaker Maggie Hadleigh-West walks down US city streets (New Orleans and New York) and when men heckle her, she turns the camera on them to ask why. None apologize. Yet her focus on the men's reactions – in turn enraging and hilarious – resists the urban scene as masculinist by her demand for a response. When she stops one man and accuses him of harassment, he responds by saying: "How did I harass her? I said, 'Good morning, young lady. Have a nice day.' Was it harassment?" Maggie Hadleigh-West retorts, "Was it necessary to say it to her ass?" She weaves personal stories about harassment and its impacts on girls' and women's lives, and also questions the continuum of violence against woman from the spoken to the physical (the film ends with a harrowing recording of a 911 emergency call from a woman being raped).

8.6   Summary and Conclusions

Everyone has vastly different experiences in and of cities across the globe (or across the street), but one thing is certain: all experiences matter. This chapter provided some conceptual frameworks for thinking about difference and how it is reproduced through people's everyday geographies and in critical urban research itself. While social differences shape many of the difficulties that people face, whether through poverty, homophobia, violence against women, or racial segregation, social differences also provide individuals with their sense of uniqueness, identity, and pleasure.

We considered issues of inequality and how powerful status quo interests work to devalue the range of diverse urban lives and spaces. People's urban experiences are greatly impacted by the norms that proscribe values of place and living, like whiteness, middle class consumption, adultism, ableism, and heterosexuality. Gentrification, race and neighborhood change, youth and consumption, and homelessness are examples to think about how injustices occur when someone's race, income, gender, sexuality, disability, or age (or all of these) help to determine the ways that they *can* live their lives in particular urban spaces. By examining cosmopolitan identities, we also argued that social differences always involve questions of power and privilege, disempowerment and struggle; these questions imply a difficulty in imagining a shared vision for urban life among very different people. Finally, we introduced the emotions of city life to argue that feelings offer important insights into urban life.

8.7 Further Reading

- Bondi and Rose (2003) offer accessible overviews of feminist contributions to urban geographies. Recent reviews of feminist geographies can be found in Wright (2010a, 2010b). A useful discussion of queer geographies can be found in Brown and Knopp (2008).
- Urban geographies of children and youth offer experiences of the city from shorter heights (Young, 2003; Jeffrey, 2010; Thomas, 2011).
- Decentering whiteness in the West is an important part of critical anti-racist geographies (Pulido, 2000, 2006; Nayak 2003; McKittrick, 2006; Ehrkamp, 2010; Mahtani, 2014).
- See the special issue on homelessness in the journal *Urban Geography* guest edited by Klodawsky and Blomley (2009).
- The study of dis/ability in urban geography is growing rapidly. See the special issue on "Children, young people, and disability" in the journal *Children's Geographies* (Pyer *et al.*, 2010), Gleeson (2013), and Davidson (2010) on autism.

Chapter 9

Molding and Marketing the Image of the City

Urban Geography: A Critical Introduction, First Edition. Andrew E.G. Jonas, Eugene McCann, and Mary Thomas.
© 2015 Andrew E.G. Jonas, Eugene McCann, and Mary Thomas. Published 2015 by John Wiley & Sons, Ltd.

9.1   Introduction

Paris, London, Barcelona, Berlin, and Amsterdam would seem to have little in common with cities like Bradford (UK), Chisinau (Moldova), Duisburg (Germany), Vilnius (Lithuania), and Lodz (Poland). And, according to a study commissioned by the think tank, City Mayors, the two groups of cities are indeed very different in terms of their **brand** "strength." According to the authors of the study, "A city's brand is an overall image and set of associations that resides in people's heads" (City Mayors, 2008; see also City Mayors, 2010). The authors' purpose was to gauge which European cities the people they surveyed found most recognizable and desirable as places to visit. The result was a ranking of 72 of the continent's largest cities in

Brand. In the context of cities, a brand is an overall image of, and set of associations about, a city that is developed through a concerted strategy by local growth coalitions. Brands are not natural or static. Instead, they are directed at various audiences and changed over time to keep them fresh and successful. They are also questioned and contested by other groups in society.

terms of: their "assets" (tourist attractions, good food and shopping, low costs, good weather, walkability, and convenient public transit); their recognizability and media exposure; and their ability to leverage these assets to attract tourists. The fact that five of the cities we list above do not need to be explicitly identified by their respective countries, while the other five most definitely do, should tip you off to which have high levels of "brand strength" and which the study defined as poor performers with little or no marketing identity.

There are whole industries that have developed to market products in cities (Figure 9.1) but also to market cities as commodities to specific audiences in order for cities to leverage their place characteristics and attract investment and other forms of revenue (Box 9.1). The highly visible tip of this city marketing iceberg is the city **slogan**. Particularly notable in this regard is Las Vegas' "What Happens Here Stays Here" catchphrase, which continues a long North American and European tradition following historic exemplars like "I ♥

Slogan. A pithy, striking, evocative, and memorable phrase that operates as the leading edge of a larger advertising campaign, brand, or political agenda. The most successful transcend their original purpose – for example, "What happens in Vegas stays in Vegas."

New York," developed in the 1970s, and "Glasgow's Miles Better," from the 1980s. But city slogans are a global phenomenon and business and political elites in Africa ("Johannesburg: A World-Class African City"; Nairobi: "The Green City in the Sun"), Asia ("Uniquely Singapore," "Definitely Dubai") and elsewhere increasingly seek to "imagineer" their city's identity for largely economic purposes (Rutheiser, 1996). Mega-events and cultural festivals, such as the Olympics, World's Fairs, and the European City of Culture designation are other spectacular instances in which cities and their identities are reshaped and strictly governed as urban elites' compete with one another to gain global brand dominance (Waitt, 1999; Shoval, 2002; Klauser, 2012; McCann, 2013; Hubbard and Wilkinson, 2014).

It is what happens below the glossy surface of the slogans and the mega-events – the strategies involved in shaping city images, the historical, political economic forces

Figure 9.1   The junction of Yonge and Dundas Streets in downtown Toronto, Canada. Urban built environments are not only thoroughly branded but cities themselves have become brands. Photo: Eugene McCann.

Box 9.1   The "Best" Places to Live?

An attention to place branding is by no means confined to European cities. In the United Sates, for example, similar ranking exercises are a staple of popular media discourse and economic development practice. Cities are advertised and analyzed in terms of their quality of life, their "business climates," their actual climates, their attractiveness for certain groups in the population (from technology investors, to sports fans, to the much vaunted "creative class" (Florida, 2002)), and in terms of a myriad of other characteristics. Much is made, for example, of *Money* magazine's annual "Best Places to Live" issue (Time Inc., 2009), where the editors evaluate cities and towns across the country in terms of their cost of living, cultural and recreational amenities, health care facilities, taxes, and so on. Over time, this and other magazines' repetition of a relatively consistent narrative about which cities are "best," produces a popular mental map of certain cities that are paragons of the good life, good business, and good governance. In the case of *Money's* "Best Places to Live," Austin, San Francisco, Seattle, and Minneapolis–St. Paul, along with Rochester, MN (because of its health care facilities) and Madison, WI (because of facilities associated with its university and its lake-front location) are consistent top performers, reflecting the magazine's ranking criteria that place heavy weight on a mix of good weather, high levels of amenity, low taxes, and available services, especially health care (McCann, 2004; Figure 9.2 and Table 9.1).

Urban politicians and business leaders take this free publicity seriously. It is considered both an honor and an objective validation of good city management. Indeed, in certain cases, good city management is actually the focus of these sorts of popular evaluations of cities: in 2009, the popular Canadian news magazine, *MacLean's*, ranked Burnaby, BC, Saskatoon, SK, and Surrey, BC, as its top three "best governed" cities, based on the cost and quality of municipal services, for example (Coyne, 2009). As long as the images of the cities presented by the media are considered positive by local business and political elites, they are welcomed as a generator of interest that can, with effort and skill, be converted into tourist revenue, new residents, and new business investment.

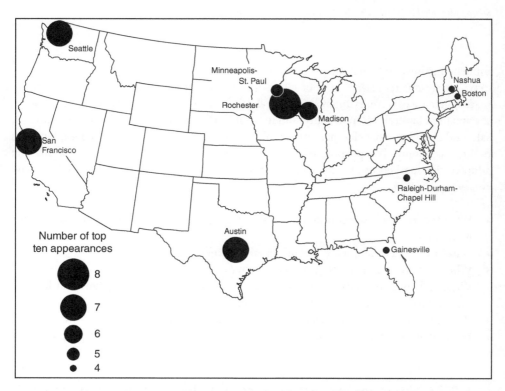

Figure 9.2   Cities regularly appearing in *Money's* top ten, 1987–2002. Between 1987 and 2002, *Money's* rankings have featured Rochester, MN eight times, more than any other city; Austin, TX, San Francisco, CA, and Seattle, WA have appeared seven times; Madison, WI, six times; Minneapolis–St. Paul, MN, five times; and Boston, MA, Gainesville, FL, Nashua, NH, and Raleigh–Durham–Chapel Hill, NC, have each appeared four times. Source: McCann (2004). Used with permission of Sage Publications.

Table 9.1 Top criteria for choosing a city according to *Money's* surveys of its subscribers. 1997 was the last year in which *Money* published a full list of the criteria. In 1998 it published the top five: clean water, low crime rate, clean air, good schools, and low property taxes.

1994	1995	1996	1997
1 Low crime rate	Clean water	Low crime rate	Low crime rate
2 Clean water	Clean air	Clean water	Clean water
3 Clean air	Low crime rate	Clean air	Plentiful doctors
4 Plentiful doctors	Plentiful doctors	Plentiful doctors	Clean air
5 Many hospitals	Many hospitals	Many hospitals	Many hospitals
6 Strong state government	Strong state government	Housing appreciation	Good schools
7 Low income taxes	Low income taxes	Good schools	Housing appreciation
8 Low property taxes	Low property taxes	Low property taxes	Low property taxes
9 Housing appreciation	Housing appreciation	Low income taxes	Strong state government
10 Affordable medical care	Good schools	Strong state government	Low income taxes

Source: McCann (2004). Used with permission of Sage Publications.

influencing those strategies, their social consequences, the interests they serve, the way they draw on certain representations of cities, and the way they facilitate the (re)shaping of place – that are of primary interest to critical urban geographers. Their work problematizes the apparent naturalness, normality, and inevitability of treating cities like commodities for sale, and they show that city marketing is a social process with a history, a geography, and a political economy. The purpose of this chapter is to explore a number of questions that address city marketing and its wider historical, social, and geographical contexts and consequences:

- What theories and concepts do critical urban geographers use to help them analyze city marketing?
- What are the key components of urban entrepreneurialism?
- Who is involved in marketing cities and why?
- What audiences or markets are targeted by urban marketing campaigns and how do these reinscribe social inequalities and differences in cities?
- What are the key strategies used in shaping urban marketing images?
- What political struggles surround the (re)shaping of cities for marketing purposes?

9.2 Contemporary Perspectives on Urban Entrepreneurialism

The intellectual touchstone of most critical urban scholarship on city marketing is David Harvey's analysis of **urban entrepreneurialism** (Chapter 7; Harvey, 1989). The notion of urban entrepreneurialism is characterized by the willingness of the neoliberalized (Chapter 2) state at the local level – often in combination with governance actors and institutions at other scales – to initiate, rather than simply manage the effects of, urban economic development. For Harvey, this neoliberal urban entrepreneurialism has a three-fold focus:

i. Attempts by local actors to "lure highly mobile flexible production, financial and consumption flows" to their city (Harvey, 1989: 11; Logan and Molotch, 1987; DuPont, 2011). These attempts entail the creation of public–private partnerships, where state powers and resources are used in innovative ways to support and enhance traditional business-led booster strategies aimed at competing with other cities for inward investment.

ii. The utilization of **speculative economic development strategies** marked by "risk absorption by the local (rather than the national or federal) public sector [distinguishing it] from earlier phases of civic **boosterism** in which private capital seemed generally much less risk averse" (Harvey, 1989: 7; Clarke and Gaile: 1989; Leitner, 1990).

iii. A reorientation of state priorities toward the neoliberalized speculative construction of spectacular *places*, from business parks to mega-developments to sports stadia to gentrified neighborhoods, that may have economic and cultural impacts only in certain parts of a city and that likely reduce local government's long-standing "managerialist" concerns with the provision of housing, education, and so on.

> **Speculative economic development strategies.** Investing in urban development – for example, building office parks or highways – or in other development-related practices – for example, workforce training –not because a buyer, user, or employer is already committed but as a way of stimulating investment. The phrase, "If you build it, they will come," represents the most optimistic version of this risk-taking mindset.

> **Boosterism.** A term referring to the enthusiastic promotion of a cause, idea, institution, person, or place. Civic, or place, boosterism refers to the promotion of places, whether towns, cities, regions, or countries. "Boosters" are those, from both the private and public sectors, who engage in this promotion or marketing. The interests that drive them toward boosterism range from the economic to simply civic pride, although these two usually work in tandem.

Urban entrepreneurialism entails, Harvey argues, some combination of a number of economic development strategies. Attempts to create and enhance local competitive advantages in the realm of production form one trusted strategy. This includes the following: the continual training of the local labor force so that businesses see the city as an attractive place to open an office or factory; the funneling of venture capital to key new enterprises that are being nurtured in the city, such as high technology or biotechnology start-ups; and the provision of tax breaks or custom-prepared sites to potential investors.

A second strategy entails efforts to enhance the city's character and reputation as a place of consumption and culture, particularly for higher income residents and visitors, through investments in the beautification of the built environment, entertainment and recreation facilities, spectacular events, and marketing efforts to make the city seem to have a high quality of life. The purpose is to make the city "appear as an innovative, exciting, creative, and safe place to live, to play, and consume" (Harvey, 1989: 9). These strategies are often combined with continued attempts to maintain a competitive position with respect to the transfer of funds from other levels of government, even as the form of these transfers changes (e.g., from block grants to defense contracts).

Harvey suggests that the entrepreneurial stance now taken by the public sector, characterized by government's willingness to underwrite inter-city competition for investment and speculative development, benefits multinational corporations by allowing them to play one city off against another in, for example, a competition for a new office or manufacturing facility. He contends that the pressure to create a "good business climate" acts as 'an "external coercive power' over cities to bring them into line with the discipline and logic of capitalist development" (Harvey, 1989: 10). This coercion sets business and political elites on a "treadmill" of continual innovation, a pressure that is manifest in what he perceptively identifies as the "serial reproduction of 'world trade centers' or of new cultural or entertainment centers, of waterfront development, of post-modern shopping malls" and so on (Harvey, 1989: 10). These are, he continues, "innovations and investments designed to make particular cities more attractive. ... [that have, however] quickly been imitated elsewhere, thus rendering any competitive advantage ... ephemeral" (Harvey, 1989: 12). This further underscores the key distinguishing feature of contemporary entrepreneurial urbanism: the assumption of considerable risk from speculative development by the local public sector.

Another key contribution of Harvey's (1989) paper, and the one which will frame much of the rest of this chapter, is his foregrounding of what he calls "the revival of [civic] boosterism" (Harvey, 1989: 4) and associated practices of image making, symbolism, promotion, and city marketing. What Harvey identifies as having been revived since the 1970s is a practice of **place marketing** that has occurred in various forms on both sides of the Atlantic since at least the middle of the nineteenth century. So, contemporary urban entrepreneurialism is not new, but it is distinguished from previous forms of boosterism by the increased assumption of risk by the local state that, with the rise of neoliberalism as a dominant political ideology, has been compelled to act less as a manager and regulator and more as an entrepreneur and pliant facilitator of capital investment.

> **Place marketing.** The broad set of activities focused on boosting a place and, thus, making it more enticing to a range of audiences who might invest or spend money in it. Since the rise of **neoliberalism** (Chapter 2) in the late twentieth century, place marketing has become much more an activity in which local governments engage.

Reflecting on the first decade of academic research inspired by the entrepreneurial thesis, Andrew Wood (1998: 121–122) noted that a great deal of the research has involved case studies of places which exhibit signs of the entrepreneurial stance, many of which were particularly concerned with the "new boosterism." While noting the value of these case studies, he critiques the literature for a lack of attention to entrepreneurialism's impacts on inequalities beyond those centered on class, for a lack of attention to how the new spectacular landscapes of the entrepreneurial city are "actually experienced and interpreted by residents," for lacking much attention to how entrepreneurialism might be questioned and resisted, for not specifying how exactly changes in urban governance influence broader political economies, and for tending to avoid the direct application of Harvey's framework and, instead, simply using the original argument as "a *preface to* rather than a *framework for* the study of particular processes or phenomena" (Wood, 1998: 122, his emphases, see also Hall and Hubbard, 1996).

We will return to some of these issues below but, for now, we will explore the ways in which the identities of cities – their built environments, their economies, their societies and cultures – are shaped through and for city marketing. In doing so, we will rely both on the language of the entrepreneurial city thesis and on case studies that illustrate urban entrepreneurialism's operations and effects. Harvey's work, and how it has been used by critical geographers, offers a useful framework through which to understand how, why, in whose interests, and at whose expense cities have been neoliberalized (Brenner and Theodore, 2002) and are marketed as commodities in the global market.

9.3   Who Markets Cities and to Whom? Key Actors and Audiences

Which actors are involved in shaping the identity of contemporary cities through marketing and whose interests are served by their activities? Certainly, the types of business interests evident in nineteenth and early twentieth century city boosterism are also central to contemporary entrepreneurial urbanism. In fact, these locally dependent place entrepreneurs, or **rentiers** (Logan and Molotch, 1987), are crucial to the process because their economic interests are based in drawing rent from land and buildings in a specific city (see the discussion of the **growth coalition** in Chapter 7). Therefore, it is generally in their interests to advocate for policies that will attract more population and business, intensify land uses, and increase land values in their place.

In order to achieve this goal, rentiers (i.e., developers, construction companies, property financiers, the real estate industry, etc.) must bring local politicians – a group that is as much, or more, locally dependent than they are – into a local

> **Rentiers.** A French word referring to people who receive a fixed sum of money from a particular source on a regular basis, for example, rent payments. Landlords, then, are one type of rentier. In cities, rentiers are what Cox and Mair (1988) call locally dependent capitalists, in that their income and profit comes from regularly drawing rent or other income from land and property. Given their economic relationship to local land and property, it is in their interests to band together to boost their place, so that, with more demand for land, their income and profits will increase.

growth coalition (Chapter 7). These actors join with other institutions and groups who view their interests – economic or otherwise – as lying with local economic growth. The other institutions include local media, utilities, local arts and entertainment organizations, and universities, all of whom also have a primary interest in seeing their place grow (Logan and Molotch, 1987; Jonas and Wilson, 1999; Leslie and Hunt, 2013).

Another set of actors whose interests ally them with the growth coalition are mobile consultants and gurus who travel from city to city advising business and political elites – and anyone else who will listen – on how best to design their economy, their built environment, their cultural activities, and, of course, their marketing strategies. The recent boom in demand for these consultants and the current ability of the most prominent of them to command massive fees for their services speaks directly back to the rise of urban neoliberalism. Reductions in city revenues and budgets have not only encouraged policy makers to be entrepreneurial in the pursuit of investment but have also forced the downsizing and outsourcing of many internal local state activities, including planning, which while always relying somewhat on outside contractors and consultants, now rely on their services to a greater extent. The economic restructuring has also forced a frenzied attention to the latest trends in policy innovation, which can be purchased "off the shelf" and quickly implemented in the hope of both saving money and getting a jump on other cities (McCann and Ward, 2011).

It is already evident from the discussion above that members of growth coalitions tend to have more than one audience in mind when they set about shaping a city's identity. Clearly, potential business investors are an extremely important target of marketing efforts. Entrepreneurial city boosters must be continually on the look-out for investors who will bring jobs, tax revenues, and other spin-offs to the local area. In some cities, local economic development professionals are willing to entertain just about any potential investor while their counterparts in other cities seek to develop "clusters" of economic activity in areas of biotechnology or software design, for example, and are, therefore, more focused on pitching their narrative to select companies. In either case, potential investors are enticed with talk of a generally "business friendly" environment, backed up by various tax incentives, a willing and well-trained workforce, ongoing economic growth, an already existing cluster of similar businesses and suppliers, help with customized facilities, and proximity or ease of transportation.

These attributes are frequently combined with stories about the high quality of life CEOs, their families, and other highly valued workers will enjoy in a particular city. These and other potential residents are a second important audience for city marketing. They are enticed with the promise of jobs and abundant career opportunities, low cost living, and high quality of life, encompassing everything from proximity to attractive natural environments and recreational opportunities adjacent to the city, to bike paths, high quality recreational facilities and spectator sports, good schools and colleges, abundant "high" and "street" culture, and so on. Marketers, in other words, seek to present their city as an economic boomtown and, simultaneously, an ideal hometown. Among potential residents and workers who have become particularly coveted since the turn of the millennium in North America have been the so-called **creative class** of young workers employed in the technology and design industries (Florida, 2002), even as this strategy has been severely criticized (Creative Class Struggle, n.d.; Peck, 2005; Wilson and Keil, 2008; Kotkin, 2013). Cities pursuing this market niche have sought to highlight their vibrant neighborhoods, coffee shops, active (rather than spectator) recreational opportunities, diversity, cosmopolitanism, "cool," and "buzz."

A third audience that is always squarely in the sights of city marketers are tourists. This group, like the others, can be differentiated into subgroups depending on the

Creative class. A putatively distinct socioeconomic grouping in contemporary society in the **global North**. Richard Florida (2002), who developed the idea and has become a consultant employed by many cities interested in attracting this group of people, argues that it is comprised mostly of young people who create new ideas and technologies in engineering, architecture and design, arts and entertainment, and education. His argument is that while, in the past, workers

Figure 9.3 A worker rests at a construction site in Datong, Shanxi Province, China, in 2011. The site is part of a tourist-oriented redevelopment program that aims to reconstruct Datong's urban center as a replica of the city's days as the capital of the Jin Dynasty (1115–1234 CE). To make way for the construction, almost two thirds of the inner city's original residents were relocated to suburban high-rise housing sites. Photo courtesy of Max Woodworth.

nature of the place they might visit and what they might do when they are there. They are not only "holidaymakers," but might also be "conventioneers" – people in town for a meeting, conference, trade show, and so on. The "brand strength" ranking to which we referred at the beginning of the chapter is based on cities' attractiveness to tourists of various sorts, something that is taken seriously by local businesses (Figure 9.3). Thus, in urban tourist branding, potential tourists, as well as tour companies, hotel chains, and travel agents, will be told a story about a city that highlights its particular attributes, whether they be good weather, interesting historical sites, nightclubs, or high

travelled to where the jobs were, now members of this Creative Class seek out places where they want to live, and it is up to employers to follow them. Thus, in urban policy terms, he argues that cities must make themselves attractive to the tastes and needs of the Creative Class in order to attract investment. While popular among many politicians, this notion has been roundly critiqued both for the quality of the research upon which it is based and the political, economic, and social consequences of its arguments (including providing a justification for gentrification). Peck (2005) provides a forceful critique.

quality convention centers and meeting facilities, all of which have been serially reproduced across the urban landscape in recent years (Sanders (2005) provides a critical evaluation of the glut in North American convention space).

A fourth, audience – a "niche" one, but still one that urban policy makers take seriously – is representatives of other cities and members of the wider community of urban planners, governance experts and so on. Cities engage in what might be called "policy boosterism" when engaging with these groups. They strive to out-compete others in reducing greenhouse gas emissions, for example, while, in a seeming paradox, they are also willing to share their innovations and practices with their peers (McCann 2013).

A fifth and frequently overlooked audience for city marketing narratives is the local audience. The local population's support for a particular growth agenda is crucial to the long-term operation of a growth machine. If an electorate turns against a particular form of development – one that seeks to make suburban single-family neighborhoods denser with more apartments, for example – significant changes in the composition of local politics may occur at the next election. If well-organized groups of activists – opposing urban expansion into rural areas, for instance – use protests, letter writing campaigns, and law suits to slow down or stall the development approval process, fears will emerge about lost economic opportunities, as investors look for more stable and predictable business environments elsewhere. Therefore, the local audience finds itself the target of a particular strand of place marketing, one that is intended to legitimize existing policies, strategies, and visions of development and to foster a hegemonic sense of community and common purpose – what Logan and Molotch (1987: 62) call "we feelings," and what Cox and Mair (1988) refer to as localist ideology. These narratives play up what is good about a particular city and its people – from its sports teams, to its scenery, to its high ranking on the sorts of league tables we mentioned above. They are intended to convince the general population that the growth machine's particular vision for the (always growing) future of the city benefits *all* of its residents equally, even when it stems from the economic interests of a narrow strata of society – what Logan and Molotch (1987) call the myth of value-free development.

It is important to note here that appeals to "we feelings" involve appeals to emotion, that is, strategies are used and appeals are made that bring on visceral feelings that shape our normative positions about how cities should be (Chapter 8). Music, visuals, and so on draw out deep feelings of belonging identity, and place attachment. They also stimulate desires for betterment and play on fears of what might happen to a city, to jobs, to livelihoods, if everyone does not "get on board" with the local economic development strategy. When effective, these emotional campaigns are remembered for longer than verbal slogans and detailed narratives about places (Chapter 11).

While acting "defensively" to counter opposition and maintain "we feelings," internally oriented city marketing also seeks to set goals and agendas for the future, offering a clear vision for community feeling to coalesce around. As Chang (1997), in his discussion of Singapore's tourism strategies, notes:

> [I]mages are studiously crafted as goals to be achieved rather than as embodiments of what is already existing. By analogy, tourism imaging strategies also may serve as a goal to which the city and its people can aspire rather than just a statement about what the city has to offer to visitors. Indeed advertising images create experiences on the part of tourists, which locals and local societies must in turn fulfill if they wish to continue to be a destination area. (Chang, 1997: 546)

There are various forms of these goals, not only in the realm of tourism. They include general ones (to be a more prosperous city, to be a more sustainable city), to more time limited and specific ones (to attract the new assembly plant or the next Olympics Games). In each case, they are promoted by certain actors with specific interests to other members of the local community with the hope of gaining their support. In this regard, city marketing is powerful and political. It involves the strategies of various groups seeking to shape cities in ways that satisfy their interests. We now turn to a more detailed discussion of these strategies.

9.4   Making the Pitch: The Strategies and Politics of Shaping Urban Identities for the Market

The actors involved in creating and promoting a particular image of a city do so not only with specific audiences in mind but, necessarily, via audience-specific narratives that are intended to seduce a specific group. Thus, there is no single marketing strategy in most large cities. Rather, there are a number of interrelated and (ideally) mutually reinforcing strategies. In this section, we will discuss some of the most prevalent and important ones by focusing on how cities are "written" and "re-written" both in textual/representational terms and also in a physical sense.

Imagineering the built environment as a resource for production and consumption

First, there is the careful use of the built and physical environments to represent the productive resources a city offers – physical infrastructure that allows the production of goods and services – and local opportunities for consumption of goods, services, sights, "buzz," and ambience (Degen, 2008, 2014). There is an intent by the actors described above to present what they see as the most attractive essence of their city to the world via an assemblage of cut-and-pasted tangible and intangible elements of its landscape, economy, society, and culture (Waitt, 1999). This **imagineering** is not only captured in a slogan and a logo but also involves the careful managing and presentation of specific images and narratives of the city through city web sites, marketing brochures, and, where possible, via stage-managed media events.

> **Imagineering.** A term originally used by the Walt Disney Corporation. It suggests a conscious attempt to mold the world through imagination and imaginative work. It is particularly useful in the context of our discussion of place marketing because it brings together the representational and the material aspects of the practice.

On the production side, business and political elites will direct the attention of potential investors toward the available stock of offices, factory buildings, warehouses, and appropriately zoned land that are available or that could be built in the city. This infrastructure is complemented by good road, rail, or air links, depending on the needs of specific investors. Local economic development professionals emphasize how prospective investors might fit their businesses into the existing landscape, how they might be permitted to shape the existing built environment to their own needs, and how the state at the local and other levels will help their integration into the city through a range of incentives, favorable tax arrangements, and so on.

Of course, marketing for the purpose of enhancing a city's productive capacity cannot be fully separated from marketing efforts that represent cities as objects and places for consumption. As we have already suggested, the CEOs or upper-level managers who may be enticed to a city because of its productive infrastructures are also interested in whether there are good restaurants, safe streets, and a vibrant culture for them to consume in the city. Carefully managed images of urban landscapes are often central to consumption-oriented marketing narratives.

People as resources for production and consumption

The strategic representation of a city's landscape is intertwined with a second set of marketing strategies: those involving urban populations as a whole or, more commonly, specific urban social groups. This connection is evident, for example, in a full-page advertisement in *The New Yorker* magazine. In it, the government of the province of Ontario, Canada, represented itself as open and welcoming to business. Over a glossy shot of Toronto's lakefront skyline, featuring the CN tower and surrounding office buildings, the advertisement made the following marketing pitch:

NESTLED BESIDE FOUR GREAT LAKES, YOU'LL FIND ONE IMMENSE TALENT POOL.

Otherwise known as the Ontario workforce: the G7's most educated. … But brainpower is not Ontario's only advantage: Ontario's economic hub, Toronto, is the third largest financial center in North America. And Ontario's low combined federal/provincial corporate income tax rate – lower that the U.S. federal/state average – helps create a cost-effective business environment. All of which make Ontario an ideal business location. That's why **the world works here**. (Government of Ontario, 2009: 11, capitalization and emphasis in original; see also www.investinontario.com)

The magazine's elite readers are, it seems, being tempted to imagine their businesses in Toronto, and by extension Ontario, through the inviting image and through the glowing description of the local population as a production resource.

Again, it is not unusual for urban elites to sell sanitized, decontextualized stories about certain groups within their populations. One would not expect them to highlight the *lack* of formal education or appropriate talents within their population! And in terms of selling the city as an object and space of consumption, ethnic minorities are often central to myths about the vibrancy and diversity of multicultural cities. Certain groups' food and culture are frequently commodified and used by elites, especially in Europe and North America to "spice up" the image of their cities, often with the aid of ethic entrepreneurs (Binnie *et al.*, 2006b; Volkan and Rath, 2012).

This everyday deployment of minority group identities (and the conscious, active participation of many members of those groups) in image making is also reflected in the rise of city marketing aimed specifically at lesbian, gay, bisexual, transgender, and queer (LGBTQ) populations. While LGBTQ people are still discriminated against in most parts of the world,

Figure 9.4 A float at the Vancouver Pride Parade. Note how the symbolism and slogans on this float combine two of Vancouver's marketing images: a city that is LGBTQ friendly and also a city that is green, sustainable, or "natural." Photo courtesy of Charlie Smith.

some city governments and business leaders have identified an economic opportunity in their LGBTQ populations. They have engaged in strategic attempts to attract "gay dollars" by defining their cities as welcoming to sexual diversity and, more specifically, by promoting gay neighborhoods and annual Pride Parades (Figure 9.4) as tourist destinations (Box 9.2).

Managing and policing the Imagineered city

While urban landscapes and social groups are frequently employed by marketers to create specific identities for cities, critical geographers also note how urban branding can provoke the physical and practical re-shaping, policing, and managing of urban spaces and urban experiences. Perhaps the two most obvious examples of this aspect of city marketing are the reshaping of built environments to enhance or correspond to a marketing goal, often creating "stage set" places to be consumed, and the channeling of tourists through an urban landscape in a circuit that connects numerous stage sets while avoiding or ignoring other parts of the city.

Think of your own experiences as a tourist in an unfamiliar city, or even as a visitor to another part of your own city (Figure 9.5). Tourist maps, guidebooks, directional signs, information booths, tourist office staff, and even those ubiquitous "hop-on, hop-off" double-decker buses are a great resource. They allow you to hit all the highlights with maximum efficiency and (hopefully) without getting your purse stolen, or worse. Furthermore, many of these "highlights" are the results of the purposeful reworking of existing landscapes into new, spectacular settings. The most renowned examples of these "stage set" developments include Baltimore's Harborplace development and the surrounding Inner Harbor and Boston's Faneuil Hall Market Place but examples of "festival spaces" intended to contribute to revamped city images and economies can be found across the world.

Box 9.2   Gay Pride and Gay Dollars in Vancouver, BC

Speaking in anticipation of the city's 2007 Pride Parade and Festival, then-mayor of Vancouver, Sam Sullivan, celebrated the event, which attracts around 500 000 people from Canada and beyond to the streets around the Davie Village neighborhood (Vancouver's "gay village"). The summertime festival is one of the largest events of its type and serves a number of purposes: to have fun, to build community by bringing members of the city's lesbian, gay, bisexual, transgender, and queer community together with their friends and supporters from the city and elsewhere, to promote the vibrancy and health of the community and its members, and to showcase Canada's diversity.

For the mayor, the event "demonstrates our community's commitment to inclusiveness and human rights" (Sullivan, 2007) while a colleague on the city council and a member, like Sullivan, of the city's right-leaning political party, characterized it as "an opportunity to celebrate our successes and renew our resolve to combat discrimination and intolerance" (quoted in Sullivan, 2007). A third city councilor, an openly gay member of a left-leaning party, added, "The Pride Parade and festival is one of Vancouver's premier events. In addition to celebrating our diversity, the parade helps reinforce Vancouver as a primary destination for GLBT travelers" (quoted in Sullivan, 2007). His comments resonated with a consultant's report published to much fanfare the previous year that ranked Vancouver as Canada's top gay tourism destination; a city where visitors "appreciate 'being able to walk down the street hand in hand, being able to walk on the beach and have their arms around each other'" (CBC News, 2006, quoting a local organizer of gay weddings).

Many cities are marketed to gay tourists who, it is hoped, will spend so-called "gay dollars" or "pink pounds" when they attend Pride Parades, for example (yet, their strategies are targeted, depending on their audience; Hunter, 2011). More generally, many urban elites seek to promote and market their cities as tolerant. Yet, even relatively tolerant cities like Vancouver witness hate crimes and other forms of homophobia (Catungal and McCann, 2010). Thus, a gay-friendly marketing image, like all elements of urban brands, must be constantly managed by those whose interests (both social and economic) it serves.

Yet, as a tourist, the enjoyment you might derive from these sights/sites is tempered by the deep-down nagging feeling that you are seeing someone else's version of the city – pre-packaged and relatively sanitized. You might feel, and with good reason, that you are being channeled through a well-managed set of spaces that correspond to a carefully constructed brand and that are intended to make you feel welcomed, safe, stimulated (within certain bounds!), and ready to spend your tourist dollar. This feeling may become particularly irksome when, on your travels, you encounter one of those signs telling you to take a photograph on this spot, facing in that direction, so you capture the classic, stage-managed view of the harbor, temple, monument, or interesting ethic community. It is hard to escape this feeling since, even if you try to break out of the standard circuit, the tourist industry also

Figure 9.5   Stage set landscape: Consuming Sydney Opera House and Harbour Bridge. Photo by Eugene McCann.

provides you with the "Off the Beaten Path" alternative, complete with its own must-see sights/sites, maps, guidebooks, and so on. Indeed, most of us have internalized the hegemonic script of what to experience and consume in cities to such an extent that, even if we understand the script critically, we tend to fall into it when visitors come to town – especially visitors who are of a different generation from us. When we have to entertain young children or our parents, for example, we jump on the predetermined, comfortable tourist carousel.

Brand managers are aware of the latent skepticism and creeping weariness with which any audience greets a marketing message. Every brand – its slogan, its logo, its iconic social and landscape elements – is fragile and has a shelf life. Indeed, the fragility of the brand seems to be all the more apparent in the context of what Harvey referred to as "serial reproduction," where the crowding of the global marketplace with look-alike landscapes (its Disneyfication or "Guggenheimization") compels other growth coalitions to innovate and find new marketing styles and strategies to better differentiate their city and compete with others.

One strategy is the one-off mega-event like the Olympics (Box 9.3, Figure 9.6), but it is important to note that urban entrepreneurial strategies and their attendant politics are not

Box 9.3 The Olympics and Contemporary City Marketing

Beijing's 2008 Olympic extravaganza was an unabashed image-making exercise, characterized by the pre-Games clearing of some of the city's oldest neighborhoods, extravagant new architecture, artificially good air quality, and a strict prohibition on protests (Broudehoux, 2012; Shin, 2012). Its opening ceremony is widely reported to have cost $300 million and featured a lip-synching child singer, digitally enhanced fireworks, and a group of children supposedly representing China's 56 ethnicities who were all, in fact, from the majority Han population. Beijing might be the most extreme example of the way urban and national elites carefully and strategically use Olympic Games to manage the image and identity of places for economic and political purposes, but its extremes only highlight the more general process of marketing through mega-events. By the same token, mega-events of all kinds and degrees of extremity highlight the key elements of the more general process of city marketing.

Made-for-media images do not happen by chance. They are classic examples of the careful training of the eye and selective story-telling that accompanies both one-off city marketing campaigns and also the more prosaic marketing strategies that are common to most cities. If they succeed, the city's "brand strength" will increase in the eyes of tourists, potential residents, and prospective investors who are looking for a city to consume. As Waitt (1999) and others have noted, the "Olympic Movement" as its proponents romantically refer to it, or the "Olympic Industry" as skeptics call it (Lenskyj, 2000; Shaw, 2008), frequently sparks controversy when it comes to town. For every glowing tale of actual or potential "legacies" of the Games, anecdotes and analyses abound about the negative impacts of the Olympics on city budgets (Montreal paid off its debt for the 1976 games in 2006), on low income populations (homeless and poor people are often targeted and displaced in the run-up to Olympic Games (Centre on Housing Rights and Evictions, n.d.)), on urban infrastructures (long-standing worries about Olympic "white elephants" have been strengthened by news that Beijing famed Bird's Nest Stadium has become nothing more than a failing tourist site since the games [Lim, 2012]), and on civil liberties during and after the events (in post-9/11 Olympics, "security" and surveillance are considered "legacies" and "deliverables" whereby CCTV and other infrastructures developed to police the Games will remain indefinitely (Boyle and Haggerty, 2009).

These cautionary examples are raised by opponents of Olympic bids as reasons why cities should reject the games. In this regard, the decision of the citizens of Denver to turn down an opportunity to host the 1976 games is frequently cited. The recent Vancouver winter games were vehemently, if unsuccessfully, opposed by various groups, including those who could see better uses for the public funds involved in hosting the event ("Healthcare Before Olympics," was one popular slogan) and those among the local First Nations who saw the games as a further insult in a long history of dispossession ("No Olympics on Stolen Land'). As the games neared, and costs to taxpayers increased, local negative opinion rose. Yet, it must be said that for the large numbers of people from Greater Vancouver and beyond who spent time in the city's crowded streets during the Olympics it will be regarded as a wonderfully happy party, even as taxpayers lost $100 million when the developer of the Olympic Village went bankrupt and the former athletes' accommodations did not sell on the condominium market as expected (Mason, 2014).

Figure 9.6 One of the most photogenic images of the 1992 Barcelona Games was of the diving competition, held at an outdoor pool on Montjuïc, a hill overlooking the city. As the divers propelled themselves off the high board, their flight was framed by the spectacular view of the city stretched below them, punctuated by Gaudi's multispired cathedral in the distance. Photographer Jerry Lodriguss captured the American diver Mary Ellen Clark in this image. Used with permission of *Philadelphia Inquirer*.

only focused on one event. Rather, they go on for years, sometimes in public but often behind the scenes, and entail the careful monitoring of the branding strategy, including decisions on which elements of the built environment and society to bring to the foreground. Frequently, they also entail reinvention, where even the most successful brands, like that of Las Vegas, are scrapped and created anew.

This constant managing of the brand also involves the explicit managing and policing of the branded spaces of the city, so that its public spaces – and even its people, or at least those who are on public view in spaces likely to be traversed by tourists or business people – correspond to and enhance, or at least do not cause too much damage to, the city's image. This managing and policing of cities is now frequently the purview of **Business Improvement Districts (BIDs)** (Chapter 7) or their equivalents (Ward, 2007). These are private organizations funded by special localized levies and taxes that have, under conditions of **urban entrepreneurialism**, assumed the formerly public functions of managing clearly delimited areas of the city (frequently the downtown area).

These private governance agencies and their employees, often called "ambassadors," provide advice and directions to tourists, operate street-sweeping services in their area and contract with private security firms to enforce bylaws and guard against so-called "quality of life" crimes (e.g., panhandling (begging for money in public spaces), public intoxication, graffiti tagging, and sex work). BIDs, then, are inspired by and seek to rein-force some of the central myths of city marketing – the city as safe and friendly, fun, and without obstacles to commerce. They do so in ways that have frequently been shown to have negative impacts on certain already-marginalized populations, such as homeless people and others who choose to, or have no option but to, live the majority of their lives in public spaces (Mitchell, 2003; Mitchell and Heynen, 2009). From this perspective, the critical literature also argues to that this constant policing and manicuring of the urban built and social environments is contrary to many widely held ideas about what a city should be – a place where difference can be encountered, literally face-to-face, and that can be, as a result, a place where society can be strengthened through the spark and buzz of difference. Others, however, argue that the way in which homeless people and other marginalized groups are treated in cities is more complex and differs depending on con-text (Cloke *et al.*, 2010; DeVerteuil, 2012).

Nonetheless, many have noted that the attempts by tourist agencies, Chambers of Commerce, and BIDs to manage the urban environment in correspondence with a par-ticular marketing strategy are often armored with a hard edge of high technology and "zero tolerance" policing strategies. These strategies frequently involve the blanketing of city neighborhoods with closed circuit television surveillance (CCTV), the (re) introduction of neighborhood police stations, and the strict enforcement of laws for even the most minor infrac-tions, under **broken windows policing**. While many applaud the "cleaning up" of cities where these tactics are deployed, others argue that this sharp edge of image-conscious urban governance marks an new high (or low) point in a mean-spirited, revanchist (i.e., vengeful) war against the poor, and particularly the homeless, in contemporary cities.

Broken windows policing. A controver-sial approach that stresses rapid response to minor crimes and blemishes on the built environment (e.g., vandalism, pan-handling, graffiti, and broken windows). The idea is that a quick response will dis-courage both minor and also major crimes in the future. Associated with urban politicians such as Rudy Giuliani of New York, it has been critiqued for the questionable evidence upon which it is based and the harsh, "revanchist," approaches to low income and homeless people that it tends to encourage.

Many of these strategies and the poli-tics around them are epitomized by Times Square in New York – a place argued to be the contemporary center of revanchist policies toward the urban poor. In the 1990s, under the guidance of Mayor Giuliani and a private–public development partnership, this neigh-borhood, which was renowned as a "red light" district but was also regarded by many as the vibrant heart of the city, was transformed into what proponents see as the welcoming face of the new tourist- and business-friendly Manhattan and what skeptics regard as a bland, and literally Disneyfied, space of consumption (featuring a Disney store, a Disney theater, and a studio of Disney-owned ABC Television). The Square has its own BID, whose street cleaners patrol constantly, a police substation, and is in midtown Manhattan, a neighbor-hood where almost every square foot of public space is covered by at least one CCTV cam-era. Of course, the re-written square is also the site of the annual, internationally televised street party to welcome the New Year – an event staged to convey the city's image as a friendly, safe, vibrant and fun, if sometimes chilly, place.

The politics of maintaining a city's image

If urban entrepreneurialism, image making, marketing and branding have become hegemonic in cities across the globe in recent decades, they have become so in the true sense of that word: these ideologies and practices are widely prevalent and taken for granted but they are by no means accepted by all nor are they incontrovertible. Rather, they are always in the process of being questioned and disrupted by skeptics and opponents of growth machine tactics and, on the other hand, they are continually being tended, adjusted, and legitimized by those business and political elites whose interests are closely tied to their operation. Thus, we can always see a contentious *politics* of image making in the entrepreneurial city. This might be evident in the public sphere, as certain marketing efforts are questioned in terms of their costs and social implications. But another form of politics – centered on persuasion and negotiation – can be found in the inner workings of growth coalitions as leaders try to make their message clear and persuasive while keeping all coalition members "on message" and "on the same page."

The attempt to "rebrand" the small cities of Cambridge, Kitchener, and Waterloo, ON, as "Canada's Technology Triangle" (CTT) is a striking example of how difficult it is to keep all members of a growth coalition focused, "on message," and willing to put aside their differences and specific interests in favor of a common marketing and governance strategy. Located 100 km southwest of Toronto, the three cities, along with neighboring Guelph, were first branded as the CTT in the late 1980s. As Joseph Liebovitz (2003) notes, the point was to create a new identity for the cities that showed them to be more than traditional manufacturing centers, to be leveraging the technology spin-offs from their local universities, and to be emerging from the perceived shadow of the more economically powerful Toronto region. Yet, coming up with a marketing image was only the start of what turned out to be a delicate political balance.

Liebovitz's account suggests that the development of the CTT brand demanded a change in how key actors perceived and practiced their role in the region. It also entailed the difficult political task of building what he calls "institutions of associative governance," which could "generate collaboration, trust and agreement among actors" (Liebovitz, 2003: 2637), thus allowing them to work together in ways that would achieve their common goals. In turn, the success of these new marketing and governance arrangements depended on strong and long-lasting bonds of trust and cooperation among the various public and private institutions whose interests rested in local economic development. This was an immense and politically delicate task, since economic development interests in each city were used to competing with each other for inward investment; the CTT model asked them to change their ways and share "leads" (i.e., information on potential investors). Similarly, local politicians saw the interests of their local constituents as paramount and had to be persuaded to think and act regionally while public and private sector actors found it difficult to completely understand or trust each other. Furthermore, differences among elements of the regional business community – between representatives of the traditional manufacturing economy and the newer high technology "upstarts," specifically – raised further barriers to cooperation and the development of a shared marketing and economic development strategy (Liebovitz, 2003).

Thus, while the CTT survives as "typically the first point of contact for enterprises outside the Waterloo Region interested in start-up, expansion, or relocation" to the region and while it continues coordinate local actors to offer potential inward investors economic development services, including data and networking opportunities, site location assistance, and tours of potential sites (http://www.techtriangle.com), Liebovitz notes that attempts over the years to build trust and institutional frameworks that keep the various actors and interests on the same page have been extremely difficult. It is, in other words, one thing to brand a place with a new catchy or evocative slogan, but it is quite another (highly complex and political) task to turn the diverse interests that exist in the place toward the single purpose of maintaining and enhancing the local economy and brand (Bathelt and Munro, 2012).

9.5   Summary and Conclusions

The identities of cities, their marketing brands or images, their role as competitive entities, and the use of their built environments and people as commodities to be sold in the global market place are not natural or inevitable. A critical perspective on the phenomenon of city image making and marketing seeks to denaturalize the phenomenon, identifying the *social* processes involved in creating cities as marketable commodities. It also asks the basic critical and political question: *For whom?* Whose interests benefit from the shaping of a city's identity to fit a marketing strategy? Whose interests, on the other hand, are damaged or ignored in the drive for "brand strength"? To address these questions it is necessary to engage in two related analytical tasks that are a feature of critical approaches to urban geography. Firstly, we must historicize the topic, that is, to show how the marketing of cities by a combination of business and political elites, for example, is not natural, inevitable, or even particularly long-standing and to trace its emergence from a particular point in the past. A second, related analytical task is to contextualize the development of contemporary city marketing by identifying the specific social contexts – institutional, political, economic, geographic, and so on – in which it developed.

Harvey's framework for analyzing urban entrepreneurialism in general and, particularly, the "new boosterism," as he called it, provides the starting point for a critical analysis. We have seen how contemporary city marketing is the product of a specific historical and social context, specifically since the 1970s in the major industrial cities of Europe and North America. At this time, and in this place, city governments saw the tax revenues and transfers of funds from higher levels of government that they once relied on to provide municipal services dry up due to revolts against taxation among citizens, spurred by a wider shift in the dominant ideology regarding what government is for and how it should act. In line with this hegemonic ideal of small government, partnered with and acting like business, urban elites in Western cities identified public–private partnerships and an entrepreneurial stance as the best ways to attract revenues to fill the gap left by the reduction in tax revenues and government transfers. To do so, public sector institutions accepted increasing amounts of risk by underwriting investments made in speculative developments and, thus, the willingness to "take the hit" if investments in new malls, sports stadia, or industrial parks failed to bear profits for their private sector partners. This contextualization allows us to demystify and denaturalize the glossy marketing images, catchy slogans, and extravagant megaevents that epitomize urban entrepreneurialism.

We also identified the main actors involved in imagineering cities and their interests in being involved (largely members of local growth machines, interested in intensifying the uses of and raising the value of land in the city in order to reap more profit from their locally fixed investments and activities). We have specified the key audiences that are the targets of marketing strategies (potential business investors, residents, and tourists, as well as local people). We then unpacked the various types of strategies used in contemporary city marketing (representing the built environment and the city's people as resources for production and consumption, managing and policing the most salable spaces for the entrepreneurial city), and the continual politics of keeping all the interests involved in selling the city "on message."

9.6   Further Reading

- Find the marketing websites or documents of the place where you live. Remember, there may be multiple sources – separate economic development and tourism websites for example. Start by identifying the slogans and images used to entice people to the place. What do they show, what do they not show, and what narrative, representational, and emotional strategies do they use? Then delve deeper. Who are the actors involved, which specific audiences do they seem to be targeting, what incentives or other types of help (such as tax breaks to industry) are they offering?
- If you are interested in this element of urban geography, it is important to read the classics: Harvey (1989) and Logan and Molotch (1987).
- Scout the web for oppositional and critical activist reactions to and campaigns around upcoming mega-events. As this book goes to press, the most obvious recent target has been the Brazilian World Cup, but by the time you read this, there will no doubt be new mega-events and new critiques on the horizon. Five Ring Circus is a critical online film on the Vancouver Winter Olympics: http://www.thefiveringcircus.com.

Chapter 10

Nature and Environment in the City

Urban Geography: A Critical Introduction, First Edition. Andrew E.G. Jonas, Eugene McCann, and Mary Thomas.
© 2015 Andrew E.G. Jonas, Eugene McCann, and Mary Thomas. Published 2015 by John Wiley & Sons, Ltd.

10.1   Introduction

William Cronon (1991) points out that the city has, all too often, been represented as separate from, or outside, our experiences of **nature**. This distinction has roots in the Western philosophical tradition of separating nature from society, and placing "Man" as a superior force or shaper of "Nature." In the ancient Greek and the Roman Empires, for example, this dualism meant that the city represented order and civilization, the antithesis of an unbridled nature; anything outside the city was savage, untamed, and uncivilized – in the lap of the gods, as it were. Even when colonists fled Europe for the Americas in the fifteenth and sixteenth centuries, they were simultaneously awed and appalled by nature's raw beauty, power, and abundance, and they took their views of nature–society dualism with them, belittling and demolishing indigenous ways of knowing the natural world through colonialism and conquest.

> **Nature.** Nature is a useful term for thinking about how society and cities are tied to other elements of the world. This is especially the case if we think of ourselves as part of nature and our products – from everyday commodities to cities – as natural. We are obviously natural, as much as we often cling to social/natural distinctions and boundaries. And concrete high-rises are natural in that they are formed from raw materials by natural beings (us). Thinking of cities and societies as connected to nature can reorient our relationships (see the definition of **urban metabolism**).

With the onset of industrialization, a new metropolitan sensibility toward nature took hold. Urban planners, politicians, and residents began to view nature in the city differently, bestowing it with a progressive meaning. No longer seen as separate from the city, untamed and wild, nature could serve a wider economic and social purpose, such as providing energy and material resources for industrial growth or, through the construction of public parks, playgrounds, and garden districts, combating social unrest in the industrial city. People began to think about nature's relationship to the city less in terms of wilderness or pristine landscapes and more through the instrumental concept of the urban environment. Planners also began to seek to mitigate nature's impact, for instance in the construction of levees or in the training of populations for disaster events (Figure 10.1). These forms of engaging nature, however, still maintain society's hold over the natural world, and problematically assume that urban society and nature are separate domains.

In the latter part of the twentieth century, growing awareness of environmental pollution and mounting anxiety about global warming and growing worldwide energy consumption gave a further inflection to this modern urban environmental sensibility. In movements emphasizing **sustainable development**, nature is seen to be a continuing resource for economic growth, but only if consumption does not contribute to environmental degradation or pollution. Whether this is even possible remains to be seen. Humanity and its reliance on fossil fuels have irrevocably shifted environmental systems on a planetary scale.

Despite new consciousness about environmental protection, you might still think that looking for nature in the city is counterintuitive. For if what is outside the city – suburbs, countryside, rurality, and nature – is not what urban theorists study, how can one study the ways in which cities transform nature and, in doing so, transform urban society and

地震 ＝ 津波 ➡ 避難
EARTHQUAKE ＝ TSUNAMI REFUG
(TIDAL-WAVES)

すぐ高いところへあがってください
Move to the higher places to avoid Tsunami.

神奈川県・藤沢市
KANAGAWA · FUJISAWA CITY

Figure 10.1　A tsunami warning sign in Fujisawa in Kanagawa Prefecture, Japan, informs viewers in Japanese and English to move to higher ground after an earthquake. Photo: Eugene McCann.

Sustainable development. Sustainability is a term used to define processes that balance energy inputs and outputs so that they can continue to operate (i.e., be sustainable). Sustainable development is a term that highlights the ideal of meeting the material needs of the present population without compromising those of future generations. The term has many critics who question whether development at present rates can ever be sustainable and who suggest that it is often associated with corporate "greenwashing." Critics also argue that sustainable development often focuses on the environment and economy but not on sustaining or improving society. On the other hand, those who subscribe to it are motivated to seek out ways to address the socio-natural challenges we currently face as a society.

politics? To think about this question, consider the case of a catastrophic hurricane named Katrina that came ashore on the Gulf Coast of the United States in August 2005. Hurricane Katrina made landfalls in Florida, Louisiana, and Mississippi, causing the deaths of 1800 people, and its storm surge was felt from Texas to Florida. Most spectacularly, Katrina breached the massive levees protecting the city of New Orleans from the waters of the Mississippi Delta, resulting in wholesale destruction of property and at least 1500 deaths in Louisiana alone. Thousands of homes and livelihoods were destroyed in the city's many low and moderate income neighborhoods. In the worst-hit Lower Ninth and Upper Ninth wards, where at least 75% of households self-identify as African–American, less than 20% of lots damaged by flooding have since been reoccupied. Initial media attention was focused on sporadic instances of looting that followed Katrina, eventually leading to criticisms of racist media representation of this environmental disaster and its victims. The horribly inadequate responses to the disaster by the federal and state governments also raised scrutiny and many pondered why, in this case, the disaster efforts were so poorly implemented. The social and cultural fabric of a great American city has been irrevocably transformed by both the natural disaster and the political and economic processes put in place to respond (or not) to it (see also Derickson, 2014).

The perception that cities like New Orleans are only "victims" of natural disasters tends to overlook the fundamental role of cities and urban societies in producing and transforming nature (Braun and Castree, 1998). In this chapter, we will consider how nature is a concept utilized for different urban purposes, and we suggest that cities are as "natural" as any other place. Critical geographers continue to push against the separation of nature and society into discrete categories.

The following questions drive our discussion of nature in the city in the chapter:

- Is nature separate from the city or a fundamental constituent of patterns of urban growth and development?
- How do cities, urban infrastructures, and land uses come to represent particular nature-society ideas and relations?
- What sorts of natural and social conditions have given rise to different meanings and ideas of the modern urban environment?
- How are the boundaries between the city and nature negotiated, regulated, and contested?
- Is the concept of the sustainable city in conflict with urban economic development?

10.2　Nature in the Modern Metropolis

Locating nature in the city represents a significant challenge to conventional wisdom. The visible landmarks of the city are tall buildings, bustling streets, bright lights, steel and glass, traffic and noise, pollution, and so forth. These objects appear far removed from our assumed encounters with the natural environment. In the city we might assume that our experience of nature is often limited to what we see on TV, in the movies, on the internet, or at the zoo or botanical garden. Yet while city people can find temporary escape from urban life in public parks and gardens (Figure 10.2), or by visiting local beaches and attending summer camps, whether or not these spaces should be seen as "natural" immediately raises a set of challenging theoretical and definitional issues.

For one, the city can only exist through its intimate interrelationships to a geography extended far beyond city limits. Environmental historians such as William Cronon and Donald Worster illustrate that nature of cities by detailing the massive reach of urban consumption and resource reliance. Cronon (1991) writes about Chicago – the very same city that inspired the neo-classical zonal model of urban structure – but he does not confine his gaze to the ecology of inner city districts, such as the stockyards of the south side or the lumber mills of the Chicago River basin. Instead, he expands his view of ecological zones and resource flows well beyond the city limits: to the forests and prairies of the Midwest and

Figure 10.2 Community garden in the Cascade neighborhood of Seattle, WA. In the USA, community gardening grew out of movements to preserve farmland in the city. One of the first of these was Seattle's "P-Patch" program, which began in the 1970s. The City of Seattle now has a zoning policy for community gardens. Photo: Andy Jonas.

the slopes of the Rocky Mountains. Cronon shows how these agricultural and natural spaces have resourced Chicago and how, in turn, "nature's metropolis" has transformed the vast exurban spaces of the Great American West by means of flows of capital, labor power, and traded commodities.

Writing about the development of hydraulic civilizations – those cultures dependent upon the harnessing of water for irrigated crops and urban development – Donald Worster (1985) deploys the powerful metaphor of the "flow of power in history" to demonstrate how nature (water) is corralled for human uses under the capitalist state mode. Worster may not have had specifically a metropolitan-scale environmental sensibility in mind but it is does not take much imagination to link his discussion of the taming of the American West by means of the waters of the Colorado River to the growth of the metropolitan economy of Southern California and, eventually, to the modern landscape of freeways and suburban sprawl (Reisner, 1986). Such ideas about the relationship between the flow of water, power, politics, and the growth of cities have recently been taken up and expanded in new directions by critical urban geographers, such as Gandy (2002), Kaika (2005), Pincetl and Katz (2007), and Meehan (2013), to name just a few in the field of scholarship known as **urban political ecology** (UPE) (see also Box 10.1).

Box 10.1   Urban Metabolism

Urban political ecology (UPE) offers a way of approaching nature–city relationships from a critical theoretical perspective. Central to UPE research are concepts of socionature and nature-urban metabolism (Swyngedouw, 1996). Cities incorporate human institutions and practices involving the appropriation and transformation of nature under different modes of production. As David Harvey (2000: 207) puts it, "[w]e are sensory beings in a metabolic relation to the world around us. We modify the world and in doing so change ourselves through our activities and labor". Drawing on the metaphor of urban metabolism, Swyngedouw (1996) argued that urban social relationships operate and evolve through complex interactions with the natural environment. For instance, the growth of the industrial capitalist city involved harnessing fixed physical resources, including raw materials, chemicals, and biological products (animals, bodies, etc.), and linking them together in material and social flows comprised of extensive chains of production, manufacturing, distribution and consumption.

Urban metabolism also enhances our awareness of social differences and inequalities. The internal differentiation of urban space, such as the expansion of suburbs or the movement of capital back into the city through gentrification, arises from our interactions with external nature and the uneven circulation of capital through the built environment. Resulting social injustices in the city, such as those associated with housing shortages or the lack of access to parks and open space, reflect not so much a fixed spatial pattern of the city as a dynamic set of socio-natural relations of production and consumption. Whereas mainstream research on the city has often ignored nature and the environment, or perhaps has treated it as a separate sphere of human activity and politics (Carlin and Emel, 1992), UPE seeks to examine the internal and symbiotic relationships between nature, production, and consumption, and resulting patterns of urban inequality (Heynen *et al.*, 2006).

Social urban geographers are also interested in nature. Take, for example, summer activities for young people involving visits to the countryside. Vanderbeck (2008) examined a program in New York City, the Fresh Air Fund, which arranges for "inner city" black and Latino children to spend portions of their summers living with host families, many of whom are identified as white, in rural Vermont. Vanderbeck suggests that such programs serve to reinforce particular racialized imaginative geographies of city and country and reinforce the idea that whiteness rather than the encounter with

Urban political ecology. Urban political ecology (UPE) is a strand of thinking that has emerged in urban geography in recent years as a way to think about the relationships between society and nature. It emphasizes the connections, rather than separation, between cities and nature. It focuses on flows that disrupt easy notions about the separation between societies and nature, or easy definitions of where the city ends. Moreover, the inclusion of the word *political* in the term is important. It indicates that the way in which social groups in cities engage with nature (whether by enjoying good quality drinking water, access to park space, or being exposed to pollution, etc.) is in no way "natural" but, instead, is a characteristic of uneven power relations in society.

nature *per se* represents a long-term solution to urban inequalities. Some further questions that follow from this research might be: Do such activities enhance our sense of the difference between city and countryside? Or do such programs remind us of life in the city? Cities certainly shape our experiences of nature; but in what sense are cities themselves natural? Or are they unnatural? We explore these questions in the following sections.

Urban metabolism

Urban metabolism suggests that social and economic lives in the city are deeply intertwined with nature. In considering the idea of urban metabolism, we can perhaps start by recognizing that urban places are fundamentally connected to the countryside through an already-transformed nature. What this means is that many of the products that go into making cities (concrete, steel, glass, bricks, etc.) must first be made from raw materials, many of which come from areas surrounding, next to, or underneath our cities, such as gravel pits, aquifers, fields, farms, mines, estuaries, and so forth. These raw materials are processed and made into useful commodities. This, in turn, involves combining labor power (the skills and capacities of workers) with various means of production (processing facilities, assembly lines, etc.).

Urban metabolism. In biology, "metabolism" refers to all the physical and chemical processes through which an organism's life is maintained. It focuses attention on change (the Greek root of the word means change) and on flows of chemicals and energy in and out of organisms. Not surprisingly, then, scholars interested in questioning or standard understanding of the separation between (urban) society and nature have picked up the term "metabolism." They use it to highlight the interconnectedness and ever-changing relationships between nature and society as well as the important ways in which humans, by changing nature, also change.

The city – and more generally the urban scale – is the place where labor power is concentrated at the point of nature's production and circulation (Smith, 1984). Some urban places have grown up around the extraction of natural resources such as coal, water, clay, and iron ore, and now increasingly natural gas; others have developed as ports attracting trade, natural resources, and flows of capital. Nature also makes its way into the city through various engineering projects, land use, infrastructure, planning, power, and politics. For example, contemplating the burgeoning skyline of Manhattan, Matthew Gandy writes, "The architectural ebullience of the modern city has intensified a perception that the scale and dynamism of New York owes more to the raw power of nature than to the prosaic efforts of human labor" (Gandy, 2002: 2).

If the boundary between nature and the city is difficult to detect, it is arguably even harder to grasp the more abstract idea that cities are produced from the social interaction of human labor with nature. Urban production processes generate by-products, some of which are

Figure 10.3   In Kochi, India, raw sewage flows just below the sidewalk and is covered with concrete blocks. In even minor rain storms, the sewage overflows its trenches and pollutes low-lying areas. Many cities in the global South, like Kochi, lack sufficient waste water treatment facilities, and often only very wealthy areas with new construction projects can access this luxury. Rapid urban growth, along with poverty, also presents a major challenge to building new pipeline and infrastructure. Photo: Mary Thomas.

toxic to the environment, while others can be made socially useful even as they are toxic in production (e.g., plastic bottles made from petroleum can be used to make park benches even if their production increased the carbon load in the atmosphere). One important legacy of industrial production in the city is the presence of various noxious and polluting facilities, such as trash-burning power plants, waste disposal facilities, chemical industries, sewage treatment plants, fuel refineries, landfills, and toxic dumps. For a variety of reasons, such facilities have tended to cluster in certain urban neighborhoods and districts but not in others. In Columbus, OH, for example, the city's trash-burning power plant and a major sewerage treatment facility are located in the far south of the city, a pattern dictated in part by the county's river drainage system. In other cities, like Kochi, India, much of the city's raw sewage runs just below the sidewalk and is dumped into the ocean unprocessed (Figure 10.3).

Research notes a strong correlation between the location of low income and minority households and the spatial distribution of toxic facilities (Bullard, 2000). **Environmental racism** suggests that

Environmental racism. Toxic and polluting facilities such as waste treatment plants are often to be found in urban neighborhoods that are populated by minorities and people of color. The concept of environmental racism captures the strong association between land uses contributing to environmental degradation and the location of minority and low income communities in close proximity.

racial and ethnic minorities are more vulnerable to pollution and industrial hazards than whites. Laura Pulido (2000) shows that this is largely due to the fact that poor people and people of color are more likely to reside in urban areas zoned for industrial uses. Whites and middle class people do not, therefore, carry the same relation to and interaction with toxic environments as do poor people and people of color. Pulido suggests that whites have the privilege to decide to live far away from industry, which reinscribes a racial order that works in the benefit of whites and their health and quality of life (Pulido, 2000: 15). Thus, environmental racism is a term that insinuates the low values placed on *both* poor people of color (racism) and environmental degradation simultaneously. This process occurs over time and space through property valuation, economic change, access to labor for industry, and so on. As such, there is rarely an easy fix to environmental racism (but see Chapter 12 on environmental justice movements and racism).

Positive environmentalism

Positive environmentalism grew out of class struggles in the industrial nineteenth century city, which led to the spatial and social distancing of the middle and upper classes from the working class. Positive environmentalism suggested that clean, utopic, leisure spaces in the city would aid in class harmony and would also provide working class people and immigrants outlets for their class resentments. In short, by encouraging the different classes to mix with each other, it was believed that environmental reforms such as the construction of urban parks and open spaces would produce greater social harmony. Such projects not only profoundly transformed class relations and the character of the built environment but also altered the experience and meaning of nature in the city.

> **Positive environmentalism.** Positive environmentalism grew out of class struggles in the nineteenth century city, which led to the spatial and social distancing of the middle and upper classes from the working class. By encouraging the different classes to mix with each other, it was believed that environmental reforms such as the construction of urban parks and open spaces would produce greater social harmony. Such projects not only profoundly transformed class relations and the character of the built environment but also altered the experience and meaning of nature in the city.

Increasingly at that time, urban problems of disease, poverty, social unrest, and drunken and disorderly behavior were documented with the use of modern science and technology. In the 1870s and 1880s, new technologies, such as photography and forensic criminal science – the later popularized by fictional characters such as Sherlock Holmes – fostered new images of the urban environment, which shaped ideas of how the environment could influence human behavior. In turn, photography brought the working class and immigrant city to the viewership of those upper class people living at some remove from the crowded, often unsanitary, and violent conditions of cramped housing.

Working in the notorious Five Points district of lower Manhattan, Jacob Riis captured photographic images of extreme poverty, overcrowding, disease, pollution, criminality, and death. He published many of these images in *How the Other Half Lives* (Riis, 1890), a book

Figure 10.4 Bandit's Roost by Jacob Riis. This image of the notorious Five Points district in Lower Manhattan was captured by Riis circa 1890. Riis's striking photographic images of New York's slums horrified the City's upper classes, prompting calls for urban social reforms. Many of these reforms were inspired by the belief that social conditions could be improved by changing the environment in which the lower classes lived, i.e., positive environmentalism. Photo credit: The Museum of the City of New York/Art Resource, NY, used with permission.

which horrified New York's upper and middle classes. It reminded those living in the mansions of Madison Avenue of the spatial proximity of the urban poor and the poor's proximity to waste and dirt (Gagen, 2000). For nineteenth-century reformers, moreover, such images soon cemented in their minds the need to establish a positive link between the urban environment and human behavior (Figure 10.4).

In a classic study of the industrial city, Rosenzweig (1983) comments on the role of parks and recreation in the harmonization of factory time and playtime. Park planning not only brought the urban masses closer to nature but also sought to integrate them into the moral order of industrial capitalist society (Boyer, 1978). The late nineteenth century was a period when cities were marked by growing tensions among working classes, immigrants, trades unions, and employers. Industrial capitalists engaged in social and environmental experiments in the belief that these would habituate workers into the rhythms of production and the assembly line. The latter were decidedly "unnatural" given that many new arrivals in the city were used to the very different rhythms of life in the countryside. It was believed that urban festivals that celebrated certain dates, seasons, national symbols, or identities would remind recent immigrants of the more positive aspects of rural life back in their country of origin. These activities helped to sustain a sense of loyalty to the company, the community, and even the American nation at large. Nevertheless, public festivals and urban parks also created opportunities for different urban social classes to mix and engage in a variety of activities seemingly beyond the direct surveillance of factory owners and regulatory control of urban authorities. The social boundaries separating the city and nature thus remained porous and malleable.

Ric Burns' documentary series, *New York* (Burns, 2009), captures the emergence of the modern political view of the urban environment during the Progressive Era. In one episode, Burns examines through photography, music, poetry, and commentary the economic and political conditions leading up to the establishment of Central Park, one of a number of great public works projects designed by Frederick Law Olmstead for America's cities. It was believed that urban parks brought light and air back into the city and would remedy many urban ailments, not least of which were crime and social disorder. This was also a time of crisis in New York's politics. Upper and middle class apprehensions about the growing power of the urban political machine were personified by Mayor William "Boss" Tweed, the leader of the Tammany Hall machine, who was eventually charged with corruption and imprisoned. For opponents of the political machine, urban reforms were seen as a means of socializing and disciplining the working classes. Burns skillfully portrays how emerging ideas of positive environmentalism enabled the upper, middle, and lower classes to mix together in a bold new democratic experiment.

In colonial cities, positive environmentalism worked somewhat differently. As William Glover argues in his book, *Making Lahore Modern: Constructing and Imagining a Colonial City*, the material settings of the city were designed and organized by the British colonizers to "irrigate [Lahore's] residents with a flow of salutary effects…as though [the process of urban design] were an extension of nature itself" (Glover, 2008: xxi). Colonizers were intent on "morally improving" the Indian subject through colonialism, and they designed open boulevards, public parks, and new construction to forcefully instill European sensibility in the colonial city. One example Glover dwells on in the case of Lahore is the construction of the bungalow, a house type meant to offer a more "hygienic" and bourgeois abode than Indian townhouses. Glover points out that "houses in the colonial city distributed homely comforts unevenly across the fault lines of race and class" (Glover, 2008: xxvii). European settlers themselves gained access to public parks and bungalows, while their colonized servants largely did not.

Disease, life, and death in the modern city

Toward the end of the nineteenth century, reformers in major cities such as London, Chicago, and New York were horrified to discover that working people were on a daily – and, given long hours of work, nightly – basis exposed to unhealthy urban environments: pollution, raw sewage, disease, noise, dirt, and noxious odors. When the critical novelist Upton Sinclair wrote about conditions in Chicago's meatpacking industry in *The Jungle*, he deliberately drew upon this somewhat sinister metaphor of nature to evoke a picture of how mass production was fused with the flesh and blood of humans and animals (Sinclair, 1906). His attack on the meatpacking industry motivated subsequent reforms in the regulation of the food industry. By then, it was already well know that the spread of deadly diseases such as cholera was related

Box 10.2   Parks as Urban Utopias

By the early twentieth century, industrialists and liberal reformers began to champion regional environmental planning as a solution to a wide range of infrastructural and environmental problems associated with urbanization, ranging from social unrest to poverty and disease. The control of nature (and with it the control of labor power) brought improvements in water supply and sewage disposal, the development of extend networks of parks and urban parkways, and the creation of green spaces and garden cities, as well as ideas of the city beautiful (Mumford, 1961). As Harvey (2000) documents, environmental themes – of nature, the countryside, and harmonious social relations – contributed to a broad range of utopian visions of the city, which became embodied in different approaches to architecture, design, and planning in cities as varied as London, Paris, New York, Baltimore, and Barcelona.

In turn-of-the-century Barcelona, the architect and designer Antoni Gaudi became involved in the design of an exclusive residential enclave for the city's upper classes. Gaudi's patron was the industrialist Eusebi Güell, who had inherited a large family consortium of textile and shipping industries and wanted to use his wealth and influence to build a model community located on farmland recently purchased just outside the city. The original plan for what became known as Parc Güell was to create a gated community, with a marketplace fashioned after Roman Forum, expansive gardens, an ornately decorated entranceway, benches shaped like lizards and snakes, and carriageways and viewpoints hewn into the hillside using shapes and patterns that echoed the fauna and flora of the surrounding Catalan countryside (Figure 10.5). Wealthy residents were encouraged to purchase lots on the site. But Gaudi's project failed to attract sufficient bidders and the architect turned his attention instead to the construction of the spectacular cathedral of Sagrada Familia, a project that was never completed in his lifetime. Today, Park Güell is enjoyed as a public space by a wide range of people, including international tourists and local families.

to the location of urban water supply sources. Planners and urban authorities sought to promote the idea that environmental reforms could resolve urban health problems.

Themes from nature were often harnessed for utopian experiments in the city (Box 10.2). But the harnessing of nature through urbanization also called for mundane (functional) infrastructure projects, such as integrated metropolitan water supply and sewage systems. These once demanded major public investments to manage new technological challenges and environmental risks. If earlier urban reforms helped to eliminate many environmental problems and diseases from the city, the harnessing of nature in the form of large-scale urban development projects has now exposed cities and their residents to the potential for dramatic urban fiscal-cum-environmental crises (Gandy, 2002). In one infamous case in June 1969, the heavily polluted Cuyahoga River in Cleveland, OH, caught fire. More poignantly, in 1984 the residents of Bhopal, India, were exposed to deadly toxic gases accidently released by a giant facility of a major international chemical company, resulting in thousands of deaths and disfigurements, and years of legal action for compensation on the part of affected families and surviving relatives.

Figure 10.5   Parc Güell in Barcelona, Spain, was originally designed to be an exclusive
residential enclave for the city's bourgeoisie but is now a public park and World Heritage site.
Photo: Andy Jonas.

New health threats to urban society have emerged, such as *E. coli*, AIDS, SARS, and bird flu.
The rapid spread of these viruses has prompted work on the idea that some global cities are
"global" precisely because they are vectors of diseases and pandemics, which have origins in
the countryside and places outside the city (Keil, 2005). Urban publics are also differently
constructed and regulated in relation to the treatment of viruses and infectious diseases
such as AIDS (Brown, 2009). Nature in the form of the carcasses of animals, the blood and
sweat of workers, the spread of diseases, viral infections, and so on is infused into the very
lifeblood – or death-blood – of the city and its residential geographies.

10.3   Regulating Nature and Environment in the City

During the twentieth century, public awareness of the impact of urban development on the
rate of consumption of natural resources grew and deepened, transforming into a range of
pressures on the state to regulate the growth of cities, contain urban sprawl, and address

energy shortages. The 1970s energy crisis exposed modern urban society to the natural and ecological limits of the western capitalist model of economic development. Advanced capitalist countries had come to rely on energy-dependent urban forms, locking economic growth into particular resource-and-technology based trajectories (Walker and Large, 1974; Huber, 2013). No longer was environmentalism simply about protecting charismatic endangered species, such as golden eagles and grizzly bears in areas of wilderness and national parks often far removed from the city. Urban environmentalism has allowed people to rethink the relationships between city and nature.

Regulating the boundaries between city and countryside

At the end of World War II, the idea of a green belt surrounding major conurbations came into being in Great Britain. This was a protected zone of fields and open space, enshrined in national planning legislation, which was used to contain urban sprawl. New Towns – free-standing master-planned communities sanction by the state – became another tool of national Keynesian economic planning, concentrating the working class in "overspill" settlements at the edge of major conurbations. The construction of motorways and suburban New Towns resulted in the selective development of agricultural land yet also provided housing and industrial sites on a mass scale. By these means, workers and the British countryside have been culturally and politically integrated into the national urban system.

Our awareness of the boundary between the city and the country is often shaped by the social and political contexts in which we observe and assess the landscape around us. An open field next to the city may be seen, variously, as an environmental resource, a land use planning tool, a wildlife corridor, or an opportunity to build affordable homes. Environmental and land use policy tools like green belts in the United Kingdom and urban growth limits in the United States are often used to regulate the boundary between city and nature. But this is a conflict-ridden process; it gives rise to the geopolitics of nature–city relations in which spaces of environmental regulation and growth control come into tension with those of urban development and territorial governance (Dierwechter, 2008). Even where the boundary does not exist, except perhaps as an imaginary line on the map or perhaps in the imaginations of residents, property owners, and planners, ideas of where the city ends and nature begins are emotionally felt and profoundly contested (Huber and Currie, 2007).

At one level, the struggle to define the limits of the city might simply be due to the fact that cities and metropolitan areas are growing bigger, spreading out into surrounding open spaces, wilderness areas, and public lands, consuming agricultural land and open space. In this respect, the boundary constantly shifts with the outward movement of the suburban frontier. On another level, however, such growth brings suburban economic values and interests in conflict with those of the exurban. Once used to regulate the boundaries between nature and the city, new environmental and land use policies are variously mobilized or contested by suburban property owners, middle classes, developers, and growth interests in order to defend property values and lifestyles (Feldman and Jonas, 2000). The encroachment of the city into surrounding natural ecosystems demands increasingly sophisticated instruments of environmental governance in order to regulate neoliberal patterns of growth (Robertson, 2004).

Re-imagining nature in the entrepreneurial city

Critical urban research recognizes that environmental knowledges and imaginaries have changed over the course of time as service economy cities have restructured from spaces of production to sites of newer economic activities, such as producer services and high technology industries (Keil and Graham, 1998). Facing dramatic changes to the economic base, older urban-industrial centers have confronted particular challenges in terms of improving their image to adjust to the changing locational demands of the new economy. Decades of industrial contamination have rendered many former urban-industrial sites unusable yet many people continue to live in close proximity to such sites. Urban centers have to overcome the negative environmental stereotypes commonly associated with the industrial past; for example, images of smokestacks and chimneys bellowing out toxic pollutants. However, it has also become possible to incorporate environmental themes into the marketing of new urban developments – and even to convert old smokestacks into public parks (Figure 10.6).

Such changes in regimes of urban representation – the dominant practices by which cities are marketed to attract investors and visitors – is a theme taken up by Short (1999), who has examined urban place promotion strategies in the United States. One increasingly dominant theme is how images of the industrial city once devoid of natural environmental signifiers have been replaced by more benign images of industry in harmony with the urban environment. Short refers to the particular case of Syracuse in the US state of New York.

Figure 10.6 Landschaftspark in Duisburg Nord, Germany. The site of a former steel plant, the park memorializes industry and encourages enjoyment of a former toxic environment, and, thus, of the industrial past, too. Photo: Mary Thomas.

Recent promotional images of the city have restored the lakefront to a prominent position. The image of high rise buildings dominating the skyline is set against a pristine lakeside view. This image is seen to be emblematic of the city's attractiveness to business and stands in contrast with earlier promotional images of smokestacks, which were used to convey the idea that Syracuse was once a progressive industrial city.

Cities draw on these environmental themes to market themselves as tourist attractions and venues for international conferences and public events. Vancouver made an economic virtue of hosting the Winter Olympics in 2010, using a logo that represents a rock symbol from the Inuit (Figure 10.7 and Box 10.3; also Chapter 9). The development and marketing of cities has involved the deployment of new forms of urban environmental technology and ecological knowledge (Harvey, 1996). Cities incorporate environmental knowledge in their products, plans, place names, images, iconography, and mythology. Newcastle is still

Figure 10.7   An inukshuk in the city of Vancouver, Canada. The plaque at its base reads: "This ancient symbol of the Inuit culture is traditionally used as a landmark and navigational aid and also represents northern hospitality and friendship." The plaque goes on to explain that the corporate sponsor of the inukshuk, Coast Hotels & Resorts, provides lighting to make "this welcoming symbol visible at night." The Aboriginal rock symbol is therefore invoked as a marketing technique. Photo: Eugene McCann.

Box 10.3 Environment, Symbolism, and the Image of the City

In urban geography, the relationship between image, environment, and the city is closely associated with the work of Kevin Lynch. Lynch's studies of mental maps provided important clues about social behavior in the city. In *The Image of the City*, published in 1960, Lynch argued that human perception of the city could be broken down into basic structural elements, such as districts, paths, centers, landmarks, and edges (Lynch, 1960). The intensity with which each of these elements featured in mental maps was a function of how people interacted with different parts of the city on a daily basis. An individual's perceptions of the city and its environment could vary depending on the social importance attributed to any given element of the built environment. A study of the mental maps of residents of Los Angeles, CA, showed that upper and middle class residents saw the city as being organized around important physical features such as parks, lakes, beaches, and the ocean. However, the corresponding mental maps of lower income residents tended to include a much smaller geographic area, often devoid of physical features and limited to neighborhoods in the vicinity of downtown Los Angeles (Orleans, 1973).

Studies of urban images replaced static models of urban land use with dynamic images of the city based on human movement, perception, and behavior. As such, the analysis of mental maps could be regarded as an example of early critical thinking on the city. Although these studies tended to focus on the role of individuals, there was a growing appreciation that images of the urban environment could, in turn, shape collective attitudes and behaviors. Iconography featuring landmarks and images of the natural environment now play an important part in the marketing of cities. When the Vancouver, BC, hosted the Winter Olympics in 2010, the logo that was used to market the city during the games was based on a representation of a rock symbol, the inukshuk, used by the Inuit in the Arctic region (the inukshuk is figured on the flag of Nunavut, Canada). However, the logo courted controversy. Opponents of the games claimed that Inuit symbols had been appropriated solely for the benefit of the Vancouver Winter Olympics at the expense of a contextual and historical understanding of its use and circulation by Inuit themselves.

associated with coal long after mining ceased, much as Pittsburgh is with steel and Chicago meatpacking. Even when certain forms of environmental knowledge and artefacts disappear from the urban landscape, today's urban dwellers can re-encounter simulated nature by visiting museums, public gardens, and aquariums, or shopping at local farmers markets.

In the City of Bremerhaven, near Bremen in northern Germany, the local authorities have encouraged business ventures and tourist attractions to develop around the theme of adaption to climate change. One popular venue is the Klimahaus®, which takes the visitor on a journey around the world along the eight degrees east line of longitude, showing how climate change might impact upon different places and people, urban and rural alike (http://www.klimahaus-bremerhaven.de/en.html). By way of contrast, in Las Vegas, NV, it is possible to shop, eat, swim, gamble, and be entertained by lions and pink flamingos all in the same place. In these re-naturalized urban settings, experiences of nature and the country-side are simulated, repackaged, or performed specifically for consumption. Likewise in new suburban spaces of consumption, such as enclosed shopping malls, leisure centers, country parks, zoos, and themed attractions, nature's production is lent a distinctly suburban aesthetic.

New ideas of city–nature relations further shape the trajectory of urban development politics. Nevarez (2003) argues that new forms of capital increasingly seek out locations where urban environmental values are in sync with the competitive demands of the new economy. Referring to an elite-driven process of constructing "desirable places," he shows how smaller towns and cities in coastal California seek to incorporate positive environmental values into the marketing of place. The positive quality of life in such new economy places is contrasted with that of the bigger inland cities of California, where crime and racism are seen as deterrents to potential employers. The critical message is as follows: modern urban environmental improvements, such as the creation of green open space and parks or attempts to set up and attract clean or ecologically friendly industries might be beneficial to the economic and environmental health of a city and its residents, yet also play into the hands of the promoters of urban and suburban development (Logan and Molotch, 1987; Heynen, 2006).

10.4 The Urban Sustainability Fix: Towards Low Carbon Cities

The increasingly complex social, economic, and environmental problems in urbanizing settings demand a critical interdisciplinary perspective on urban sustainability (Wolch, 2007). The origins of the concept of urban sustainability go back to the 1987 Brundtland Commission report, which defined sustainable development as meeting the material needs of present generations without compromising those of future generations. In addressing the environmental impact of economic growth, urban authorities have become targets for criticism due to the fact that urban development depends on the high mass consumption of energy resources and land (Low *et al.*, 2000; Huber, 2013). Indeed, rapid urbanization in countries like China and India represents the antithesis of steady-state or "no growth" economic policies. However, some researchers have challenged this assumption by pointing to how cities can play a constructive role in sustainable development (Satterthwaite, 1997). As McManus (2004: 5) argues, it is possible to challenge the idea of cities as "growth vortexes" by demonstrating examples of how they can be turned into artefacts of resource renewal, proper environmental protection, recycling, and sustainable development.

The principle of sustainable urban development recognizes that actions need to be taken that over the long term balance the growth and development of urban systems with their environmental resource base (Lake, 2000). If taken at face value, environmentally sustainable urban development appears incompatible with urban entrepreneurialism (Haughton and While, 1999). Yet, the same cities which engage in competition with each other for investment also tend to be those that aggressively pursue environmental agendas. Examples include urban authorities signing up to international agreements on locally sustainable development, such as **Local Agenda 21**, or places participating in global climate change initiatives or annual World Urban Forum conferences.

Critical studies of urban regimes have demonstrated that urban take-up of strategies such as Local Agenda 21 tends to correlate with the presence of alliances between public

Local Agenda 21. Following the Earth Summit held in Rio de Janeiro in 1992, Agenda 21 was promoted as a global program of action for sustainable development. Subsequently, Local Agenda 21 (LA21) was identified as the formal mechanism for translating this global program into local initiatives to be undertaken in cities and communities throughout the world. By signing up to LA21, urban authorities were required to identify specific actions and policy measures that would facilitate the transition to environmentally, socially, and economically sustainable communities.

Urban sustainability fix. As urban authorities, politicians, businesses, and residents have become more aware of the relationship between environmental improvements and promoting urban development, critical interest in sustainable urban development has grown. The concept of the urban sustainability fix suggests that cities seek to introduce sustainability measures that do not conflict with economic development and are not likely to trigger public opposition. In the process, sustainability often removes the more controversial urban development projects out of the democratic arena.

officials and wealthy and middles class residents capable of influencing public policy and the urban environmental regime (Lake, 2000; Bulkeley and Betsill, 2002). Likewise, there are tangible fiscal and social benefits to be gained by marketing particular public spaces in the city as green and environmentally sustainable. Urban public spaces can be seen as sustainable if they, variously, meet community social needs or help to promote economic development. However, it does seem that tensions between different practices, meanings, and politics of sustainability are characteristic of cities undergoing major economic and social transformations (Parès and Sauri, 2007).

Cities in different countries have responded to growing pressures and demands for environmental regulation by engaging in a search for an **urban sustainability fix** (While *et al.*, 2004b). This concept refers to how political responsibility for balancing economic competitiveness with social provision and environmental protection has been pushed downwards from the national to the urban scale, forcing cities to be selective in how environmental, social and economic sustainability objectives are met (Figure 10.8). Given economic pressures facing cities, it seems that sustainable development might have lost much of its progressive meaning in terms of promoting alternative visions of the city and urban politics.

Indeed, Keil (2007) describes sustainable development as a master concept that is deployed by powerful economic and political interests to serve neoliberal urban economic agenda rather than progressive social and environmental goals. For example, in London and the South East of England, the UK state is interested in building "sustainable communities" in high growth regions as an answer to problems of housing shortages for professionals and "key workers" operating in the service economy rather than a way of addressing issues like water shortages, aging infrastructure, social alienation, urban decline, and environmental pollution. However, even if sustainable development is not incompatible with urban and regional growth, it nevertheless "provides policymakers and a range of communities with alternative ways of thinking about economic development, social justice and resource use ... and can challenge neoliberal inspired growth agendas and modes of regulation" (Raco, 2005: 330).

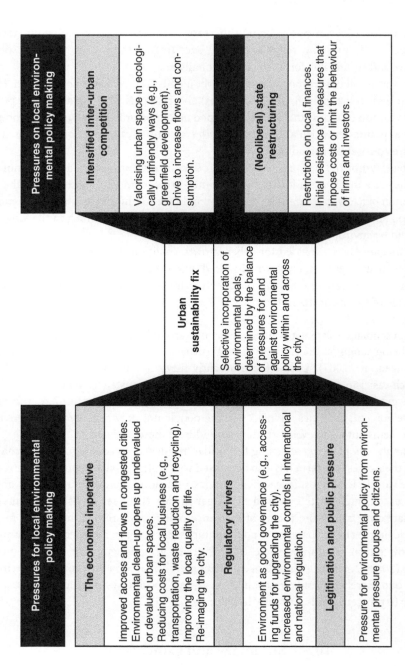

Figure 10.8 The urban sustainability fix. Source: While *et al.*, 2004b. Used with permission of John Wiley and Sons Ltd.

Jonas *et al.* (2010) suggest that the search for an urban sustainability fix is leading cities to adopt various strategies in order to reduce carbon emissions. They highlight the following urban environmental trajectories:

- The drive for a low carbon economy increases our awareness of the wider resource dependence of cities and regions, thereby encouraging the pursuit of more socially inclusive and sustainable forms of city-regionalism.
- Nation-states will pass responsibility for carbon emissions reduction onto urban localities and their constituent firms (workplaces) and residents (living places). The pursuit of a low carbon economy therefore could open up opportunities for a new environmental urban politics in which alternative growth trajectories can be seriously debated. But there are constraints, including:
  - ○ Urban authorities are pressured to introduce market incentives in environmental policy as a mechanism for stimulating inter-urban competition; therefore, the promotion of a low-carbon urban economy could further lubricate inter-urban competition and intensify neoliberal forms of urban development, which in the long term could be environmentally damaging;
  - ○ As incentives are provided for urban growth coalitions to purse low-carbon public investment strategies, costs are displaced onto others, including poorer urban residents; in this case, the pursuit of carbon reduction strategies could become a new means of social control in the city.

Some urban scholars fear that a political consensus around global concerns such as climate change is being sought at the expense of local (urban) dissention, discussion, and democracy (Swyngedouw, 2007). Unlike the inherently fuzzy notion of urban sustainability, it seems much easier to measure and predict the impact of, for instance, temperature rises on urban life and livelihoods or to estimate the environmental impact of different forms of urban development. Yet cities are places where people not only can learn about environmental problems but also develop strategies to address these problems.

Increasingly, city planners are using terms like "resilience" to accede to climate change's impact on their cities (the term has also been used widely in response to threats of terrorism around the world). Urban resilience refers to cities' mitigation against natural forces, adjusting practices to contend with events like stronger storms, rising sea levels, and warmer climates. Adaptation is the core theme of resilience policies, whereas sustainability focuses more on seeking to change practice to adjust natural systems (e.g., reduce carbon consumption to slow global warming). Some critical urban geographers, like MacKinnon and Derickson (2012), suggest that resilience policies merely maintain the capitalist system and the status quo. Rarely do resilience policies seek new social or economic structures; they usually try to protect what is currently in place.

10.5 Summary and Conclusion

Critical urban geographers incorporate ideas of nature and environment into the analysis of the modern city. Cities provide a range of opportunities for examining the metabolic relations linking people to the natural world. Urban political ecology (UPE) examines the flows, connections, and metabolisms that link cities to the natural environment. Nature, in turn, is produced and urbanized through its metabolic relations with the city. Particular urban spaces and attendant flows of materials and resources embody this metabolic relationship. If cities were once thought of separate from nature, a critical approach to UPE seeks to show how nature is ever-present in the city in many forms. Cities represent a particular assemblage of distant and proximate natural, cultural, physical, and social processes. The city has no limits – real or imagined – where the critical study of nature is concerned.

In recent times, we have been encouraged by the global media to associate particular cities, such as New Orleans, Tacloban, or Port-au-Prince, with environmental crisis and natural disaster. Powerful though these images are, we must also see nature as having a profound cultural imprint on the totality of urban experience; in short, nature produces particular cultures and politics of urban place, and vice versa. Thus, in spite of the devastating impact of Hurricane Katrina, New Orleans remains a natural city in many other ways, for example in its connections to the Mississippi Delta region through jazz, the blues, food, engineering, canals, sewage systems, railroads, and agricultural products. The rebuilding of New Orleans depends in part on thinking how these connections are re-established, strengthened, or perhaps in some cases drastically altered. It is important to recognize that the long-term solution to rebuilding inner city wards in New Orleans devastated by flooding does not just mean building new houses. It also involves building up social networks and community relations, especially given that due to years of prior economic and political neglect many properties and communities in these wards were already abandoned and blighted prior to the flooding. In these and other respects, the cultural, economic, and political landscapes of cities incorporate complex environmental histories and geographies, which are shaped and remolded by flows of capital, commodities, people, knowledge, and natural resources over time.

Recognizing social forms of nature in the city allows you to explore a range of new questions about around environmental racism, social justice, and urban sustainability. But the reassertion of ideas of nature and culture into critical urban theory also throws up new intellectual challenges. There is a concern that the new focus on urban environmental problems such as climate change has placed emphasis on cultures of consumption at the expense of knowledge of wider changes in work, production, the state, and capitalism. Your knowledge of the relationship between urban entrepreneurialism and environmental sustainability or resilience might come at the expense of appreciating environmental activism and the role of urban environmental movements in challenging current economic and social priorities.

10.6   Further Reading

- Several excellent documentaries tell the many stories of horror and hope in Katrina New Orleans, including director Spike Lee's *When the Levees Broke* (2006). *Trouble the Water* (dirs. Lessin and Deal, 2008) has harrowing footage by Kimberly Rivers Roberts as the storm hits and as she and her family deals with its aftermath.
- On imagining environmental disaster in the city, see Davis (1999). See Dominey-Howes *et al.* (2013) for why researchers and planners need to think about lesbian, gay, transgender, and intersexual people's experiences in disasters.

- A good overview and discussion of urban political ecology can be found in Volume 35:5 of the journal *Antipode* (2003); using critical UPE concepts, Robbins (2007) discusses in detail the particular case of the lawn chemical industry and its role in shaping suburban life in the United States. Feminist approaches to political ecology insist that women's lives are consistently made more difficult with environmental degradation. See, for example, Rocheleau *et al.* (2013).
- There is an extensive literature on the environment and racism. For recent cases, see Gibson-Wood and Wakefield (2013) on a Hispanic environmental justice movement in Toronto, and Loyd (2014) on the entwined history of health rights and civil rights in Los Angeles.
- Food scholarship in critical urban geography provides examples of how corporate interests and moral geographies shape eating as well as food production. See Guthman (2013) on food and obesity; Agyeman and McEntee (2014) on food justice and urban political economy; and Tornaghi (2014) on urban agriculture.
- Chapters in Gibbs and Krueger (20007) examine the political economy of urban sustainability. The standard reference for critical urban research on climate change and urban governance is Bulkeley and Betsill (2002) and for the urban sustainability fix it is While *et al.* (2004b). See Rice (2014) on for a recent consideration of climate governance in US Pacific Northwest cities. See Braun and Wakefield (2014) on how resilience governing works in the United States.

Chapter 11

Urban Arts and Visual Cultures

Urban Geography: A Critical Introduction, First Edition. Andrew E.G. Jonas, Eugene McCann, and Mary Thomas.
© 2015 Andrew E.G. Jonas, Eugene McCann, and Mary Thomas. Published 2015 by John Wiley & Sons, Ltd.

11.1 Introduction

Graffiti is ubiquitous in the world's cities and has been written and scratched on walls and the surfaces of buildings for centuries. Is it art or vandalism? The answer to that question, of course, depends on perspective, placement, and the dominant ways that cultural and financial value becomes attached to different art forms. It is rare that a gang tag gets labeled as "art," after all. On the other hand, some graffiti artists gain notoriety and fame, not to mention wealth. For example, Banksy, the pseudonymous British street artist, began painting on outdoor walls in Bristol in the early 1990s, but now his fame is global and some of his art fetches millions of dollars. Entire sections of buildings hosting Banksy murals have even been stolen (no easy feat), only to resurface at art auctions later. Yet, most of his work

Figure 11.1 Banksy graffiti on the exterior wall of Bristol's Sexual Health Clinic, 2006. Photographed by Richard Cocks (Own work, Banksy Graffiti (Park Street) Close shot) [CC-BY-SA-2.5 (http://creativecommons.org/licenses/by-sa/2.5) or CC-BY-2.0 (http://creative commons.org/licenses/by/2.0)], via Wikimedia Commons.

is unsolicited by the owners of the property on which it appears, so it could easily be considered vandalism.

The cultural and artistic value of the art is open to debate, and its placement in public venues and its distribution through social media means that many people can weigh in with their opinions. The city of Bristol even held an online public referendum in 2006 to ask its residents if one piece of Banksy clandestine art should stay or go (Figure 11.1). Its tongue-in-cheek depiction of a secret lover dangling from a window while her business-suited husband searched for the culprit was painted on the wall of a Bristol Council Sexual Health Clinic. The result of the city's referendum? Citizens said, yes, keep it. Alas, the graffiti was painted over by Bristol's graffiti-removal contractors within a month, presumably a mistake (Figure 11.2).

In this chapter we will consider a full range of urban visual cultures, with a focus on images, representation, art, architecture and design, and artists. The chapter starts by considering what counts as art and where. It then considers an example of an American sports team logo to explain how dominate meanings are produced over time and space through visual images. Throughout the chapter, we examine the ways that cities emphasize design, new construction, and public art in order to script symbolisms promoting elite cultural status, social advancement, and economic development. This will include an examination of skyscrapers in New York, Dubai, and Kuala Lumpur, which seeks to illustrate these cities' emerging roles over time in the global economy.

Figure 11.2 Banksy mural painted in New York City, on 1 October 2013, as part of a month-long Banksy residency in the city. The image went through several iterations, with other graffiti artists altering it, and within a day had been painted over completely. In the fluid world of public art, no work can be guaranteed forever. The nature of public street art – including its devaluation as a scourge – makes preservation extremely challenging. Image used with permission of the Pest Control Office.

The goal of the chapter is to consider the visual symbols in and of urban spaces and those who create and contest them. The chapter encourages an approach to visual urban culture that emphasizes a critical geographic standpoint because it is important to remember that elite visual representations of urban spaces, cities, and urban economic and social development are almost never fully inclusionary and democratic. By the end of the chapter, you should be able to critically analyze how and why artistic and design symbols come to be differently valued by particular interests in cities. After reading this chapter, you should be able to answer the following questions and offer examples illustrating their importance:

- What tools do critical urban geographers use to analyze visual representations and art?
- What is visuality?
- What is the artistic mode of production?
- Using the skyscraper as an example, how can we understand some urban design and large-project construction to be nationalist in scope?
- How can a critical perspective help you to dispute the dominant visualities of different cities?

11.2   Art, Aesthetics, and Urban Space

While graffiti art (like Banksy's) is most often uninvited, other forms of art placed in public urban space are commissioned by cities, businesses, or public–private initiatives. The goals of public art works are contingent on the political and economic processes that led to their placement. Examples include murals commissioned by neighborhood groups to counter the ubiquity of tags and graffiti and to promote a neighborhood's dominant official identity.

Other public art works include attempts to illustrate a city's interest in highlighting its diversity and commitment to multiculturalism, for instance, to evidence its specific history in civil rights protests. In the US state of Alabama, Birmingham's Kelly Ingram Park faces the Civil Rights Institute and the 16th Street Baptist Church, the site of a Klu Klux Klan bomb attack in 1963 that killed four young African–American girls. The installations by artist James Drake (Figure 11.3) bring the violence that civil rights protestors faced to life for contemporary park goers. The park is also a symbol of Birmingham city's attempts to move beyond its history as a segregationist and racist city, which in the 1960s earned it the nickname "Bombingham." The park's public sculptures and installations encourage participants in its space to see Birmingham as a multicultural, modern city that reflects on its racist past but also transcends it.

Aesthetics refers to the study of art; the word also insinuates beauty and a pleasing appearance. Within the study of aesthetics, central questions include: What counts as art? What is beauty and how it is determined and judged? While these questions have stimulated debate for as long as there has been philosophy, contemporary critical social scientists tend to focus on the possible elitism of aesthetics, in particular the ways that distinctions between high art and popular culture get made and enforced. Thinking about aesthetics and

> **Aesthetics.** Aesthetics refers to art or beauty and can define an approach guiding particular artistic work (e.g., the Impressionist aesthetic).

Figure 11.3 Police Dog Attack (1993) by artist James Drake (b. 1946), Kelly Ingram Park, Birmingham, AL, USA. The sculpture, which must be entered to walk the path through the park, evokes the terror that Civil Rights marchers experienced in 1963 as the Birmingham Police attempted to pacify African–Americans' resistance to Jim Crow segregation. Source: Used with permission of the Artists Rights Society (ARS), New York. Photo by Mary Thomas.

power can help critical urban geographers examine how public art for parks gets commissioned and designed, or how graffiti art gets valued or possibly preserved, or how the full range of art and design get represented and reproduced in various urban marketing strategies.

Critiquing the distinction between high and low art, and the values attached to different art forms and spaces, helps us to understand why the graffiti and tags of some neighborhood gangs do not get normatively evaluated as "art" whereas spray paintings by Banksy now hang in expensive art galleries. Banksy was able to transcend the barrier between low and high art (even if the artist himself oftentimes resists that move) because the art establishment deemed his art valuable. Galleries hang it, presses publish books on it, collectors pay inordinate sums for it, and the popular press reports on his antics regularly. The use of social media is important in this example, too, as Banksy employs Twitter, YouTube, and Instagram to publicize and politicize his work, while fans pin favorite images of his art to Pinterest for large online audiences to consume. All of these media contribute to the buzz about his art, in turn elevating the cultural value of his work and mysterious image, which has become something of a brand itself.

Evaluating art also involves implicit racial, class, and imperial biases. These all matter for how markets set prices of art and for how artists from around the world are judged and represented. In short, there is **ideology** at work in art (Bourdieu, 1984, 1993). While the answer to "what counts as art" has exploded in the twentieth and twenty-first centuries,

> **Ideology.** Ideology is a set of ideas, including myths, ideals, and beliefs, and so on. Ideology can be both conscious and unconscious, since beliefs are often framed by things we do not necessarily think about carefully. Ideology is not objective, since things like myths are influenced by feelings and can be highly biased. Ideologies are the products of social, economic, and political relations, and dominant ideologies are powerful systems of thinking that shape how we all come to see and value the world.

such that graffiti now hangs in some of the most prestigious museums in the world, elite institutions (like museums and galleries), journalism (think about art critics and their role in judging art), and collectors (millionaires and billionaires) continue to play predominant roles in determining art's value. And ongoing bias for "Western" art means that artists located in places outside of Europe and North America cannot easily break into high-end art markets (although the wealth in the Middle East and East Asia is beginning to change that). In the West there is also a distinct racial hegemony to the production of visual artistic production (from high art to television), such that racial minorities have a difficult time succeeding financially as artists.

That is not to say that art only reflects ideologies of the elite, wealthy, or global urban classes. In fact, artists have played critical roles in protesting and resisting elitist and exclusionary ideologies. Art can exceed the dominance of elite classes (Adorno, 1997) and forge representations that resist oppression. Banksy's critique of the high art establishment is tied to his choice of medium: the ephemeral, public streetscape. The value of spray paint on a building is cheap, and only becomes highly valuable through an art establishment that makes it more permanent through its proclamations and adoration. There is thus a kind of irony involved in Banksy's graffiti, which the artist exploits to make a point about elitism. When he had a month-long residency in New York, for example, he set up a kiosk manned by an elderly person in Central Park to sell his art anonymously for $60 a canvas. By and large, the work did not sell, because it was just spray paint on canvas! If people had known it was Banksy art, however, it would have been a mob scene. But without his name, the stenciled spray could not sell.

Another example is the Chinese artist Ai Weiwei who uses his designs, installations, and sculptures to protest the Chinese government's extreme censorship (see also Box 11.3). Ai became very well known in the West after he denounced the Beijing 2008 Olympics. This denunciation was remarkable given that he was central to the design idea for the iconic Beijing National Stadium, which came to be known as the "Bird's Nest." Ai's criticism of China's Olympics was vociferous and well publicized outside of the country. He famously said the Olympic effort was a "pretend smile," a phrase picked up widely in Western media. In an interview with the *New York Times* in 2008 during the Games, he explained his choice of words:

> I did say it's a "pretend smile." I was questioning whether it's possible for a society that doesn't have democracy to excite the joys and celebrations of its people. And is it possible for such a society to win international recognition and approval when liberty and freedom of expression are lacking? There are all kinds of efforts under way that are means for stricter and tighter control. When these new security rules and restrictions are put in place, how can one smile and perform, cheer and pose? (http://beijing2008.blogs.nytimes.com/2008/08/04/chinas-olympic-crossroads-birds-nest-designer-ai-weiwei-on-beijings-pretend-smile)

The Nest was one of the most celebrated visual representations of Beijing during the Games and its "New China, New Beijing" campaign. Yet the legacy of the representation should include not just the aesthetic qualities of design, nor even the outspoken persona of Ai. The Nest's legacy can also represent the controversy around the construction boom in Chinese cities more generally, which displaces millions of residents and leads to the destruction of centuries-old *hutongs* (narrow alleyways with courtyard houses).

In order to evaluate the messages of visual representations, many critical urban geographers have brought the lessons of art scholarship to their critical urban analyses. For example, one art scholar, Rosalind Deutsche, critiques urban geographer David Harvey. In an influential article published in 1991 called "Boys Town," she pointedly takes Harvey to task for ignoring "the emergence of a feminist voice" in contemporary aesthetics (Deutsche, 1991: 6) and for reducing the analysis of urban space, the built environment, and the production of meaning to economic "metatheory" (Deutsche, 1991: 18). In other words, Deutsche specifically faulted Harvey for assuming that capitalist economic relations "determine the meaning" of social life (Deutsche, 1991: 13).

Deutsche insists that feminist theories of visual culture bring important lessons about power to an understanding of representation in art and urban design. Representations derive from particular subjects and their interests and reflect ideologies and standpoints that seek to prioritize some beliefs over others. Feminist artists and art critics, Deutsche argues, teach us that we can look at images as "constructed relationships whose meaning arises in a historical meeting of image, viewer and the spatiotemporal circumstances of their existence" (Deutsche, 1991: 28). Unless we can learn to look critically and differently at representations, we fail to see the resistant messages of some artistic productions. Thus, approaching images and aesthetics critically means also interrogating how we see, look, and understand images, and how images do work in the world to sustain and prioritize certain relationships and spaces over others. Representations do not, after all, merely reflect reality, they also produce reality. A critical understanding of visual culture entails analyzing representations for meanings they forward *and* disrupt.

11.3 Visuality

How does an image hold meaning for you? The term **visuality** is one that scholars use to invoke the complicated relations, histories, and spaces that go into the production of images. The visual studies scholar Nicholas Mirzoeff even refers to an image as an "archive" (Mirzoeff, 2011: xv), since images can only be seen and communicated after a lot of work has gone into their production over time and space.

Take, for example, the image of a major US city's National Football League (NFL) mascot, shown on a bottle "suit" that sells at the Washington Redskins online store for US$8.00 (Figure 11.4).

What messages about "redskins" go into the circulation of this image?

Visuality. Anything that can be seen is visual, and visuality is a term that refers to how particular images come to be and how one learns to see. Visuality comes from the history of images, from knowledge production, from your own subject position and experience, and from relations ranging from the social to the economic. In short, visuality refers to the historical and geographical framing of any one image.

Figure 11.4 Redskins Bottle Suit. This purchase would cost you $8.00 at the Redskins online team store, or you could choose from hundreds of other items featuring the Native profile and feathers icon. Photo by Mary Thomas.

How has it come to be a symbol of masculine sports, competition, a profitable franchise, and a US city?

That story would itself require a textbook, but start with one moment in time and place: the nineteenth century cigar store. The Redskins mascot image exists in part because of the wide use of wooden statues of "Indians" to represent tobacco stores on the streets of towns and cities in the United States and even in the United Kingdom. Wherever the statues were found, consumers were sure to be able to buy tobacco. The chiseled face in profile on the NFL logo is reminiscent of the stereotype of "Indians" that was widely reproduced in the carving of these statues. The representation of "Indians" could work as a common communicator of a tobacco business due to stereotypes and fables of "Indians" as users of "peace pipes." The global use of tobacco did follow European conquest of North America, so the image's archive must include the geographies of **settler colonialism**. The removal of "Indians" from tribal lands and the use of the statue icon in towns and cities is a geographic displacement of nineteenth-century Native experience, too.

The imagery of the "Indian" wooden statues had feathers or headdresses, were darkly stained red, and were almost always male bodies, often with bare chests. Just search for "wooden Indian statue" or "cigar store Indian" on the Internet, and you can find a wide range of these antique statues for sale. These ubiquitous images of "Indians" inscribed the legibility of the

> **Settler colonialism.** Colonialism occurs when one political entity takes over another and exploits it for its resources. Settler colonialism refers to the type of colonialism that establishes a new population after conquest in the colonialized territory. Canada, the United States, Australia, and South Africa are examples of settler colonies.

Native body through stereotypically chiseled, red, male, feathered visuality. The "Indian" in profile on the Redskins logo is an authoritative representation of subservience, "savage" warrior brutality, and conquest. A racist stereotype is promulgated by the visuality of the cigar store statue, and over time and space became ingrained in ideas about who "Indians" were and are. This is the power of visual stereotypes to affect the real lives of oppressed and marginalized social and racial groups.

The cigar store statue also worked in the interests of white settler businesses, just as the "Redskin" logo is a symbolic commodity for a sporting franchise owned not by Native Americans but an American billionaire. Native Americans do not profit from its trademark. The male strength of the warrior is meant to represent the powerful football players on the team and has become a symbol of a city's sports team – but at what cost to Native Americans? And for whose profit?

The Executive Director of the National Congress of American Indians (NCAI), Jacqueline Pata, said, in October 2013, that no professional sports team has put an "Indian" mascot on their team since 1964. This is evidence that contemporary US American cities (and colleges, since Native mascots are used by some US colleges and universities, like the Florida State University Seminoles) know better than to introduce a new mascot using Native imagery. Yet the symbol persists in a way that racist Black depictions of slaves has not (for example, the mammy symbol used to sell pancake syrup on Aunt Jemima products has been removed). That the profile is even used to sell an NFL beer bottle suit is itself an image of the relationship between sports and alcohol, and the practice of partying and watching football.

An NCAI report on the use of Native imagery for mascots draws a direct link between the branding and marketing of highly profitable professional sports and the "mocking" of Native identity. The NCAI claims that the term redskin "originates from a time when Native people were actively hunted and killed for bounties, and their skins were used as proof of Indian kill. Bounties were issued by European companies, colonies, and some states, most notably California" (NCAI, 2013: 10). The visuality of the Redskin depends on authority of colonialism and its viewpoint.

A resistant visuality of the Redskin logo demands that viewers and consumers of professional American sports (in this case of the NFL, America's most popular professional league) confront the archive of Native genocide, white settler racism, and capitalism's imprint in urban sports. After all, why does the team resist a name change? In large part because the logo is a brand, is highly profitable, and represents a city's identity in a national league – these are difficult to replace from the perspective of the team's ownership, since all rely on a long history of circulation and representation to ensure profitability. Yet, as the NCAI reports, the "commercialization of race" through the use of "Indian" marketing symbols perpetuates harm (NCAI, 2013: 17) by commodifying Native bodies and reproducing an archive of violence that affects all Native people.

That the Redskins call Washington, DC, home is not incidental; US President Barack Obama has even chimed in his opinion that the NFL team should consider a name change. The city of Washington, DC, does not even host the stadium for the Redskins; rather the team plays its home games in Landover, MD. Whenever discussion arises about relocating the team back from the suburbs and in the US's Capitol city, the controversy over the name resurfaces (Box 11.1). *The Washington Post* newspaper reported in 2013 that the city Mayor, Vincent Gray, suggested that a move would require "a name change, or at least discussion of one" (http://www.washingtonpost.com/blogs/mike-debonis/wp/2013/01/09/redskins-name-change-should-be-discussed-vincent-gray-says). While the team's owners resist changing the team logo and name, there is little doubt that the image promulgates a racist

Figure 11.5   Portland, OR, markets itself as a green city, welcoming to alternative mobilities, such as bicycles. However, the irony of the city's branding is obvious in this visual representation, since "Welcome to America's Bicycle Capital" overlooks a busy downtown parking lot. Photo: Eugene McCann.

Box 11.1 Visual Imagineering

In Chapter 9: City Marketing, we examined urban entrepreneurialism and branding in order to understand the role of the state in promoting economic development and growth. The chapter suggested that particular interests benefit from shaping a city's image and identity, which are historically and geographically specific. However, what is common to urban branding and marketing is the priority to promote a city's economic and political power, especially in its competition with other cities.

Representations of a city as "world class" seek to create that city's standing; they do not merely reflect an existing standing. Therefore, representations within marketing campaigns seek to change the ways particular cities are seen globally. Visual representations are central to these enterprises and often come out of an ideological position foregrounding business development and social advancement (Figure 11.5). Consider the fact that marketing campaigns would never highlight images of poverty, urban decay and poor infrastructure, or displacement, despite the fact that cities also have all of these things. The power of visuality in urban branding can only work if such "negative" images are omitted.

Yet, as critical urban geographers, we can interrogate the images that do make it to marketing campaigns, ask whose interests they serve, what emotions they are meant to elicit, and what kinds of positions are meanwhile left out and silenced. **Aesthetics** (the study of art) can provide useful tools to critically examine urban representations and the role of artists in contesting dominant, elite urban positions. Resistance to elite interests in a city comes both from new representations and the interrogation of existing ones.

slur and a visuality of Native Americans that represents US settler sovereignty over indigenous autonomy in arguably the world's most politically and militarily powerful city.

11.4   The Artistic Mode of Production

Deutsche's critique of Harvey's overwhelming reliance on economic metatheory does not insinuate that understanding capitalism's role in the production of art has no place in a critical urban geography. It just means that there is more to the story than capital relations. According to urban studies scholar Sharon Zukin, the twentieth century harkened a new era for art in the United States. Art became "capitalized" (Zukin, 1982: 177), but that capitalization relied not solely on market forces but also on a wide range of state practices, city residents, and socioeconomic relations. In her book, *Loft Living: Culture and Capital in Urban Change*, Zukin argues that art was a central force in urban real estate development in New York City. Old industrial buildings left vacant in the wake of globalization meant scores of underutilized, decrepit, yet centrally located and available sites for urban lofts and artist studies. Zukin shows that young people and artists moved into Lower Manhattan and gave birth to neighborhoods like SoHo (Zukin, 1982: 16). Rents were ridiculously cheap in the late 1960s and 1970s, allowing artists to have huge living and studio spaces. But Zukin insists that this loft movement was no mere market driven, supply and demand process of property exchange, or a straightforward case of gentrification. Rather, loft living became an "aesthetic conjuncture" (Zukin, 1982: 15). She writes:

> On the one hand, artists' living habits became a cultural model for the middle class. On the other hand, old factories became a means of expression for a "post-industrial" civilization. A heightened sense of art and history, space and time, was dramatized by the taste-setting mass media. This suggests that the supply of lofts did *not* create demand for loft-living. Instead, demand was a conjunctural response to other social and cultural changes. (Zukin, 1982: 15)

The social and cultural changes to which she refers include a shift in the center of art production and consumption from Europe to the United States in the post-World War II era. The local US state also poured huge amounts of money into the development of the arts in those decades, for example, the construction of museums and performance spaces. At the federal level, money similarly flowed to the arts. Consider the creation of national governmental agencies like the National Endowment of the Arts (formed by the US Congress in 1965), which granted money to sustain the arts in areas of education, urban infrastructure, and artist fellowships. Cities were almost exclusively the sites of these investments.

The social and cultural changes include, too, art itself. While the urban infrastructures for art were growing mid-century – all those galleries, museums, cultural centers – the production of art grew to feed the machine of consumption and vice versa. Zukin calls this a "process of valorization" of art (Zukin, 1982: 177). Upper class and corporate consumption of art put artists to work at levels not previously experienced, and the state investment in the arts was a key aspect to this growth of artists' productivities. The revalorization of real estate through loft living slotted into this story as repurposed old industrial infrastructure became artist living spaces. A new identity was born, too, as the chic artistic sensibility of loft living spread to nonartist populations in time (what Zukin called the "cultural model for the middle class").

While real estate markets and financial speculation fluctuate, such as with the mortgage market crash in 2008, there remains a demand for repurposed buildings in many cities in the twenty-first century. Industrial buildings become upscale condominiums after capital investment allows their redevelopment. Artists may very well have squatted or rented those old buildings before being priced out as condominium renovations increase the costs of real estate. Of course, artists themselves may have pushed out even poorer residents earlier, in effect being gentrifiers themselves. We might tend to romanticize artists in our assumptions that they resist capital and commercialization and seek new social and economic formations. That might be true for some artists, but there are also those who profit from speculative development of their art and also of real estate. And there are plenty of artists like Banksy and Ai who overtly critique existing art production, venue, and materiality, yet manage to get very rich in the process.

But no matter our opinions on the value of art and its politics, it is important that we remember Zukin's arguments that artists can never individually affect markets for art or real estate, nor are they a uniform group (also see Ley, 2003; Mathews, 2010). Zukin's work reminds us to think through the complex urban geographies of art, state influence and investment, urban form, housing infrastructure, capitalism, and accumulation. Here we could also add to the list creative urban marketing, so that urban forms of public art and the presence of artist communities become symbols of a city's world class status.

11.5   Architecture, Verticality, and the Nation

Architectural design and the construction of new buildings are further examples of what Zukin called "aesthetic conjuncture." Here, we examine these themes through the case of the skyscraper – and the role of this urban form in both national identity and an international competition in world class symbolism (Box 11.2). Importantly, in many cases the choices cities make about supporting big development projects – as well

---

Box 11.2   Urban Verticality: High Up and Deep Down

In an article called "Getting off the ground: on the politics of urban verticality," Stephen Graham and Lucy Hewitt suggest that urban scholars tend to privilege the city's horizontalism over its verticality. Horizontalism, they say, gets prioritized through conceptualizing space as networks, relations, connections, mobilities, assemblages, and other terms which "flatten" space rather than extend it up and down (Graham and Hewitt, 2012: 73). Verticality, in contrast, would challenge the idea that we can have a perspective on urban societies and space from solely a top-down viewpoint. Verticality would contribute to what the authors call a "fully *volumetric* urbanism" (Graham and Hewitt, 2012: 74) that entails "the radical horizontal extension of cities and urban regions *and* the engineering of unprecedented numbers of both super-high and super-deep structures" (Graham and Hewitt, 2012: 75).

One example of volumetric urbanism that Graham and Hewitt provide is "Google Earth urbanism." Google Earth, they argue, forces urban scholars to "update" a top-down view of the city to one "where this view has very rapidly become radically assessable, zoomable and pannable in a myriad of mobile and (near) real-time ways" (Graham and Hewitt, 2012: 75). Yet Google Earth, remember, has been developed by a corporation heavily reliant on US military technoscience (Graham and Hewitt, 2012: 76; see also the list of what organizations gave data to Google Earth for Figure 11.6). Google is also a large corporation and one that, not surprisingly, wants to profit from its project. The use of Google Earth depends on broadband access (highly uneven globally) and the provision of good resolution, up-to-date images is sketchy. In short, "unevenness in data resolution favors central, high-technology and highly urbanized capitalist heartlands" (Graham and Hewitt, 2012: 76–77).

Finally, Graham and Hewitt's examination of Google Earth also points to its power of visual representation for shaping city form. Both "city boosterists" and urban designers are now driven by the question of how they will look through Google Earth. One example of design is the Palm and World developments of Dubai – the city which also boasts the Burj Khalifa (Figure 11.6). Graham and Hewitt point to Dubai as a site of extreme "urban spectacularization" (Graham and Hewitt, 2012: 78). Even if other cities cannot muster the elites and their finances to such spectacular visual and developmentalist ends, Google Earth urbanism affects cities just about everywhere with its reach, surveillance apparatus, and corporate prerogatives.

Figure 11.6   Dubai's Palm and World developments from Google Earth. These artificial islands are made largely of sand dredged from the Persian Gulf. Source: NASA/GSFC/MITI/ERSDAC/JAROS, and U.S./Japan ASTER Science Team (http://earthobservatory.nasa.gov/IOTD/view.php?id=7040)

as their efforts at urban branding and marketing – are also features of **nationalism**. This section examines several examples tying the city to the nation by examining the visual representation, urban aesthetics, and architecture of skyscrapers. Skyscraper development continues to evidence a competitive urbanism to be the highest, although this race is regionally more present in Asia in the twenty-first century.

Urban geographer Mona Domosh, in a series of articles from the late

> **Nationalism.** Nationalism refers to feelings and expressions of pride in one's country. Nationalism often evidences sentiments of superiority over other nationalities and is, therefore, not solely a positive term.

1980s, argues that New York City's nineteenth-century construction of skyscrapers conveyed messages to the urban populace, the nation, and the world about the city's power and prestige. "As symbols," she writes, "skyscrapers embody the intentions of the particular group of people who built them" (Domosh, 1988: 322). In the 1800s, New York's elites class – its entrepreneurs and merchants, financiers, and politicians – were "striving for appropriate material expression" (Domosh, 1988: 324) to reflect their economic and social status. Ornate structures, lavish residences, and, eventually, the first skyscrapers (after the development of the elevator starting in the 1870s) fulfilled their desire to symbolize power through the urban built environment. Domosh claims that "to the elite of New York who saw skyscrapers as aesthetic objects, the message was one of cultural legitimacy" (Domosh, 1988: 322). Skyscrapers evidenced this group's "rise to 'nobility,'" especially situated as they were close to both City Hall Park and also on the wide, impressive Broadway (Domosh, 1988: 327).

But the new skyscrapers were more than just symbols of class status. They were also specifically embodied representations of male power and rising corporate power. It is no wonder that feminist, urban, and architectural theorists (and even Sigmund Freud himself!) point to the phallic power represented in vertical buildings. And, as pointed out in Chapter 6, the consolidation of the business district in many US central cities also motivated the rise of the suburb and the spatial removal of middle class women, as well as the ghettoization of poor immigrants and people of color in the city. As corporations and male labor defined many symbols of the central US city, the symbols of suburbanization was decidedly feminine and domestic, while racist and xenophobic "ghetto" symbols came to signify urban poverty, decay, and devaluation.

Domosh further insists that "New York skyscrapers can be understood as expression of the shifting global economy that led to New York's rise as the capital of capitalism" (Domosh, 1988: 341). Here it is not difficult to draw a comparison between early skyscraper construction in nineteenth-century New York to the dizzying heights of the massive skyscrapers of today's Asia (Figure 11.7). For example, in Malaysia, according to geographer Tim Bunnell (1999), large scale infrastructure and skyscraper projects have been directly related to the government's desire to "put Kuala Lumpur on the world map," as Prime Minister Mahathir stated at the unveiling of the first phase of the construction of a new city center (Bunnell, 1999: 7). The Petronas Twin Towers are centerpieces of the city center and were the highest buildings in the world after completion in 1996, until they lost that standing in 2004 to Taipei 101. They are named for the Malaysian state oil company whose headquarters occupy half of one building. In the case of Kuala Lumpur, it is certainly not difficult to see the foundational role capital plays in design and representation.

Bunnell's examination of the Towers' design points to the use of Tower images in national and corporate marketing. The Towers represent Malaysia's quest to be recognized as a "developed nation" with "Malaysian modernity" (Bunnell, 1999: 12), with urban Kuala Lumpur the heart of the nation's economy. The Towers' design also sought to consolidate the identity of the nation itself. Bunnell writes: "Official representations of the building, political and commercial, do powerful work in defining an appropriate version of the nation and an aspirational vision of national development" (Bunnell, 1999: 6).

Central to the definition of the Malaysian nation is an attention to Islam. While Western media tend to fetishize the height of skyscrapers exclusively in the competition for highest, they may miss the Muslim motifs in the Petronas Twin Towers' design and

Figure 11.7　See Chapter 3 for an image of the Petronas Towers. Seen here, the dizzying heights of Shanghai's skyline, showing specifically the Lujiazui Finance and Trade Zone of the central business district of Pudong New Area. Formerly agricultural fields and small factories, the area was developed in the 1990s and 2000s as a special development zone with favorable policies for the finance and service industries. Photo courtesy of Max Woodworth.

conceptualization. Bunnell insists that Islam in Malaysia is "associated with regional or pan-national identity, not a national one" so that the Petronas Towers' Islamic motifs are intended as an architectural sign of the *Melayu Baru* ("new Malay") and the modern Muslim. He writes, "The building thus offers a new international vantage point for a modern pan-national Islam which is to be practiced nationally by *Melayu Baru*" (Bunnell, 1999: 11). Bunnell effectively situates the role of skyscraper representation in one city's (and nation's) efforts to demonstrate its regional and global development.

Yet, even as early as 1996, Anthony King warned that a Western notion of urban modernity exemplified by the skyscraper were being displaced by "ecological, energy, social and health concerns [which are considered] as more appropriate measures and signifiers of the modern city" (King, 1996: 111). His insinuation that Asia was coming to the race for the tallest at an obsolete moment now seems overstated. New technologies have allowed even big buildings to be vastly more energy and water efficient. And, sometimes, the imperatives of nationalism trump desires for **green architecture**.

While gigantic United States skyscraper construction virtually stopped as central cities gave way to suburban economic development and construction in the 1990s, the events of 9/11 brought the symbolic power of the skyscraper back to the core of the national project. When the Twin Towers fell to a terrorist attack, the

Green architecture. Green architecture denotes that the design and construction, or remodeling, of buildings was done in a way to minimize environmental impact. Central features of green architecture include energy efficiency, the use of recycled and reclaimed materials instead of new ones, water use minimization, and construction practices that do not pollute.

Figure 11.8 Construction of One World Trade Center. Photo: Andy Jonas.

reconstruction of One World Trade Center became an urgent priority for those wishing to reassert American power (Figure 11.8). It has since become a nationalist visual representation of resilience and a dedication to preserving the memory of those who died at "Ground Zero." The visuality of One World Trade Center promotes American military hegemony, corporate priorities, and nationalistic resistance to the amorphous "War on Terror." At a height of 541.3 meters (1776 feet – do not let the significance of this number escape you – the spire at the top of the building ensures this height to invoke the year the US Declaration of Independence was signed), the site can now boast New York's and the United States' tallest building.

Currently, Dubai's Burj Khalifa skyscraper (828 meters, or 2717 feet, high) ranks as the highest skyscraper in the world. In Jedda, Saudi Arabia, the firm Saudi Binladin Group has begun construction on the Kingdom Tower (Burj al Mamlakah). The tower will reach a kilometer into the sky (3281 feet). These projects evidence the Middle East's energy wealth (the cost of the Kingdom Tower is currently estimated at $30 billion) and also the shift in the region to more diversified service economies not solely reliant on energy production. Obviously, the symbolic statement of these gigantic towers fit into an economic, social, historical, and geographic trajectory that equates height with power and prestige (McNeill, 2009). The competition to be biggest continues.

Figure 11.9 Installation view, *Remembering*, by Ai Weiwei for the façade of Haus der Kunst, Munich, as part of the exhibition 2009/2010. The façade of the museum is a mural made of children's backpacks. The 9000 backpacks spell "She lived happily for seven years in this world." The sentence comes from one mother's elegy for her daughter killed in the 2008 Sichuan earthquake. Source: © Ai Weiwei. Used by permission of Ai Weiwei. Photo by Jens Weber, München. Used by permisson of Haus der Kunst.

11.6   Museums and Memorialization

Museums, art galleries, and installation spaces are central sites in cities for gathering visual productions for public viewership (Box 11.3). They are also key places for the social and cultural production of memory. If you look at Figure 11.10, for example, the artist, Ai Weiwei, photographs an important place where a resistance struggle and subsequent brutal repression occurred: Tiananmen Square. In Beijing, Tiananmen is a huge square (440 000 square meters or 109 acres) with a long history as a symbolic place of government, empire, and revolution – and of protest. Most famously in recent decades, in April 1989, a large, months-long student protest in the square called for reform of the Communist Party and an end to corruption and the censorship of the press, among many other demands. Tens of thousands – and more at times – people converged in the square in protest, sit-ins, demonstrations, and hunger strikes. The forceful display was too much dissent for Party leadership to tolerate. In early June martial law was declared, and the army was dispatched to clear the square. It is not known how many young people lost their lives to gunfire and tanks. Ai's

Box 11.3 Art as Activism: The Case of Ai Weiwei

In the documentary film, *Ai Weiwei: Never Sorry* (dir. Alison Klayman, 2012), the Chinese artist/activist claims that "life is much more interesting when you make a little bit of effort" (Figures 11.9 and 11.10). Ai's insistent work at exposing the corruption of the Chinese state certainly has made his life interesting. After the Sichuan earthquake in 2008, he and his team of activists focused on the many cases of schools which crumbled in the disaster and led to thousands of student deaths. Called tofu construction, the shoddy buildings contained subpar concrete. The money "saved" by skimping on construction materials went into corrupt officials' pockets. Ai and others gathered the names and birthdays of the dead children – something the government refused to release – and used his popular blog as the venue to disseminate the scale of suffering from the province. He and his team found 5212 student victims, and the list was posted on the one-year anniversary of the quake (Figure 11.9).

In the film Ai proclaims, "Blogs and the Internet are great inventions for our time because they give regular people an opportunity to change public opinion." Although the government shut down his blog after the student names were posted, Ai began using Twitter to send updates, messages, and images to his followers. When an Ai studio under construction was demolished by the Chinese state, presumably in retaliation for his activism and criticism against the government, he Tweeted a photo of himself in front of the destruction @aiww with the following statement (translated to English): "What can they do to me? None other than deportation, kidnapping and imprisonment, or make me completely vanish" (November 19, 2009 05:41:06).

In April, 2011, he did disappear, sparking an international frenzy of protest against China. After 81 days, he was released and charged with tax evasion. Despite bans by the Chinese state on his use of social media or in granting interviews, at the end of the film, *Never Sorry*, he says the following to an English language interviewer: "I think that art certainly is the vehicle for us to develop any new ideas, to be creative. ... I think there is a responsibility for any artist to protect freedom of expression." He remains very active on Twitter.

middle finger communicates his outrage quite simply; the photo is a memorialization to the struggle for democracy as well as an insult to the Chinese state for its blatant murdering of students seeking democratic reform.

Tiananmen Square does not have a memorial honoring the student protestors. Who and what events gain a public memorial in public spaces and in museums is of keen interest to critical urban geographers. If you think about what sorts of public spaces hold memorials, you will come up with a long list of examples, from museums, monuments, cemeteries, statuary, the naming of public buildings and streets, historical preservation sites, plaques – the city is saturated with memorialization. Often, the aim of such sites of memory is to create and sustain a nationalist identity. The proliferation of memory sites has accompanied nation-building projects for the past several hundred years; consider the many squares in Europe celebrating war heroes and famous battles, like Trafalgar Square in London, which

Figure 11.10   Ai Weiwei, *Study of Perspective – Tiananmen Square. 1995–2003*. Ai took similar photos and distributed them via Twitter at various global landmarks, including the Eiffel Tower in Paris and the White House in Washington, DC. See his Twitter postings @aiww (@aiwwenglish). Source: Used by permission of Ai Weiwei. Digital image used by permission of The Museum of Modern Art/Licensed by SCALA / Art Resource, NY.

commemorates the naval victory over France and Space in the Napoleonic Wars in the early nineteenth century. Another example is the Arc de Triomphe at the Avenue des Champs-Élysées, which commemorates the dead of the Revolutionary and Napoleonic Wars.

The making of memorials and museums is an especially important process of political and national transition and involves urban elites seeking to design images and symbols to capture and reflect the "new" order. The process of memorialization therefore attempts to fix a time – like the triumph of battle – in public space. However, despite the fact that urban elites are by far the overwhelming force in the creation of memorials and museums, their power can be limited in the act of viewing and experiencing the spaces themselves. Elites in this case include wealthy funders and donors, city planners, boards of directors, government officials, and celebrities who champion their causes. But public art and the production of art – visuality, too – are socially and culturally consumed by many different people and groups; images and installations are mulled over, hated, paining, scary, lovely, or none or all of the above at once. Most importantly, the many divergent experiences of urban spaces of memory are in the present, not the past.

Karen Till, in her important book *The New Berlin: Memory, Politics, Place* (2005), examines the process of memorializing the Holocaust in Berlin, Germany. She writes, "Through place making, people mark social spaces as haunted sites where they can return, make contact with their loss, contain unwanted presences, or confront past injustices" (Till, 2005: 8). In Germany, and in Berlin more particularly, where many of the nation's memorials to the Holocaust are sited, Till suggests that Germans "continue to negotiate their contradictory feelings of being haunted by a dark national past in the present." She continues:

> *Places of memory* are created by individuals and social groups to give a shape to felt absences, fears, and desires that haunt contemporary society. … People speak of historic sites as eyewitnesses to the past or describe landscapes as original artifacts and traces … from another time; they believe that by visiting these places they can experience, and perhaps work through, their contradictory emotions associated with feeling haunted by the past, including fear, anger, guilt, shame, sadness, longing, and unease. By representing places in these ways, people create social spaces definted by contemporary needs and desires; they emplace their social dreams and hopes for the future. (Till, 2005: 9; emphasis in original)

Till's book is a fascinating examination of how a city, a nation, its artists, citizens, planners, and government officials, struggle with how to aestheticize horror, torture, genocide, and trauma (see Chapter 13 for more on Till and to see a photo of the Holocaust Memorial).

Memorials and museums are political in the sense that their construction and curation involve intense negotiation about whose past becomes a visible public space. In some cases, citizen groups establish alternative places of memory when they feel that "official" and national narratives have forgotten or omitted their experiences. In Cape Town, South Africa, the District Six Museum offers an exhibition showing how one neighborhood was destroyed in the consolidation of **apartheid** rule. As Charmaine McEachern (1998) explains, District Six was a part of Cape Town known in the nineteenth and early twentieth century for its racial diversity and working class populations. When the National Party gained control over the South African government in 1948, white apartheid rule – which was de facto rule for decades – became de jure rule, that is, by law. A central piece of apartheid legislation was the Population Registration Act of 1950, which McEachern writes,

> **Apartheid.** Apartheid is an Afrikaans word ("apartness") that denotes the extreme structures of racial segregation in South Africa in 1948–1994 when the National Party held power in government. Racial segregation was a key feature of colonial rule in South Africa, but after 1948 a series of laws and policies cemented white rule. Millions of black and colored South Africans were removed from cities and towns under apartheid rule.

> sought comprehensively to enforce racial difference by controlling non-white populations in terms of residence. Apartheid was thus a spatial system. … In particular, the city, the urban, was central to policy. The city was seen as white, built by whites for whites, so that access to the cities by non-whites for whatever purpose, residential or employment, had to be strictly controlled through the Group Areas Act in order to maintain this correct relationship between whiteness and urbanization. Non-whites were to live and work in the urban areas only on white terms. (McEachern, 1998: 501)

Black South Africans, mixed raced people, and those of Asian descent were forced nation-wide to move to the townships or peripheral urban areas – four million people over

25 years – and in District Six, tens of thousands of people (upwards of 65 000; McEachern, 1998: 502) lost their homes to apartheid's bulldozers by the mid-1960s.

Apartheid rule finally ended in 1994 with the election of Nelson Mandela, whose release from prison in 1990 after 27 years' confinement began the dismantling of apartheid's legal and political apparatus. District Six Museum formed in late 1994 in one of the few buildings from the neighborhood to survive demotion – a Methodist Church. Photographs of District Six before its destruction form the bulk of the exhibition, and McEachern describes the powerful testimony of the "survivors" of District Six who accompany visitors and tell stories about living and struggling with apartheid's cruel, racist rule. In fact, the museum's focus on struggle and resistance is the core holding together the fragments of its collection: old street signs, objects saved from the rubble piles, a map of local history filled in by visitors. The District Six Museum now provides what the apartheid nation did not: a place in urban space.

11.7 Summary and Conclusions

A critical visuality in urban geography questions the overtly communicated meanings of images by exploring the latent ways that representation works. Utilizing the tools of aesthetics and visuality, the chapter showed that images circulate by evoking contextual meanings that are necessary for communication. Those contextual meanings result as much through processes of exclusion, since evaluating what you see from a critical standpoint means also asking what is not visible or included in an image. We therefore examined how to analyze images by placing them in a geographic and historic trajectory through which meanings are made and also valued. Using examples like graffiti art, an urban sports franchise logo, a public park sculpture, and places of memory, the chapter suggests that images and representations do important work in constructing meanings in specific urban spaces. Central questions to ask when engaging a critical visuality include: from whose perspectives do representations stem? For whose benefit they are reproduced? How might we disrupt elitist images in order to advance more diverse or inclusionary representations of urban life and space?

In the chapter the example of the artistic mode of production illustrated that the economic capitalization of art is vital to an examination of urban form, design, identity, and neighborhood. But that example also insisted that we think not just about capitalism but also state involvement in the arts, urban identities, and the role of art production and aesthetics themselves when we think about gentrification and loft living. The examples of skyscrapers and memorialization further brought the importance of nationalism to an analysis of urban form and design.

Urban branding and marketing are vital ingredients in any city's quest for regional and global development, and interrogating the images and architectural design that are utilized for marketing purposes can help us understand how elite subjects foreground their own visions in their quest for development. Thus, a critical visuality also insists that we seek to expose the limits of all images and their representational exclusions. A resistant visuality places the limits and exclusions of images at the center of analysis in order to claim more inclusionary representations of urban life and space.

11.8   Further Reading

- You can take a virtual tour of District Six Museuam at its website, www.districtsix.co.za.
- Derek Gregory's blog, *geographical imaginations; war, space and security*, at www.geographicalimaginations.com, provides many insightful musings about visuality and war-making over time.
- Harriet Hawkins (2012) provides a great overview on geography and art.
- See Cameron McAuliffe (2013) on the management and urban policy related to graffiti in Sydney, Australia.
- Dean Rader's (2011) book, *Engage Resistance: American Indian Art, Literature, and Film from Alcatraz to the NMAI*, examines Native American artistic production from visual art to the movies.
- *Visual Methodologies* by Gillian Rose (2001) is a textbook to help students understand how to read images and also how to integrate them in research analysis.
- Stephen Legg (2011) considers memory-making in postcolonial India; see also his historical urban geographies of Delhi (Legg, 2005)
- Suggested Documentary Films:
  - *Ai Weiwei: Never Sorry* (dir. Alison Klayman, 2012). A documentary film on the Chinese dissident artist, his worldwide fame, and his struggles with the Chinese state. A second documentary on Ai, *The Fake Case* (dir. Andreas Johnsen, 2014), considers his post-detention politics.
  - *Exit Through the Gift Shop* (dir. Banksy, 2010). Banksy's film about street art.
  - *The Art of the Steal* (dir. Don Argott, 2009). A documentary film that narrates the struggle over the Barnes collection after the owner of the private collection dies and demands in his will that the collection (valued at over $25 billion) remain far away from the urban elite. The collection is eventually placed in downtown Philadelphia against his wishes and to the benefit of the city's tourist economy.
  - The National Film Board of Canada has a multimedia, multiyear documentary called *Highrise: The Towers in the World, World in the Towers*. The interactive documentary is at http://highrise.nfb.ca. The segment called "Out My Window" contains reflections from people around the world on living high in cities, and an interactive storybook called, "A Short History of the Highrise."

Chapter 12

Alternative Urban Spaces and Politics

Urban Geography: A Critical Introduction, First Edition. Andrew E.G. Jonas, Eugene McCann,
and Mary Thomas.
© 2015 Andrew E.G. Jonas, Eugene McCann, and Mary Thomas. Published 2015 by John Wiley & Sons, Ltd.

12.1   Introduction

Over several weeks in early 2011, tens of thousands of Egyptians – young and old, men and women – staged anti-government protests in Tahrir Square in the center of Cairo. The target of their protests was the Western-government-backed regime of President Hosni Mubarak that had been in power since the 1980s. The protests focused international attention on civil rights, low wages, and economic mismanagement by the Egyptian state. Following several weeks of tension, the Egyptian army eventually came out in support of the civil uprising, forcing President Mubarak to leave office in February 2011. He was replaced by a military junta, the Supreme Council of the Armed Forces. After democratic elections were held throughout the country, in June 2012, Mohamed Morsi became the President of Egypt. Further urban protests in July 2013 led to Morsi himself being ousted and a new wave of violence on the streets of Cairo followed the coup. Given the years of tumult and protest in Tahrir Square leading to drastic shifts of governance, it has become a symbol of the Arab Spring, a movement seeking democratic reform throughout the Middle East region.

Cities and their public spaces have long been associated with mass demonstrations against the authority of ruling elites. Similar protests in Tiananmen Square in Beijing two decades earlier than Tahrir Square led to the Chinese state authorities sending in tanks to crush massive student-led protests (Chapter 11). In both cases, urban spaces – buildings, streets, boulevards and public squares – became powerful symbols of both democracy and repression. For critical urban geographers, the study of protests reveals the importance of the **urban public realm** in struggles against wider forces of change such as globalization, state repression and the erosion of citizenship rights. However, there is also a sense that the struggle for survival in the city often occurs on a much more mundane basis (Figures 12.1 and 12.2).

In Chapter 7, for instance, we considered how mainstream institutions of urban governance often reflect the interests of powerful alliances between the state and capital (in the form of urban **growth coalitions**). While you should not underestimate the influence of such mainstream urban political interests, conventional accounts of urban politics often downplay or overlook completely the activities and voices of ordinary people. In doing so, such accounts serve to conceal the rich tapestry of urban development pathways and, thereby, deny the possibility of **alternative urban spaces and politics**.

Urban public realm. The urban public realm refers to the extent to which physical spaces of the city are accessible to ordinary urban residents. Public access is governed by prevailing rules and norms that apply to the use and exchange of property, both public and private. In the neoliberal city the scope of the public urban realm is progressively narrowed by the intrusion of private property relations into public spaces.

Alternative urban spaces and politics. Economic and political spaces of the city that actively oppose or replace dominant economic systems and mainstream uses of urban space can be described as alternative. The development of these alternative urban spaces usually involves ordinary people engaging with and challenging mainstream political institutions. The assumption is that such alternative urban spaces and politics have a wider social and economic purpose than is usually possible given the constraining influence of mainstream power structures in the city.

Figures 12.1 and 12.2   Public space is ubiquitously posted with rules and regulations in many European, North American, Australian, and Japanese cities. In Figure 12.1, a sign informs the public in Sydney that drinking in the "alcohol-free zone" can result in a visit from the police. In Figure 12.2, Tokyo city warns you not to smoke on the street. Photos: Eugene McCann.

Much of what urban protest is all about today relates to what Henri Lefebvre (1968) referred to as *le droit à la ville*, which translates into **the right to the city** (Chapter 2). The concept of the right to the city seeks to capture the relationship between the production of urban space, on the one hand, and the struggle for political identity and economic survival on the part of the working class, the homeless, and the dispossessed, on the other hand. Critical urban scholars now recognize that urban-based struggles around redevelopment, gentrification, or outright state repression open up all sorts of opportunities for resistance against dominant power structures. Threats to the right to the city, such as the erosion of the urban public realm by private sector redevelopment, shift our attention to the role of ordinary people in shaping urban political space in a much more democratic and socially inclusive fashion than hitherto possible under mainstream or modernist visions of **citizenship** and public participation (Rossi and Vanolo, 2012: chapter 5).

There is, of course, a rich tradition of radical research on urban social movements in the **global South** (Chapter 2) that has already revealed the diversity of the urbanization experience for the poor, the working class, the dispossessed, and other "ordinary people" (Castells, 1983). Such movements have afforded slum dwellers, factory workers, and migrants with access to basic resources – food,

Citizenship. In contrast to the commonly understood notion of citizenship as a status conferred by the national state and entailing certain rights (e.g., to a vote) and responsibilities (e.g., to pay taxes), citizenship is also a concept used by academics and activists to both identify the ways in which people in cities claim rights and responsibilities related less to their official status and more to their inhabiting of place. Urban citizenship may then involve people who are not part of the traditional citizenry (e.g., undocumented immigrants) and is more likely to be evident in protests than in traditional forms, like voting.

shelter, income, and a political voice – necessary for economic survival. Such basic material concerns are not unique to residents of cities of the global South. Indeed, many critical scholars want to draw attention to similar sorts of grassroots struggles now occurring in cities in the **global North** (Chapter 2), such as the rise of anti-capitalist movements like Occupy (Chapter 1). Although global cities remain important centers of economic and political power, the public spaces within them afford grassroots organizations opportunities to challenge institutions of global governance and, in doing so, to develop alternative approaches to the use and exchange of urban space. One of the tasks of the critical urban geographer is to uncover this sense of a city's "otherness": in other words, to reveal how urban space can be used a resource to be deployed against the more socially, politically, and economically regressive aspects of globalization, neoliberal austerity, and state political repression.

The main purpose of this chapter is to examine the city as potential site of alternative economic and political spaces. The sorts of questions it addresses are:

- What alternative urban development trajectories are politically possible?
- How is the right to the city expressed today?
- What is the basis of citizenship and public participation in the city?
- What urban development processes are eroding the urban public realm?
- How are environmental and social justice movements connecting together in the city?
- Where in the city can we look for alternative economic spaces?

The chapter argues that critical urban research can make a crucial contribution to postcapitalist politics by making the connection between the production of urban space and the emergence of all sorts of struggles around public space, citizenship, housing, and economic survival in the city.

12.2 Beyond Mainstream Urban Development Politics

The story of urban development since the 1980s has for the most been written from the perspective of what happened in industrial cities in Western Europe and North America after the collapse of the Fordist manufacturing economy; namely, the restructuring of cities into postindustrial service and financial centers, the gradual withdrawal of the state from social welfare provision in the city, and the rise of urban entrepreneurialism (Chapters 3 and 7). For the past 20 years or so, the business of urban politics has been conducted around a received discourse of growth, with only occasional references made to the distributional aspects of urban development. You might, therefore, be forgiven for thinking that *all* cities regardless of their differences in terms of size, location, economy, and politics are engaged in the same neoliberal, entrepreneurial activities, promoting almost identical strategies of urban redevelopment (Jessop *et al.*, 1999). You might further come to the conclusion that the main beneficiaries of this "growth at all costs" model of urban development are business participants in the urban growth coalition, broadly conceived. The capacity for ordinary people operating outside these arrangements to engage in alternative strategies and politics of urban development is often restricted to rhetorical actions and short-lived protests. The limits placed on public participation in urban development are further exacerbated by the fact that urban politicians and policy-makers have greater resources at their disposal and prefer to copy "best practice" policies in other cities rather than consult with their local electorates. The net effect of all of this is to produce a global landscape of urban uniformity rather than one of political diversity and difference, or so it seems.

Nevertheless, you might want to question the idea that there is a generic neoliberal model of entrepreneurial urban development that sweeps around the world unaffected by its encounters with ordinary people and unopposed by urban residents. The conventional argument that there was a distinct rupture between the pre-Fordist urban order and the present neoliberal urban regime is far too simplistic. Even under the current neoliberal regime of urban austerity there are marked differences in the experiences of individual cities (Hackworth, 2007; Peck, 2012). Some approaches to urban governance do recognize these differences but in focusing on, for instance, variations in the characteristics of urban regimes, they fail to look much beyond mainstream political structures and examine how ordinary residents make alternative urban spaces and politics. As Williams and Pendras (2013: 291) argue, urban scholarship often fails "to clearly distinguish between those qualities that define dominant neoliberal cities and the less comprehensive and forceful business presence in other cities." They call our attention to consider examples of cities where political conditions might make alternative urban development pathways more viable, in other words, to look beyond mainstream urban institutions and power structures and examine more closely the role of ordinary people and grassroots organizations in shaping the city from below.

In Chapter 4, we already suggested that we need to focus less on self-selected examples of global cities and more on "ordinary cities," that is, how ordinary people shape the economic and political life of a city irrespective of its size, location, or global economic significance (Robinson, 2006). The same principle applies in our search for alternative urban political spaces: we need more examples of where conventional growth coalitions have failed to coalesce and/or grassroots organizations have proven successful in challenging major urban redevelopment schemes and proposing alternatives. A case in point is Lexington, KY, where an unusual coalition of church ministers, residents, and developers came together around the rezoning of a former industrial site owned by major tobacco company (McCann, 2002). The future of this property was up for grabs in the 1990s both because of the size of the site (450 acres) and the fact that it represented a significant shift in the urban economy from industrial branch plans to new commercial services and light industry. It also came at period of growing urban conflicts: involving environmentalists around open space in the city and the African–American community over issues of economic equity. While those opposed to the rezoning proposals had some successes, the developers eventually took the matter out of the urban political arena and used the courts to get the proposal approved, but not in the way they had originally planned.

Williams and Pendras (2013) conclude from this that those advocating alternative approaches to urban development can have some successes but also face many challenges. Often, no one group or political agenda – not even a conventional business-led growth coalition – is able to control or shape the way cities develop, resulting in a kind of political stasis. In such cases, it might be possible for residents and grassroots environmental and social justice organizations to mobilize their wider political and social networks in order to pursue alternative approaches to urban politics. We now consider how alternative urban spaces and politics can be connected to new struggles over the right to the city and the urban commons.

12.3   The Right to the City and the New Urban Commons

Our knowledge of the economic revival of cities in the global North has been profoundly shaped by recent theorizations of neoliberal urban development. At the same time the urbanization process has extended and deepened on a global scale (Chapter 3). Processes that initially took place in the eighteenth and nineteenth centuries in Europe and North America, such as the displacement of peasants from agricultural land, rural–urban migration, and the growth of industrial cities and slums, now characterize the cities of the global South, too (Davis, 2006b). Yet global urbanization and the further dispossession of the urban poor continue to have profound significance for struggles around urban space in the global North; we should not think that dispossession only occurs contemporarily in the less developed world.

Two concepts that help to shed light on these issues are: (i) the right to the city; and (ii) the new urban commons. In this section, we consider how these concepts help critical urban geographers to explore the relationship between the production of urban space and alternative urban spaces and politics.

The right to the city

The right to the city was a phrase used by Henri Lefebvre in *Le Droit à la Ville* (1968) in reference to the rights of those who inhabit the city. Note that Lefebvre was writing in the 1960s, a time of growing urban social unrest in North America and Western Europe. In Detroit, decades of housing segregation had led to the so-called "race riots" of 1967. In 1968, the student movement was active in the streets and boulevards of Paris (and in many other cities around the world) challenging state authority and the growing influence of transnational capital. A new generation of urban activists seemed empowered to challenge state authority. Inspired by these incipient urban movements for revolutionary change, Lefebvre constructed an argument about how the working class could secure a more democratic route to socialism through active political participation in the transformation of urban space. For him, the city contained particular spatial organizations that made this possible. In order to more fully appreciate Lefebvre's ideas, we need to think about how present urban forms reflect the intensification of various processes that continue to deny urban masses their right to the city.

The right to the city concept can be broken down into two components (Mitchell, 2003; Purcell, 2008). First, there is the **right to participation**. This is the idea that ordinary residents of the city have a right to play an active role in the democratic production of urban space but are prevented from doing so by the actions of the dominant ruling class. The city has become a crucible of struggles around citizenship and political identity; struggles which we shall return to later on in

Right to participation. Emerging out of the concept of **the right to the city** (Chapter 2), the right to participation refers to the role of urban residents in shaping urban space in a democratic and participatory fashion. It is generally believed that in the neoliberal city the demands of private interests are met far more readily than the needs of the public (i.e., ordinary people). You can assume that a critical urban geographer has an important part to play in promoting the right to participation.

Right of appropriation. The right of appropriation refers to claims by ordinary people for greater control over how space is used in the city. It is manifested in the struggle on the part of urban resident to access and occupy urban spaces (e.g., buildings and public squares). However, the exercise of this particular right is compromised by the power of private interests to shape and unduly influence urban redevelopment in and around public spaces.

this chapter. Second, there is the **right of appropriation**. This means all inhabitants of the city should have equal opportunities to access physical space. In the neoliberal city where private sector redevelopment often encroaches on urban public space, the right of appropriation has come to refer to the right to occupy urban space and engage in various acts of democratic protest and resistance to global change. However, the exercise of this particular right is, in turn, constrained by the exclusionary and privatized character of urban development in the neoliberal city, which we will shortly consider in the context of a discussion of the new urban enclosures.

In the capitalist city, the redevelopment of physical space (i.e., buildings, streets, squares, etc.) has become a highly organized process involving the exchange of property, both private (e.g., corporate office blocks, condominiums, etc.) and public (i.e., open space, parks, and buildings owned by the state or another public authority). The process of urban development often involves property owners exercising rights in an exclusionary manner. This happens when owners use state powers, such as zoning or **eminent domain** (Chapter 7), to keep out other undesirable uses.

The process of urban development often involves various acts of privatization, exclusionary zoning, control, displacement, and eviction. Edward Soja writes:

> Not only are residences becoming increasingly gated, guarded, and wrapped in advanced security, surveillance, and alarm systems, so too are many other activities, land uses, and everyday objects in the urban environment, from shopping malls and libraries to razor-wire protected refuse bins and spiked park benches to stave off incursions of the homeless and hungry. Microtechnologies of social and spatial control infest everyday life and pile up to produce a tightly meshed and prisonlike geography punctuated by protective enclosures and overseen by ubiquitous watchful eyes. (Soja, 2010: 42–43, cited in Hodkinson, 2012: 501)

Due to urban development and the exercise of private property rights, urban residents are often denied access to public spaces in the city (Figures 12.3 and 12.4). Nevertheless, legitimate democratic claims can be made on such spaces by redefining the scope of the public urban realm.

Homelessness is one arena where struggles over the right to the city seem to have intensified. In Chapter 7, we examined the housing question in relation to planning and the urbanization process in capitalist society. Although the causes of homelessness are complex and relate in part to the housing question (Chapter 8), homelessness itself is the condition of not having a fixed or permanent place of residence. In a capitalist system, this usually means not having access to one's own private house, rental accommodation or, failing that, to a temporary shelter or room provided by a public authority. At the same time, the

Figures 12.3 and 12.4 Plaça de George Orwell in Barcelona, complete with a "Big brother" stencil. The sign lets people know that they are under surveillance. Video surveillance is a common form of "microtechnologies of social and spatial control" referred to by Soja. Photos: Eugene McCann.

homeless need to have access to jobs as well as shelter and services, all of which are often most accessible in the inner city (especially since the poor and homeless typically do not have access to a car or cannot afford public transport). Therefore, the struggle to provide even temporary accommodation for the homeless often involves a struggle for access to physical space in the heart of the inner city.

A fairly typical scenario is when advocates for the homeless come into conflict with those involved in transforming downtown areas into consumption spaces that are attractive to urban professionals, gentrifiers, and tourists. How does this happen? Perhaps it involves forcibly relocating the homeless, passing laws that exclude people from particular urban spaces, and/or monitoring public behavior. In the Skid Row district of Los Angeles, for instance, there have been numerous efforts over the years to enforce an old city ordinance that prevents people from sleeping, lying, or sitting on public sidewalks. The police presence in Skid Row is perhaps the largest concentration anywhere in the United States (Stuart, 2013). Activists have criticized the ordinance for specifically targeting the local homeless population and argue that its enforcement is part of a city-wide plan to "tidy up" certain districts prior to redevelopment. At the same time, the police shift the homeless into rehabilitation programs that only address individual pathologies (e.g., drug addiction) without addressing the absence of affordable housing and the issues of equable economies, racism, and systemic violence (Stuart, 2013).

The new urban commons

The struggle for the right to appropriation in the city focuses our attention on the changing nature of public space in the city or what we have called the urban public realm. We tend to take for granted public space in the city: usually you can walk freely around public parks, visit squares and monuments, hang out on street corners, and watch the world go about its business without fear of sanction by urban authorities (provided you follow basic rules such as respecting the rights of others to use the same spaces as yourself). Typically, the boundaries between the public realm and private space in the city are well defined: signs tell you where and when you can visit a public park, and notices saying "Private Property" warn you not to enter a gated community or private land. In many situations, however, the boundaries are not so clear and there is room for negotiation, protest, and outright struggle.

For Staeheli and Mitchell (2008) the struggle over the use and regulation of public space is becoming common feature of life in the neoliberal city today; this is due to the increasing intrusion of private property relations into the public urban realm via private-sector-led urban redevelopment processes such as gentrification, the construction of downtown shopping malls, and the creation of tourist spaces and sports venues. As Blomley (2008b) argues, private landowners and developers often work in partnership with state or local authorities to enforce their legal rights to demolish and/or redevelop private property in a district or area undergoing redevelopment. Such redevelopment is often a direct challenge to someone else's vision of the use of adjacent property, such as a park, community garden, playgrounds, or a community facility, or, in the case of Figure 12.5, a strip club denoting "low class" sex work and urban blight (see also Hubbard, 2011). So there is a sense in which the public's right to have access to *any* urban space is something that is held in common by *all* urban residents rather than reducible to individual ownership rights. The enclosure of the urban space by private redevelopment calls into question the degree of "publicness" of the city and creates conditions for struggles on the part of urban residents to reclaim their right to the city.

> **The new urban commons.** The new urban commons involves a struggle on the part of ordinary residents to claim back the city and to view it as resource held in common by the people rather than a tool of a privileged and wealthy minority.

The **new urban commons** provides a theoretical discourse for understanding growing resistance to the variety of enclosure practices associated with the redevelopment of the city (Hodkinson, 2012). The idea of enclosure itself harks back to Karl Marx's arguments about how the development of capitalism and the emergence of the industrial city led to the creation of a landless class of wage laborers, who had neither direct control of the means of production nor access to land and property once held in common. In light of this, the new urban commons becomes a metaphor for thinking about ways of resisting the variety of enclosure processes operating in the city today, such as neoliberal housing policy.

Focusing on the United Kingdom, Stuart Hodkinson (2012) argues that there has been a neoliberal turn away from the post-war collectivist model of public housing provision (i.e., what was known as public housing in the United States and council housing in the United Kingdom) towards the private market and private financing arrangements. The privatization of public housing began in the 1980s under the Conservative Government of Prime Minister Margaret Thatcher and has continued under the current Coalition government through schemes such as "Right-to-Buy," which gives tenants of council housing the right

Figure 12.5 Condominium construction in this downtown Seattle neighborhood will have widespread effects on the surrounding areas. Who decides when US$1 million apartments are more "appropriate" to urban space than a strip club? Photo: Eugene McCann.

to purchase and own their homes outright. Such schemes have severely depleted the accumulated stock of public rental (council) housing: from 31.4% of housing stock in 1979 to 16.1% in 2012. In the meantime, greater powers have been given to private landlords and developers to shape the market for "affordable housing," which today means housing not just affordable to the urban working class but also so-called "key workers": people employed in urban services industries such as teachers, nurses, police officers, and so forth.

As more and more low and middle income earners are denied access to public rental housing, or are unable to afford down payments on mortgages for private home ownership, many households have been displaced into the private rental market, which in Hodkinson's (2012: 512) view "has in turn been subject to further enclosure processes such as strengthening landlords' power to evict, the removal of rent controls and a succession of cuts to housing benefit." How might today's urban commoners contest these sorts of enclosures? One answer involves new urban social movements embracing the right to the city as enshrined, for instance, in the right to have access to affordable public housing.

Another space in the city where the new urban commons has served as a powerful anti-capitalist discourse involves the Occupy movement. Born in the wake of the global financial crisis, Occupy began in September 2011 as a popular movement targeting the strategic urban centers of capitalism, most notably Liberty Square at the heart of Wall Street, New York City's financial district (http://occupywallst.org/). Inspired by popular uprisings in Tunis and Cairo, the movement seeks to expose the inherent inequality of the global economy by focusing public attention on locations in the city where the concentration of financial power is most visible. Through various acts of public demonstration and direct action, the Occupy movement seeks to wrest control of the city away from the minority financial elite and, thereby, establish the basis for a new urban commons. As the movement gathered momentum, it spread to other cities around the world, including Frankfurt (Chapter 2) and London, where the local authorities forced members of Occupy to relocate their protest camp from the heart of the City (London's financial district) to the steps of St. Paul's Cathedral, itself a recognized public gathering place symbolizing the close link between finance capital, church, and state. As Harvey (2008: 35) argued, "the right to the city, as is now constituted, is far too narrowly confined, in most cases in the hands of a small political and economic elite who are in a position to shape the city more and more after their own particular heart's desire."

12.4 The City, Citizenship, and Democracy

For much of the twentieth century democratic society was built around a state-centric vision of political participation, which was very much fixed around the political scale of the nation state. Two factors have contributed to our current state-centric view of citizenship, both of which are now deeply contested. First, the state has encouraged the cultural integration of citizens as equal members of an **imagined community** known as the nation-state (Anderson, B. 1991). To that end, urban spaces often serve to remind citizens of their loyalty to the nation through monuments, myths, symbols, signs, festivals, and events, all of which seek to appeal to certain visions of nation-statehood. Second, the state confers rights on its citizens as members of territorial units called countries, the jurisdictional limits of which represent the space of citizenship. The national political space in turn defines the spatial scope of citizen rights and responsibilities, such as the right to vote (e.g., in local or national elections), freedom of political expression (e.g., the right of assembly) and mobility (e.g., freedom to travel from one city to another across a national territory).

> **Imagined community** is that sense of belonging to a particular place, region, or country, which people often share in common despite never having met each other in person (Anderson, B. 1991). For example, when you join with other fans and sing your national anthem at a football game, you are participating in an imagined community. Likewise, particular buildings, such as museums and monuments, often convey a sense of belonging to a much wider community than the immediate urban setting. **Nationalism** is a particular kind of imagined community which is cultivated by public authorities for the greater good of the citizens (and businesses) of a given city, region, or country.

Our received view of democratic participation is, therefore, primarily seen through the lens of the nation-state, yet increasingly it seems that struggles and protests are occurring around *urban* spaces. The erosion of the modernist idea of citizenship expressed at the scale of the nation-state is opening up opportunities for new forms of political participation and expressions of protest to take place at the urban scale. An important dimension of the

Figure 12.6   A protest against forced evictions associated with the gentrification and redevelopment of inner city districts in north-eastern Spain. Photo: Andy Jonas.

rescaling of citizenship is the assertion of the right to the city by ordinary people. This is shifting the locus of political participation downwards, from the national level to the urban scale, and upwards in the sense that protest movements occurring in different cities are becoming interlinked. This is partly a function of the growth of multiscalar legal and governance systems associated with the global economy; but it is also a function of the strategic role of global cities in sustaining financial capitalism and its associated neoliberal regulatory order. So while social scientists like Saskia Sassen (2006) have talked in general terms about the denationalization of citizenship, its actual assemblage in the city is leading to all sorts of struggles around globalization, inward investment, income redistribution, human rights, political identity, and so forth. As Rossi and Vanolo (2012:159) argue, "[W]hile the advent of globalization has undermined the primacy of state-centered citizenship, the resurgence of the local scale of governance and economic development has led to the re-emergence of cities and larger metropolitan areas as crucial spaces of contention over the recognition of minority identities and a variety of shifting positionalities."

Mundane signs that the neoliberal city is a space of contention can be seen in the graffiti daubed on houses, pavements, and trains, or posters attached to walls, lamp posts, and public buildings, perhaps indicating the location of a protest meeting, a forthcoming political action, or other gestures of resistance. Colorful images, slogans, and murals sprayed or daubed in paint convey messages of opposition to gentrification, displacement, depleted public services, or surveillance in the city (Figure 12.6). Such expressions of protest in the city assume many forms – both visual and covert – and often have a broader geographic impact – symbolic and political – that extends well beyond the scale of the street, public square, or financial district. In these respects, both the visible and hidden drama of the public urban realm makes its study an exciting prospect for critical urban geographers.

The nature of democracy is being transformed through its various encounters with urban political space (Purcell, 2008). An interesting example of changing meaning of citizenship in the neoliberal city comes from Seattle, WA, which has become a center of new technology industries and the headquarters of US-based global corporations like Microsoft and Starbucks (Sparke, 2011). In 1999, Seattle became a focal point of anti-globalization protests targeted at the major trading nations. If the city was then known for its progressive anti-capitalist politics, business elites have since tried to channel grassroots social and political capital in new directions including local philanthropic endeavors. Thus, corporations like Microsoft have been actively sponsoring charitable ventures and the provision of health and social support services where the public sector increasingly fails to deliver. Here the notion that urban politics involves struggles for social provision by the state is being supplanted by new forms of political participation nurtured by global capital.

12.5   Environmental and Social Justice in the City

Social justice is a well-established theme in critical urban geography thanks to David Harvey's landmark treatise on *Social Justice in the City* (Harvey, 1973/2010). Harvey's specific focus was on how the capitalist urban condition gives rise to all sorts of class alliances, political coalitions, and revolutionary movements. This is because contemporary urbanization processes are associated with all sorts of injustices. For example, in Chapter 10 we suggested that environmental injustices in the city affect some social classes, ethnicities and races more than others. The presence of various noxious facilities, such as trash-burning power plants, chemical industries, sewage treatment plants, landfills, and toxic dumps is a direct consequence of unfettered urban industrial development. Such facilities tend to cluster around poor and minority residential neighborhoods, suggesting that non-Whites are exposed disproportionately more than Whites to certain forms of environmental pollution and industrial hazards due to locational factors. In Los Angeles, for instance, many toxic inventory release (TRI) sites are located in close spatial proximity to non-White Hispanic neighborhoods, which in turn reflects historical patterns of residential segregation and the exercise of White privilege in the housing market (Pulido, 2000).

The 1964 US Civil Rights Act established that any federal program that causes environmental injustice or discriminates on the basis of race is unlawful. The Act has encouraged activists and ordinary people in many US cities to engage in movements for urban environmental justice. For example, brownfield sites in cities have been targets of grassroots efforts to promote environmental and health improvements, along with community-based schemes to create new jobs and retrain the workforce. In Los Angeles, environmental and community partnerships have been created in many inner city neighborhoods in order to engage people of color, local charities, not-for-profit organizations, and urban planners in the promotion of more sustainable forms of urban living (Pincetl, 2003).

The concept of **just sustainability** offers a way of thinking about the potential links between environmental security, racial justice, and social equity in the city (Agyeman *et al.*,

2003). Krueger and Savage (2007) use this concept in a study of a public hospital anti-merger campaign in Boston, MA. This campaign grew up around a proposal to merge the city's public hospital with a private institution. It brought together labor unions and public service organiza-

> **Just sustainability** is the conjoining of environmental and social justice movements around the promotion of environmentally sustainable and socially equitable forms of urban development.

tions in a coalition opposed to the merger. This example of just sustainability connects environmental sustainability to the struggle for social justice in the city. Nevertheless, Krueger and Savage (2007: 221) caution us that "the sustainable development discourse does have a progressive potential but if we are interested in grappling with issues of economy, social justice, and environment the analytical entry point must extend beyond *environmental* sustainability to engage concepts of economic development and social justice."

While environmental problems still feature prominently in conflicts around the urban living place, the right of appropriation also draws our attention to the daily struggle on the part of urban residents for access to shelter, food, nutrition, health, and livelihoods. For many city dwellers in the global South, this often means confronting problems like sanitation, water shortages, flooding, disease, and insect menace on a daily basis. Studies suggest that these problems are experienced as especially threatening for the poor and low income households (Table 12.1). In cities like Bangalore in India or Accra in Ghana, richer neighborhoods – especially areas where there is a strong presence of foreign residents – may be well served by basic infrastructure and health services whereas poorer districts populated by migrants from the countryside or low-skilled factory workers have inadequate services and frequently experience problems such as power cuts. Struggles for environmental and social justice in such places are fought around issues that are experienced as immediate and health threatening, affecting livelihood strategies on the part of the urban poor.

Concerns about basic necessities also top the agenda of grassroots environment and social movements in cities in the global North. Food security has become a serious issue for many residents of cities in Europe and North America. There are two issues here: first, there is increasing concern on the part of environmental activists about the over-reliance of urban consumers on food that is globally sourced rather than locally produced; and,

Table 12.1 Environmental problems identified by householders in lower income neighborhoods in Chittagong City, Bangladesh.

Household environmental problems identified	Rank	% of mentions by those surveyed
Water shortage	1	84.4
Electricity crisis	2	82.8
Mosquito menace	3	46.7
Poor ventilation	4	30.0
Overcrowding and indoor air pollution	5	25.0
Poor sanitation, damp housing and insect menace	6	11.0

Source: adapted from Table 1 in Rahman *et al.* (2010). Used with permission of Sage Publications.

Community food security describes a situation when all residents are able to obtain safe, personally acceptable (in terms of religious or dietary restrictions, for example), nutritious food through a food system that is sustainable, maximizes healthy choices, community self-reliance, and equal access.

Right to food. A right defined by international organizations and claimed by food and poverty activists in both international and urban contexts. It has many aspects, including the expectations that governments must provide prisoners with food; in the urban context, the right to food generally refers to people's right to have equal access to enough nutritious and culturally appropriate food as they need to survive.

second, the increased cost of basic food products means that the food component of household budgets has increased, yet state support in the form of food subsidies and free meals for low income people, the elderly, or children has been reduced or cut back altogether. Consequently, the past decade or so has seen the growth of new urban-based social and environmental movements around the issues of **community food security** and **the right to food**. These movements argue that, first of all, having secure access to food is a human right and that not only should that food be acceptable and nutritious but that the provision of food should be equitable and promote self-reliance, rather than promoting dependence on charitable handouts (Hamm and Bellows, 2003; Riches, 2011; Purcell and Tyman, 2014).

One more formal approach to this issue involves local governments establishing Food Policy Councils, advisory bodies that identifies concerns with the municipal food system and provide policy recommendations to city staff and council (Mendes, 2008). For example, in 2008, an *Action Plan for Creating a Just and Sustainable Food System* was adopted by the city council in Vancouver, Canada, a city with a longstanding rhetorical commitment to sustainable urban development (http://vancouver.ca/people-programs/vancouvers-food-strategy.aspx). Examples of tangible outcomes from the Vancouver Food Policy Council include: an inventory of city-owned properties that may be available for community gardens or agriculture; rules mandating that city facilities purchase locally grown food; a commitment to creating a city composting program; and the implementation of programs linking regional farms to school cafeterias (http://www.vancouverfoodpolicycouncil.ca/what-is-food-policy).

The work of the Food Policy Council in Vancouver is set largely within a context of social movement activism around food in the city, which often addresses concerns that are beyond the mandate of the Council itself. One example is the work of the Downtown Eastside Neighbourhood House (DTES NH), which focuses on the right to food or "urban food justice" to link food access, democracy, citizenship and environmental justice in the low income neighborhood. Through its critique of charitable food provision and its efforts to reshape the neighborhood foodscape (Miewald and McCann, 2013), the DTES NH has developed a series of food-related interventions. Its Kitchen Tables Project (http://dteskitchentables.org) organizes community kitchens and provides healthy smoothies at various gathering spots in the neighborhood. It also works to engage in debate through its *Right to Food* zine (http://dtesnhouse.ca/?page_id=73#RTF) and the Right to Food Mobile Mural Project, which outlines its food philosophy, including the statement "Dignifying food = more food @ more places with no lineups [on the street, waiting for charitable food donations]." The organization's politics challenge the "commonly held myth that those living in poverty do not have nutritional knowledge or aspirations" by acknowledging "food to be a communicative instrument and hence [using] its offering as an instrument of community building" (Downtown Eastside Neighbourhood House, n.d.). In this way, resonances can be identified between struggles for survival in cities of the global North and the global South, where, in a place like Belo Horizonte, Brazil, for example, attempts to improve community food security have come to be known as global models (Box 12.1).

Box 12.1   Food Policy in Belo Horizonte, Brazil

Belo Horizonte is a city with a metropolitan population of five million people, the third-largest in Brazil. Since 1993, a municipal law has protected "the right of peoples to define their own food and agricultural policies" (Sustainable Food Cities, n.d.). Thus, the city has become a model of alternative policy making that has circulated globally (Chapter 4). As Rocha and Lessa (2009, 389) put it, "Belo Horizonte is a world pioneer in tackling food consumption, distribution and production as components of an integrated urban policy for food security leading to the development of an alternative food system – a goal which an increasing number of Food Policy Councils in North American cities have been promoting in recent years." They argue that, rather than a food system based on private market initiatives, the Belo Horizonte model's strength lies in the fact that it is a public, state initiative that coordinates private sector and civil society initiatives.

There are a number of concrete manifestations of the city's policy that have been successful locally while gaining wider notoriety. Perhaps most famous are its municipally owned and operated *Restaurantes Populares,* cafeterias that sell nutritious, balanced meals at very low cost (Figure 12.7). They operate on the basis of universal access, serving 12 000 people per day, ranging from low income families and students to homeless people and retirees. A typical, largely locally produced, lunch consists of "rice, beans, meat, vegetables, salad, and fruit (or juice)" (Rocha and Lessa, 2009: 391). Typical prices in 2014 for lunch were R$2.00 (about US$0.90), while breakfast is R$0.50 and dinner is R$1.00.

Two other programs address the retailing of groceries. The *Abastecer* program (or "ABC markets" – *AbasteCer*, which also refers to *Alimento a Baixo Custo*, meaning "low cost food") provides local produce retailers with opportunities to sell in the most popular markets if they sell a certain number of healthy products at low, fixed prices (20–50% below market prices). Through the "Straight from the Farm" (*Direto da Roça*) program, family farmers from the region surrounding Belo Horizonte are permitted to sell their produce in advantageous urban locations, often in association with ABC markets, thus reducing the cost of food for consumers by undercutting traditional retailers' mark-ups on food prices, helping to improve the economic circumstances of rural residents and dissuading migration to urban *favelas*, and also encouraging interactions between rural producers and urban consumers.

Figure 12.7   A restaurant popular in Belo Horizonte, Brazil. Photo courtesy of Felipe Magalhães.

These examples of subsidized food sales are set within a long history of urban activism in Brazil, which has made participatory democracy at the city and neighborhood scales a feature of Brazilian politics. They are also part of a much wider set of programs that are coordinated by a local state agency. These others include the public procurement of local food, school meals programs, food banks, job training in the food sector, programs to combat malnutrition among the very poor, nutritional education, and support for urban agriculture, including community and school gardens (World Future Council, 2013).

What the Belo Horizonte example shows is that, as Robinson (2006), Simone (2010), and Roy (2011a), among other postcolonial scholars argue, the global South often provides models that global North cities, like Vancouver, emulate, rather than only being the recipient of policies and theories developed in the global North (Chapters 2 and 4). Indeed, this model offers an alternative to hegemonic neoliberal models that tend to circulate globally because it is a government program, "less susceptible to cooptation or 'conventionalization' … given that it is based on collective decision making (through government) rather than individual behaviors (through consumer choices and producer decisions)." Yet, "[i]ts vulnerability lies on the vagaries of political changes in municipal administration through the electoral process, and the difficulties in constructing and maintaining true participatory governance" (Rocha and Lessa, 2009: 399). Indeed, recently, a political shift to the right in the city's municipal government and an attendant roll-out of more neoliberal policies is believed by activists to be threatening the beneficial aspects of the programs. Thus, like all alternative policies, economic models, and spaces, models like Belo Horizonte's require continual work by their supporters if they are to be spread to other places and also if they are to be defended in their original city.

The struggle for food security in cities like Vancouver and Belo Horizonte shows how environmental and social justice concerns are creating spaces for alternative urban politics. In the next section, we examine more closely at the evidence for the proliferation of alternative economic spaces in the city.

12.6 Circuits of Value and Alternative Urban Enterprises

So far we have thought about the variety of injustices and enclosures that proliferate in contemporary urban political space. Critical urban geographers have started to pay more attention to these processes, partly in response to the pervasiveness of urban entrepreneurialism. Likewise, we are now discovering that many economic enterprises found in the city do not feature in mainstream policy and academic discourse. Upon closer examination, cities are places where informal activities and alternative enterprises thrive and proliferate. Most of you will be familiar with street hawkers, buskers, panhandlers, and other signs of the informal urban economy. Although it is hard to quantify, informal enterprises can account for well over half of all basic transactions in the city. But there are many other enterprises that play a role in the formal urban economy yet do not easily fit into conventional economic categories. In that sense, alternative enterprises and the spaces they occupy are "hidden" from mainstream economic and political discourse. Typical examples of these alternative urban enterprises include local cooperatives, credit unions, complementary currencies, local exchange and trading systems, car boot and garage sales, online sales, recycling schemes, and suchlike. Such enterprises have a great variety of organizational structures; some depend upon paid or unpaid work; others involve market as well as nonmarket transactions; most operate outside global circuits of capital. As such, they are part of what is known as the diverse economy: a mixture of capitalist and noncapitalist, global and local enterprises (Gibson-Graham, 2006).

Critical urban geographers can play an important part in revealing the presence of alternative urban enterprises. This demands a grounded approach to the urban economy: looking at people whose everyday, relatively small individual economic transactions form a large portion collectively of the social and material substance of daily life in the city. Radical development geographers first contributed to our knowledge of the informal urban economy by examining the different circuits of value operating in cities in the global South. For example, Milton Santos (1977) identified two "circuits of capital" as follows: (i) the upper circuit of capital, which tends to be dominated by capitalists operating in international or national markets; and (ii) the lower circuit of capital, which is made up of labor-intensive small-scale enterprises such as traders, hawkers, small-scale services, and other independent business. While capitalists operating in the upper circuit are engaged in inter-urban transactions, enterprises in the lower circuit depend upon on intra-urban markets and social networks for the exchange and recycling of labor, goods and services. Therefore, in terms of employment and daily transactions, the lower circuit potentially covers a substantial fraction of the daily urban economy, yet it remains hidden from view (especially in terms of the attention it got from mainstream policy makers and economists).

Although the upper/lower circuit distinction is somewhat dated, seeing the urban economy as comprised of different **circuits of value** allows us to move beyond simple binaries like formal/informal or mainstream/alternative; it reveals how different urban enterprises

Circuits of value. When value in the form of money (M) and commodities (C) circulates through the urban economy, it does so via different circuits of value. Represented in its simplest form, a circuit of value is as follows: C–M–C. Some circuits are extensive and involve the recycling of previously exchanged commodities. In an alternative urban economy, the aim is to ensure that circuits of value benefit local enterprises rather than leak income out into the global economy.

and economic spaces interact with each other. The important point is that labor, commodities, and money flow into the urban economy through diverse circuits of value: therefore, we should not think of the city has having one dominant economic trajectory but rather as comprised of many different economic spaces and enterprises, some of which have the potential to be alternative in terms of their labor relations, systems of exchange, or mechanisms of redistribution.

Attempts have been made to identify some general features of alternative urban enterprises and their relationship to the mainstream economy (Fuller *et al.*, 2010). Some alternatives are variations of mainstream capitalist enterprise but, nevertheless, have a strong social or environmental ethic (i.e., "alternative capitalist" institutions). Others operate outside mainstream or global circuits of capital and allow urban residents to survive by exchanging goods and services without relying on the wider market economy. Yet still others operate in such a fashion as to preserve their local identity and autonomy; these actively seek to operate outside of, or in effect replace, the mainstream. Each of these possibilities can be further grouped into three categories: alternative-additional, alternative-substitute, and alternative-oppositional (Table 12.2).

First, additional-alternative enterprises function in the city by providing extra services and economic choices alongside mainstream capitalist enterprises. In the current financial context, this is becoming more significant in light of growing public distrust of mainstream urban economic institutions like banks. Many credit unions fall into this category because they operate under different rules to banks and building societies yet provide similar services like credit, interest, and loans that are seen as competitive and fairer. As a result, some urban activists and policy makers would like to give credit unions and other financial

Table 12.2 Key characteristics of alternative urban enterprises.

	Additional	Substitute	Oppositional
System of exchange	Market	Survival	Reciprocal
	Interest bearing	Gift	Social credit
	Complementary	Sharing	Communitarian
Type of labor	Wage	Cooperative	Nonwage
	Alternative wage	Socially necessary	Redistributive
Value	Price of labor	Needs driven	Labor time
	Exchange value	Alternative value	Use value
Political ideology	Competitive	Self-sufficient	Anti-capitalist
	Liberal	Utopian/Anarchist	Populist
Spatial scale	Global	Urban	Local-to-global

Source: adapted from Table 1 in Jonas (2013). Used with the permission of [transcript] Verlag.

cooperatives more powers and resources to compete with mainstream enterprises; yet this could compromise their ability to be alternative (Box 12.2).

Complementary currencies also fall into this category. These are alternative currencies set up in cities in towns to encourage residents to buy goods and services in local shops and

---

Box 12.2   Credit Unions as Contested Alternative Urban Enterprises in the United Kingdom

In countries like the United States, credit unions operate very much like conventional banks, providing urban residents facilities to save and borrow at low interest rates regardless of income or race. Not so in the United Kingdom: British credit unions have a low public profile and have been seen to serve only the urban poor and minority communities. This is because many credit unions were first established in those cities having significant immigrant (especially Afro-Caribbean) communities, such as London and Birmingham. Such community credit unions often drew their membership from low income housing estates and tended to be operated by volunteers based in youth centers and churches. Following financial deregulation in the 1980s and the resulting closure of local bank branches, activists sought to transform community credit unions into professionally operated financial cooperatives. The overall membership of British credit unions doubled between 1999 and 2009. By 2010, there were well over 500 active credit unions operating throughout Great Britain with total assets of GBP 674 million and 818 403 members (Jonas, 2013: 36).

Recent reforms have allowed British credit unions to draw their membership from a larger common bond area, which can encompass up to two million people and several urban localities. Credit unions now offer interest payments for savers at rates that compete with mainstream banks and building societies, prompting one British tabloid newspaper to headline as follows "Greedy banks beware: Credit unions are a fairer alternative" (Phillips, 2012; http://www.mirror.co.uk/money/personal-finance/ greedy-banks-beware-credit-unions-157988). Moreover, credit unions are viewed as less exploitative and more socially and politically legitimate urban enterprises than payday lenders and loan sharks. They have attracted the support of Justin Welby, the Archbishop of Canterbury and the head of the Church of England, who has been publicly critical of payday lenders (Welby, 2013; http://www.archbishopofcanterbury. org/articles.php/5083/payday-loans-archbishops-speech-in-the-house-of-lords).

However, critics argue that credit unions have been compromised in their role as social enterprises due to the current UK Coalition Government's Localism agenda, which relies on local social enterprises to deliver services that the state refuses to support. Moreover, there are growing concerns that the social ethic underpinning the cooperative movement in the United Kingdom (which includes credit unions) is being compromised by its links to mainstream financial institutions. Consequently, the British credit union movement remains divided between those who want to mainstream credit unions as part of the wider financial system and others who see credit unions as alternatives that can best serve the needs of the urban poor (for a lengthier discussion, see Jonas, 2013).

outlets rather than elsewhere. An example is the Lewes Pound, a local currency used by traders in a market town in the South of England (http://www.thelewespound.org). Advocates argue that complementary currencies prevent money from circulating at a wider scale as often happens with speculation on international currency markets; it means in principle that more money goes into supporting and sustaining the "real" urban economy.

Second, substitute-alternative enterprises are economic enterprises of last resort that allow people to survive in the city without necessarily having to rely on the exploitative practices of mainstream economic institutions. The development of these sorts of enterprises tends to be spontaneous, often motivated by a desire to survive, get by, or be self-sufficient. Many experiments in utopian living in the city would fall into this category; however, more typically we are thinking about the informal urban economy in this context.

Finally, oppositional-alternative enterprises are deliberately created in order to challenge and replace mainstream economic enterprises. These sorts of economic alternatives embody radically different approaches to trade and exchange and try to measure and perform labor time in a nonexploitative fashion, such that there is some sort of equivalence in the quality and quantity of labor performed. Examples of this type of enterprise include: time banking, where urban residents can exchange equivalent hours of providing a service such as gardening, plumbing, or childcare; local exchange and trading systems, where one skill or services can be traded for another; and various anti-capitalist enterprises, where experiments in socialist or communal urban living are undertaken initially at the scale of the community or city but ultimately with a view to connecting up to wider social and political movements.

12.7   Summary and Conclusions

In this chapter we considered how the nature of urban political space is changing due to the intrusion of private property relations into public space, on the one hand, and the assertion of the right to the city by ordinary people, on the other hand. On a global scale, urban spaces have become powerful sites and symbols of public protest against neoliberal urban redevelopment and the authority of ruling elites. On a more local level, the gradual erosion of the public urban realm has resulted in microgeographies of enclosure, which create various social and environmental injustices and open up a space for an alternative urban politics. We have examined how ordinary people are reclaiming their right to the city and have offered examples of the diversity of alternative economic enterprises operating in the city today.

Critical urban geographers have made – and will continue to make – valuable and insightful contributions to knowledge of struggles for a more just society. So long as cities remain important public gathering places, then we need to understand how the process of gathering is changing as urban citizens exchange political ideas and information via new social networks and technologies. In this respect, recognizing the right to the city helps to liberate ordinary citizens from the traditional spatial constraints associated with modernism and the authority of the nation state. By looking at the role of new technologies of public participation (e.g., social networking and participatory GIS), critical urban geographers are also able to help develop a normative perspective on what role democracy can play in shaping a more progressive urban future. Both as students *and* critical urban geographers you, too, are well positioned to make important interventions into our understanding of the right to participation in the city.

12.8 Further Reading

- For examples of research on alternative urban politics, we suggest you consult recent issues of *Urban Geography, Antipode, Environment and Planning D: Society and Space,* and *International Journal of Urban and Regional Research.* The paper by Williams and Pendras (2013) nicely sets out many salient issues, written from a North American perspective. Rossi and Vanolo (2012) is an accessible text on neoliberalism and urban politics written from a global perspective.
- The classic reference for the right to the city is Lefebvre (1968), later republished in English (Lefebvre, 1996). Building on his prior work on capital accumulation and urban space, Harvey (2012) brings the story of the struggle for the right to the city up to the present day and the Occupy movement. On the new urban commons and housing policy in the United Kingdom, the paper by Hodkinson (2012) is helpful.
- Staeheli and Mitchell (2008) offer a sophisticated analysis of property relations and the erosion of the urban public realm. They provide a number of interesting examples of people's movements to claim back physical space in US cities, including struggles around community gardens in New York City.
- The urban political geographer Mark Purcell has written extensively on democracy in the city (see, for example, Purcell, 2008 and his blog http://pathtothepossible. wordpress.com).
- The classic analysis of social justice in the capitalist city is Harvey (1973/2010). Castells (1983) uses examples from cities around the world to examine grassroots urban social movements. On spatial justice in the city, Soja (2010) is well worth consulting.
- For a highly influential discussion of postcapitalist politics and alternative enterprises, see Gibson-Graham (2006). The edited collections by Leyshon *et al.* (2003) and Fuller *et al.* (2010) offer original case studies of alternative economic spaces.

Chapter 13

Urban Crises

Urban Geography: A Critical Introduction, First Edition. Andrew E.G. Jonas, Eugene McCann,
and Mary Thomas.
© 2015 Andrew E.G. Jonas, Eugene McCann, and Mary Thomas. Published 2015 by John Wiley & Sons, Ltd.

13.1   Introduction

A crisis is a time of trouble, of intense difficulty, of danger. The roots of the word crisis also connote a decisive point in time – a turning point; a time for making decisions. There are many examples of social, political, environmental, and economic trouble, difficulty, and turning points in this book. In fact, the theme of crisis resonates throughout much of the critical approach to urban geography. Critical urban geographers ask questions that emphasize the importance of paying attention to injustice and inequality, which results in a lot of attention to the *effects* of injustice and inequality – the trouble, difficulty, and danger that people must live with and endure every day. Highlighting struggle, exclusion, and suffering in critical research has an obvious political dimension, since critical urban geographers are not merely noting a certain situation here and there. Instead, they seek to show the *systematic* processes that result in the effects that they find; they seek to offer solutions or perspectives that work toward new possibilities; they seek to highlight the resistance efforts of people and cities in crisis in order not only to analyze but also to motivate change.

We turn to the ongoing quests for new urban futures and your role in shaping and exploring those futures in the next and final chapter of the book. Before you get there, however, in this chapter we emphasize how crisis manifests simultaneously in national and international political contexts, on the one hand, and in urban space, on the other hand. The goal of the chapter is to help you gain a further understanding of how cities fit within broad political–economic structures and movements – and how particular people suffer from, survive with, and react to the effects of these politics. We also cover urban crises in this, separate chapter to illustrate the incredible complexity that cities' diverse inhabitants face in dealing with crises as well as the role that urban spaces play in perpetuating crisis.

We tackle these goals by describing five examples of contemporary urban crises. Unfortunately, we could have chosen countless other examples, given the tremendous range of crises to choose from in the world, from global warming to war and to hunger. The five chosen will help you see the divergent range of urban-political processes and international contexts involved, so that the chapter can illustrate the difficulty in addressing urban crises given their historical and geographic depth and complexity. The five are: urban austerity, shrinking cities, political instability, incarceration, and the militarization of urban life.

In the first and second examples, we revisit the process of urbanization through the concepts of austerity urbanism and shrinking cities. **Austerity urbanism** describes austerity measures imposed on cities in the United States in the wake of the global financial crisis in 2007–2008 (Peck, 2012). The term **shrinking cities**, on the other hand, was first used in North America in the 1970s to describe the economic decline of the central city but later was also applied to industrial cities in Eastern Europe and the former Soviet Union that began to lose population and industrial activity following the collapse of communism and the breakup of the Soviet economic bloc in the late 1980s (Martinez-Fernandez *et al.*, 2012). Processes of austerity urbanism and

> **Austerity urbanism.** Urban authorities in many cities have been forced to cut back on essential services, lay off public sector employees, control spending, and reduce debt in order to satisfy current and future fiscal obligations and meet restrictions imposed by higher levels of government. Austerity is becoming a pervasive feature of the neoliberal urban condition today.

> **Shrinking cities.** Cities (or parts of cities) which have lost population and economic activity over a sustained period of time are known as shrinking cities. Examples include former industrial cities in North America (e.g., Detroit, Cleveland), Europe (e.g., Liverpool, Dresden, Trieste), and Russia (e.g., Ivanovo).

> ***Coup d'etat.*** This is a phrase in French which translates as "stroke of state" or "blow of state." It refers to the sudden overthrow of a government. A coup replaces the overthrown government with another. Militaries are often, but not always, involved in coups.

urban shrinkage often produce similar outcomes (e.g., contracting public services, poverty, unemployment, out-migration from the city, abandoned buildings as seen in Figure 13.1) and both concepts have been applied to cities, such as Detroit and Berlin, which have experienced a combination of economic decline, population outmigration, and fiscal austerity.

In the third example, we examine the case of Bangkok, Thailand, to think through the relationship between national political unrest and urban environments. Massive demonstrations in the city in recent years illustrate the swell of social and political movements demanding reform. Several military ***coups d'état*** in the past decade in Thailand illustrate the power of the military to dictate the terms

Figure 13.1   A vacant house after foreclosure. Vacant properties are endemic in shrinking cities. Photo by Mary Thomas.

and limits of democracy and to continue the dominance of Bangkok's elite and of their benefactors on national political contexts.

In the fourth example, we turn to the alarming 30-year trend in the United States to incarcerate more people than any other country in the world. In 2012, one in 35 adults was under the supervision of the US correctional system, which includes people on parole and probation, and those in jails or prisons (from county jail to state or federal prison). That is an astonishing 6 940 000 people – 2.9% of the total adult resident population (Glaze and Herberman, 2013). The spatial distribution of incarcerated people is overwhelmingly urban and highly racialized.

In the final example, we briefly examine the increasing militarization of urban life and its relation to carceral society. Military tactics have been transplanted from battlegrounds to cities globally, bringing surveillance and military-style policing to bear on many populations (Figures 13.2 and 13.3). The effects on everyday life are profound, yet, like other crises, they are unevenly experienced by different people and regions.

The following questions are ones you should be able to answer after reading this chapter:

- How does thinking about cities in terms of crisis help us understand their role in wider politics?
- To what extent has austerity urbanism been imposed on subnational levels of government by the state?

Figure 13.2 An Israeli military patrol in a Palestinian West Bank neighborhood in Hebron/al-Khalil. Photo courtesy of Lisa Bhungalia.

Figure 13.3   Israeli soldiers at a checkpoint in Hebron/al-Khalil question Palestinian youth. Photo courtesy of Lisa Bhungalia.

- What are some of the economic, social, and political consequences of urban shrinkage?
- How does national level political unrest unfold and manifest in city spaces, and how do urban citizens respond? What are the consequences of political unrest for urban development and quality of life?
- What is the spatial concentration of the US carceral society? What groups of people are most affected by carceral societies? What is the enduring effect of carceral society policing, imprisonment, and surveillance?
- What is the militarization of urban space? How has warfare affected urban life?

13.2   Global Financial Crisis and Austerity Urbanism

Burdened by more than US$14 billion in debt obligation and a shrinking tax revenue base, the city of Detroit filed for bankruptcy on 13 July 2013, becoming the largest US city ever to have been forced to undertake such drastic measures (Rushe, 2013). The specter of urban crises like Detroit's is a recurring feature of the landscape of urbanization in the United States. In the Great Depression of the 1930s, following the collapse of the Municipal Bond Market in 1931, the credit ratings of the 20 largest cities in America, including Detroit's, were drastically downgraded. Within a matter of two years, the effects the 1929 Wall Street crash had filtered down to the level of municipal government, contributing to widespread unemployment, homelessness, poverty, and social despair in America's major cities. Not

Figure 13.4 An abandoned house in Detroit, MI. Since 1950, the City of Detroit has lost well over a million residents, making it an extreme example of urban shrinkage. According to the Detroit Blight Removal Task Force (2014), by May of 2014, 30% of Detroit's land parcels were vacant and 90% of publicly held land parcels were blighted. Photo courtesy of Stephen Hall.

until the 1950s and 1960s would fiscally stressed cities such as Detroit fully recover from the trauma of the Great Depression, and only then as the result of an unprecedented scale of state intervention in the form of federal public works programs and housing policies. Arguably for the first time in its history, the US state realized that the future of the nation depended on securing the economic stability of its cities.

The years following World War II were a period of relative economic prosperity largely built on the backs of suburbanization and urban renewal. Yet, at the same time, poverty was severe for many Americans, especially racial minorities, rural populations, and the elderly. Moreover, the rise of the suburb and the consolidation of white wealth in segregated cities meant the neglect of the poor inhabitants and neighborhoods.

By the 1960s, growing domestic tensions around Civil Rights and US intervention in Vietnam brought discontent into the streets. Detroit was one of many cities at the forefront of urban social and political upheavals during this time. Following the "race riots" of the summer of 1967, nearly a million Detroit residents (mainly white middle class households) relocated to the suburbs. Detroit never fully recovered from this mass exodus. Having peaked at two million residents in 1950, Detroit's population today stands at around 700 000 (Figure 13.4). Arguably, no city is more in need of public assistance than Detroit, yet federal and state officials argue that austerity measures are necessary to restore investor confidence in the city. But austerity urbanism and shrinkage are not just happening in Detroit; they have become global phenomena affecting numerous urban places, both large and small.

In the United States during the 1960s and 1970s, the urban crisis assumed a particular spatial form as investment and population left the central cities for the suburbs. Whereas the central cities were represented in official discourse as places of poverty, blight, crime, racial unrest, and economic decline, the suburbs were portrayed as dynamic, prosperous, safe, and attractive to investment and the white middle classes (Chapters 5 and 8; Beauregard, 2003). It was hardly a big surprise when New York City went bust in 1975 (and not for the first time in its history). When the New York City government asked for a federal bailout, a headline appeared in the New York-based paper, *The Daily News*, on October 30, 1975, which reported that US President Gerald Ford allegedly told the city to "drop dead." While President Ford apparently never made this comment, the headline nonetheless marked a significant moment in how the US state has responded to urban crisis, namely, the transition to austerity urbanism.

Austerity urbanism is an active process undertaken by the neoliberal state to downsize the public sector and cut back on welfare and other services as a prelude for restoring suitable conditions for private sector reinvestment in the city (Peck, 2012). By declaring an urban fiscal crisis, economic and political elites contrive to reassert their power over the urban political arena through measures such as the privatization of public services, the selling of state assets, asserting the financial discipline of debt, and enforcing austerity. Such measures, in turn, weaken the poor (especially children), minorities, migrants, the powerless, and those dependent on services in the city. Austerity urbanism represents a distinctive phase in capitalism in which the responsibility and costs of economic crisis and state failure are "pushed" down the state and governance hierarchy onto ordinary citizens and the spaces of urban government. As Jamie Peck (2014: 20) argues:

> Austerity politics are "push" politics in at least two senses of the word. First, and fundamentally, they involve pushing the costs, risks and burdens of economic failure onto subordinate classes, social groups and branches of government. Austerity, in this respect is concerned with social, spatial and scalar strategies of *redistribution*; it is about making "others" pay. Second, and clearly essential to the accomplishment of this ideological feat, the case for austerity must be discursively pushed, since its necessitarian appeal is far from self-evident, even if the language of "belt-tightening" and "living within our means" does appeal to a certain utilitarian commonsense. Austerity, in this respect, entails a concerted *renarration* of the financial crisis in the form of new homilies of (local) state failure, in the service of this effort to redistribute … both the costs of and the responsibility for the crisis.

What makes the current regime of neoliberal urban austerity especially insidious is that it is filtering into all reaches of urban life and also into parts of the metropolis that were assumed to be immune to fiscal problems. If the urban crisis of the 1960s and 1970s reflected a growing fiscal discrepancy between the central city and the suburbs – what became known as the metropolitan fiscal disparity problem (Cox, 1973) – today's austerity urbanism has spread beyond the jurisdictional limits of the city to the suburbs and the edge cities.

The global financial crisis of 2007–2008 has produced a new urban form known as the **subprime city** (Albers, 2012). To help you understand this connection between austerity urbanism and the subprime city, we can briefly revisit the workings of finance capital in the urban land market. You might remember from our earlier discussions (in Chapters 2, 3, and 8) that gentrification arises from efforts to close the rent gap in parts of the inner city that have experienced disinvestment and loss of population. In certain neighborhoods undergoing disinvestment, residential properties can undergo devaluation to the point where it becomes

Subprime city. Urban places at the forefront of the recent financial crisis and having high mortgage foreclosure rates are known as subprime cities. Examples of subprime cities can be found in both growing and declining urban regions of the United States and Europe.

profitable for finance capital and real estate to reinvest in those neighborhoods. In a similar way, banks and other lenders in the 1990s realized that there was an opportunity to make money in "high risk" urban housing markets, that is, residential areas hitherto avoided by mainstream banks and other financial institutions. Sometimes these were the same inner city neighborhoods that had previously been denied access to mortgage finance because of historical practices of redlining and racial discrimination (Chapter 3). In other cases, they were parts of inner suburbs starting to attract low income households, minorities, and first-time homebuyers. By charging higher rates of interest than those of conventional loans, subprime mortgage lenders saw an opportunity to profit (Figure 13.5).

Figure 13.5 A retail lender offers cash loans against car titles as collateral. The subprime lending market for automobile sales is booming in the United States. The housing mortgage market now has new restrictions on risky lending, but auto loans are not covered by the same regulations. Photo: Mary Thomas.

In the 1990s and 2000s, lenders bundled together subprime mortgages into new financial vehicles in order to squeeze extra liquidity out of capital invested in the built environment (Gotham, 2012). Given a political climate in the United States that supported financial deregulation, subprime lending was sanctioned by financial regulators and federal authorities. It produced rampant speculation in global financial markets. The resulting financial crisis of 2007–2008 led to the collapse of major financial institutions, banks, and investment houses based in New York and London. Squeezed by high interest payments and declining income, thousands of homeowners across the United States struggled to make mortgage payments and were forced to foreclose.

Subprime cities are urban places which are at the forefront of austerity measures imposed since the financial crisis. The subprime mortgage crisis put municipal finances in a "double jeopardy" because it devastated the property-tax base of cities and increased costs of municipal borrowing (Hall and Jonas, 2014). For example, between 2008 and 2011, mortgage default rates in the Detroit Metropolitan area, which includes Wayne, Macomb, and Oakland counties, averaged roughly 1 in every 39 households (as compared to the United States average of some 1 in 45 houses). Over this same period, net annual property tax receipts for municipalities throughout Metro Detroit declined by as much as 25% (Hall and Jonas, 2014).

It is not just big cities like Detroit that are in the frontline of austerity urbanism. Research by urban scholars reveals that smaller cities and suburbs in fast-growing areas of the Sunbelt, such as Florida and Southern California, face an uncertain future of fiscal stress and possible bankruptcy (Davidson and Ward, 2014). Around the world, city authorities have turned to increasingly complicated private financing arrangements in order to leverage capital and fund basic services and infrastructure (Torrance, 2009). While these new urban financing arrangements offer banks and other lenders the promise of a profitable rate of return over the medium-to-long term, they also expose urban authorities to future volatility in financial markets and political risks.

In Chapter 3, you were introduced to the idea that the global expansion of capitalism intensified processes of regional urbanization. According to some urban geographers, the future of capitalism is being fashioned around mega-urban regions, which attract growth in the form of finance, high technology, and creative industries. However, Detroit's predicament points to another, and arguably more poignant, story about urban development. Following decades of economic decline, racial segregation, and public austerity, Detroit has been turned into a poster-child of urban shrinkage, a term which is used to describe how former industrial cities can undergo an irreversible contraction of economic activity and loss of population. It appears that the same processes of capital accumulation and global expansion that generate urban growth in some parts of the world can cause profound urban economic decline and population outmigration in others. These seemingly different urban development trajectories need to be treated with equal measure because they speak to divergent urban futures and political possibilities.

13.3   Shrinking Cities

By 2030, nearly five billion people will live in cities. However, urbanization is not occurring at the same pace everywhere. While some urban geographers continue to highlight the growth of mega-urban regions in some parts of the world, in many others there are places that are not participating in these growth trends. Indeed, in countries like Germany, the United Kingdom, France, Russia, the United States, Syria (Box 13.1), and Romania, there are numerous examples of cities where the population has been shrinking, a trend which began several decades ago but seems to have become a more pervasive feature of urbanization in recent years. It has been estimated that there are well over 500 examples of shrinking cities around the world (Rieniets and Oswalt, n.d.). While many of these cities are found in the former industrial heartlands of Europe, Asia, and North America, there are also examples from countries where the national urban population is still growing, such as China, South Africa, Mexico, and Chile.

The idea that cities could shrink first appeared in studies of urban decline in North America in the 1970s, and later the concept of shrinking cities was used to describe the fate of former industrial centers in Europe (Weaver, 1977; Häußermann and Siebel, 1988; Oswalt, 2006; cited in Martinez-Fernandez *et al.*, 2012). Urban shrinkage represents a serious challenge to the idea that urban growth can be sustained through creative innovation and new rounds of investment. Instead, economic restructuring and deindustrialization can combine with demographic trends, such as outmigration and declining rates of natural increase, to induce long-term processes of structural urban decline. Rather than restructuring around new economic activities, cities can experience drastic outflows of capital investment, declining revenues, and loss of population. In some extreme cases, such as Detroit, land use

Box 13.1   War and Shrinking Cities

War and domestic conflict can wreak massive destruction on urban physical infrastructures and the built environment. Cities undergo rapid depopulation as residents look for refuge in other areas not affected by conflict. In Syria, where civil war grew from anti-government protests in 2011, 6.5 million people were in need of humanitarian assistance by mid-2013. That number represents almost one-third of the entire population of the country. Over two million people fled to neighboring countries like Turkey, Lebanon, Iraq, and Jordan, and the rest are displaced within other parts of Syria. According to the United Nations High Commission of Refugees (UNHCR), the bulk of these refugees reside in Lebanon. Lebanon's population is under five million people, so the massive influx of refugees threatens its own political, economic, and social stability.

Homs, Syria, has been the center of the rebellion against the Syrian government. The city has been a center battleground between the Syrian national authorities and rebel groups. Ruined buildings, empty streets, burnt out vehicles, and damaged infrastructure vividly convey the impacts of war on the city; urban existence has become at best precarious for the ordinary residents of Homs, and in the Old City's section, there are very few people left. Early in 2014, a three-day ceasefire was negotiated in order to allow women, children, and older men who remain trapped in certain areas of Homs to leave. Back under governmental control, with the rebels forced out after almost two years of shelling, bombing, and street warfare, up to one-third of Homs' population remains displaced in Syria and neighboring countries (Barnard, 2014).

Place annihilation. A term used to describe the total physical destruction of cities for strategic military purposes. Often it involved bombing cities with a view not just to inflicting physical damage on buildings and urban infrastructure but also destroying the social fabric and morale of the urban population.

arrangements revert to a kind of pre-industrial urban form. Abandoned buildings, rusting infrastructure, and once thriving residential districts have been taken over by weeds, grass, trees, gardens, and cultivated agriculture.

War is an obvious cause of shrinking cities, as seen in Box 13.1. The geographer Kenneth Hewitt (1983) once used the phrase **place annihilation** to describe the wholesale destruction of cities in Europe and Japan in bombing raids undertaken by Allied and German forces during World War II. If place annihilation is a strategic military objective in which the aim is to eviscerate all traces of a city, including its inhabitants, communities, and memories, urban shrinkage today is a more insidious process that eventually leads to similar outcomes, including the destruction of the social and physical fabric of the city, population outmigration, and the loss of urban livelihoods.

The effects of shrinkage on urban identity and memory

For a number of critical urban scholars, Berlin, Germany, has become an important laboratory for investigating the contradictory dynamics of urban development and shrinkage during a dramatic period of transformation. The re-unification of East and West Germany in 1990 initially offered Berlin the prospect of economic revival with its transformation into a "global city" capable of attracting international firms and the "national capital" of the reunited Germany (Cochrane and Jonas, 1999). As the Berlin Wall was torn down, new investment indeed flowed to major redevelopment projects in the city center, such as Potsdamer Platz and the outer suburbs. However, other districts in what had been East Berlin began to exhibit signs of shrinkage as people left for other areas in Berlin or the rest of Germany. Despite efforts to attract investment, Berlin's economy has oscillated between boom and bust, prompting Stefan Krätke (2004) to characterize it as a case of "worst practice" urban governance.

Alexa Färber (2014) argues that Berlin's political and financial elites have played on the themes of urban crisis and attractiveness to re-imagine the city in ways that make urban shrinkage as much a blessing as a curse (at least in terms of fostering urban regeneration). For example, much has been made of Berlin's bohemian culture, which is based upon a vibrant techno-music scene, art, architecture, high technology, and the creative industries. When combined with a surplus of vacant properties and abandoned historical sites, Berlin's creative economy has afforded opportunities for new forms of urban economic development and even a new economic identity for the city. As far as the management of simultaneous processes of urban shrinkage and economic development is concerned, Berlin should be viewed not as an exceptional case, but instead as "one of the quintessential cities in Europe" (Färber, 2014: 123).

Like other cities, Berlin's answer to shrinkage has been to make a virtue out of the situation. For instance, in 2004 the issues and challenges of urban shrinkage were aired at a public exhibition on Shrinking Cities, which was held at the Berlin Institute for

Contemporary Art. The exhibition featured the work of artists, architects, film makers, graphic designers, journalists, and scholars. Following Berlin's lead, urban scholars, photographers, and creative artists in other cities have likewise tried to capitalize on the cultural and symbolic landscapes of urban shrinkage, using ruined cities as backdrops for the depiction of life – both real and imagined – in the twenty-first century city. It has spawned some innovative work on how the contemporary urban experience is documented and re-imagined through film, photography, popular media, computer games, and the Internet.

Critical urban geographers study specific sites in the city that evoke memories of past urban lives and landscapes or offer insights into wider geographical imaginaries (e.g., nationalism, imperialism, social movements, etc.). In her powerfully evocative monograph on the making of the New Berlin after the collapse of state socialism in Eastern Europe, Karen Till (2005) draws upon critical feminist and humanistic traditions in urban geography to explore contemporary sites, locations, and landscapes of urban memory (see Chapter 11, too). Her specific focus is on developing geographically sensitive ethnographies of Jewish sites of memorialization, including the Holocaust Memorial (Figure 13.6) and the concentration camp at Sachsenhausen. These sites today evoke conflicting memories and

Figure 13.6 The Memorial to the Murdered Jews of Europe, also known as the Holocaust Memorial, in Berlin. Since the collapse of state socialism in Eastern Europe and the re-unification of Germany, Berlin has become an important laboratory for critically investigating urban development, shrinkage, and memory. Designed by architect Peter Eisenman and engineer Buro Happold. Source: Used by permission of the Foundation Memorial to the Murdered Jews of Europe. Photo courtesy of Pauline Deutz.

emotions; for Germans in particular, they generate feelings of national guilt and repentance alike. Till argues that the New Berlin has become a place where past urban landscapes might have been eviscerated by war, disinvestment, and forced depopulation but whose memories are being repackaged and commodified as tourist attractions.

13.4   National Political Unrest

National political unrest usually unfolds on the streets of cities – such as Homs, Syria (Box 13.1). While the rebels in Homs were forced from their stronghold city by the government forces of the Syrian Army, other urban-based protests have toppled national governments. Consider the millions of people who demonstrated and fought in Cairo to bring down the Egyptian government in 2011, for example. The military backed the protestors and forced the outing of the president, Hosni Mubarak, only to force the outing of his democratically elected successor in 2014 (Chapter 12). Urban protests can thus be squelched by powerful national governments and militaries, and there are all too many cases to illustrate this argument, like China with the example of Tiananmen Square in 1989 (Chapter 11).

On the other hand, city-based social and Civil Rights movements can call for drastic national change in attitude and legal structures, as with the case of the Civil Rights movement of the 1950s and 1960s in the United States. Lunch counter sit-ins, bus terminal occupations, and horrible city police responses to peaceful marches in dozens of small, segregated cities like Greensboro, NC, Nashville, TN, Richmond, VA, and Birmingham, AL, provoked national outrage and a shift in national sentiment on race relations in the United States. Federal courts and the National Guard (the reserve forces of the US Armed Forces, i.e., the military) played important roles in forcing an end to daily racial segregation across the US.

National-scale urban protest can also be unorganized and seek no clear outcome. In England in the summer of 2011, urban riots around the country began when people (mostly young men) took to the streets to protest the police killing of an unarmed Black man, Mark Duggan, in North London. The event sparked riots in at least a dozen cities across the nation for almost a week. The rioting was unplanned, unorganized, and lacked any sort of demand on part of the rioters. Urban scholars have suggested that the rioting can be sourced to the disillusionment that urban poor and minority youth, mostly men, have with the growing social and income inequality of England (Till, 2013: 74).

Bangkok, Thailand

In the rest of this section, we consider one ongoing case of national unrest in recent years: Thailand. Bangkok, its capital and by far the largest city in the country, in recent years has been the site of massive demonstrations and the forced removal of democratically elected officials by the national military. Bangkok is one of the world's **primate cities**, defined as a city that houses a disproportionate percentage of a nation's population, with at least twice the population as the next biggest city in a country. In Thailand, in part due to this condition of primacy – a condition that results in wide disparities in income and influence over national space – struggles over control of the country's government often center on the relation between Bangkok's ruling elites and less-urban and rural areas, and on wide disparities in income over national space.

The political unrest has led to economic instability as the effects of the demonstrations have strangled the city, as when demonstrators occupied Bangkok's two airports for over a week in late 2008.

Primate cities. A primate city is one that houses a disproportionate percentage of a nation's population. Primacy is a characteristic of a city that has at least twice the population of the next biggest city in a country.

The newer airport of the two, Suvarnabhumi international airport, serves as an important symbol of Bangkok's desire to gain global city status, and it is a vital hub of economic integration into global capitalism and international tourism for Thailand. In fact, the centrality of Bangkok to Thailand's national political-economic development and stability is an important aspect of the national unrest unfolding in the city. This is due to the city's dominance on national economic and political governance.

Primacy is a condition of urbanization in a country when the largest city is vastly larger than the second ranked city by population in the country; the oversized dominance of a primate city comes to have national and international ramifications. Primacy is not restricted to the **global South** or developing countries, since Paris and London are both primate cities. Paris and London both dominate their countries' economies and represent a center of political power and wealth for France and the United Kingdom. Both were, not incidentally, imperial capitals, drawing vast amounts of resources from their colonies to themselves, which in effect allowed them to consolidate urban power during their imperial reign. That power and wealth continued to grow even after colonialism lessened (both France and the United Kingdom still have colonial holdings, of course), since the wealth and capital that had accumulated over centuries allowed these cities to develop even more.

Despite the examples of Paris and London, primacy is more prevalent in the developing world. Bangkok, Thailand, is one such primate city (Glassman, 2010). It has 18 times the population of the next largest Thai city, Nonthaburi, and though it has only 14% of the country's total population, Bangkok is responsible for almost half of Thailand's gross domestic product. There is a high concentration of wealth in the city, too, which is not equally distributed. That concentration of wealth also skews economic development in Thailand toward itself, so that development flows to virtually only one city in the whole country. Bangkok's primacy also means that the city has a disproportionate share in services and benefits, including half of all physicians in the country, the majority of banking and insurance services, and most universities in the country. It also has terrible pollution, traffic congestion, and gross disparities in income. It is home to the central Thai government and its many bureaucracies, elites, the political parties, and the military.

Political unrest in Thailand plays out largely in the city streets of Bangkok (Figure 13.7). Protestors from around the country go to Bangkok to object to the city's outsized power in Thailand and of two *coups d'état* by the Royal Thai Army that came about largely for the benefit of Bangkok's urban elite. The first of the two recent coups, in 2006, deposed the democratically elected Thaksin Shinawatra whose basis of support was in the northern regions of Thailand, distant from Bangkok. Supporters of Thaksin (both rural and urban poor) formed the Red Shirts in support of his programs to address poverty and bring development to all of Thailand. The scholar Chairat Charoensin-o-larn (2013) argues that the improvement of the rural masses and urban poor under Thaksin provoked the ire of Bangkok's better off, who feel "that their security and standard of living have been gradually

Figure 13.7   "Red Shirt" protest at Ratchaprasong intersection, Bangkok, Thailand. The red shirts organized mass rallies across Thailand to mark the ousting of former Thai prime minister Thaksin by a military coup four years ago, and to commemorate the final day of the military crackdown on their protests four months ago. This gathering was at Ratchaprasong intersection, an area in downtown Bangkok that was occupied by the red shirts between 3 April 2010 and 19 May 2010, the day that the Thai military violently ended the protests and on which day the protesters set fire to many buildings across Thailand including CentralWorld in Bangkok, the largest shopping mall of Southeast Asia, here to the left of the photo. Source: Takeaway, via Wikimedia Commons, Attribution-ShareAlike 3.0 Unported (CC BY-SA 3.0)

declining" (Charoensin-o-larn, 2013: 203). The Yellow Shirt People's Alliance for Democracy supported the 2006 coup and the quelling of large Red Shirt protests in Bangkok, while the Red Shirt movement demands the end of the urban Bangkok bias.

Jim Glassman writes that "Bangkok is crucial to political outcomes not only because it is the center of political and economic power, but also because it is the center of media production" (Glassman, 2010: 1312), and the city's media controllers were decidedly anti-Thaksin. This is important because, according to Glassman, images of Red versus Yellow on international media "helped spare the coup leaders serious condemnation in international circles, given that few international observers could readily discern the deeper political conflicts underlying the street demonstrations" (Glassman, 2010: 1316). Thus, the military coup against a democratically elected official was interpreted as a popular coup internationally, with no resulting pressure to call for Thaksin's reinstatement. (That the Thai military – the coup's force – was supportive of the United States' post-9/11 counter terrorism military presence in Southeast Asia is no mere accident, either.) Bangkok's elite utilized "their disproportionate political power and media exposure to overturn" the electoral victories of Thaksin and his supporters (Glassman, 2010: 1318).

In 2010, Red Shirt protestors flooded Bangkok, filling "all roads, rails, and rivers leading to Bangkok" (Chairat, 2013: 219). After a general election in 2011, the Pheu Thai Party formed a coalition government, a political party that the Red Shirts support and which sought to reform Bangkok's hold over national economic and political systems. At the head of the government was Yingluck Shinawatra, the sister of Thaksin. After six months of intense street protest and riots between pro- and anti-governmental factions, she was removed from office in May 2014 by Thailand's Constitutional Court, the third removal of a Shinawatran in six years. The successor of Ms. Yingluck, a so-called "caretaker" government head, was deposed by a military-backed coup just three weeks later.

The years of political unrest in Thailand – the military coups, the states of emergency, the occupation of ports and government – all have profound impact on the national and urban economy. The Thai stock market fluctuates widely, international investors threaten to pull out, tourists cancel reservations, and global manufacturers like Toyota consider a withdrawal from investment monies already promised due to the ongoing unrest and disruption (Wassener, 2014). The effects on Thailand's population are profound, and the question of whether the Bangkok urban elite will allow a national-scale democracy to develop remains an open one.

13.5   The Urban Carceral Society

The population of the United States is about 5% of the world's total, yet it holds an astonishing 25% of the global prisoner population. In 2011, 1 in 50 adults in the country was on probation or parole, and 1 in every 108 adults was incarcerated. Based on government data for the last 25 years of the twentieth century, all men in the United States face a 1 in 9 lifetime likelihood of imprisonment, yet for White men the chance is 1 in 17. The shocking racialization of incarceration in the United States means that Black men, based on these trends, face a lifetime likelihood of being imprisoned at a rate of 1 in 3; for Hispanic men, the threat is faced by 1 in 6. Many critical scholars now even refer to the United States as a **carceral society**, which means that prisons and policing affect many other realms and spaces of life (Figure 13.8).

> **Carceral society.** A phrase used to denote the spread of social control from the prison to society more generally. Carceral society is associated with surveillance, behavioral correction, and social control. It is also increasingly associated with the militarization of urban space.

More than half of the prison population in the United States is Black or Hispanic, even though combined they are less than one-third of the total population nationwide (National Research Council, 2014). The National Research Council (2014) reports that poor African–American urban communities are affected by incarceration at very steep rates, and specific neighborhoods marked by high levels of poverty and racial segregation are the sources of a great deal of the prisoner populations of US cities. When incarceration is geographically and racially concentrated, so are the effects of incarceration – on particular communities, families, and cities.

The characteristics of the millions of Americans involved in the justice system (court-involved, on parole or probation, in prison or jail) are thus easy to point out: the incarcerated populations in the United States are overwhelmingly racial minorities, male, and they are predominantly younger than 40 years old. Lesbian, gay, and transgender people also have disproportionate contact with the justice system (Spade, 2011; Stanley and Smith, 2011). And undocumented migrants, largely from Mexico and other Latin American countries, also face a high risk of apprehension, imprisonment, and deportation, with millions grabbed at home and work by local and federal police in the last decade alone (DHS, 2013).

Figure 13.8   Two bail bonds companies located directly across the street from the city and county courthouses in Columbus, OH. A bail is an amount of money set by a court of law that a prisoner must pay to be released before trial; the bail acts as a surety that the prisoner will show up for trial. A bail bond agent (often referred to as a bondsman) posts bail on behalf of the prisoner in exchange for a percentage of the total bail (usually 10–15%). Prisoners or their families or friends offer collateral on this money in the form of home or car titles, or they pay cash. Photo: Mary Thomas.

Keep in mind that immigration policing far and away does not hone in on criminals only and that "apprehensions" do not necessarily count as arrests; thus, the statistics on the US prisoner population do not count these additional *millions* of people caught up in the nation's wide justice system. These examples illustrate the ways that the carceral society targets people holding the least amount of privilege in American society.

While most people in prison and jail in the United States are male, the growth of the number of women prisoners has far outpaced men. Between 1980 and 2010, the number of women in prison increased by 646%, 1.5 times faster than for men (Sentencing Project, 2012). Black women in 2011 experienced incarceration at 2.5 times the rate as whites, although the rate of white women incarceration is climbing while for black women it is declining (Sentencing Project, 2012; this growth is largely accounted for by white women's rising drug usage). Drug offenses for women are higher than for men, and the majority of women are in prison for nonviolence offenses. The majority are also mothers, which begs the question of what happens to their children when they are locked up. The answer: relatives take most of the children, but an alarming number must be placed in foster care, where abuse, poverty, and instability are too-common tales (Beam, 2013).

How did the United States – the so-called "land of the free" – become the land with the most unfree? Scholars attribute changing national and political contexts for a shift in attitude toward crime and punishment. They call this shift a retributive turn in US penal policy, since reform of prisoners has been cast away to be replaced with punitive policies, including longer minimum sentences for a variety of offenses and **three strikes laws** that can place people in prison for minor crimes, sometimes for decades. Hundreds of laws passed in the 1980s and 1990s extended sentences for many offenses, with one federal law in 1994 *requiring* states to increase sentences for violent offenses if they wanted to access federal money to build prisons (National Research Council, 2014: 71).

Compounding these retributive shifts is the growth of the **prison-industrial complex** and for-profit prisons (Gilmore, 2007). The economic gains of the carceral

> **Three strikes laws.** In some US states three strikes laws mandate harsh sentences on repeat offenders, usually on their third conviction. The phrase comes from baseball, where three strikes are allowed at bat before the batter is out. Three strikes laws have increased prison populations in states where they are mandated because the lengthy sentences means prisoners spend much more time behind bars than before these laws were enacted.

> **Prison-industrial complex.** The use of the phrase prison-industrial complex draws attention to the ways that the US prison system is integrated with for-profit companies and corporations. Private companies therefore profit from incarceration, and prisons are capitalized through the process.

society are marked, with huge profits accruing to those companies that provide goods and services for prisons – all the food, uniforms, technology, construction, and so on needed to run the massive prison infrastructure – not to mention the salaries of guards, prison administrators, social workers, and police who maintain them (Figures 13.9 and 13.10). The growth in the prison-industrial complex did not overlap with rising crime, however. In fact, crime rates have *fallen* even as the rates of incarceration have increased, although the increase in the policing and criminalization of drug possession and sales has been primarily held up as a reason for growing prison populations (National Research Council, 2014). Thus, even as crime rates fall, policing increases means that more people are arrested. Rising incarceration rates reflect changing policing practices more than changing crime rates, in other words.

A wide range of policies and institutions contribute to the retributive turn in American "justice" systems (Gottschalk, 2006), but perhaps foremost to them all is the use of law and order topics by politicians for their own electoral purposes. Elected officials – and those wishing to be elected – have often used the fear of crime to their own benefit. Urban unrest in the 1960s, for instance, was broadcast on the evening news and along with it came "public" anxiety in the face of it. This was racially bifurcated, with the "unrest" reflecting unjust racial segregation and the blatant racism that we have illustrated through this book. Changing urban economies hit poor African–American populations harder than middle class, white Americans, given their precarious positions and poor housing choices (Chapters 3, 6, 7, and 8). Middle class white Americans vote in higher numbers than other groups, especially older people who respond to law and order messaging (Flamm, 2005).

Figure 13.9   A county Sheriff's bus transports prisoners to the Franklin County Corrections Center, Columbus, OH. Photo: Mary Thomas.

Figure 13.10   Urban prisons in the United States are usually near the courts complexes. Chances are, if you have been to an American city, you have driven or walked past one and not noticed it. They are typically unmarked or with only small signs to mask their purposes. However, the security cameras and blacked out, or nonexistent, windows give them away if you look closely. Photo: Mary Thomas.

Politicians often utilize the currents of racial and class-based fear to energize voters toward their own candidacy. Law and order politicians, once in office, champion the construction of prisons in their jurisdictions, even though the economic benefit of prison placement is not certain; often rural locations lose other and divergent economic opportunities once they build prisons (Gilmore, 2007). And as Anne Bonds argues, prison construction championed by white officials, in white towns, means that economic development projects "legitimate local geographies of racialized poverty, inequality, and dispossession" (Bonds, 2013: 1390).

Another outcome of prison placement in some states is prison gerrymandering, a process through which prisoners are counted by the Census Bureau as "local" inhabitants. The Prison Gerrymandering Project web site argues that this "creates significant problems for democracy [because it] leads to a dramatic distortion of representation at local and state levels, and creates an inaccurate picture of community populations for research and planning purposes" (http://www.prisonersofthecensus.org/impact.html). For example, small towns might have a prison with enough inmates to double their local population count, allowing them to have twice the representatives in the state legislature. Or perhaps federal funding for some local program is based on a population count, so more bodies counted means the place gets more funding. The irony with prison gerrymandering is that, in most states, people convicted of a felony offense lose their voting rights. Thus, the places where prisons are located benefit from prisoner population counts, while home communities lose both population counts and citizen-voters, thereby reducing their power to influence politics or garner resources.

The US carceral society disproportionately affects poor neighborhoods of color, and not solely for the obvious reasons that more people are removed from home to be placed in prison at distant locations. The concentration of policing in certain urban neighborhoods (Black and Hispanic neighborhoods with high concentrations of racial identity and poverty) means a decimation of young male populations; it also means that the everyday quality of life for young men of color is impacted negatively (Goffman, 2014). And released prisoners returning home find stark options facing them, including a lifetime ban on public housing with some convictions, a reduction in mental health and addiction services given urban austerity cutbacks in social programs, difficulty in finding employment given the gaps in their work experience and the stigma of "convict" in their lives, traumatic engagements with their children after time away from home, and more. White returnees are much less likely to face many of these challenges, as they tend to come from urban areas that are less disadvantaged and less marked by poverty, a high police presence, and overall lack of economic opportunity (National Research Council, 2014).

The carceral society away from prison

The "land of the free" is a carceral society in more ways than just the one reflecting the number of people arrested and in prison and jail, however. The phrase "carceral society" is one meant to convey the reach of the prison into broad facets of everyday life. Thus, the carceral society is one in which the state exerts control and surveillance in a number of ways, and in which people then begin to take on the role of policing themselves, both aimed at others and on their own bodies.

Examples of the carceral society include: the wide reach of video and audio surveillance in urban space; the ubiquitous presence of police in many city places like schools, shopping centers, public transportation, and parks; an intense social focus on behavior and normalization with middle class, white, heteronormative conformity highly valued and emphasized; the political processes whereby punishment rather than reform becomes pronounced; and, perhaps most importantly, the everyday ways people come to watch each other suspiciously as they assume a constant threat all around them from criminality.

The carceral society also extends its reach through so-called counter-terrorism activities in cities. In New York City, people are encouraged by the city, state, and federal governments to watch out for "suspicious activities," and suspicion has racial, ethnic and religious tones post-9/11. New York's Division of Homeland Security urges people to "look" for terrorism by knowing its signs. One of these is "suspicious persons out of place: this may include people who are in places they should not be, as well as people who do not fit in to the daily routine of your neighborhood or community" (DHSES, n.d.).

The carceral society is, unfortunately, not America's alone. It occurs in other countries, too, such as the United Kingdom, and has become entwined with counter-terrorism tactics post-9/11. Consider the example of the 2012 Summer Olympics in London, which occurred shortly after the 2011 riots. Stephen Graham (2012a) notes that security costs for the Games would exceed half-a-billion UK pounds. World War II was the last time Britain had so many soldiers on its soil, and during the Games more were placed in the United Kingdom than in Afghanistan at the same time (Graham, 2012a: 446). The security infrastructure in London lives after the Games, too, with security cameras running, paramilitary training remembered, and military machinery placed in local police permanently, from helicopters to drones (Graham, 2012a: 448). The profits to military and police contractors are immense, a cost borne by public funds in times of austerity.

13.6   Militarization of the City, Urbanization of the Military

In the United States and the United Kingdom, the carceral society and the militarization of everyday urban life are connected. Policing in American and British cities is very much informed by military technology and training, for instance, and the war on terror in these countries has affected religious and racial minorities disproportionately through the everyday surveillance and harassment of police. The ironic outcome of increased incarceration is the fact that the US military actively recruits in prisons. As Deborah Cowen and Amy Siciliano (2011) explain, there is a "cycling of bodies from incarceration to active duty" especially in the United States, where military recruiters visit prisons and juvenile detention facilities looking to sign up service men and women among those in confinement. Increased militarization feeds its own ranks.

Cowen and Siciliano connect the military and prisons together conceptually by arguing that the governing of each is tied to the need to absorb labor, thus expanding the reach of the prison-industrial complex:

> Prisons and policing expand to absorb populations made redundant by deindustrialization, changing regional and global patterns of uneven development, and the growth of high-tech and professional industries. ... Like urban penality, national militaries also have ... [the] means of managing the poor, and of warehousing reserve armies of labour. Today, the armed forces are ever more distinguished as state institutions that can provide economic security in a competitive global economy. (Cowen and Siciliano, 2011: 1517)

The militarization of urban populations occurs as the military seeks new recruits, but there is more to the story with this example. There is also the disintegration of the spatial separation between police and military. Thus, Cowen and Siciliano argue that the military no longer simply operates outside of a country and the police inside of it. Now, rather than being the exception to the norm, the military operate in domestic city spaces, policing is done by the military in foreign places after war is over or as part of warfare, and perhaps most importantly, "targeted policing" of specific areas can occur with military training, often perfected through lessons learned during wartime.

Stephen Graham (2012b: 137) provides further explanation for some of the key forms of the militarization of urban sites:

> Practices of militarization also invariably rely on the normalization of military paradigms of thought, action and policy; (attempts at) the aggressive disciplining of bodies, places and identities seen not to befit the often masculinized notions of nation, citizenship or body (and the connections between them); and the deployment of wide ranges of propagandist material which romanticizes or sanitizes violence as a means of righteous revenge or achieving some God-given purpose. Above all, militarization and war involve attempts to forge powerful new links between cultures, states, technologies and citizenship.

Figure 13.11   Nablus, West Bank, Palestine. Photo courtesy of Lisa Bhungalia.

Box 13.2　Palestine and Urban Occupation: The Case of Gaza

Cities have always been battlegrounds. Now, according to Eyal Weizman, "The city [is] not just the site, but the very medium of warfare" (Weizman, 2006, also cited in Graham, 2012b: 151). Weizman recounts an Israeli attack in the city of Nablus in 2002 (Figure 13.11) in which soldiers "used none of the city's streets, roads, alleys or courtyards, or any of the external doors, internal stairwells and windows, but moved horizontally through walls and vertically through holes blasted in ceilings and floors" (Weizman, 2006). He claims that the Israeli Defense Forces conceptualize the city as "a flexible, almost liquid medium" (Weizman, 2006). Of course, the "liquid medium" is a lived environment, and those walls that are blasted away include many civilian homes. Weizman writes, "Civilians in Palestine, as in Iraq, have experienced the unexpected penetration of war into the private domain of the home as the most profound form of trauma and humiliation."

Perhaps this has been nowhere felt more in Palestine than in Gaza (Figure 13.12). In late 2008/early 2009, responding to rocket fire originating in Gaza and aimed at southern Israel (which injured scores but killed few), Israel attacked Gaza for 22 days. When it was finished, 1400 Palestinians were dead and 15 000 buildings were destroyed. That represents 15% of all buildings in Gaza (Weizman, 2010: 11), including hundreds of schools. An Israeli blockade of Gaza has resulted in 90% of its residents being sustained by humanitarian aid in the subsequent years, with strict controls by Israel on the number of calories and kilowatts of electrical power per resident let into the territory (Bhungalia, 2012).

Political geographer Lisa Bhungalia reports that the three-week attack indiscriminately targeted civilians and combatants, and Israeli soldiers described firing on crowds and "clearing" households by killing everyone inside, including children (Bhungalia, 2012: 269). An Israeli blockade prevented people from fleeing Gaza, effectively perpetuating death and suffering, such that, she writes, "Death in this instance was not a peripheral or secondary consequence in pursuit of some other aim" (Bhungalia, 2012: 269). Death *was* the aim.

The military state – and the lessons learned through war – came to live at home in the new militarized city. War never ends, therefore, as military logistics and infrastructure are re-placed in domestic cities. In one example, Graham describes how the US military brought tactics from Baghdad, Iraq, to New York and other cities to implant "security zones" in sites of immense economic and political importance to the nations (Graham, 2012b: 140). He argues that "these blurring processes thus sustain the imagination of all cities everywhere as key battle spaces requiring permanent targeting and mobilization within limitless imaginations of war" (Graham, 2012b: 140). From the visual images of war that are hyper-consumed through media and gaming, to the ever-present surveillance tactics of the digital city, even in peace the militarization of urban space saturates our worlds (Box 13.2, Figures 13.11 and 13.12).

Figure 13.12   Road barriers in the West Bank of Palestine are common, especially in troubled times. Roadblocks are often made by the Israeli army and are meant to restrict Palestinian mobility around the region and channel their traffic through Israeli military checkpoints. Photo courtesy of Lisa Bhungalia.

13.7   Summary and Conclusions

In this chapter we examined five examples of urban crisis in order to illustrate the ways that national and international political and economic contexts affect urban lives and liveability in cities around the world. Critical urban geographers investigate crisis in order to show that difficult situations require complex analysis. Understanding why houses stand vacant, for example, requires a view on global political economic processes of lending and austerity. Shrinking cities reflect not just changes in population dynamics but indicate structural economic and social processes beyond the flow of people out of cities. National political unrest often comes down to particular urban conflicts, or contestations over political power held by an urban elite, as is the case in Thailand. Understanding why so many African–American men are in prison requires an analysis of national law and order politics and how those politics play out in racialized formations. The ubiquity of the carceral society unfolds in the militarization of urban spaces, and militaries have a powerful presence in most of the world's cities today.

Finding the answers to questions about how and why urban inequality and injustice occur throughout the world demand our close attention to complexity and context. Finding answers also requires careful scholarship and political commitments that strive toward alternative futures. In the final chapter, we urge you to continue to think about critical urban geography in your own future and to carry your interest in critical scholarship to political endeavors.

13.8   Further Reading

- A very useful edited collection of papers on shrinking cities was published in 2012 in a special issue of the *International Journal of Urban and Regional Research*, **36**(2). The introduction by Martinez-Fernandez *et al.* (2012) has a very good summary and assessment of the literature. Two websites are worth exploring on shrinking cities, including the European Union Cluster (http://www.cluster.eu/shrinking-citiescitta-che-si-spopolono) and Shrinking Cities Project, Federal Cultural Foundation, Germany (http://www.shrinkingcities.com/detroit.0.html?&L=1).
- The theme of urban austerity is featured in the first issue of the *Cambridge Journal of Regions, Economy and Society* in 2014 (Donald *et al.*, 2014) Detroit's fiscal predicament is covered in the contributions by Reese *et al.* (2014) and Hall and Jonas (2014). Färber (2014) examines Berlin. For definitive accounts of austerity urbanism in the United States, we suggest you read recent papers by Peck (2012, 2014).
- Albers (2012) is an excellent edited collection of essays by leading urban scholars on the subprime mortgage crisis. Gotham (2012) and Wyly *et al.* (2012) examine aspects of the urban geography of the mortgage crisis in the United States.
- The urban sociologist Loïc Wacquant's (2009) *Punishing the Poor: The Neoliberal Government of Social Insecurity* offers analysis on punishment in the United States and in Europe. On the lives of those most targeted by the US carceral society, read Victor Rios (2011), *Punished: Policing the Lives of Black and Latino Boys*, and Michelle Alexander (2010), *The New Jim Crow: Mass Incarceration in the Age of Colorblindness*.
- Graham's 2011 book, *Cities Under Siege: The New Military Urbanism*, lays out an approach. Dowler (2012) suggests that militarization literatures could do a better job thinking about gender, the home, and the body, and not just global and national scales.
- *Detropia* (dir. Heidi Ewing and Rachel Grady, 2012) is a visually arresting documentary on Detroit's decline.
- *The House I Live In* (dir. Eugene Jarecki, 2012) is an examination of the "war on drugs" and how it led to the mass incarceration of millions of Americans, especially African–Americans.
- *The Battle of Algiers* (dir. Gillo Pontecorvo, 1966) is a masterpiece that fictionalizes the anti-colonial street warfare in Algeria's fight for independence from the French in the 1950s. Guerrilla and insurgent groups perfect urban warfare in resistance struggles but are coopted by military forces that incorporate their tactics over time (Weizman, 2006).

Chapter 14

Epilogue
Critical Urban Geographies and Their Futures

Urban Geography: A Critical Introduction, First Edition. Andrew E.G. Jonas, Eugene McCann, and Mary Thomas.
© 2015 Andrew E.G. Jonas, Eugene McCann, and Mary Thomas. Published 2015 by John Wiley & Sons, Ltd.

14.1   Introduction

The previous two chapters were framed by the ideas of alternatives (Chapter 12) and crises (Chapter 13). As we said at the start of Chapter 13, one connotation of the word crisis is decision. The roots of that word are also wound up with the word "critical" itself. Being critical does not mean pretending to be scientifically detached or impartial, or unbiased. Instead, being critical is all about being partial, being involved, and deciding what is right and what is wrong – or deciding that there are no simple categories to sum up complex situations. As we end this book on critical urban geography, we hope that you are now better equipped and also more energized to:

i.   analyze the geographies of cities from a critical perspective – one that encourages you to take a stance in asking and answering the critical, decisive question: *Cities for whom?*
and

ii.   decide among the various alternatives we have highlighted about how cities should be analyzed and how they should be changed for the future.

Many of the innovative critical perspectives on the city in the last 30 years – such as those stemming from political economy, feminism, postcolonialism, queer theory, and cultural geography – have grown out of critiques of models and theories of urban growth based what happened in a few cities in the **global North** during the twentieth century. The new trends and challenges of twenty-first century urbanization suggest there is always a need for new critique and fresh insight (Chapter 2).

Despite the great progress that has already been made in advancing critical urban analysis, tensions nevertheless persist between those who argue that it is possible to generate abstract urban theories based on recent urban trends in western capitalism and those who argue that we need to embrace a greater diversity of urban worlds and to study the rich complexity of urban lives.

Urban scholars like Jenny Robinson (2011b), for example, remind us that it is dangerous to over-rely upon theorizations of the urban condition based on cities in the global North. This, then, is the particular challenge facing urban theories and models that try to generalize future urban patterns and processes from the experiences of select cities like Chicago or Los Angeles (e.g., the Chicago School of social ecology or the Los Angeles School of urban theory). Robinson argues instead for the advantages of comparative theoretical frameworks, which can produce better representations of the richness of the urban experience and are sensitive to differences among various kinds of cities, not least places in the **global South** and smaller cities in the North and South. In other words, there is much more to cities and how ordinary people experience them than abstract models and theories of capitalist urbanization are ever capable of capturing.

What we would like to suggest is that having an interest in how urban difference is experienced and lived out through the lives of ordinary people is not incompatible with developing critical theories and concepts of urban development. We feel that the future of critical urban studies lies in further developing grounded concepts of **urban development** and **urban experience**. In order for this to happen, we need to engage with the multiplicity of urban worlds and expose existing tensions and contradictions in the process of **urbanization** in a variety of contexts and settings.

We also believe that an over-obsession with the structural forces and general processes of urbanization at the expense of how everyday urban worlds are actually sustained, challenged, and changed could stifle serious debate and discussion about **alternative urban spaces and politics**. To paraphrase former British Prime Minister Margaret Thatcher, the elite would have it that "there is no alternative" to **neoliberalism** and the stark prospects of unchecked planetary urban growth, **shrinking cities**, hyper surveillance, inequality, and **austerity urbanism**. Fortunately, critical urban geographers sharply disagree. They take issue with this state of affairs and are prompting discussion, debate, and dissent about the forms and possibilities of alternative urban politics. If the seeds of alternative urban development trajectories are ever-present in existing urban systems of production, circulation, and exchange, then we need to find, in effect, those spaces through which to think critically about the city. Doing so is one step in advocating for more just cities.

14.2   Ways Forward

A starting point might be to investigate the dominant discourses (or tropes) found in conventional representations of the city. Examples of such discourses touched on in this book include global cities, urban sustainability, competitive city-regionalism, urban entrepreneurialism, city marketing, and so forth. While each of these narratives does speak to different future visions of the city in its own respective way, it does not exhaust the possibilities. In this spirit, we think it is well worth your time speculating on what alternative (i.e., postneoliberal, democratic) urban worlds might look like.

To help you do this, we offer five themes around which you might want to continue your investigations into **urbanization**, urban development, urban **planning**, and urban experience. These themes are: (i) exploring interconnected urban worlds; (ii) looking for new and existing alliances and social movements in the city; (iii) rescaling knowledge of the state and citizenship around the city; (iv) revealing urban geographies of social reproduction; and (v) planning for social and environmental justice in the city (Table 14.1). We are *not* proposing a prescriptive, or exhaustive template for producing future critical urban geographies here. As we noted in Chapter 2, academics, including critical academics, cannot define the best future for cities and societies, we can merely analyze the present and suggest possible pathways to better futures. Nonetheless, these five pathways do seem to offer many exciting possibilities.

Table 14.1   Five themes for future critical urban research.

1. Exploring interconnected urban worlds
2. Looking for new and existing alliances and social movements in the city
3. Rescaling knowledge of the state and citizenship around the city
4. Revealing urban geographies of social reproduction
5. Planning for social and environmental justice in the city

Exploring interconnected urban worlds

The first theme that we hope this book has encouraged you to consider is the future role of all cities in the context of a world of growing interconnections. A critical urban geography should help you to challenge the idea that the urban represents its own separate **scale**, which can be examined in isolation from the national and the global scales. Henri Lefebvre once suggested that urbanization is caught up in a wider politics of space (Brenner and Elden, 2009). He argued that the state's role in the production of urban space (e.g., spatial planning, urban policy, etc.) reflects the growing pressures to meet the physical and social infrastructural demands of globalization.

In other words, Lefebvre seemed to be referring to the development of ever more complex and increasingly strained relations between the urban, regional, national, and global scales. For example, city officials and planners often by-pass scales such as the national in order to engage in knowledge exchange and policy learning with other cities (Chapter 4). For these reasons, it is useful to look not just at social relations within cities but also to how the "urban" stretches across space to form inter-urban, regional, national, and global social relations and networks. Each of these perspectives represents a different way of seeing the urban in a relational fashion, as part of a world of flows, inter-scalar connections, and inter-urban relations rather than as self-contained urban territories.

Seeing the city through this relational approach also allows you to question other ways in which the urban scale has been categorized and containerized, including the idea of the "global city" discussed in Chapter 4. Instead, we encourage you to consider the diversity of ways in which cities are being globalized and how, in turn, this worlding of cities challenges received understandings of urban territory, scale, and identity (Chapter 2; Roy and Ong, 2011). There is a need to bring a greater variety of national and regional settings into our critical view of urbanization, and consider how western concepts of territory, sovereignty, and political identity are challenged by the emergence of new and other urban forms. The urbanization of the global South and its connections to cities in the global North have a wide range of ramifications, such as enhancing the role of the development state in international competition, fostering new urban-based political struggles around sovereignty and territorial identity, and, above all else, challenging national urban development pathways based on western models of neoliberalism and free-market capitalism. As you saw in Chapters 3 and 7, one response to this new world of inter-urban competition has been attempts by nation-states to reorganize territory into extended urban regions or city-regions. In an interconnected urban world, the relations between the urban, regional, national, and international scales are very much up for grabs.

Looking for new and existing alliances and social movements in the city

Our second suggestion is to examine the ways in which **regional urbanization** could be motivating the formation of new territorial alliances and social movements within and across urban spaces. Harvey (1985a) once suggested that the contradictions of capitalism can throw up a variety of unexpected class and territorial alliances around urban regions. In Chapter 7, for instance, we examined the ways in which locally dependent businesses and local governments participate in urban **growth coalitions** in order to attract investment and jobs to urban localities threatened by capital mobility. Urban and regional alliances also engage with higher levels of the state in order to leverage resources and draw down corresponding powers into the urban locality. These processes of urban-region territorial organization seem to throw doubt upon the capacity of existing urban political arrangements to deal with the various challenges created by capital mobility, spatial agglomeration, economic development, and land use intensification. Indeed, one of the central urban problems today is how to forge effective urban and regional alliances and social movements in order to offset some of the negative distributional consequences of neoliberal urban development.

One trend worth noting is the further balkanization of urban regions into smaller self-governing entities, including special purpose districts, gated communities, and new privatized forms of suburban governance (Chapter 7). The proliferation of private neighborhood governance in global cities like Sydney, Australia, provides evidence of this "granular" scale of urban politics (McGuirk and Dowling, 2011). As edge-urban settlements engage more vigorously in economic development, the functional political ties between cities and suburbs become weaker and the opportunities to establish a more re-distributional metropolitan polity are undermined. There is a real danger that inner urban and suburban spaces lacking in appropriate governance capacities or suffering from the fiscal effects of urban austerity and the subprime mortgage meltdown will be deprived of essential investments in basic social and physical infrastructures. These marginalized and excluded urban spaces and populations might want to enter into new urban and regional alliances in order to participate in key decisions around the future planning and governance of the metropolitan region.

There are urban counter-movements emerging and operating already which are raising issues of social redistribution. As we saw in Chapters 5 and 6, alliances are being forged around **living wage** campaigns to support the growing army of informal, low paid, and casual labor in the city. These new urban social movements carry with them different understandings and assumptions about engagement and participation in the economic development of city-regions. Other urban-regional distributional struggles might develop around a range of issues like challenging tax subsidies for private investors, reforming urban politics, providing childcare, strengthening spatial planning, promoting environmental justice, delivering infrastructure to poor and disenfranchised communities, providing affordable housing, and introducing better democratic governance in cities. Tracking the organizational geographies of urban social and economic justice movements represents a pressing and worthwhile area for critical urban inquiry.

Rescaling knowledge of the state and citizenship around the city

The third challenge facing critical urban geography relates to the future role of **the state** and citizenship in urban development. Work on shrinking cities and austerity urbanism has exposed the damaging effects of state withdrawal on the physical and social fabric of the city. There is no doubt that cities and metropolitan areas are becoming bigger and more complex to manage under existing state jurisdictional and regulatory arrangements. In response, supranational organizations traditionally not involved in urban development, such as the European Union (EU) and the Organisation for Economic Cooperation and Development (OECD), have started to take a greater interest in urban policy. But there are many as-yet-unmet urban challenges demanding new forms of state intervention, such as the fallout of economic crisis, infrastructure deficit, climate change, food security, and so forth. As a critical urban geographer, you might be interested in investigating what spaces and scales of the state are emerging around the future economic and infrastructural development of cities.

It is not just the state that is being rescaled as a result of new patterns and processes of urban development, so too are concepts and practices of democracy. Saskia Sassen (2006) has argued persuasively that **citizenship** has been progressively "denationalized" in response to globalization. The growth of urban-based protests and struggles for citizenship in countries like Tunisia and Egypt signify aspects of this denationalization process; as also does the Occupy movement in North America and Europe. The urban rescaling of citizenship prompts urban political geographers such as Mark Purcell (2007) to argue that we need to develop new critical approaches to democracy in order to allow more progressive urban futures to flourish. This does not mean a return to an idealized space of democracy as represented by the city-states of ancient Greece. Instead, it means we need to develop a far richer understanding of new scales of political participation and activism in the city.

For example, recognizing **the right to the city** (Chapters 2 and 12) injects new life into the analysis of urban politics and the struggle for access to physical space in the neoliberal city. Likewise, public art and graffiti can be studied as creative outlets for expressing dissatisfaction with certain aspects of urban life today (Chapter 11). But these do not exhaust the possibilities. Cities and urban spaces are at the forefront of anti-capitalism protests, democratic movements, queer protests, access struggles for people with disabilities, anti-racism campaigns, migrant rights movements, and separatist struggles. Others are caught up in debates about national welfare policy, austerity, and labor market restructuring. Yet others are entangled in actions around food security, transportation, health, and environmental protections. As a critical urban geographer, you have a role to play in revealing the diverse spaces and scales around which struggles for citizenship and the "right to the city" are being played out.

Revealing urban geographies of social reproduction

If there has been considerable progress in understanding how cities have globalized in an economic sense, this has all-too-often come at the expense of knowledge of the lives of ordinary urban residents. David Wilson (2009) suggests that the **trope** of globalization has become so normalized in official discussions and imaginaries of the city that it has scripted a language of urban development from which the everyday struggles for survival on the part of the poor and minorities in the city are excluded. He describes the urban condition facing racial minorities and the poor in America as follows:

> Today, in the shadows of shiny gentrified blocks and gleaming downtown skyscrapers, many poor African-American neighborhoods in America continue to suffer. Globalization continues to afflict these already punished terrains in ways that are now well chronicled … But the impact of globalization on these communities has another dimension. Less recognized is that globalization, as a kind of cultivated imagining that is aggressively spoken, is widely put in the service of neoliberal urban politics (via diverse kinds of communicating) that deepens the production of these disadvantaged communities. Here, what globalization is thought to be by people is

seized and wielded like a cudgel to punish and discipline planning measures, social welfare programs, and urban policy. Planning, political expediency, and opportunistic pronouncements of a new ominous reality meld into one potent political force. In the process, the public often comes to casually accept an "entrepreneurializing" of cities that afflicts these racialized communities. (Wilson, 2009)

The "global trope," as he puts it, encourages neoliberal principles to pervade urban policy discourses, thereby reinforcing the social predicament of those left behind in the city.

Several chapters in this book have encouraged you to problematize the "global trope" and investigate urban social geographies of the everyday. In Chapters 5 and 7, for example, we suggested that neoliberal globalization discourses profoundly shape the urban labor market and the living place. However, these discourses fail to deliver a message about the practical experiences and challenges surrounding the struggle for social reproduction in the city (Chapters 6 and 8). The daily struggle in the city for food, shelter, and work are not resolved simply through the "trickle down" effects of neoliberal urban development. For these reasons, Helen Jarvis (2007) argues that there are many "home truths" yet to be learned about how ordinary people get by in the city. Given that conditions of social under-provision and inequality exist throughout the city, actually-existing struggles for social reproduction remain urgent priorities for your investigation.

Planning for social and environmental justice in the city

Perhaps you were first motivated to study cities because you wanted to plan a better urban future. You are not alone in this respect. Urban planning encompasses a wide range of urban practices and interventions. As such, it is not immune to the pressures of globalization and neoliberal urban development we have examined in this book. Indeed, over the past three decades or so it seems the market has often trumped the voice of ordinary citizens and social planners in the allocation of resources and decisions affecting planning and the built environment. In responding to this state of affairs, Susan Fainstein (2010) encourages urban planners to embrace a different approach based upon meeting the criteria of diversity, democracy, and equity. On this, we agree with Fainstein. But this is not a simple task; we need additional means and concepts for planning for a more environmentally sustainable and socially just urban future.

For these reasons, Rob Krueger and Lydia Savage (2007) express a preference for the concept of **just sustainability** over mainstream planners' interest in equity and sustainable development. They argue that planning discourses of equity and sustainability often seem inadequate in the face of the broad array of social, environmental, and economic issues and challenges to be found in the city today. One major challenge for mainstream planning is that there are huge vested economic interests in preserving environmentally and socially unsustainable urban forms, such as suburban sprawl and the carbon economy. Indeed, you should not underestimate the capacity for developers and urban governments to structure land use patterns in ways that continue to promote urban growth and extract value from the built environment and that rely on petroleum products to be cheaply accessible. Nonetheless, questions of environmental and social justice, housing affordability, and improved health are starting to feature much more centrally in the search for a more progressive **urban**

sustainability fix (Chapter 10). Your task as a critical urban geographer is to look for the spaces of the city where stronger connections between progressive forms of economic development, environmental reforms, and planning for social justice can be nurtured.

14.3   Final reflections and Conclusions

In writing this book, our aim has been to push for analyses of cities that are grounded in the contemporary urban experience in all its diversity, albeit mindful of historical forces of urbanization and urban development. Unlike other texts which give separate treatments to the urban economy, urban social space, and urban politics, we show how critical urban geographers look at these urban spheres as integral. We also tried to strike a balance between recognizing the virtues of situated urban geographies and the wider connections and flows operating between cities around the world. For us, this is potentially the most fruitful way forward. In our view, then, a truly critical urban geography means:

- Using the city as a lens for proposing and developing critical concepts that help to shed light on how wider (capitalist, colonialist, racist, misogynist, heteronormative) social processes, relations, and power structures can change. This involves seeing urban space relationally as part of an interconnected and diverse world.
- Developing insights about the city and its various peoples and spaces that are socially relevant and politically engaged. This includes (but is not limited to) thinking about the different ways in which urban space is used a site of radical intervention and alternative forms of political action.
- Revealing the experiences, lives, practices, struggles, and words of ordinary urban residents and diverse social groups rather than exclusively those of urban elites. This requires moving beyond a critique of dominant neoliberal representations of the city to expose the "ordinary geographies" of the city in all their forms.

Another of our aims in this book has been to propose that knowledge of city issues should not be exclusively the domain of urban experts. Cities should be seen as ordinary insofar as we can all participate in the urban experience and express our opinions and views about how cities should and can develop. Nonetheless, it helps to have a set of critical concepts with which to engage and participate in an open and democratic urban polity. Otherwise you end up by resorting to common-sense explanations for urban events and processes which are steeped in problematic assumptions about the status quo. Our intention has been to arm you with the ideas, concepts, and images that invite discussion, participation, critical comment, and hearty debate. At the very least, we hope that this book has fueled your critical interest in the city and its diverse geographies.

Glossary

Abjection   A process of casting away those who are different than the self because the different, other person represents a threat to the self. Abjection often involves disgust, fear, and repulsion.

Accumulation   The drive to accumulate capital is definitive of capitalism. Capitalism is a system that exploits social relationships, so that wealthier classes can profit from the labor power of poorer classes. Excess capital comes from the difference between the labor power of the working classes plus the cost of production, and the money paid for the goods they produce. Thus, the ability to accumulate capital under capitalism involves the production process as well as the social relations of waged labor. When labor and production costs are kept low, then accumulation is higher. The drive to accumulate means that capital is always searching for ways to maximize accumulation.

Adjustable rate mortgage   An adjustable rate mortgage (ARM) is a way to borrow money to buy property. In this type of mortgage, the interest rate fluctuates with the market, rather than being a fixed rate. If the interest rate rises, so does the mortgage payment. Thus, the risk of the rising costs of credit is passed to the consumer rather than being held primarily by the financial institution offering the mortgage.

Advanced Producer Services (APS)   Services that transnational corporations need if they are to operate effectively in many different contexts across the world. They include: insurance, banking, financial, real estate, legal, accounting, and advertising services, business consulting, and professional organizations. They are offered by APS firms who contract with corporations. These firms tend to cluster in certain major cities, like New York, London, Hong Kong, and Tokyo. Thus, their presence has a great deal to do with those cities being defined as global cities.

Urban Geography: A Critical Introduction, First Edition. Andrew E.G. Jonas, Eugene McCann, and Mary Thomas.
© 2015 Andrew E.G. Jonas, Eugene McCann, and Mary Thomas. Published 2015 by John Wiley & Sons, Ltd.

Aesthetics   Aesthetics refers to art or beauty and can define an approach guiding particular artistic work (e.g., the Impressionist aesthetic).

Alternative urban spaces and politics   Economic and political spaces of the city that actively oppose or replace dominant economic systems and mainstream uses of urban space can be described as alternative. The development of these alternative urban spaces usually involves ordinary people engaging with and challenging mainstream political institutions. The assumption is that such alternative urban spaces and politics have a wider social and economic purpose than is usually possible given the constraining influence of mainstream power structures in the city.

Apartheid   Apartheid is an Afrikaans word ("apartness") that denotes the extreme structures of racial segregation in South Africa in 1948–1994 when the National Party held power in government. Racial segregation was a key feature of colonial rule in South Africa, but after 1948 a series of laws and policies cemented white rule. Millions of black and colored South Africans were removed from cities and towns under apartheid rule.

Austerity urbanism   Urban authorities in many cities have been forced to cut back on essential services, lay off public sector employees, control spending, and reduce debt in order to satisfy current and future fiscal obligations and meet restrictions imposed by higher levels of government. Austerity is becoming a pervasive feature of the neoliberal urban condition today.

Bid rent theory   assumes that the most expensive land is that located closest to the city center. Under bid rent theory, land's value decreases outward. Much like the concentric circles in a bullseye, the best target is at the center. The phrase "bid rent" comes from the idea that businesses or people would offer a price (bid) for prime location (rent), but that they might be outbid by others. This theory is thought to allow us to predict where certain land uses will predominate in a city.

Boosterism   A term referring to the enthusiastic promotion of a cause, idea, institution, person, or place. Civic, or place, boosterism refers to the promotion of places, whether towns, cities, regions, or countries. "Boosters" are those, from both the private and public sectors, who engage in this promotion or marketing. The interests that drive them toward boosterism range from the economic to simply civic pride, although these two usually work in tandem.

Brand   In the context of cities, a brand is an overall image of, and set of associations about, a city that is developed through a concerted strategy by local growth coalitions. Brands are not natural or static. Instead, they are directed at various audiences and changed over time to keep them fresh and successful. They are also questioned and contested by other groups in society.

Broken windows policing   A controversial approach that stresses rapid response to minor crimes and blemishes on the built environment (e.g., vandalism, panhandling, graffiti, and broken windows). The idea is that a quick response will discourage both minor and also major crimes in the future. Associated with urban politicians such as Rudy Giuliani of New York, it has been critiqued for the questionable evidence upon which it is based and the harsh, "revanchist," approaches to low income and homeless people that it tends to encourage.

Business Improvement Districts (BIDs)   This is the most common term for a number of similar organizations operating around the world, sometimes with other designations, like Business Improvement Associations (BIAs). They are areas of cities with clear boundaries within which businesses pay a special levy on top of their regular taxes. The board of the BID, comprising largely of local business representatives, is then permitted to take that extra revenue and decide how to use it within the district. Often, its uses include advertising for the District, extra street cleaning, private security, or special events. Critics accuse BIDs of being undemocratic because the decision to set one up and the control of how to use the extra revenue are not subject to a full democratic vote among the whole population of the area.

Carceral society   A phrase used to denote the spread of social control from the prison to society more generally. Carceral society is associated with surveillance, behavioral correction, and social control. It is also increasingly associated with the militarization of urban space.

Caring labor   is paid and unpaid work that involves the care of others who are typically in close proximity to the worker. Examples include day care workers, nurses, teachers, wait staff, and therapists. Feminists like Paula England and Nancy Folbre have argued that aid care workers experience a disadvantage in the wage labor market because care work is associated with love, or the requirement that such care be done for emotional reasons and not economic ones.

Central Business District (CBD)   The core of the city, where transport networks converge and land uses are dominated by retail and office functions. Commonly, especially in older global North cities like Chicago, this area has the densest land uses and the highest land prices. Since the mid-twentieth century in the global North, traditional CBDs face competition from suburban office and retail locations, often located at the junctions of major highways.

Circuits of value   When value in the form of money (M) and commodities (C) circulates through the urban economy, it does so via different circuits of value. Represented in its simplest form, a circuit of value is as follows: C–M–C. Some circuits are extensive and involve the recycling of previously exchanged commodities. In an alternative urban economy, the aim is to ensure that circuits of value benefit local enterprises rather than leak income out into the global economy.

Citizenship   In contrast to the commonly understood notion of citizenship as a status conferred by the national state and entailing certain rights (e.g., to a vote) and responsibilities (e.g., to pay taxes), citizenship is also a concept used by academics and activists to identify the ways in which people in cities claim rights and responsibilities related less to their official status and more to their inhabiting of place. Urban citizenship may then involve people who are not part of the traditional citizenry (e.g., undocumented immigrants) and is more likely to be evident in protests than in traditional forms, like voting.

Commodification   is the process by which an object, product, capacity, or even labor, a belief, representation, or piece of land is converted into an element of market exchange by being assigned a price. Once mediated by money, commodities are frequently more able to circulate through markets, being bought and sold.

Community   A group of people who share commonalities of culture, values, or interests. While often thought of in terms of local territories or neighborhoods (a view stemming at least in part from the Chicago School's use of the term), communities are often scaled (stretched across the world, especially in the context of advances in communication technologies), and neighborhoods are almost always defined by numerous, overlapping and intersecting communities. Community is not pre-given or natural. It is a social product that is continually being produced and reproduced through social practices.

Community food security   describes a situation when all residents are able to obtain safe, personally acceptable (in terms of religious or dietary restrictions, for example), nutritious food through a food system that is sustainable, maximizes healthy choices, community self-reliance, and equal access.

Contingent labor   covers a range of developments in how labor is regulated and recruited, such as the growth of casual employment and short-term (e.g., zero hour) labor contracts, along with the replacement of welfare with workfare as a system of state support for the unemployed. The rise of contingent labor suggests that for many the work–life balance has become more precarious, since employers have much more freedom to lay off workers, and the state can impose stringent conditions on how the unemployed receive public assistance.

Cosmopolitanism   Defined in terms of elite groups having the ability to traverse space and manage difference in their travels. A second definition refers to more of us: people who may not be cosmopolitan elites but now accept difference as a basis for constructing unity.

Coup d'etat   This is a phrase in French which translates as "stroke of state" or "blow of state." It refers to the sudden overthrow of a government. A coup replaces the overthrown government with another. Militaries are often, but not always, involved in coups.

Creative class   A putatively distinct socioeconomic grouping in contemporary society in the **global North**. Richard Florida (2002), who developed the idea and has become a consultant employed by many cities interested in attracting this group of people, argues that it is comprised mostly of young people who create new ideas and technologies in engineering, architecture and design, arts and entertainment, and education. His argument is that while, in the past, workers travelled to where the jobs were, now members of this Creative Class seek out places where they want to live, and it is up to employers to follow them. Thus, in urban policy terms, he argues that cities must make themselves attractive to the tastes and needs of the Creative Class in order to attract investment. While popular among many politicians, this notion has been roundly critiqued both for the quality of the research upon which it is based and the political, economic, and social consequences of its arguments (including providing a justification for gentrification). Peck (2005) provides a forceful critique.

Development   has many meanings, ranging from the global scale (international development), to the scale of the individual (personal development or self-improvement). For our purposes, it refers to the creation, destruction, and recreation of urban built environments over time – land, buildings, and infrastructure – for the purposes of producing and utilizing value of different sorts. It is driven by the interests of specific **elite** groups, often referred to as **growth coalitions** or growth machines.

Dynamic dependencies   refers to the complex, intimate, and evolving relationships between employers, employees, and the social geography of the city. It used to be the case that the labor requirements of local employers were studied separately from the patterns of social life in the city. However, urban geographers now recognize that employers are very dependent on exploiting the social dynamics linking the workplace to the living place. These dynamic dependencies strongly influence how and why employers recruit their labor force from different areas in the city.

Edge cities and boomburbs   Edge cities are places at the outer reaches of major metropolitan areas that have attracted new office developments and retail activities but not necessarily housing. Boomburbs are residential suburbs comprised of master-planned estates that have grown exceptionally quickly and, consequently, tend to be lacking in supporting employment and infrastructure.

Elites   are small groups of people that control large amounts of capital, political power, or social and cultural influence. Their power is often exercised through institutions, such as the **state**, that mediate, facilitate, and occasionally limit their ability to satisfy their interests.

Embodied experience   Embodied experience denotes that the body of the human is a context and space of all experience. Humans never have an experience that is not embodied, as even thoughts depend on a body to happen. Every body, too, is specific in terms of its size, shape, color, age, ability, gender, and so on. Therefore, embodied experiences are also racial, gender, sexual experiences (to name just a few).

Eminent domain   involves the taking (i.e., acquisition or regulation) of private property by government agencies in situations where there is deemed to be an overriding public interest. Typically in the United States, it involves a municipal government exercising its police power to assemble land and acquire property prior to undertaking a program of urban renewal or redevelopment. Eminent domain is controversial because it removes the control of the redevelopment process out of the hands of local residents and property owners. Moreover, the affected residents and property owners do not always receive just compensation for any losses incurred following the compulsory purchase of their homes and properties.

Emotions   Visceral feelings that are brought on by our understandings of how cities are and should be, and by encounters with difference. They shape our normative positions about how cities should be.

Environmental racism   Toxic and polluting facilities such as waste treatment plants are often to be found in urban neighborhoods that are populated by minorities and people of color. The concept of environmental racism captures the strong association between land uses contributing to environmental degradation and the location of minority and low income communities in close proximity.

Epistemology   How we know the world. It highlights the ways in which the knowledge we develop about the world is conditioned by our approaches to it and beliefs about it. An approach like the Chicago School's, with its ecological metaphors, brings one particular knowledge of the world to the fore, as do the positivist approaches of bid-rent theorists, and the postcolonial approaches of Robinson and others.

Exclusionary zoning   involves the exercise of local land use authority to keep out locally undesirable land uses from the city. In the United States, it has contributed to metropolitan disparities in levels of fiscal effort and service provision.

Flexible work   The demise of mass production has been linked to the emergence of more flexible forms of work. Flexible work covers a range of practices such as nonstandard working hours, job sharing, working from home, and part-time work. It is increasingly seen as a solution to the challenges of managing the work–life balance in the city. From a geographical perspective, flexible labor systems have tended to flourish well away from the traditional urban heartlands of mass production and, especially, in locations where workers are less unionized (e.g., suburbs and rural towns). However, feminist urban geographers question whether labor flexibility is an inevitable spatial outcome of the demise of Fordism. Instead, it has encouraged the rise of new gender divisions in the workplace as more and more women enter the urban labor market. Notably, flexible work allows employers to pay women lower wages than their male counterparts.

Fordism   Fordism describes the system of mass production adopted by the Ford Company during the early years of the twentieth century. This system of production and its ability to be very profitable at large scales became generalized across the US political economy within decades. Fordism shaped urban development by linking mass production to mass consumption. The working class could afford to buy the products (cars, domestic appliances) it was producing. Thus, both production (the assembly line) and social relationships (of wage labor and consumers simultaneously) are implied in the term Fordism.

Gentrification   is the process by which urban neighborhoods, usually the home of low income residents, become the focus of reinvestment and (re)settlement by middle classes. This process is seen in the redevelopment and upgrading of housing and retail landscapes. Socially, it is frequently represented by displacement of existing residents as rents and property taxes rise. The process is now expressly encouraged by many local states, which hope to gain more amenities and higher tax revenues. While originally associated with the redevelopment of older buildings, the process now also includes "new build" gentrification, where neighborhoods are razed and new buildings are built from scratch.

Global cities literature   A literature in geography and urban studies that emerged in the 1980s around the term "world cities" before adopting the term "global cities" in the 1990s. Still, the terms are used in combination and sometimes interchangeably. The literature is focused on understanding the ways in which cities are related to the organization of the contemporary global economy. A key argument is that certain cities are "global" because they are locations of intense bundles of "command and control" functions which allow firms to maintain their global operations.

Global North global South   Over the years, the uneven development of the world and its cultural differences have been defined by general terms, including First World, Third World, West, Non-West, Developed, Less Developed, Core, and Periphery. Global North and global South are the commonly accepted general terms in contemporary critical geography largely because they do not necessarily connote a hierarchy in the ways that most of the others do.

Globalizing cities   A term used to indicate that being a global city is, for some cities, a goal that their elites strive towards, while, for others, it is a status that is always in process and must be maintained and developed. In either case, the point is that globalization and urbanization are socio-spatial processes that never find an end state.

Green architecture   Green architecture denotes that the design and construction, or remodeling, of buildings was done in a way to minimize environmental impact. Central features of green architecture include energy efficiency, the use of recycled and reclaimed materials instead of new ones, water use minimization, and construction practices that do not pollute.

Greenfield sites   Greenfield sites are areas of undeveloped land targeted for capitalist development. The opposite of a greenfield site is a brownfield site, which is an industrial area of land that has been abandoned. Many brownfield sites are environmentally polluted.

The urban **growth coalition**   is an alliance of business organizations and local government actors, whose interest is in the further expansion of the local (city) or regional economy. It unites and mobilizes around the shaping of land use policies and other instruments of urban development with a view to enticing further investment and growth to the locality. The term "growth coalition" is derived from the writings of the sociologists Harvey Molotch and John Logan (Logan and Molotch, 1987) and has been widely used in critical urban geography (see Jonas and Wilson, 1999 and the discussion of **rentiers** in Chapter 9).

Hegemony   and "hegemonic" are terms often used in a general sense as synonyms for dominant and widespread. More technically, the concept refers to a variety of coercive and noncoercive strategies used by a ruling class to control and regulate the behavior of other classes. What is crucial, in both senses, is that hegemony is never complete, that is, a class or idea is never completely dominant. It can, and likely will, be questioned, resisted, and perhaps overturned at some point in the future.

Heteronormativity   The idea that men and women fall into distinct categories and that a corresponding sexual pairing between them is the only correct way to express desire. Heteronormativity denotes a binary relationship between femininity/masculinity, so that feminine men are not "normal," nor are masculine women. Thus, heterosexuality requires gendered norms, not just sexual ones.

HOPE VI   is a US federal program that provides funding to revitalize public housing areas, largely in inner city locations. The funding aims to redevelop large scale public housing projects that are in disrepair into mixed-use developments. This process encourages privatization of public housing. In many cities, developers can pay fines instead of fulfilling affordable housing requirements, so the loss of public housing is not replaced with different options for the poor.

Ideology   Ideology is a set of ideas, including myths, ideals, and beliefs, and so on. Ideology can be both conscious and unconscious, since beliefs are often framed by things we do not necessarily think about carefully. Ideology is not objective, since things like myths are influenced by feelings and can be highly biased. Ideologies are the products of social, economic, and political relations, and dominant ideologies are powerful systems of thinking that shape how we all come to see and value the world.

Imagined community   is that sense of belonging to a particular place, region, or country, which people often share in common despite never having met each other in person (Anderson, B. 1991). For example, when you join with other fans and sing your national anthem at a football game, you are participating in an imagined community. Likewise, particular buildings, such as museums and monuments, often convey a sense of belonging to a much wider community than the immediate urban setting. **Nationalism** is a particular kind of imagined community which is cultivated by public authorities for the greater good of the citizens (and businesses) of a given city, region, or country.

Imagineering   A term originally used by the Walt Disney Corporation. It suggests a conscious attempt to mold the world through imagination and imaginative work. It is particularly useful in the context of our discussion of place marketing because it brings together the representational and the material aspects of the practice.

Informal labor   refers to work in the informal sector. The informal sector is typically economic activity that is unregulated, untaxed, and may even include examples of criminal or illegal activity. Examples can range from street hawkers to cash-only workers mowing the lawn, from prostitutes and drug sellers to agricultural day-laborers or maids. Migrants, women, and children form the bulk of the informal sector's laborers, as they have less access to formal and legal sector employment.

International division of labor   Labor is unevenly valued across space. In the past, colonial or imperial states, and now, transnational corporations, can take advantage of this unevenness by locating to places where labor is cheap and plentiful. Under colonialism, labor was often coerced by the power of the gun and then by the introduction of capitalist economies that required people to have wages to pay for basic needs. The international division of labor refers to the global asymmetry of labor value and connotes the power of capital to exploit labor by moving between places. It is vital to remember that the regulation of labor by states affects the international division of labor. For example, state policies that protect labor by supporting fair labor practices, unionization, and worksite safety might deter transnational corporations from hiring in that place. Thus, the international division of labor also becomes uneven through state policy, and the lack of policy encourages transnational, capitalist investment in places where labor is not only cheap, but less regulated and protected by the state.

Just sustainability   is the conjoining of environmental and social justice movements around the promotion of environmentally sustainable and socially equitable forms of urban development.

Keynesian spatial policies   Keynesian spatial policies are geographically targeted measures implemented by the state in order to bolster aggregate demand in the economy. During the Great Depression of the 1930s, the British economist John Maynard Keynes argued that state monetary and fiscal policies were necessary in order to correct market inefficiencies and offset the effects of downturns in the business cycle. After World War II, many countries implemented Keynesian economic policy measures in order to ensure that the productivity gains achieved with Fordism were realized by corresponding increase in aggregate (national) demand. Such measures were often targeted at regions and cities where economic activity and demand lagged behind the national average. In this way, Keynesian policies often had an explicitly spatial component.

Labor control regime   refers to a social need in capitalism for employers to develop social mechanisms for integrating workers into the production system (e.g., assembly-line mass production). This need arises because workers, in theory, can sell their labor power (i.e., capacity to work) to any employer, and, moreover, they tend to resist exploitative work practices. It also reflects that fact that workers usually require appropriate supervision by employers, not just within the immediate workplace but also in terms of fostering good relations with the wider community. The *local* labor control regime means the place-specific labor control practices through which workers are integrated into the workplace.

Labor geographies   is a reference to the variety of ways in which workers are organized across space and how, in turn, space shapes workers' organizations (e.g., trades unions). For example, the membership of national trade unions representing the service sector might be made up of workers mainly based in major cities where service industries are concentrated. As a result, trade union practices and policies can reflect urban service workers' interests, such as their demands for a **living wage**.

Living wage   A living wage is the amount of salary a worker should receive to cover the cost of a standard of living that is deemed decent, normal, and acceptable to the majority of the population. A living wage is, therefore, well above minimum wages set by law in most countries, since minimum wages often only allow people to live at or below the poverty line. A living wage would increase costs of business, but is more just because the distribution of income is spread more equally in society.

Local Agenda 21   Following the Earth Summit held in Rio de Janeiro in 1992, Agenda 21 was promoted as a global program of action for sustainable development. Subsequently, Local Agenda 21 (LA21) was identified as the formal mechanism for translating this global program into local initiatives to be undertaken in cities and communities throughout the world. By signing up to LA21, urban authorities were required to identify specific actions and policy measures that would facilitate the transition to environmentally, socially, and economically sustainable communities.

Methodology   is the process of combining approaches (theories, concepts, etc.) with specific methods (surveys, interviews, observation) and analyses in order to produce a research project. Methodology is always closely related to one's research questions and is not merely about the practicalities of methods.

Mobilities   defines a particular, relatively recent, "turn" among social science researchers, especially sociologists, geographers, and anthropologists. Their central argument is that the social sciences have tended to focus on the world as if it is not in constant motion or have tended to "freeze" the mobile world in order to study it. Instead mobilities scholars seek to understand and explain the world by starting from the assumption that movement is fundamental to how it works and to people's lives. This leads to the study of a range of topics from the experiences and infrastructures of urban transportation to the character of international migration. Yet, mobilities scholars are careful not to suggest that the world is nothing but flows. They note, as Harvey and Massey both do in their own ways, that the world operates through tensions between fixities and mobilities and between local embeddings and global interconnections.

Myth   A narrative about the world that is not necessarily completely untrue, although it tends to resonate with and support particular of interests over others. Myths resonate deeply with their audience and provide an agenda and legitimacy for action.

Nationalism   Nationalism refers to feelings and expressions of pride in one's country. Nationalism often evidences sentiments of superiority over other nationalities and is, therefore, not solely a positive term.

Nature   Nature is a useful term for thinking about how society and cities are tied to other elements of the world. This is especially the case if we think of ourselves as part of nature and our products – from everyday commodities to cities – as natural. We are obviously natural, as much as we often cling to social/natural distinctions and boundaries. And concrete high-rises are natural in that they are formed from raw materials by natural beings (us). Thinking of cities and societies as connected to nature can reorient our relationships (see the definition of **urban metabolism**).

Neoliberalism (and neoliberalization)   Neoliberalism is an ideology that has become widespread since the 1980s. Its followers, including most contemporary politicians, believe that the competitive free market is the most efficient way of organizing the economy and society in general. It is manifest in government programs to privatize formerly public institutions and economic sectors, from health care to housing, and to deregulate industries like finance. In cities, it is manifest in the outsourcing of state activities to the private sector (e.g., refuse collection) and the reframing of cities as competitive entities and as commodities to be sold (see **urban entrepreneurialism**). Thus, its rhetoric is that of "smaller government," although, in reality, the process of *neoliberalization* happens through the actions of state institutions that facilitate privatization and deregulation. The process is also highly crisis prone. Therefore, the state is often needed to bail out the worst failures of neoliberalism (as in the recent economic crisis). Needless to say, neoliberalism is a major focus of political debate around the world.

New regionalism The belief that government should operate at larger territorial scales than the neighborhood, city, or county levels. New regionalism suggests that metropolitan-wide planning and economic development does a better job than disconnected local governments, and that economies operate beyond local jurisdictions and, therefore, so too should planning. In the main, it has led to the creation of new regional collaborative arrangements between local governments, civic groups, and business organizations across metropolitan areas.

The new urban commons The new urban commons involves a struggle on the part of ordinary residents to claim back the city and to view it as resource held in common by the people rather than a tool of a privileged and wealthy minority.

Norms Norms are idealized and enforced representations of social hierarchies of power that gain everyday, mainstream acceptance over long periods of time and through complex workings of power. Norms are impersonal social forces that shape how subjects experience life and how spatial exclusion forms over time (Sibley, 1995).

Path-dependent urban development Urban development often follows spatial patterns that reflect the built environment needs and infrastructural requirements of the wider production system and supporting social and political institutions. For example, urban scholars sometimes distinguish between Fordist and post-Fordist patterns and pathways of urban development in order to highlight their different urban development trajectories.

Patriarchy is the systematic domination of men over women. Patriarchy is sustained by the everyday exploitation of women, the practices that prioritize men's work and needs over women's, and also by social structures such as heteronormative marriage that place men in positions of authority and power over women. Patriarchy is not universal, since the domination and exploitation of women take very different forms throughout the world and affect women to greater and lesser extents.

Place refers to locations imbued with meaning. Place is always being reworked and redefined by the people who live in it and forces stretching beyond it. In this sense, place can be understood as "**scaled**": regions, nations, and even the globe can be understood in some ways to be places, as can localities.

Place annihilation A term used to describe the total physical destruction of cities for strategic military purposes. Often it involved bombing cities with a view not just to inflicting physical damage on buildings and urban infrastructure but also destroying the social fabric and morale of the urban population.

Place marketing The broad set of activities focused on boosting a place and, thus, making it more enticing to a range of audiences who might invest or spend money in it. Since the rise of **neoliberalism** in the late twentieth century, place marketing has become much more an activity in which local governments engage.

Planning has many connotations. This book's focus is on urban and regional planning, which is a set of practices that emerged at the end of the nineteenth century to manage flows of investment into and around urban regions and to address crises (health, sustainability, etc.) that emerge with **development**. **Zoning** is an example of such a planning practice. Historically, planning was the purview of a few visionaries, funded by private donors, and often intent on designing model alternatives to the polluted, crowded industrial city. By the mid-twentieth century, planning had become a professionalized, bureaucratized **state** institution. Increasingly, since the 1980s, the **neoliberalization** of the state has meant that more elements of planning have been made private (e.g., the rise of private consultants contracting with the state). While many worry about the anti-democratic potential of this shift, others see hope in its ability to bring a wider range of voices to the table.

Policy mobilities   A recent approach to the study of how policy is made in global context. It focuses on the socially produced and circulated forms of knowledge that address how cities are governed. The fundamental part of this approach is the argument that policies are not "merely" local. Instead, it is argued that they develop in, are conditioned by, travel through, connect, and shape various places, spatial scales, networks, policy communities, and institutional contexts. Studies of policy mobilities are, therefore, studies of the practices, contexts, and politics of making (urban) policy in a global context.

Positive environmentalism   Positive environmentalism grew out of class struggles in the nineteenth century city, which led to the spatial and social distancing of the middle and upper classes from the working class. By encouraging the different classes to mix with each other, it was believed that environmental reforms such as the construction of urban parks and open spaces would produce greater social harmony. Such projects not only profoundly transformed class relations and the character of the built environment but also altered the experience and meaning of nature in the city.

Postcolonialism   In one sense, the term refers to an epoch: the present period after most formal colonialism has ended (although it is important to note that former colonizers still maintain many economic advantages rooted in their former colonial adventures). More pertinent is the definition of postcolonialism as a set of related critical approaches. Postcolonial analytical and political approaches: take seriously the power of naming, categorizing, and language (see **global North/global South**); critique dualistic thinking like East/West and the ways that dualism stigmatizes certain people and places outside of Europe and North America; emphasize the importance of acknowledging researchers' identity and social position in analyses; question "Development" when understood as a singular trajectory toward some ideal form of advancement; and seek to locate dominant theories in particular places so that they cannot be assumed to be universally true or real beyond the very specific contexts of their origin (thus "provincializing" or "decentering" them).

Power (A)   is commonly thought of as being something that some people or institutions, such as elites like the members of growth coalitions, possess and wield. Others, in this view, tend to be powerless. There is much truth to this view, yet power can also be usefully understood to be widely distributed in society and always productive of capacities to make change, even among those who might normally be seen to be powerless. Critical geographers, as a group, use the concept in both these ways. Fundamentally, power is the result of social interactions in the present, in the past, and always in places. It is a key concept when studying urban politics, broadly defined, where coalitions of like-minded people come together to enhance their capacities and, thus, their interests.

Power (B) can also mean   The ability to act or the capacity to influence others. Power relations means that some groups have historically and geographically been able to do both of these more than others.

Primate cities   A primate city is one that houses a disproportionate percentage of a nation's population. Primacy is a characteristic of a city that has at least twice the population of the next biggest city in a country.

Prison-industrial complex   The use of the phrase prison-industrial complex draws attention to the ways that the US prison system is integrated with for-profit companies and
corporations. Private companies therefore profit from incarceration, and prisons are
capitalized through the process.

Regional urbanization   Today's mega-urban agglomerations appear to grow not so much
outwards from a single urban core but rather inwards from multiple centers often located
at the metropolitan periphery. In doing so, they spread across many local jurisdictions,
coalescing into larger regional territories which, in some cases, generate more economic
activity than entire countries. Examples include the Yangtze River Delta (Greater
Shanghai) region in China, Greater Tokyo in Japan, and Malaysia's Multimedia Super
Corridor around Kuala Lumpur.

Rent gap   As land and property values in parts of the central city undergo decline, a gap
emerges between the actual value of property (ground rent) and its potential value should
the property ever be redeveloped to its "highest and best use." Gentrification processes
occur when developers and property owners purchase and rehabilitate such property and
sell or rent it at a higher value than the cost of initial acquisition, thereby closing the rent
gap. The rent gap describes *in theory* what happens to property values in former working
class districts the city. In reality, patterns of investment and disinvestment can change
dramatically from block-to-block and neighborhood-to-neighborhood in any given city.

Rentiers   A French word referring to people who receive a fixed sum of money from a
particular source on a regular basis, for example, rent payments. Landlords, then, are one
type of rentier. In cities, rentiers are what Cox and Mair (1988) call locally dependent
capitalists, in that their income and profit comes from regularly drawing rent or other
income from land and property. Given their economic relationship to local land and
property, it is in their interests to band together to boost their place, so that, with more
demand for land, their income and profits will increase.

Right of appropriation   The right of appropriation refers to claims by ordinary people for
greater control over how space is used in the city. It is manifested in the struggle on the
part of urban resident to access and occupy urban spaces (e.g., buildings and public
squares). However, the exercise of this particular right is compromised by the power of
private interests to shape and unduly influence urban redevelopment in and around public spaces.

Right to food   A right defined by international organizations and claimed by food and
poverty activists in both international and urban contexts. It has many aspects, including
the expectations that governments must provide prisoners with food; in the urban context, the right to food generally refers to people's right to have equal access to enough
nutritious and culturally appropriate food as they need to survive.

Right to participation   Emerging out of the concept of **the right to the city**, the right to
participation refers to the role of urban residents in shaping urban space in a democratic
and participatory fashion. It is generally believed that in the neoliberal city the demands
of private interests are met far more readily than the needs of the public (i.e., ordinary
people). You can assume that a critical urban geographer has an important part to play in
promoting the right to participation.

The right to the city   is a phrase coined by Henri Lefebvre in 1968 to describe working
class struggles for political participation and access to physical space in the city. The right
to the city is a central concept in contemporary urban activism and in urban geographical

scholarship. It focuses attention on the role of ordinary people in opposing the erosion of the **urban public realm** by private sector redevelopment and in shaping urban political space in a much more democratic and socially inclusive fashion than hitherto possible under mainstream or modernist visions of citizenship and public participation.

Scale is a conceptual arrangement of space. It is commonly thought of in terms of levels – the local, national, global, and so on. And there is some truth to this. Yet, human geographers understand scale as a social product, tied up with power and politics (see **space**). While scales appear natural, fixed, separate, and ahistorical, they are, in fact, produced and often interconnected for certain purposes by particular interests. Think of the European Union, NAFTA, or even the nation-state or the municipality. All have very specific and relatively recent histories (it is not so long ago that none of them existed in their present form). All involve drawing new lines on maps, creating territories, and, thus, assigning certain powers to particular scales and allowing certain activities to take place, while others are disallowed (see **state**). Scales are social and political, and they are performed and produced by social action. Therefore, they are powerful and can be changed ("rescaled"), for better or worse.

Settler colonialism Colonialism occurs when one political entity takes over another and exploits it for its resources. Settler colonialism refers to the type of colonialism that establishes a new population after conquest in the colonialized territory. Canada, the United States, Australia, and South Africa are examples of settler colonies.

Shrinking cities Cities (or parts of cities) which have lost population and economic activity over a sustained period of time are known as shrinking cities. Examples include former industrial cities in North America (e.g., Detroit, Cleveland), Europe (e.g., Liverpool, Dresden, Trieste), and Russia (e.g., Ivanovo).

Slogan A pithy, striking, evocative, and memorable phrase that operates as the leading edge of a larger advertising campaign, brand, or political agenda. The most successful transcend their original purpose – for example, "What happens in Vegas stays in Vegas."

Social difference The ways that people are divided into categories are socially determined. Social difference is a phrase that insists that the categories used to separate and segregate people are constructed and enforced over time and space. For example, "race" is a category that comes from a colonial past and through which "whiteness" was valued over "blackness," leading to the justification of slavery and colonial conquest. Critical scholars therefore insist that social differences are never just reflections of our identities but also derive from inequality.

Social exclusion The process of stigmatizing and marginalizing certain groups and identities in society. This tends to have economic as well as social and cultural dimensions. Social exclusion involves the definition of groups as nonnormal, and it has a spatial process: people being cast out of and prohibited entry into "normal" urban spaces defined by mainstream categories of race, health, national status, class privilege, sexuality, and so on (Sibley, 1995).

Social reproduction refers to the myriad of ways that the workforce is sustained and replenished under capitalism. These include childbirth and child rearing and regenerating the body through food, sleep, pleasure, and daily care. Without reproduction, production would cease, and capitalism would therefore collapse.

Socio-spatial process A phrase indicating the mutually constitutive relationship between society – the organization of society into groups or classes, the development of cultural mores, and so on – and space – the organization of built environments, landscapes, and so on. How a society operates, understands itself, and is governed is reflected by the spaces (urban and otherwise) that it produces. Furthermore, the legacies of geographies that came before necessarily structure and define the character of contemporary society. The addition of the word "process" indicates that this relationship between society and space is historical and dynamic.

Space   is a term with many connotations. Most contemporary critical geographers agree that space is both something absolute – the physical, material spaces of the world – and is also socially produced. In this sense, space is a concept that refers to the relationships between society – human practices, representations, institutions, ways of life, and so on – and the spaces that society produces (see **socio-spatial process**). Space then, is very much defined in terms of relationships with other beings and things as well as in relation to power and to change over time.

Spatial entrapment hypothesis   Many women are spatially restricted in their job search area and choice of career paths due to various domestic responsibilities. The spatial entrapment hypothesis proposes that the *only* forms of employment available to women are low wage, service sector jobs, which are typically located in close spatial proximity to their suburban places of residence. Consequently, women are trapped in suburban labor markets dominated by low wage, service sector employment.

Spatial fix   is a phrase indebted to the work of Marxist geographer David Harvey. He argues that capitalism attempts geographical expansion and restructuring to address its inability to grow indefinitely. In general terms, a spatial fix is a geographic solution or attempted solution to problems of accumulation, control, and stasis.

Spatial science   emerged in geography in the 1960s as many geographers rejected ideographic (descriptive) approaches in favor of nomothetic (law generating) approaches. Major foci are the interactions of objects in space and the diffusion of phenomena across space, which geographers seek to quantify, measure, and model and, thus, explain and predict. While critical urban geography has tended to orientate toward qualitative, rather than quantitative analyses, there is no necessary reason why spatial science approaches cannot contribute to critical analyses of cities.

Spatiality   is a term geographers use to indicate that space and society are mutually constitutive (see **space** and **socio-spatial process**).

Speculation   Investing in buildings or land, not primarily to use, but to hold for a period of time, in the hope that its price on the market will increase so that they can then be sold again for a profit.

Speculative economic development strategies   Investing in urban development – for example, building office parks or highways – or in other development-related practices – for example, workforce training –not because a buyer, user, or employer is already committed but as a way of stimulating investment. The phrase, "If you build it, they will come," represents the most optimistic version of this risk-taking mindset.

State, the   A set of institutions, including government and the law, that govern and exercise control over a particular territory. The term usually refers also to the people who work in state institutions – its agents, such as urban planners or police officers. Societies invest rights in the institutions of the state, such as the right to tax and to enforce laws. States are also charged with responsibilities, including providing infrastructure, social services, and so on. States' functions, rights, and responsibilities are divided among different scales.

Urban geography deals with both the "local state" – planning, for example – and the ways in which provincial and national state bureaucracies, policies, and actions impact on cities

Structural adjustment programs Structural adjustment programs, or SAPs, result from the policies of the International Monetary Fund (IMF) and the World Bank. In order for countries to access loans from the IMF, or development funds from the World Bank, they must agree to conditions that require a range of changes to national fiscal policy, social spending, and privatization. SAPs encourage foreign investment by insisting on the reduction of trade barriers, through an emphasis on direct export and the extraction of resources for the global market. SAPs also require states to deregulate labor and privatize land and industry.

Subprime city Urban places at the forefront of the recent financial crisis and having high mortgage foreclosure rates are known as subprime cities. Examples of subprime cities can be found in both growing and declining urban regions of the United States and Europe.

Subprime lending Banks and brokers offer subprime loans to people who have poor credit histories or who are at higher risk of being unable to pay back loans. Subprime loans carry higher interest rates and, therefore, this form of credit is more costly to borrowers than prime loans – and, correspondingly, they are more profitable for lenders. Legacies of racism in American financial institutions affect the ability of minority people to access prime lending, even when their credit histories were rated very highly. Brokers and banks can, therefore, potentially profit from structural racism by selling subprime loans to racial minorities in the United States.

A **suburb** is an area outside of a town or city and is considered to be primarily a residential area. Suburbanization includes, however, the spread of not just people's housing outside the core city but also industry, businesses, and commercialized leisure. Suburbs are often represented as North American inventions and require mobility, as they are often ill-served by poor public transport networks. Therefore, suburbs especially developed around automobility and highway infrastructures.

Sustainable development Sustainability is a term used to define processes that balance energy inputs and outputs so that they can continue to operate (i.e., be sustainable). Sustainable development is a term that highlights the ideal of meeting the material needs of the present population without compromising those of future generations. The term has many critics who question whether development at present rates can ever be sustainable and who suggest that it is often associated with corporate "greenwashing." Critics also argue that sustainable development often focuses on the environment and economy but not on sustaining or improving society. On the other hand, those who subscribe to it are motivated to seek out ways to address the socio-natural challenges we currently face as a society.

Sweat equity is a term used to the increase in value of a building, usually a dwelling, that comes from the labor put into renovations by its owners, rather than paying a contractor to do the work. By sweating to decorate and upgrade their house, these owners hope to see its value in the marketplace increase. The term is commonly associated with gentrifiers who move into older historic buildings (houses, lofts, etc.) early in a neighborhoods' gentrification when even small physical upgrades can translate into significant increases in value.

Tax increment financing (TIF) is a mechanism for financing urban redevelopment that is widely used by cities in the United States and, to a lesser extent, also in other countries like the United Kingdom. In the United States, redevelopment legislation allows local governments to establish a public-private redevelopment agency which has powers to set up a designated a tax increment district (TID) for any part of a city deemed in need of redevelopment due to low property values or "blight." Working with private developers, the agency raises money by selling bonds in order to fund infrastructure and improve the development prospects of the TID. As redevelopment occurs, property tax revenues rise and, in theory, the increment (i.e., the tax above the pre-redevelopment amount) is used to pay off the bonds. However, TIF is controversial because other public entities such as school districts, which also rely on property tax revenues, do not always receive their share of the tax increment. Despite requirements to spend TIF revenue on affordable housing, this designated revenue is often not spent on such housing. Finally, there is a lack of public accountability because TIF bonds do not require voter approval.

Three strikes laws In some US states three strikes laws mandate harsh sentences on repeat offenders, usually on their third conviction. The phrase comes from baseball, where three strikes are allowed at bat before the batter is out. Three strikes laws have increased prison populations in states where they are mandated because the lengthy sentences means prisoners spend much more time behind bars than before these laws were enacted.

Trope. A representation with an overwhelming image and message not likely to be read in alternative ways. They are often "taken for granted" and thus are difficult to question.

Uneven development A process and condition that is both the product of and, crucially, the inevitable result of capitalist development. Uneven development can be expressed at all scales, from different levels of development in various parts of the world, to differences in development from neighborhood to neighborhood in a city. This concept (and most evidence) contradicts classical economists' argument that the economy tends toward equilibrium.

Urban ecology an iteration of the Chicago School's human ecology approach, borrows ecological concepts like invasion and succession, in an attempt to explain the organization of society in cities. This approach has been roundly critiqued and is no longer a prominent approach in urban geography, although it continues to provide an historical reference point.

Urban entrepreneurialism refers to the investment-friendly strategies used by urban authorities to entice companies and entrepreneurs to their jurisdictions. One sign of urban entrepreneurialism is the proliferation of public–private partnerships around the redevelopment of the city. Entrepreneurialism is one manifestation of **neoliberalism** and **neoliberalization**.

Urban metabolism In biology, "metabolism" refers to all the physical and chemical processes through which an organism's life is maintained. It focuses attention on change (the Greek root of the word means change) and on flows of chemicals and energy in and out of organisms. Not surprisingly, then, scholars interested in questioning or standard understanding of the separation between (urban) society and nature have picked up the term "metabolism." They use it to highlight the interconnectedness and ever-changing relationships between nature and society as well as the important ways in which humans, by changing nature, also change.

Urban political ecology Urban political ecology (UPE) is a strand of thinking that has emerged in urban geography in recent years as a way to think about the relationships between society and nature. It emphasizes the connections, rather than separation, between cities and nature. It focuses on flows that disrupt easy notions about the separation between societies and nature, or easy definitions of where the city ends. Moreover, the inclusion of the word *political* in the term is important. It indicates that the way in which social groups in cities engage with nature (whether by enjoying good quality drinking water, access to park space, or being exposed to pollution, etc.) is in no way "natural" but, instead, is a characteristic of uneven power relations in society.

Urban public realm The urban public realm refers to the extent to which physical spaces of the city are accessible to ordinary urban residents. Public access is governed by prevailing rules and norms that apply to the use and exchange of property, both public and private. In the neoliberal city the scope of the public urban realm is progressively narrowed by the intrusion of private property relations into public spaces.

Urban renewal generally refers to extensive state-led redevelopment in mid-twentieth century Europe and in North America. It frequently razed established neighborhoods and replaced them with new retail districts, housing projects, and highways. State bureaucrats wielded their urban renewal powers not only to address self-evident urban problems but also to define certain neighborhoods and people (especially racial minorities and low income people) as problems to be remedied or banished. The term is less used today, largely due to its negative connotations, but the state's fondness for erasure of the old in favor of the newly built is still evident. Urban renewal has long been an object of political struggle, often related to anti-gentrification politics.

Urban sustainability fix As urban authorities, politicians, businesses, and residents have become more aware of the relationship between environmental improvements and promoting urban development, critical interest in sustainable urban development has grown. The concept of the urban sustainability fix suggests that cities seek to introduce sustainability measures that do not conflict with economic development and are not likely to trigger public opposition. In the process, sustainability often removes the more controversial urban development projects out of the democratic arena.

Urbanism is often used to refer to urban design (architecture, etc.). In this book, its other meaning is more prominent: ways of life that define cities in specific historical periods. These ways of life, of course, shape and are shaped by the design of urban built environments.

Urbanization is a term that refers to the clustering of population in increasingly large, dense, and diverse, cities over time. It also suggests the increasing globalization of cities' and urban processes' influence. Both of these processes indicate the relationship between the (re)organization of space and changes in the character of societies and economies.

Visuality Anything that can be seen is visual, and visuality is a term that refers to how particular images come to be and how one learns to see. Visuality comes from the history of images, from knowledge production, from your own subject position and experience, and from relations ranging from the social to the economic. In short, visuality refers to the historical and geographical framing of any one image.

Zone in transition A key term in the Chicago School's ecological diagramming of cities. The zone in transition is the area around the Central Business District of global North industrial cities where a mix of land uses is found and where a general transition from residential uses to retail, office, and light industrial uses was identified by the Chicago sociologists.

Zoning Cities are often separated into different zones, which then have restrictions attached to them in terms of what kinds of buildings and uses can be placed within them. Common examples include restrictions on the height of buildings, for instance in residential districts seeking to restrict high-rise development. A common use-based example is the restriction on types of businesses that can operate in certain areas, for instance a ban on industry, warehousing, or adult entertainment in residential areas. Zoning is a core feature of urban land-use planning.

References

Abu-Lughod, J. (1999) *New York, Chicago, Los Angeles: America's Global Cities.* Minneapolis, MN, University of Minnesota Press.

Adorno, T. (1997) *Aesthetic Theory* (trans. R. Hullot-Kentor). Minneapolis, MN, University of Minnesota Press.

Agyeman, J. and J. McEntee (2014) Moving the Field of Food Justice Forward Through the Lens of Urban Political Ecology. *Geography Compass* **8**: 211-220.

Agyeman, J., R. Bullard and B. Evans (2003) *Just Sustainabilities: Development in an Unequal World.* Cambridge, MA, MIT Press.

Albers, M.B. (ed.) (2012) *Subprime Cities: The Political Economy of Mortgage Markets.* Chichester, John Wiley & Sons Ltd.

Alexander, M. (2010) *The New Jim Crow: Mass Incarceration in the Age of Colorblindness.* New York, The New Press.

Amin, A. and N. Thrift (1992) Neo-Marshallian Nodes in Global Networks. *International Journal of Urban and Regional Research* **16**: 571–587.

Amin, A., D.B. Massey and N.J. Thrift (2000) *Cities for the Many not the Few.* Bristol, Policy Press.

Ancien, D. (2011) Global City Theory and the New Urban Politics Twenty Years On: the Case for a Geohistorical Approach to the (New) Urban Politics of Global Cities. *Urban Studies* **48**: 2473-2494.

Anderson, B. (1991) *Imagined Communities: Reflections on the Origin and Spread of Capitalism.* London, Verso.

Anderson, K. (1991) *Vancouver's Chinatown: Racial Discourse in Canada, 1875–1980.* Quebec City, McGill-Queen's University Press.

Anderson, K. and S. Smith (2001) Editorial: Emotional Geographies. *Transactions of the Institute of British Geographers* **26** (1): 7–10.

Argott, D. (dir.) (2009) *The Art of the Steal.* IFC Films.

Urban Geography: A Critical Introduction, First Edition. Andrew E.G. Jonas, Eugene McCann, and Mary Thomas.

© 2015 Andrew E.G. Jonas, Eugene McCann, and Mary Thomas. Published 2015 by John Wiley & Sons, Ltd.

Attoh, K.A. (2011) What Kind of Right is the Right to the City? *Progress in Human Geography* **35** (5): 669–685.

Banister, J. (2013) *China's Manufacturing Employment and Hourly Labor Compensation, 2002–2009*. Washington DC, United States Department of Labor, Bureau of Labor Statistics. http://www.bls. gov/fls/china_method.htm (last accessed 14 October 2014).

Banksy (dir.) (2010) *Exit Through the Gift Shop*. Revolver Entertainment.

Barnard, A. (2014) Homs Emerges as Turning Point in Shaping Syria's Future. *New York Times*, **22** April. http://www.nytimes.com/2014/04/23/world/middleeast/syria.html?_r=0 (last accessed 14 October 2014).

Bathelt, H. and A.M. Munro (2012) Regional Growth Dynamics: Intra-Firm Adjustment vs. Organizational Ecology. In: M. Fromhold-Eisebith and M. Fuchs (eds.) *Industrial Transition New Global-Local Patterns of Production, Work, and Innovation*. Aldershot, Ashgate, pp. 135-154.

Beam, C. (2013) *To the End of June: the Intimate Life of American Foster Care*. New York, Houghton Mifflin Harcourt.

Beauregard, R. A. (2003) *Voices of Decline: The Postwar Fate of US Cities*. New York, Routledge.

Beaverstock, J.V., R.G. Smith, and P.J. Taylor (1999) A Roster of World Cities. *Cities* **16** (6): 445-458.

Beaverstock, J., R.G. Smith, and P.J. Taylor (2000) A New Metageography in World Cities Research. *Annals of the Association of American Geographers* **90** (1): 123-134.

Berman, M. (1982) *All that is Solid Melts into Air: The Experience of Modernity*. New York, Simon and Schuster.

Best, U. (2009) Critical Geography. In: R. Kitchin and N. Thrift (eds.) *The International Encyclopedia of Human Geography*, Vol. **2**. Oxford, Elsevier, pp. 345–357.

Bhungalia, L. (2012) Im/mobilities in a "Hostile Territory": Managing the Red Line. *Geopolitics* **17** (2): 256-275.

Binnie, J., J. Holloway, S. Millington, and C. Young (2006a) Introduction: Grounding Cosmopolitan Urbanism: Approaches, Practices and Policies. In: J. Binnie, J. Holloway, S. Millington, and C. Young (eds.) *Cosmopolitan Urbanism*. New York, Routledge, pp. 1–34.

Binnie, J., J. Holloway, S. Millington, and C. Young (eds.) (2006b) *Cosmopolitan Urbanism*. New York, Routledge.

Blomley, N. (2008a) The Spaces of Critical Geography. *Progress in Human Geography* **32** (2): 285-293.

Blomley, N. (2008b) Enclosure, Common Right and the Property of the Poor. *Social Legal Studies* **17**: 311-331.

BLS (Bureau of Labor Statistics) (2013) *International Labor Comparisons: Manufacturing in China*. Washington, DC, United States Department of Labor, Bureau of Labor Statistics. http://www. bls.gov/fls/china.htm (last accessed 14 October 2014).

Bondi, L. (1991) Gender Divisions and Gentrification. *Transactions of the Institute of British Geographers* **16**: 190–198.

Bondi, L. and D. Rose (2003) Constructing Gender, Constructing the Urban: a Review of Anglo-American Feminist Urban Geography. *Gender, Place and Culture: A Journal of Feminist Geography* **10** (3): 229–245.

Bondi, L., J. Davidson, and M. Smith (2005) Introduction: Geography's "Emotional Turn." In: J. Davidson, L. Bondi, and M. Smith (eds.), *Emotional Geographies*. Aldershot, Ashgate, pp. 2–16.

Bonds, A. (2013) Economic Development and Relational Racialization: "Yes in My Backyard" Politics and the Racialized Reinvention of Madras, Oregon. *The Annals of the Association of American Geographers* **103** (6): 1389–1405.

Bose, P.S. (2008) Home and Away: Diasporas, Developments and Displacements in a Globalising World. *Journal of Intercultural Studies* **29** (1): 111–131.

Bourdieu, P. (1984) *Distinction: A Social Critique of the Judgement of Taste.* Cambridge, MA, Harvard University Press.

Bourdieu, P. (1993) *The Field of Cultural Production.* New York, Columbia University Press.

Boyer, P.S. (1978) *Urban Masses and Moral Order in America, 1820–1920.* Cambridge, MA, Harvard University Press.

Boyle, P. and K.D. Haggerty (2009) *Olympic-size Questions About Surveillance and Privacy.* Vancouver, Straight.com. http://www.straight.com/news/philip-boyle-and-kevin-d-haggerty-olympic-size-questions-about-surveillance-and-privacy (last accessed 14 October 2014).

Braun, B. and N. Castree (eds.) (1998) *Remaking Reality: Nature at the Turn of the Millennium.* London, Routledge.

Braun, B. and S. Wakefield (2014) Governing the Resilient City. *Environment and Planning D: Society and Space* **32** (1): 4–11.

Brenner, N. (1998) Global Cities, Glocal States: Global City Formation and State Territorial Restructuring in Contemporary Europe. *Review of International Political Economy* **5** (1): 1–37.

Brenner, N. (2002) Decoding the Newest "Metropolitan Regionalism" in the USA: A Critical Overview. *Cities* **19**: 3–21.

Brenner, N. (2009) What is Critical Urban Theory? *City* **13** (2–3): 198–207.

Brenner, N. (2013) Theses on Urbanization. *Public Culture* **25**: 85–114.

Brenner, N. and S. Elden (eds.) (2009) *State, Space, World: Selected Essays, Henri Lefebvre.* Minneapolis, MN, University of Minnesota Press.

Brenner, N. and R. Keil (eds.) (2006) *The Global Cities Reader.* New York, Routledge.

Brenner, N. and N. Theodore (eds.) (2002) *Spaces of Neoliberalism: Urban Restructuring in North America and Western Europe.* Malden, MA, Blackwell Publishers Ltd.

Brenner, N., P. Marcuse, and M. Mayer (eds.) (2011) *Cities for People, Not for Profit: Critical Urban Theory and the Right to the City.* New York, Routledge.

Bridgman, B., A. Dugan, M. Lal, *et al.* (2012) Accounting for Household Production in the National Accounts, 1965–2010. *Survey of Current Business*, Washington, DC, US Bureau of Economic Analysis. http://www.bea.gov/scb/pdf/2012/05%20May/0512_household.pdf (last accessed 14 October 2014).

Broudehoux, A.M. (2012) The Social and Spatial Impacts of Olympic Image Construction: The Case of Beijing 2008. In: H.J. Lenskyj and S. Wagg (eds.) *The Palgrave Handbook of Olympic Studies.* New York, Palgrave Macmillan, pp. 195–209.

Brown, M. (2009) Public Health as Urban Politics, Urban Geography: Venereal Biopower in Seattle 1943–1983. *Urban Geography* **30**: 1–29.

Brown, M. and L. Knopp (2008) Queering the Map: The Productive Tensions of Colliding Epistemologies. *Annals of the Association of American Geographers* **98** (1): 40–58.

Browne, K. (2007) A Party with Politics? (Re)making LGBTQ Pride Spaces in Dublin and Brighton. *Social and Cultural Geography* **8** (1): 63–87.

Buckley, M. (2013) Locating Neoliberalism in Dubai: Migrant Workers and Class Struggle in the Autocratic City. *Antipode* **45** (2): 256–274.

Bulkeley, H. and M. Betsill (2002) *Cities and Climate Change.* London, Spon Press.

Bullard, R.D. (2000) *Dumping in Dixie: Race, Class and Environmental Quality*, 3rd edn. Boulder, CO, Westview Press.

Bunge, W. (1969) *The Detroit Expedition: Discussion Paper No. 1.* East Lansing, Michigan State University. http://freeuniversitynyc.org/files/2012/09/FieldNotesIDGEI.pdf (last accessed 14 October 2014).

Bunnell, T. (1999) Views from Above and Below: The Petronas Twin Towers and/in Contesting Visions of Development in Contemporary Malaysia. *Singapore Journal of Tropical Geography* **20** (1): 1–23.

Burns, R. (dir.) (2009) *New York: A Documentary Film.* New York, Steeplechase Films.

Butler, J. (1993) *Bodies That Matter: on the Discursive Limits of "Sex."* London and New York, Routledge.

Calavita, N. and F. Ferrer (2004) Behind Barcelona's Success Story – Citizen Movements and Planners' Power. In: T. Marshall (ed.), *Transforming Barcelona*. London, Routledge, pp. 47–64.

Carlin, S. and J. Emel (1992) A Review of Literature on the Urban Environment. *Urban Geography* **13**: 481–489.

Casellas, A. and M. Pallares-Barbera (2009) Public-Sector Intervention in Embodying the New Economy in Inner Urban Areas: the Barcelona Experience. *Urban Studies* **46**: 1137–1155.

Castells, M. (1977) *The Urban Question.* Cambridge, MA, MIT Press.

Castells, M. (1983) *The City and the Grassroots: a Cross-Cultural Theory of Urban Social Movements.* Berkeley, CA, University of California Press.

Castree, N., B.M. Coe, K. Ward, and M. Samers (2004) *Spaces of Work: Global Capitalism and the Geographies of Labour*. London, Sage.

Catungal, J.P.C. and E.J. McCann (2010) Governing Sexuality and Park Space: Acts of Regulation in Vancouver, BC. *Social and Cultural Geography* **11** (1): 75–94.

CBC News Online (2006) *Vancouver Tops for Gay Tourism*. British Columbia, CBC News. http://www.cbc.ca/news/canada/british-columbia/vancouver-tops-for-gay-tourism-1.570562 (last accessed 14 October 2014).

Census of Philippines (2010) *2009 Survey on Overseas Filipinos Table*. Manila, National Statistics Office.

Chairat, C. (2013) Redrawing Thai Political Space: the Red Shirt Movement. In: T. Bunnell, D. Parthasarathy and E.C. Thompson (eds.) *Cleavage, Connection and Conflict in Rural, Urban and Contemporary Asia*. New York, Springer Publications, pp. 201–221.

Chang, T.C. (1997). From Instant Asia to Multi-Faceted Jewel: Urban Imaging Strategies and Tourism Development in Singapore. *Urban Geography*, **18** (6): 542–562.

Checkoway, B. (1984) Large Builders, Federal Housing Programs, and Postwar Suburbanization. In: W. Tabb and L. Sawers (eds.) *Marxism and the Metropolis*. New York, Oxford University Press, pp. 152–173.

Chinai, R. (2002) Mumbai slum dwellers' sewage project goes nationwide. *World Health Organization Bulletin* **80** (8): 684–685.

Centre on Housing Rights and Evictions (n.d.) Reports on Mega-Events. http://www.cohre.org/topics/mega-events (last accessed 14 October 2014).

City Mayors (2008) *Paris, London and Barcelona are Europe's Top City Brands*. http://www.citymayors.com/marketing/city-brands.html (last accessed 14 October 2014).

City Mayors (2010) *Cities Have to Develop Into Successful Brands*. http://www.citymayors.com/marketing/city-branding.html (last accessed 14 October 2014).

Clarke, S.E. and G.L. Gaile (1998) *The Work of Cities*. Minneapolis, MN, The University of Minnesota Press.

Clarke, S.E. and G.L. Gaile (1989) Moving Toward Entrepreneurial Economic Development Policies: Opportunities and Barriers. *Policy Studies Journal* **17** (3): 574–598.

Cloke, P., J. May, and S. Johnsen (2010) *Swept Up Lives: Re-Envisioning the Homeless City*. Hoboken, NJ, John Wiley & Sons, Inc.

Cochrane, A. and A.E.G. Jonas (1999) Reimagining Berlin: World City, National Capital, or Ordinary Place? *European Urban and Regional Studies* **6**: 145–164.

Cochrane, A. and K. Ward (eds.) (2012) Theme Issue: Researching Policy Mobilities: Reflections on Method. *Environment and Planning A* **44** (1): 5–51.

Coleman, M. (2009) What Counts as the Politics and Practice of Security, and Where? Devolution and Immigrant Insecurity After 9/11. *Annals of the Association of American Geographers* **99** (5): 904–913.

Coleman, M. (2012) The "Local" Migration State: the Site-specific Devolution of Immigration Enforcement in the U.S. South. *Law and Polity* **34** (2): 159–190.

Constable, N. (2014) *Born Out of Place: Migrant Mothers and the Politics of International Labor*. Berkeley, CA, University of California Press.

Cowen, D. and A. Siciliano (2011) Surplus Masculinities and Security. *Antipode* **43** (5): 1516–1541.

Cox, K.R. (1973) *Conflict, Power and Politics in the City: A Geographic View*. New York, McGraw Hill.

Cox, K.R. (1993) The Local and the Global in the New Urban Politics: a Critical View. *Environment and Planning D: Society and Space* **11**: 433–448.

Cox, K.R. and A.J. Mair (1988) Locality and Community in the Politics of Local Economic Development. *Annals of the Association of American Geographers* **78**: 307–325.

Cox, K.R. and Jonas, A.E.G. (1993) Urban Development, Collective Consumption and the Politics of Metropolitan Fragmentation. *Political Geography* **12**: 8–37.

Coyne, A. (2009) Our Best (and Worst) Run Cities. *MacLean's Magazine* **27 July**: 14–20.

Creative Class Struggle. (n.d.) Creative Class Struggle blog. http://creativeclassstruggle.wordpress.com/ (last accessed 8 October 2014).

Cronon, W. (1991) *Nature's Metropolis: Chicago and the Great West*. New York, W.W. Norton and Company.

Davidson, J. (2010) "It Cuts Both Ways": A Relational Approach to Access and Accommodation for Autism. *Social Science and Medicine* **70** (2): 305–312.

Davidson, M. and K. Ward (2014) "Picking Up the Pieces": Austerity Urbanism, California and Fiscal Crisis. *Cambridge Journal of Regions, Economy and Society* **7**: 81–97.

Davis, M. (1986) *Prisoners of the American Dream*. London, Verso.

Davis, M. (1991/2006) *City of Quartz: Excavating the Future in Los Angeles*. New York, Verso Books.

Davis, M. (1999) *Ecology of Fear: Los Angeles and the Imagination of Disaster*. London, Picador.

Davis, M. (2006a) Fear and Money in Dubai. *New Left Review* **41**: 47–68.

Davis, M. (2006b) *Planet of Slums*. London, Verso.

Dawe, P. and A. Martin (2001) *In Our Back Yard: A Vision For a Small City*. Cambridge, P. Dawe Consulting Ltd.

Degen, M. (2008) *Sensing Cities: Regenerating Public Life in Barcelona and Manchester*. New York, Routledge.

Degen, M. (2014) The Everyday City of the Senses. In: R. Paddison and E. McCann (eds.) *Cities and Social Change: Encounters with Contemporary Urbanism*. Thousand Oaks, CA, Sage, pp. 92–111.

Delany, S.R. (1999) *Times Square Red, Times Square Blue*. New York, NYU Press.

Derickson, K. (2014) The Racial Politics of Neoliberal Regulation in Post-Katrina Mississippi. *Annals of the American Association of Geographers*. **104**: 889–902.

Derudder, B., M. Hoyler, P.J. Taylor and F. Witlox (eds.) (2012) *International Handbook of Globalization and World Cities*. Cheltenham, Edward Elgar.

Detroit Blight Removal Taskforce (2014) *Detroit Blight Removal Taskforce Plan* http://report.timetoendblight.org/ (last accessed 14 October 2014).

Deutsche, R. (1991) Boys Town. *Environment and Planning D: Society and Space* **9** (1): 5–30.

DeVerteuil, G. (2006) The Local State and Homeless Shelters: Beyond Revanchism? *Cities* **23** (2): 109–120.

DeVerteuil, G. (2012) Does the Punitive Need the Supportive? A Sympathetic Critique of Current Grammars of Urban Injustice. *Antipode* **46** (4): 874–893.

Dewey, S. (2011) *Neon Wasteland: On Love, Motherhood and Sex Work in a Rust Belt Town*. Berkeley, CA, University of California Press.

DHS (United States Department of Homeland Security) (2013) *2012 Yearbook of Immigration Statistics*. Washington DC, United States Department of Homeland Security, Office of Immigrant Statistics. http://www.dhs.gov/sites/default/files/publications/ois_yb_2012.pdf (last accessed 14 October 2014).

DHSES (New York State Division of Homeland Security and Emergency Services) (n.d.) *Safeguard New York*. Albany, NY, New York State Division of Homeland Security and Emergency Services, Office of Counter Terrorism. http://www.dhses.ny.gov/oct/safeguardNY/documents/Safeguard NY.pdf (last accessed 14 October 2104).

Dierwechter, Y. (2008) *Urban Growth Management and its Discontents.* New York, Palgrave.

Dikeç, M. (2002) Police, Politics, and the Right to the City. *GeoJournal* **58** (2–3): 91–98.

Dominey-Howes, D., A. Gorman-Murray and S. McKinnon (2013) Queering Disasters: on the Need to Account for LGBTI Experiences in Natural Disaster Contexts. *Gender, Place and Culture* **21** (7): 905–918.

Domosh, M. (1988) The Symbolism of the Skyscraper: Case Studies of New York's First Tall Buildings. *Journal of Urban History* **12**: 320–345.

Domosh, M. and J. Seager (2001) *Putting Women in Place: Feminist Geographers Make Sense of the World.* New York, Guilford.

Donald, B., A. Glasmeier, M. Gray, and L. Lobao (2014) Austerity in the City: Economic Crisis and Urban Service Decline? *Cambridge Journal of Regions, Economy and Society* **7**: 3–15

Dowler, L. (2012) Gender, Militarization and Sovereignty. *Geography Compass* **6** (8): 490–499.

Downtown Eastside Neighbourhood House (n.d.) *Our Food Philosophy.* Vancouver, BC, Downtown Eastside Neighbourhood House. http://dtesnhouse.ca/?page_id=15 (last accessed 14 October 2014).

Duneier, M. (1999) *Sidewalk.* New York, Farrar, Straus, and Giroux.

Dupont, V.D. (2011) The Dream of Delhi as a Global City. *International Journal of Urban and Regional Research* **35** (3): 533–554.

Durkheim, E. (1893/1997) *The Division of Labor in Society.* New York, Simon and Schuster.

Ehrenreich, B. and A.R. Hochschild (eds.) (2002) *Global Women: Nannies, Maids, and Sex Workers in the New Economy.* New York, Owl Books.

Ehrkamp, P. (2010) The Limits of Multicultural Tolerance? Liberal Democracy and Media Portrayals of Muslim Migrant Women in Germany. *Space and Polity* **14** (1): 13–32.

Elwood, S. (2006) Beyond Cooptation or Resistance: Urban Spatial Politics, Community Organizations, and GIS-Based Spatial Narratives. *Annals of the Association of American Geographers,* **96** (2): 323–341.

Engels, F. (1845/1987) *The Condition of the Working Class in England.* London, Penguin.

Engels, F. (1872/1935) *The Housing Question.* New York, International Publishers.

England, K.V.L. (1991) Gender Relations and the Spatial Structure of the City. *Geoforum* **22** (2): 135–47.

England, K.V.L. (1993) Suburban Pink Collar Ghettos: the Spatial Entrapment of Women? *Annals of the Association of American Geographers* **83**: 225–242.

England, K.V.L. (1996) *Who Will Mind the Baby? Geographies of child care and working mothers.* New York, Routledge.

England, P. and N. Folbre (1999) The Cost of Caring. *Annals of the American Academy of Political and Social Science* **561**: 39–51.

Etherington, D. and M. Jones (2009) City Regions and New Geographies of Uneven Development and Inequality. *Regional Studies* **43**: 247–265.

European Revolution (2011) *A Lecture at the University of #occupylondon, Subject: Power, Value and Abstraction.* Take the Square. http://takethesquare.net/2011/11/01/a-lecture-at-the-university-of-occupylondon-subject-power-value-and-abstraction/ (last accessed 14 October 2014).

Ewing, H. and R. Grady (dirs.) (2012) *Detropia.* ITVS.

Fainstein, S. (2010) *The Just City.* New York, Cornell University Press.

Färber, A. (2014) Low-budget Berlin: Towards an Understanding of Low-budget Urbanity as Assemblage. *Cambridge Journal of Regions, Economy and Society* **7**: 119–136

Feldman, T. and A.E.G. Jonas (2000) Sage Scrub Rebellion? Property Rights, Political Fragmentation, and Conservation Planning in Southern California Under the Federal Endangered Species Act. *Annals of the Association of American Geographers* **90**: 256–292

Fenster, T. (2005) The Right to the Gendered City: Different Formations of Belonging in Everyday Life. *Journal of Gender Studies* **14** (3): 217–231.

Fincher, R., and J. Jacobs (eds.) (1998) *Cities of Difference*. New York, Guilford Press.

Flamm, M. (2005) *Law and Order: Street Crime, Civil Unrest, and the Crisis of Liberalism*. New York, Columbia University Press.

Flint, A. (2011) *Wrestling with Moses: How Jane Jacobs Took on New York's Master Builder and Transformed the American City*. New York, Random House.

Florida, R. (2002) *The Rise of the Creative Class: and How It's Transforming Work, Leisure, Community and Everyday Life*. New York, Basic Books.

Florida, R. and A. Jonas (1991) US Urban Policy: the Postwar State and Capitalist Regulation. *Antipode* **23**: 349–384.

Frey, W.H. (2012) *Population Growth in Metro America Since 1980: Putting the Volatile 2000s in Perspective*. Washington DC, The Brookings Institution, Metropolitan Policy Program. http://www.brookings.edu/~/media/research/files/papers/2012/3/20%20population%20frey/0320_population_frey.pdf (last accessed 14 October 2014).

Friedmann, J. (1986) The World City Hypothesis. *Development and Change* **17** (1): 70-83.

Friedmann, J. and G. Wolff (1982) World City Formation: an Agenda for Research and Action. *International Journal of Urban and Regional Research* **6** (3): 309-344.

Fuller, D. (2008) Public Geographies: Taking Stock. *Progress in Human Geography* **32** (6): 834–844.

Fuller, D. and K. Askins (2007) The Discomforting Rise of "Public Geographies": A "Public" Conversation. *Antipode* **39** (4): 579–601.

Fuller, D. and K. Askins (2010) Public Geographies II: Being Organic. *Progress in Human Geography* **34** (5): 654–667.

Fuller, D., A.E.G. Jonas and R. Lee (eds.) (2010) *Interrogating Alterity: Alternative Economic and Political Spaces*. Farnham, Ashgate.

Fyfe, N.R. and J.T. Kenny (eds.) (2005) *The Urban Geography Reader*. New York, Routledge.

Gagen, E. (2000) An Example to Us All: Child Development and Identity Construction in Early 20th Century Playgrounds. *Environment and Planning A* **32**: 599-616.

Gandy, M. (2002) *Concrete and Clay: Reworking Nature in New York City*. Cambridge, MA, MIT Press.

Gans, H.J. (1962) *The Urban Villagers: Group and Class in the Life of Italians-Americans*. New York, Free Press.

Garreau, J. (1991) *Edge City: Life on the New Frontier*. New York, Doubleday.

Gibson-Graham, J.K. (2006) *A Postcapitalist Politics*. Minneapolis, MN, University of Minnesota Press.

Gibson-Wood, H. and S. Wakefield (2013) "Participation", White Privilege and Environmental Justice: Understanding Environmentalism Among Hispanics in Toronto. *Antipode* **45**: 641-662.

Gilmore, R. (2007) *Golden Gulag: Prisons, Surplus, Crisis, and Opposition in Globalizing California*. Berkeley, CA, University of California Press.

Glass, R. (1964) Introduction: Aspects of Change. In: Centre for Urban Studies, University College, London (ed.), *London: Aspects of Change*. London, MacGibbon and Kee, pp. xiii–xlii.

Glassman, J. (2010) "The Provinces Elect Governments, Bangkok Overthrows Them": Urbanity, Class and Post-democracy in Thailand. *Urban Studies* **47** (6): 1301–1323.

Glaze, L. E. and E. J. Herberman (2013) *Correctional Populations in the United States, 2012*. Washington DC, Bureau of Justice Statistics. http://www.bjs.gov/index.cfm?ty=pbdetailandiid=4909 (last accessed 14 October 2014).

Gleeson, B. (2013) The Geographical Imagination and Disability. In: M. Wappett and K. Arndt (eds.) *Foundations of Disability Studies*. New York, Palgrave Macmillan, pp. 69–81.

Glover, W. (2008) *Making Lahore Modern: Constructing and Imagining a Colonial City*. Minneapolis, MN, University of Minnesota Press.

Goffman, A. (2014) *On the Run: Fugitive Life in an American City*. Chicago, IL, University of Chicago Press.

Gordon, D.M. (1984) Capitalist Development and the History of American Cities. In: W.K. Tabb and L. Sawers (eds.) *Marxism and the Metropolis*. New York, Oxford University Press, pp. 21–53.

Gotham, K. F. (2012) Creating Liquidity Out of Spatial Fixity: the Secondary Circuit of Capital and the Restructuring of the US Housing Finance System. In: M.B. Albers (ed.) *Subprime Cities: The Political Economy of Mortgage Markets*. Chichester, John Wiley & Sons Ltd, pp. 25–52.

Gottmann, J. (1961) *Megalopolis: The Urbanized Northeastern Seaboard of the United States*. New York, The Twentieth Century Fund.

Gottschalk, M. (2006) *The Prison and the Gallows: the Politics of Mass Incarceration in America*. Cambridge, Cambridge University Press.

Government of Ontario (2009) Invest in Ontario Advertisement. *New Yorker* **12 October**: 11.

Graham, S. (2011) *Cities Under Siege: the New Military Urbanism*. New York, Verso Books.

Graham, S. (2012a) Olympics 2012 Security: Welcome to Lockdown London. *City* **16** (4): 446–451.

Graham, S. (2012b) When Life Itself is War: On the Urbanization of Military and Security Doctrine. *International Journal of Urban and Regional Research* **36** (1): 136–155.

Graham, S. and L. Hewitt (2012) Getting Off the Ground: on the Politics of Urban Verticality. *Progress in Human Geography* **37** (1): 72–92.

Gramsci, A. (1971) *Selections From the Prison Notebooks*. London, Lawrence and Wishart.

Grant, R. and J. Nijman (2002) Globalization and the Corporate Geography of Cities in the Less-Developed World. *Annals of the Association of American Geographers* **92** (2): 320–340.

Gregory, D. (2009) Geography. In: D. Gregory, R. Johnston, G. Pratt, *et al.* (eds.) *The Dictionary of Human Geography*. Hoboken, NJ, John Wiley & Sons, Inc., pp. 287–295.

Gregory, D. (n.d.) *Behind the Lines*. geographical imaginations; war, space and security. www.geographicalimaginations.com (last accessed 14 October 2014).

Gregory, D., R. Johnston, G. Pratt, *et al.* (eds.) (2009) *The Dictionary of Human Geography*. Hoboken, NJ, John Wiley & Sons, Inc.

Griffin, E. and L. Ford. (1980) A Model of Latin American City Structure. *Geographical Review.* **70** (4): 397–422.

Guthman, J. (2013) Too Much Food and Too Little Sidewalk? Problematizing the Obesogenic Environment Thesis. *Environment and Planning A* **45**: 142-158.

Hackworth, J. (2007) *The Neoliberal City: Governance, Ideology and Development in American Urbanism*. Ithaca, NY, Cornell University Press.

Hadleigh-West, M. (1998) *War Zone*. USA, Film Fatale Inc Productions.

Hage, G. (2000) *White Nation: Fantasies of White Supremacy in a Multicultural Society*. New York and London, Routledge.

Hall, S. and A.E.G. Jonas (2014) Urban Fiscal Austerity, Infrastructure Provision and the Struggle for Regional Transit in "Motor City". *Cambridge Journal of Regions, Economy and Society* 7: 189–206.

Hall, S., Massey, D., and Rustin, M. (2013). After neoliberalism? The Kilburn manifesto. *Soundings*, 1: 3–19. http://www.lwbooks.co.uk/journals/soundings/manifesto.html (last accessed 14 October 2014).

Hall, T. and P. Hubbard (1996) The Entrepreneurial City: New Urban Politics, New Urban Geographies? *Progress in Human Geography* **20**: 153-174.

Hall, T. and P. Hubbard (eds.) (1998) *The Entrepreneurial City*. Chichester, John Wiley & Sons Ltd.

Hamm, M.W. and A.C. Bellows (2003) Community Food Security and Nutrition Educators. *Journal of Nutrition Education and Behavior* **35** (1): 37–43.

Hannam, K., M. Sheller and J. Urry (2006) Mobilities, Immobilities and Moorings. *Mobilities* **1** (1): 1-22.

Hanson, S. and G. Pratt (1992) Dynamic Dependencies: a Geographic Investigation of Local Labor Markets. *Economic Geography* **68**: 373–405.

Hanson, S. and G. Pratt (1995) *Gender, Work and Space*. London, Routledge.

Harvey, D. (1973/2010) *Social Justice and the City*. Athens, GA, University of Georgia Press.

Harvey, D. (1982/2006) *The Limits to Capital*. New York, Verso.

Harvey, D. (1985a) *The Urbanization of Capital*. Baltimore, MD, The Johns Hopkins University Press.

Harvey, D. (1985b) *Consciousness and the Urban Experience*. Baltimore, MD, The Johns Hopkins University Press.

Harvey, D. (1989) From Managerialism to Entrepreneurialism: the Transformation of Urban Governance in Late Capitalism. *Geografiska Annaler* **71B**: 3-17.

Harvey, D. (1996) *Justice, Nature and the Geography of Difference*. Oxford, Blackwell.

Harvey, D. (2000) *Spaces of Hope*. Oxford, Blackwell.

Harvey, D. (2003) The Right to the City. *International Journal of Urban and Regional Research* **27** (4): 939–941.

Harvey, D. (2008) The Right to the City. *New Left Review* **53**: 23–40.

Harvey, D. (2012) *Rebel Cities: From the Right to the City to the Urban Revolution*. London, Verso.

Haughton, G. and A. While (1999) From Corporate City to Citizens City? Urban Leadership *After Local Entrepreneurialism in the UK Urban Affairs Review* **35**: 3-23.

Häußermann, H. and W. Siebel (1988) Die schrumpfende Städt und die Städtsoziologie [The Shrinking City and Urban Sociology]. In: J. Friedrichs (ed.) *Soziologische Stadtforschung: Kölner Zeitschrift für Soziologie und Sozialpsychologie* **29**: 78–94.

Hawkins, H. (2012) Geography and Art. An Expanding Field: Site, the Body and Practice. *Progress in Human Geography* **37** (1): 52–71.

Hewitt, K. (1983) Place Annihilation: Area Bombing and the Fate of Urban Places. *Annals of the Association of American Geographers* **73**: 257–284.

Heynen, N. (2006) Green Political Ecologies: Towards a Better Understanding of Inner-city Environmental Change. *Environment and Planning A* **38**: 499-516.

Heynen, N., M. Kaika and E. Swyngedouw (2006) *In the Nature of Cities: Urban Political Ecology and the Politics of Urban Metabolism*. Abingdon, Routlege.

Hochschild, A. (2002) Love and Gold. In: B. Ehrenreich and A. Hochschild (eds.) *Global Women: Nannies, Maids, and Sex Workers in the New Economy*. New York, Henry Holt and Company, pp. 15–30.

Hodkinson, S. (2012) The New Urban Enclosures. *City: Analysis of Urban Trends, Culture, Theory, Policy, Action* **16**: 500–518.

Hoyt, H. (1933) *One Hundred Years of Land Values in Chicago*. Chicago, IL, University of Chicago Press.

Hoyt, H. (1939) *The Structure and Growth of Residential Neighborhoods in American Cities*. Washington, Federal Housing Administration.

Hubbard, P. (2011) *Cities and Sexualities*. London, Routledge.

Hubbard, P. and E. Wilkinson (2014) Welcoming the World? Hospitality, Homonationalism, and the London 2012 Olympics. *Antipode*. doi: 10.1111/anti.12082.

Huber, M. (2013) *Lifeblood: Oil, Freedom, and the Forces of Capital*. Minneapolis, MN, University of Minnesota Press.

Huber, M.T. and T.M. Currie (2007) The Urbanization of an Idea: Imagining Nature Through Urban Growth Boundary Policy in Portland, Oregon. *Urban Geography* **28**: 705-721.

Hunter, J. (2011) Tour Operators Forbidden from Marketing Vancouver as Gay-Friendly in China. *Globe and Mail* **7 November**. http://www.theglobeandmail.com/news/british-columbia/tour-operators-forbidden-from-marketing-vancouver-as-gay-friendly-in-china/article4183091/ (last accessed 8 October 2014).

ILO (International Labour Organization) (2010) *Women in Labour Markets: Measuring Progress and Identifying Challenges*. Geneva, ILO.

INURA (International Network for Urban Research and Action) (2003) *An Alternative Urban World is Possible: A Declaration for Urban Research and Action*. France, INURA. http://www.inura.org/INURA%20declaration.html/declaration_220.pdf (accessed 14 October 2014).

ITUC (International Trade Union Confederation) (2011) Hidden Faces of the Gulf Miracle. *Union View #21*. Brussels, ITUC. http://www.ituc-csi.org/hidden-faces-of-the-gulf-miracle,9144?lang=en (accessed 14 October 2014).

Jacobs, J. (1961) *The Death and Life of Great American Cities*. New York, Random House.

Jacobs, J. (1984) *Cities and the Wealth of Nations*. New York, Random House.

Jarecki, E. (dir.) (2012) *The House I Live In* Eugene. Charlotte Street Films.

Jarvis, H. (2005) *Work/Life City Limits: Comparative Household Perspectives*. Basingstoke, Palgrave Macmillan.

Jarvis, H. (2007) Home Truths About Care-less Competitiveness. *International Journal of Urban and Regional Research* **31**: 207–214.

Jayne, M., S.L. Holloway, and G. Valentine (2006) Drunk and Disorderly: Alcohol, Urban Life and Public Space. *Progress in Human Geography* **30** (4): 451–468.

Jeffrey, C. (2010) *Timepass: Youth, Class and the Politics of Waiting*. Cambridge, Cambridge University Press.

Jeffrey, C. and C. McFarlane (2008) Performing Cosmopolitanism. *Environment and Planning D: Society and Space* **26** (3): 420–427.

Jessop, B., J.A. Peck, and A. Tickell (1999) Retooling the Machine: Economic Crisis, State Restructuring, and Urban Politics. In: A.E.G. Jonas and D. Wilson (eds.) *The Urban Growth Machine: Critical Perspectives Two Decades Later*. Albany, NY, State University Press of New York, pp. 141–159.

Johnsen, A. (dir.) (2014) *The Fake Case*. Rosforth Film.

Jonas, A.E.G. (1991) Urban Growth Coalitions and Urban Development Policy; Postwar Growth and the Politics of Annexation in Metropolitan Columbus, Ohio. *Urban Geography* **12**: 197–225.

Jonas, A.E.G. (1992) Corporate Takeover and Community Politics: the Case of Norton Company in Worcester. *Economic Geography* **68**: 348–372.

Jonas, A.E.G. (1998) Investigating the Local-Global Paradox: Corporate Strategy, Union Local Autonomy and Community Action in Chicago. In: A. Herod (ed.) *Organizing the Landscape*. Minneapolis, MN, University of Minnesota Press, pp. 325–350.

Jonas, A.E.G. (2013) Interrogating Alternative Local and Regional Economies: The British Credit Union Movement and Post-binary Thinking. In: H.-M. Zademach and S. Hillebrand (eds.) *Alternative Economies and Spaces: New Perspectives for a Sustainable Economy*. Bielefeld, transcript Verlag, pp. 23–42.

Jonas, A.E.G. and L. McCarthy (2009) Urban Management and Regeneration in the United States: State Intervention or Redevelopment at All Costs? *Local Government Studies* **35**: 299–314.

Jonas, A.E.G. and L. McCarthy (2010) Redevelopment at All Costs? A Critical Review and Examination of the American Model of Urban Management and Regeneration. In: J. Diamond, J. Liddle, A. Southern, and P. Osei (eds.) *Urban Regeneration Management: International Perspectives*. London, Routledge, pp. 31–59.

Jonas, A.E.G. and D. Wilson (eds.) (1999) *The Urban Growth Machine: Critical Perspectives Two Decades Later*. Albany, NY, State University Press of New York, pp. 37–54.

Jonas, A.E.G., A. While and D. Gibbs (2010) Carbon Control Regimes, Eco-state Restructuring and the Politics of Local and Regional Development. In: A. Pike, A. Rodriguez-Posé and J. Tomaney (eds.) *Handbook of Local and Regional Development*. New York, Routledge.

Kaika M. (2005) *City of Flows: Nature, Modernity and the City*. New York, Routledge.

Kanarinka (2013) *The Detroit Geographic Expedition and Institute: A Case Study in Civic Mapping*. Cambridge MA, Massachusetts Institute of Technology Center for Civic Media. http://civic.mit.edu/blog/kanarinka/the-detroit-geographic-expedition-and-institute-a-case-study-in-civic-mapping (last accessed 14 October 2014).

Katz, C. (1998) Disintegrating Developments: Global Economic Restructuring and the Eroding of Ecologies of Youth. In: T. Skelton and G. Valentine (eds.) *Cool Places: Geographies of Youth Cultures*. London and New York, Routledge, pp. 130–144.

Katz, C. (2001) Vagabond Capitalism and the Necessity of Social Reproduction. *Antipode* **33** (4): 709–728.

Katz, C. (2004) *Growing up Global: Economic Restructuring and Children's Everyday Lives.* Minneapolis, MN, University of Minnesota Press.

Keil, R. (2005) Progress Report – Urban Political Ecology. *Urban Geography* **26**: 640–651.

Keil, R. (2007) Sustaining Modernity, Modernizing Nature: the Environmental Crisis and the Survival of Capitalism. In: R. Krueger and D.C. Gibbs (eds.) *The Sustainable Development Paradox.* Guilford, London, pp. 41–65.

Keil, R. (2011) The Global City Comes Home: Internalised Globalisation in Frankfurt Rhine-Main. *Urban Studies* **48**: 2495–2518.

Keil, R. and J. Graham (1998) Reasserting Nature: Constructing Urban Environments After-Fordism. In: B. Braun and N. Castree (eds.) *Remaking Reality: Nature at the Turn of the Millennium.* London, Routledge, pp. 100–125.

Kelly, P.F. (2001) The Political Economy of Labor Control in the Philippines. *Economic Geography* **77**: 1–22.

Kempadoo, K. and J. Doezema (1998) *Global Sex Workers: Rights, Resistance, and Redefinition.* New York and London, Routledge.

King, A. (1996) Worlds in the City: Manhattan Transfer and the Ascendance of Spectacular Space. *Planning Perspectives* **11** (2): 97–114.

Kitchen, R. and N. Thrift (2009) *International Encyclopedia of Human Geography.* Oxford, Elsevier.

Kitchin, R. and R. Law (2001) The Socio-Spatial Construction of (In)accessible Public Toilets. *Urban Studies (Routledge)* **38** (2): 287–298.

Klauser, F.R. (2012) Interpretative Flexibility of the Event-City: Security, Branding and Urban Entrepreneurialism at the European Football Championships 2008. *International Journal of Urban and Regional Research* **36** (5): 1039–1052.

Klayman, A. (dir.) (2012) *Ai Weiwei: Never Sorry.* United Expression Media.

Klodawsky, C. and N. Blomley (2009) Rights, Space, and Homelessness. *Urban Geography* **30** (6): 373–376.

Klodawsky, F. and N. Blomley (2010) Rights, Space and Homelessness: Part II. *Urban Geography* **31** (6) [Special section].

Knopp, L. (1990) Some Theoretical Implications of Gay Involvement in an Urban Land Market. *Political Geography Quarterly* **9**: 337–352.

Knopp, L. (1995) Sexuality and Urban Space: a Framework for Analysis. In: D. Bell and G. Valentine (eds.) *Mapping Desire: Geographies of Sexualities.* London and New York, Routledge.

Knowles, C. (2000) *Bedlam on the Streets.* London and New York, Routledge.

Knox, P. (ed.) (1993) *The Restless Urban Landscape.* Englewood Cliffs, NJ, Prentice Hall.

Kobayashi, A. (2013) Critical "Race" Approaches. In: N. Johnson, R. Schein, and J. Winders (eds.) *The Companion to Cultural Geography.* Chichester, John Wiley & Sons Ltd, pp. 57–72.

Kotkin, J. (2013) *Richard Florida Concedes the Limits of the Creative Class.* The Daily Beast. http://www.thedailybeast.com/articles/2013/03/20/richard-florida-concedes-the-limits-of-the-creative-class.html (last accessed 14 October 2014).

Krätke, S. (2004) City of Talents? Berlin's Regional Economy, Socio-spatial Fabric and "Worst Practice" Urban Governance. *International Journal of Urban and Regional Research* **28**: 511–529.

Krueger, R. and D.C. Gibbs (eds.) (2007) *The Sustainable Development Paradox.* Guilford, London.

Krueger, R. and L. Savage (2007) City-regions and Social Reproduction: A "Place" for Sustainable Development? *International Journal of Urban and Regional Research* **31**: 215–223.

Kushner, D. (2009) *Levittown: Two Families, One Tycoon, and the Fight for Civil Rights in America's Legendary Suburb.* New York, Walker and Company.

Lake, R.W. (2000) Contradictions at the Local Scale: Local Implementation of Agenda 21 in the USA. In: N. Low, B. Gleeson, I. Elander, and R. Lidskog (eds.) *Consuming Cities: the Urban Environment in the Global Economy After the Rio Declaration.* London, Routledge, pp. 70–90.

Lang, R.E. and J. LeFurgy (2007) *Boomburbs: the Rise of America's Accidental Cities*. New York, Brookings Institution.

Lauria, M. (ed.) (1997) *Reconstructing Urban Regime Theory: Regulating Urban Politics in a Global Economy*. Thousand Oaks, CA, Sage.

Lauria, M. and L. Knopp (1985) Towards an Analysis of the Role of Gay Communities in the Urban Renaissance. *Urban Geography* **6**: 387–410.

Lee, S. (dir.) (2006) *When the Levees Broke*. HBO Films.

Lees, L. (2009) Urban Geography. In: D. Gregory, R. Johnston, G. Pratt, *et al.* (eds.) *The Dictionary of Human Geography*. Hoboken, NJ, John Wiley & Sons, Inc., pp. 784–787.

Lees, L., T. Slater and E. Wyly (2008) *Gentrification*. New York, Routledge.

Lefebvre, H. (1968) *Le Droit à la Ville [The Right to the City]*. Paris, Anthropos.

Lefebvre, H. (1996) *Writings on Cities* (trans. and eds. E. Kofman and E. Lebas). Cambridge, MA, Blackwell.

LeGates, R.T. and F. Stout (eds.) (2011) *City Reader*. New York, Routledge.

Legg, S. (2005) Sites of Counter-memory: The Refusal to Forget and the Nationalist Struggle in Colonial Delhi. *Historical Geography* **33**: 180–201.

Legg, S. (2011) Violent Memories: South Asian Spaces of Postcolonial Anamnesis. *Cultural Memories* **4**: 287–303.

Leitner, H. (1990) Cities in Pursuit of Economic Growth: The Local State as Entrepreneur. *Political Geography Quarterly* **9** (2): 146–710.

Leitner, H. and P. Ehrkamp (2006) Transnationalism and Migrants' Imaginings of Citizenship. *Environment and Planning A* **38**: 1615–1632.

Leitner, H. and E. Sheppard (2003) Unbounding Critical Geographic Research on Cities: The 1990s and Beyond. *Urban Geography* **24** (6): 510–528.

Lenskyj, H.J. (2000) *Inside the Olympic Industry*. Albany, NY, State University of New York Press.

Leonard, S.J. and T.J. Noel (1990) *Denver: Mining Camp to Metropolis*. Niwot, CO, University of Colorado Press.

Leslie, D. and M. Hunt (2013) Securing the Neoliberal City: Discourses of Creativity and Priority Neighborhoods in Toronto, Canada. *Urban Geography* **34** (8): 1171–1192.

Lessin, T. and C. Deal (dirs.) (2008) *Trouble the Water*. Zeitgest Films.

Ley, D. (1983) *A Social Geography of the City*. New York, Harper and Row.

Ley, D. (2003) Artists, Aestheticisation and the Field of Gentrification. *Urban Studies* **40** (12): 2527–2544.

Ley, D. (2004) Transnational Spaces and Everyday Lives. *Transactions of the Institute of British Geographers* **29** (2): 151–164.

Leyshon, A., R. Lee and C. Williams (eds.) (2003) *Alternative Economic Spaces*. London, Sage.

Li, W., Y. Zhou, G. Dymski, and M. Chee (2001) Banking on Social Capital in the Era of Globalisation: Chinese Ethnobanks in Los Angeles. *Environment and Planning A* **33**: 1923–1948.

Liebovitz, J. (2003) Institutional Barriers to Associative City Regional Governance: The Politics of Institution-building and Economic Governance in "Canada's Technology Triangle". *Urban Studies* **40** (13): 2613–2642.

Lim, L. (2012) *China's Post-Olympic Woe: How To Fill An Empty Nest*. Washington, DC, National Public Radio. http://www.npr.org/2012/07/10/156368611/chinas-post-olympic-woe-how-to-fill-an-empty-nest (last accessed 14 October 2014).

Logan, J. and H.L. Molotch (1987) *Urban Fortunes: the Political Economy of Place*. Berkeley, CA, University of California Press.

Low, N., B. Gleeson, I. Elander, and R. Lidskog (eds.) (2000) *Consuming Cities: the Urban Environment in the Global Economy After the Rio Declaration*. London, Routledge.

Loyd, J. (2014) *Heath Rights are Civil Rights: Peace and Justice Activism in Los Angeles, 1963–1978*. Minneapolis, MN, University of Minnesota Press.

Luebker, M., Y. Simonovsky, and M. Oelz (2011) *Domestic Work Policy Brief 5: Coverage of Domestic Workers by Key Working Conditions Laws*. Geneva, International Labour Office. http://www.ilo.

org/wcmsp5/groups/public/---ed_protect/---protrav/---travail/documents/publication/wcms_157509.pdf (last accessed 14 October 2014).

Lund Hansen, A. (2008) Walking Through a Liquid Forest of Symbols. *Liminalities: A Journal of Performance Studies* **4** (1). http://liminalities.net/4-1/spacewars.htm (last accessed 14 October 2014).

Lynch, K. (1960) *The Image of the City*. Cambridge, MA, MIT Press.

Lynd, R.S. and H.M. Lynd (1929/1957) *Middletown: A Study in Modern American Culture*. San Diego, CA, Harcourt Brace Jovanovich.

MacKinnon, D. and K. Derickson (2012) From Resilience to Resourcefulness: a Critique of Resilience Policy and Activism. *Progress in Human Geography* **37** (2): 253–270.

MacLeod, G. and M. Jones (2011) Special issue: Renewing Urban Politics. *Urban Studies* **48** (12): 2443–2472.

Mahtani, M. (2014) Toxic Geographies: Absences in Critical Race Thought and Practice in Social and Cultural Geography. *Social and Cultural Geography* **15** (4): 359–367.

Marcuse, P. (2009) From Critical Urban Theory to the Right to the City. *City* **13** (2–3): 185–197.

Marcuse, P. and R. van Kempen (eds.) (2000) *Globalizing Cities: A New Spatial Order*. Malden, MA, Blackwell Publishers Ltd.

Markusen, A. and A. Gadwa (2010) *Creative Placemaking* (White Paper). The Mayors' Institute on City Design, National Endowment of the Arts. http://arts.gov/sites/default/files/CreativePlacemaking-Paper.pdf (last accessed 14 October 2014).

Martin, D.G. (2003) "Place-framing" as Place-making: Constituting a Neighborhood for Organizing and Activism. *Annals of the Association of American Geographers* **93** (3): 730–750.

Martin, N. (2010) The Crisis of Social Reproduction Among Migrant Workers: Interrogating the Role of Migrant Civil Society. *Antipode* **42** (1): 127–151.

Martinez-Fernandez, C., C. Audirac, S. Fol, and E. Cunningham-Sabot (2012) Shrinking Cities: Urban Challenges of Globalization. *International Journal of Urban and Regional Research* **36**: 213–225.

Marx, K. and F. Engels (1970) *The German Ideology*. London, Lawrence and Wishart.

Mason, G. (2014) Olympic Village Proves to be a Costly Lesson for Vancouver. *The Globe and Mail* **29 April**. http://www.theglobeandmail.com/news/british-columbia/olympic-village-proves-to-be-a-costly-lesson-for-vancouver/article18317203/ (last accessed 14 October 2014).

Massey, D. (1984) *Spatial Divisions of Labour*. London, Macmillan.

Massey, D. (1991) A Global Sense of Place. *Marxism Today* **35** (6): 24–29.

Massey, D. (1994) *Space, Place and Gender*. Cambridge, Polity Press.

Massey, D. (2005) *For Space*. London, Sage.

Massey, D. (2011) A Counterhegemonic Relationality of Place. In: E. McCann and K. Ward (eds.) *Mobile Urbanism: Cities and Policymaking in the Global Age*. Minneapolis, MN, University of Minnesota Press, pp. 1–14.

Mathews, V. (2010) Aestheticizing Space: Art, Gentrification, and the City. *Geography Compass* **4** (6): 660–675.

Mayer, M. (2009) The "Right to the City" in the Context of Shifting Mottos of Urban Social Movements. *City* **13** (2–3): 362–374.

McAuliffe, C. (2013) Legal Walls and Professional Paths: The Mobilities of Graffiti Writers in Sydney. *Urban Studies* **50** (3): 518–537.

McCann, E. (2002) The Cultural Politics of Local Economic Development: Meaning-making, Place-making and the Urban Development Process. *Geoforum* **33**: 385–98.

McCann, E. (2004) "Best Places": Inter-Urban Competition, Quality of Life, and Popular Media Discourse. *Urban Studies* **41** (10): 1909–1929.

McCann, E. (2007) Inequality and Politics in the Creative City-Region: Questions of Livability and State Strategy. *The International Journal of Urban and Regional Research* **31**: 188–196.

McCann, E. (2008) Expertise, Truth, and Urban Policy Mobilities: Global Circuits of Knowledge in the Development of Vancouver, Canada's "Four Pillar" Drug Strategy. *Environment and Planning A* **40** (4): 885–904.

McCann, E. (2011a) Urban Policy Mobilities and Global Circuits of Knowledge: Toward a Research Agenda. *Annals of the Association of American Geographers* **101** (1): 107–130.

McCann, E. (2011b). Points of reference: Knowledge of elsewhere in the politics of urban drug policy. In: E. McCann and K. Ward (eds.) *Mobile Urbanism: Cities and Policymaking in the Global Age*, Minneapolis, MN, University of Minnesota Press, pp. 97–122.

McCann, E. (2013) Policy Boosterism, Policy Mobilities, and the Extrospective City. *Urban Geography* **34** (1): 5–29.

McCann, E. and K. Ward (eds.) (2011) *Mobile Urbanism: Cities and Policymaking in the Global Age*. Minneapolis, MN, University of Minnesota Press.

McCann, E., A. Roy, and K. Ward (2013) Assembling/Worlding Cities. *Urban Geography* **34** (5): 581–189.

McDowell, L. (1991) Life Without Father and Ford: the New Gender Order of Post-Fordism. *Transactions of the Institute of British Geographers* **16** (4): 400–419.

McEachern, C. (1998) Mapping the Memories: Politics, Place and Identity in the District Six Museum, Cape Town. *Social Identities: Journal for the Study of Race, Nation and Culture* **4** (3): 499–521.

McFarlane, C. (2008a) Sanitation in Mumbai's Informal Settlements: State, "Slum", and Infrastructure. *Environment and Planning A* **40** (1): 88–107.

McFarlane, C. (2008b). Postcolonial Bombay: Decline of a Cosmopolitanism City? *Environment and Planning D: Society and Space* **26** (3): 480–499.

McGuirk, P. (2004) State, Strategy, and Scale in the Competitive City: A Neo-Gramscian Analysis of the Governance of "Global Sydney." *Environment and Planning A* **36**: 1019–1043.

McGuirk, P. and R. Dowling (2011) Governing Social Reproduction in Masterplanned Estates: Urban Politics and Everyday Life in Sydney. *Urban Studies* **48**: 2611–2628.

McKittrick, K. (2006) *Demonic Grounds: Black Women and the Cartographies of Struggle*. Minneapolis, MN, University of Minnesota Press.

McManus, P. (2004) *Vortex Cities to Sustainable Cities: Australia's Urban Challenge*. Sydney, NSW, University of New South Wales Press.

McNeill, D. (1999) *Urban Change and the European Left: Tales from the New Barcelona*. London, Routledge.

McNeil, D. (2009) *The Global Architect: Firms, Fame and Urban Form*. New York, Routledge Press.

Meehan, K. (2013) Disciplining de facto Development: Water Theft and Hydrosocial Order in Tijuana. *Environment and Planning D: Society and Space* **31** (2): 319–336

Mendes, W. (2008) Implementing Social and Environmental Policies in Cities: the Case of Food Policy in Vancouver, Canada. *International Journal of Urban and Regional Research* **32**: 942–967.

Miewald, C. and E. McCann (2013) Foodscapes and the Geographies of Poverty: Sustenance, Strategy, and Politics in an Urban Neighborhood. *Antipode* **46** (2): 537–556.

Mirzoeff, N. (2011) *The Right to Look*. Durham, NC, Duke University Press.

Mitchell, D. (2003) *The Right to the City: Social Justice and the Fight for Public Space*. New York, Guilford.

Mitchell, D. and N. Heynen (2009) The Geography of Survival and the Right to the City: Speculations on Surveillance, Legal Innovation, and the Criminalization of Intervention. *Urban Geography* **30** (6): 611–632.

Mitchell, K., S. Marston, and C. Katz (eds.) (2004) *Life's Work: Geographies of Social Reproduction*. Oxford, Blackwell.

Mullings, B. (2009) Neoliberalization, Social Reproduction and the Limits to Labour in Jamaica. *Singapore Journal of Tropical Geography* **30**: 174–188.

Mumford, L. (1961) *The City in History*. London, Penguin.

Nagel, C. (2002) Constructing Difference and Sameness: The Politics of Assimilation in London's Arab Communities. *Ethnic and Racial Studies* **25** (2): 258–287.

National Research Council (2014) *The Growth of Incarceration in the United States: Exploring Causes and Consequences*. Washington, DC, The National Academies Press.

Nayak, A. (2003) *Race, Place and Globalization: Youth Cultures in a Changing World*. New York, Berg.

NCAI (National Congress of American Indians) (2013) *Ending the Legacy of Racism in Sports and the Era of Harmful Indian Sports Mascots*. http://www.ncai.org/resources/ncai-publications/Ending_the_Legacy_of_Racism.pdf (last accessed 14 October 2014).

Nelson, K. (1986) Female Labor Supply Characteristics and the Suburbanization of Low-Wage Office Work. In: M. Storper and A.J. Scott (eds.) *Production, Work, Territory*. Boston, MA, Allen and Unwin, pp. 149–171.

Nevarez, L. (2003) *New Money, Nice Town: How Capital Works in the New Urban Economy*. London, Routledge.

O'Dougherty, M. (2006) Public Relations, Private Security: Managing Youth and Race at the Mall of America. *Environment and Planning D: Society and Space* **24**: 131–154.

Orleans, P. (1973) Differential Cognition of Urban Residents. In: R. Downs and D. Stea (eds.) *Image and Environment*. Chicago, IL, Aldine, pp. 115–130.

Oswalt, P. (ed.) (2006) *Shrinking Cities. Volume 1: International Research*. Ostfildern-Ruit, Germany, Hatje Cantz Verlag.

Oswin, N. (2008) Critical Geographies and the Uses of Sexuality: Deconstructing Queer Space. *Progress in Human Geography* **32** (1): 89–103.

Oswin, N. (2010) The Modern Model Family at Home in Singapore: a Queer Geography. *Transactions of the Institute of British Geographers* **35** (2): 256–268.

Oswin, N. (2012) The Queer Time of Creative Urbanism: Family, Futurity, and Global City Singapore. *Environment and Planning A* **44**: 1624–1640.

Pacione, M. (2009) *Urban Geography: A Global Perspective*. New York, Routledge.

Pain, R. (1991) Space, Sexual Violence and Social Control: Integrating Geographical and Feminist Analyses of Women's Fear of Crime. *Progress in Human Geography* **15** (4): 415–431.

Painter, J. (2000) Critical Human Geography. In: D. Gregory, R. Johnston, G. Pratt, *et al.* (eds.) *The Dictionary of Human Geography*. Malden, MA, Blackwell Publishers Ltd, pp. 126–128.

Parès, M. and D. Sauri (2007) Integrating Sustainabilities in a Context of Economic, Social and Urban Change: The Case of Public Spaces in the Metropolitan Region of Barcelona. In: R. Krueger and D.C. Gibbs (eds.) *The Sustainable Development Paradox*. London, Guilford, pp. 160–191.

Park, R.E. and E. W. Burgess (1925/1967) *The City*. Chicago, IL, University of Chicago Press.

Parnell, S. and E. Pieterse (2010) The "Right to the City": Institutional Imperatives of a Developmental State. *International Journal of Urban and Regional Research* **34** (1): 146–162.

Parnreiter, C. (2012) More than an Ordinary City: The Role of Mexico City in Global Commodity Chains. In: B. Derudder, M. Hoyler, P.J. Taylor, and F. Witlox (eds.) *International Handbook of Globalization and World Cities*. Cheltenham, Edward Elgar, pp. 437–446.

Parr, H. (1997) Mental Health, Public Space and the City: Questions of Individual and Collective Access. *Environment and Planning D: Society and Space* **15**: 435–454.

Parr, H. (1999) Delusional Geographies: The Experiential Worlds of People During Madness/Illness. *Environment and Planning D: Society and Space* **17** (6): 673–690.

Parr, H. and J. Davidson (2011) Psychic Life. In: V.J. Del Casino, Jr., M.E. Thomas, P. Cloke, and R. Panelli (eds.) *A Companion to Social Geography*. Hoboken, NJ, John Wiley & Sons, Inc., pp. 275–292.

Parr, H., and R. Butler (1999) New Geographies of Illness, Impairment and Disability. In: R. Butler and H. Parr (eds.) *Mind and Body Spaces: Geographies of Illness, Impairment and Disability*. London and New York, Routledge, pp. 1–24.

Peck, J. (1996) *Work-Place*. New York, The Guilford Press.

Peck, J. (2001) *Workfare States*. New York, The Guilford Press.

Peck, J. (2005) Struggling with the Creative Class. *International Journal of Urban and Regional Research* **29**: 740–770.

Peck, J. (2012) Austerity Urbanism. *City: Analysis of Urban Trends, Culture, Theory, Policy, Action* **16**: 626–655.

Peck, J. (2014) Pushing Austerity: State Failure, Municipal Bankruptcy and the Crises of Fiscal Federalism in the USA. *Cambridge Journal of Regions, Economy and Society* **7**: 17–44.

Peck, J. and N. Theodore (2001) Contingent Chicago: Restructuring the Spaces of Temporary Labor. *International Journal of Urban and Regional Research* **25**: 471–496.

Peck, J. and N. Theodore (eds.) (2010) Mobilizing Policy, Special Theme Issue. *Geoforum* **41** (2): 169–226.

Peck, J. and A. Tickell (1994) Searching for a New Institutional Fix: the *After*-Fordist Crisis and Global-Local Disorder. In: A. Amin (ed.) *Post-Fordism: A Reader*. Oxford, Blackwell, pp. 280–316.

Peck, J. and A. Tickell (2002) Neoliberalizing Space. In: N. Brenner and N. Theodore (eds.) *Spaces of Neoliberalism: Urban Restructuring in North America and Western Europe*. Malden, MA, Blackwell Publishers Ltd, pp. 33–57.

Phelps, N.A. and F. Wu (eds.) (2011) *International Perspectives on Suburbanization: A Post-Suburban World?* Basingstoke, Palgrave Macmillan.

Phillips, T. (2012) Greedy banks beware: Credit unions are a fairer alternative. *Mirror*, 11 January 2012. http://www.mirror.co.uk/money/personal-finance/greedy-banks-beware-credit-unions-157988 (last accessed 13 October 2014).

Pincetl, S. (2003) Nonprofits and Park Provision in Los Angeles: An Exploration of the Rise of Governance Approaches to the Provision of Local Services. *Social Science Quarterly* **84**: 979–1002.

Pincetl S. and B. Katz (2007) The Imperial Valley of California: Sustainability, Water, Agriculture and Urban Growth. In: R. Krueger and D.C. Gibbs (eds.) *The Sustainable Development Paradox*. London, Guilford, pp. 268–299.

Pollard, J.S. (1995) The Contradictions of Flexibility: Labor Control and Resistance in the Los Angeles Banking Industry. *Geoforum* **26**: 121–138.

Pontecorvo, G. (dir.) (1966) *The Battle of Algiers*. Igor Film and Casbah Film.

Popkin, S.J. (2007) *Testimony Prepared for the Hearing on S. 829 HOPE VI Improvement and Reauthorization Act, June 20, 2007*. Washington, DC, U.S. Senate, Committee on Banking, Housing, and Urban Affairs, Subcommittee on Housing, Transportation, and Community Development. http://www.urban.org/UploadedPDF/901088_HOPE_VI.pdf (last accessed 14 October 2014).

Pratt, G. (2012) *Families Apart: Migrant Mothers and the Conflicts of Labor and Love*. Minneapolis, MN, University of Minnesota Press.

Pulido, L. (2000) Rethinking Environmental Racism: White Privilege and Urban Development in Southern California. *Annals of the Association of American Geographers* **90** (1): 12–40.

Pulido, L. (2006) *Black, Brown, Yellow and Left: Radical Activism in Los Angeles*. Berkeley, CA, University of California Press.

Purcell, M. (2002) Excavating Lefebvre: The Right to the City and its Urban Politics of the Inhabitant. *GeoJournal* **58** (2–3): 99–108.

Purcell, M. (2003) Citizenship and the Right to the Global City: Reimagining the Capitalist World Order. *International Journal of Urban and Regional Research* **27** (3): 564–590.

Purcell, M. (2007) City-regions, Neoliberal Globalization and Democracy: A Research Agenda. *International Journal of Urban and Regional Research* **31**: 197–206.

Purcell, M. (2008) *Recapturing Democracy: Neoliberalization and the Struggle for Alternative Urban Futures*. London, Routledge.

Purcell, M. and S.K. Tyman (2014) Cultivating Food as a Right to the City. *Local Environment*. http://www.tandfonline.com/doi/full/10.1080/13549839.2014.903236 (last accessed 16 October 2014).

Pyer, M., J. Horton, F. Tucker, *et al.* (2010) Special Issue: Children, Young People, and Disability: Challenging Children's Geographies? *Children's Geographies* **8** (1): 1–78.

Raco, M. (2005) Sustainable Development, Rolled-out Neoliberalism and Sustainable Communities. *Antipode* **37**: 324–347.

Rader, D. (2011) *Engage Resistance: American Indian Art, Literature, and Film from Alcatraz to the NMAI.* Austin, TX, University of Texas Press.

Rahman, M.M., G. Haughton and A.E.G. Jonas (2010) The Challenges of Local Environmental Problems Facing the Urban Poor in Chittagong, Bangladesh: A Scale-sensitive Analysis. *Environment and Urbanization* **22** (2): 561–578.

Reese, L.A., G. Sands and M. Skidmore (2014) Memo from Motown: is Austerity Here to Stay? *Cambridge Journal of Regions, Economy and Society* **7**: 99–118.

Reisner, M. (1986) *Cadillac Desert: The American West and Its Disappearing Water.* New York, Viking Penguin Books.

Rice, J. (2014) Public Targets, Private Choices: Urban Climate Governance in the Pacific Northwest. *The Professional Geographer* **66**: 333–344.

Riches, G. (2011) Thinking and Acting Outside the Charitable Food Box: Hunger and the Right to Food in Rich Societies. *Development in Practice* **21** (4–5): 768–775.

Rieniets, T. and P. Oswalt (n.d.) *Shrinking Cities.* Turin, Cluster Srl. http://www.cluster.eu/shrinking-citiescitta-che-si-spopolono/ (last accessed 14 October 2014).

Riis, J. (1890) *How the Other Half Lives: Studies Among the Tenements of New York.* New York, Scribner & Sons.

Rios, V. (2011) *Punished: Policing the Lives of Black and Latino Boys.* New York, NYU Press.

Robbins, P. (2007) *Lawn People: How Grasses, Weeds and Chemicals Make Us Who We Are.* Philadelphia, PA, Temple University Press.

Robertson, M.M. (2004) The Neoliberalization of Ecosystem Services: Wetland Mitigation Banking and Problems in Environmental Governance. *Geoforum* **35**: 361–373.

Robinson, J. (2002) Global and World Cities: a View from Off the Map. *International Journal of Urban and Regional Research* **26** (3): 531–554.

Robinson, J. (2006) *Ordinary Cities: Between Modernity and Development.* New York, Routledge.

Robinson, J. (2008) Developing Ordinary Cities: City Visioning Processes in Durban and Johannesburg. *Environment and Planning A* **40** (1): 74–87.

Robinson, J. (2011a) The Spaces of Circulating Knowledge: City Strategies and Global Urban Governmentality. In: E. McCann and K. Ward (eds.) *Mobile Urbanism: Cities and Policymaking in the Global Age.* Minneapolis, MN, University of Minnesota Press, pp. 15–40.

Robinson, J. (2011b) Cities in a World of Cities: the Comparative Gesture. *International Journal of Urban and Regional Research* **35**: 1–23.

Rocha, C. and I. Lessa (2009) Urban Governance for Food Security: the Alternative Food System in Belo Horizonte, Brazil. *International Planning Studies* **14** (4): 389–400.

Rocheleau, D., B. Thomas-Slayter and E. Wangari (2013) *Feminist Political Ecology: Global Issues and Local Experience.* New York, Routledge Press.

Rogers, C. (2011) *From Gautreaux to MTO: Racial Discipline and Neoliberal Governance in Housing Policy.* Unpublished Dissertation, The Ohio State University.

Rogers, C. (2013) Overview. In: C. Roger and J. Powell (eds.) *Where Credit is Due: Bringing Equity to Credit and Housing after the Market Meltdown.* Lanham, MA, University Press of America, pp. 1–22.

Rose, G. (2001) *Visual Methodologies.* Thousand Oaks, CA, Sage.

Rosenzweig, R. (1983) *Eight Hours for What We Will: Work and Leisure in an Industrial City.* Cambridge, Cambridge University Press.

Rossi, U. and A. Vanolo (2012) *Urban Political Geographies: A Global Perspective.* London, Sage.

Roy, A. (2009) The 21st Century Metropolis: New Geographies of Theory. *Regional Studies* **43**: 819–830.

Roy, A. (2011a) Conclusion: Postcolonial Urbanism: Speed, Hysteria, Mass Dreams. In: A. Roy and A. Ong (eds.) *Worlding Cities: Asian Experiments and the Art of Being Global*. Hoboken, NJ, John Wiley & Sons, Inc., pp. 307–335.

Roy, A. (2011b) Re-Forming the Megacity: Calcutta and the Rural–Urban Interface. In: A. Sorensen and J. Okata (eds.) *Megacities: Urban Form, Governance, and Sustainability*. Tokyo, Springer: 93–109.

Roy, A. and A. Ong (eds.) (2011) *Worlding Cities: Asian Experiments and the Art of Being Global*. Chichester, John Wiley & Sons Ltd.

Rushe, D. (2013) Detroit Becomes Largest City to File for Bankruptcy in Historic "Low Point". *The Guardian* **18 July**. http://www.theguardian.com/world/2013/jul/18/detroit-formally-files-bankruptcy (last accessed 14 October 2014).

Rutheiser, C. (1996) *Imagineering Atlanta: The Politics of Place in the City of Dreams*. New York, Verso.

Samara, T.R., S. He, and G. Chen (eds.) (2013) *Locating Right to the City in the Global South*. New York, Routledge.

Samers, M. (1998) "Structured Coherence": Immigration, Racism and Production in the Paris Car Industry. *European Planning Studies* **6**: 49–72.

Sandercock, L. (1998) *Towards Cosmopolis: Planning for Multicultural Cities*. New York, John Wiley & Sons, Inc.

Sandercock, L. (2003) *Cosmopolis II: Mongrel Cities of the 21st Century*. London, Continuum.

Sanders, H.T. (2005) *Space Available: The Realities of Convention Centers as Economic Development Strategy*. Brookings Institution. http://www.brookings.edu/reports/2005/01cities_sanders.aspx (last accessed 14 October 2014).

Santos, M. (1977) Spatial Dialectics: The Two Circuits of Urban Economy in Underdeveloped Countries. *Antipode* **9**: 49–60.

Sassen S. (1991) *The Global City*. Princeton, NJ, Princeton University Press.

Sassen, S. (1994/2012) *Cities in a World Economy*. Thousand Oaks, CA, Sage.

Sassen, S. (2001) *The Global City: New York, London, Tokyo*. Princeton, NJ, Princeton University Press.

Sassen, S. (2002) Locating Cities on Global Circuits. *Environment and Urbanization* **14** (13): 13–30.

Sassen, S. (2006) *Territory, Authority, Rights: From Medieval to Global Assemblages*. Princeton, NJ, Princeton University Press.

Satterthwaite, D. (1997) Sustainable Cities or Cities that Contribute to Sustainable Development? *Urban Studies* **34**: 1667–1691.

Saunders, P. (1981) *Social Theory and the Urban Question*. London, Hutchison.

Scott, A.J. (1980) *The Urban Land Nexus and the State*. London, Pion.

Scott, A.J. (1982) Production System Dynamics and Metropolitan Development. *Annals of the Association of American Geographers* **72**: 185–200.

Scott, A.J. (1988) *Metropolis: From the Division of Labor to Urban Form*. Berkeley and Los Angeles, CA, University of California Press.

Scott, A.J. (1998) Multimedia and Digital Effects: and Emerging Local Labor Market. *Monthly Labor Review* **March**: 30–38.

Scott, A.J. and E. Soja (eds.) (1996) *The City: Los Angeles and Urban Theory at the End of the Twentieth Century*. Berkeley and Los Angeles, CA, University of California Press.

Scott, A.J. (ed.) (2001) *Global City-Regions: Trends, Theory, Policy*. Oxford, Oxford University Press.

Scott, J.W. (1991) The Evidence of Experience. *Critical Inquiry* **17**: 773–797.

Sentencing Project (2012) *Factsheet: Incarcerated Women*. Washington, DC, The Sentencing Project. http://www.sentencingproject.org/doc/publications/cc_Incarcerated_Women_Factsheet_Dec2012final.pdf (last accessed 14 October 2014).

Shaw, C. (2008). *Five Ring Circus: Myths and Realities of the Olympic Games*. New York, New Society Publishers.

Shaw, W. (2007) *Cities of Whiteness*. Malden, MA, Blackwell Publishers Ltd.

Shin, H.B. (2012) Unequal Cities of Spectacle and Mega-events in China. *City* 16 (6): 728-744.

Short, J. (1999) Urban Imagineers: Boosterism and the Representation of Cities. In: A.E.G. Jonas and D. Wilson (eds.) *The Urban Growth Machine: Critical Perspectives Two Decades Later*. Albany, NY, State University Press of New York, pp. 37-54.

Shoval, N. (2002) A New Phase in the Competition for the Olympic Gold: The London and New York Bids for the 2012 Games. *Journal of Urban Affairs* 24 (5): 583-599.

Sibley, D. (1981) *Outsiders in Urban Societies*. Oxford, Basil Blackwell.

Sibley, D. (1995) *Geographies of Exclusion: Society and Difference in the West*. London and New York, Routledge.

Simmel, G. (1903/2002) The Metropolis and Mental Life. In: G. Bridge and S. Watson (eds.) *The Blackwell City Reader*. Malden, MA, Blackwell Publishers Ltd, pp. 11-19.

Simon, D. (1995) The World City Hypothesis: Reflections from the Periphery. In: P.J. Taylor and P.L. Knox (eds.) *World Cities in a World-System*. Cambridge, Cambridge University Press, pp. 132-155.

Simone, A. (2001) On the Worlding of African Cities. *African Studies Review* 44 (2): 15-41.

Simone, A. (2010) *City Life from Jakarta to Dakar: Movements at the Crossroads*. New York, Routledge.

Sinclair, U. (1906) *The Jungle*. New York, Doubleday.

Slater, T. (2004) North American Gentrification? Revanchist and Emancipatory Perspectives Explored. *Environment and Planning A* 36 (7): 1191-1213.

Slater, T. (2011) Gentrification of the City. In: G. Bridge and S. Watson (eds.) *The New Blackwell Companion to the City*. Chichester, John Wiley & Sons Ltd, pp. 571-585.

Smith, M.P. (2000) *Transnational Urbanism: Locating Globalization*. Malden, MA, Blackwell Publishers Ltd.

Smith, N. (1979) Toward a Theory of Gentrification: A Back to the City Movement by Capital, Not People. *Journal of the American Planning Association* 45: 538-548.

Smith, N. (1984) *Uneven Development*. Oxford, Blackwell Publishers Ltd.

Smith, N. (1996) *The New Urban Frontier: Gentrification and the Revanchist City*. New York and London, Routledge.

Smith, N. and P. Williams (eds.) (1986) *Gentrification of the City*. Boston, MA, Allen and Unwin.

Social Science Bites (2013) *Doreen Massey on Space*. Thousand Oaks, CA, Sage. http://www.socialsciencespace.com/2013/02/podcastdoreen-massey-on-space/ (last accessed 14 October 2014).

Soja, E. (2000a) *Postmetropolis: Critical Studies of Cities and Regions*. Oxford, Blackwell.

Soja, E. (2000b) The stimulus of a little confusion: A contemporary comparison of Amsterdam & Los Angeles. In: L. Deben, W.F. Heinemeyer, and D. van der Vaart (eds.) *Understanding Amsterdam: Essays on Economic Vitality, City Life and Urban Form*, Amsterdam, Het Spinhuis, pp. 117-142.

Soja, E. (2010) *Seeking Spatial Justice*. Minneapolis, MN, University of Minnesota Press.

Soja, E. (2011) Regional Urbanization and the End of the Metropolis Era. In: G. Bridge and S. Watson (eds.) *The New Blackwell Companion to the City*. Chichester, John Wiley & Sons Ltd, pp. 679-689.

Spade, D. (2011) *Normal Life: Administrative Violence, Critical Trans Politics, and the Limits of Law*. Brooklyn, South End Press.

Sparke, M. (2010) Global Seattle. *Association of American Geographers Newsletter* 45 (11): 1 and 10-11.

Sparke, M. (2011) Global Geographies. In: M. Brown and R. Morrill (eds.) *Seattle Geographies*. Seattle, WA, University of Washington Press, pp. 48-70.

Staeheli, L. and D. Mitchell (2008) *The People's Property? Power, Politics and the Public*. Abingdon, Routledge.

Stanley, E. and N. Smith (eds.) (2011) *Captive Genders: Trans Embodiment and the Prison Industrial Complex.* Oakland, CA, AK Press.

Stedman Jones, G. (1984) *Outcast London: A Study in the Relationship Between Classes in Victorian Society.* London, Penguin.

Storper, M. (2013) *Keys to the City.* Princeton, NJ, Princeton University Press.

Storper, M. and A.J. Scott (1989) The Geographical Foundations and Social Regulation of Flexible Production Complexes. In: J. Wolch and M. Dear (eds.) *The Power of Geography: How Territory Shapes Social Life.* Boston, MA, Unwin Hyman, pp. 21–40.

Storper, M. and R. Walker (1989) *The Capitalist Imperative: Territory, Technology and Industrial Growth.* New York, Blackwell.

Stuart, F. (2013) From "Rabble Management" to "Recovery Management": Policing Homelessness in Marginal Urban Space. *Urban Studies* 51 (9): 1909–1925.

Sullivan, S. (2007) Local and Regional Elected Officials Invited to Participate in 2007 Vancouver Pride Parade (Press Release). Vancouver, BC, City of Vancouver, Mayor's Office. http://www.samsullivan.ca/local-regional-elected-officials-invited-to-participate-in-2007-vancouver-pride-parade/ (last accessed 8 October 2014).

Sustainable Food Cities (n.d.) *International Inspiration.* http://sustainablefoodcities.org/resources/internationalinspiration (last accessed 14 October 2014).

Swanson, K. (2010) *Begging as a Path to Progress: Indigenous Women and Children and the Struggle for Ecuador's Urban Spaces.* Athens, GA, University of Georgia Press.

Swyngedouw, E. (1996) The City as a Hybrid: On Nature, Society and Cyborg Urbanization. *Capitalism, Nature, Socialism* 7: 65-80.

Swyngedouw, E. (2007) Impossible "Sustainability" and the Postpolitical Condition. In: R. Krueger and D.C. Gibbs (eds.) *The Sustainable Development Paradox.* London, Guilford, pp. 13-40.

Tabb, W. and L. Sawers (eds.) (1984) *Marxism and the Metropolis.* New York, Oxford University Press.

Taylor, P.J., P. Ni, B. Derudder, *et al.* (eds.) (2012) *Global Urban Analysis: A Survey of Cities in Globalization.* New York, Routledge.

Temenos, C. and E. McCann (2013) Geographies of Policy Mobilities. *Geography Compass* 7 (5): 344-357.

Thomas, M.E. (2005) Girls, Consumption Space, and the Contradictions of Hanging out in the City. *Social and Cultural Geography* 6 (4): 587–605.

Thomas, M.E. (2011) *Multicultural Girlhood: Racism, Sexuality, and the Conflicted Spaces of American Education.* Philadelphia, PA, Temple University Press.

Till, J. (2013) The Broken Middle: the Space of the London Riots. *Cities* 34: 71–74.

Till, K. (1993) Neotraditional Towns and Urban Villages: The Cultural Production of a Geography of "Otherness." *Environment and Planning D: Society and Space* 11: 709–732.

Till, K. (2005) *The New Berlin: Memory, Politics, Place.* Minneapolis, MN, University of Minnesota Press.

Time Inc. (2009) Best Places to Live. *Money.* http://time.com/money/collection/best-places-to-live/ (last accessed 8 October 2014).

Tipple, G. and S. Speak (2009) *The Hidden Millions: Homelessness in Developing Countries.* New York and London, Routledge Press.

Tornaghi, C. (2014) Critical Geography of Urban Agriculture. *Progress in Human Geography* 38 (4): 551–567.

Torrance, M. (2009) Reconceptualizing Urban Governance Through a New Paradigm for Urban Infrastructure Networks. *Journal of Economic Geography* 9: 805–822.

United Nations (2012) *World Urbanization Prospects: The 2011 Revision.* New York, United Nations, Department of Economic and Social Affairs, Population Division. http://esa.un.org/unpd/wup/pdf/WUP2011_Highlights.pdf (last accessed 15 October 2014).

Valentine, G. (1996) (Re)negotiating the "Heterosexual Street": Lesbian Productions of Space. In: N. Duncan (ed.) *Body Space.* New York and London, Routledge, pp. 146–155.

Valentine, G. (2014) Living with Difference: Geographies of Encounter. In: R. Paddison and E. McCann (eds.) *Cities and Social Change: Encounters with Contemporary Urbanism*. Thousand Oaks, CA, Sage, pp. 75–91.

Vancouver Coastal Health (n.d.) *Insite User Statistics*. http://supervisedinjection.vch.ca/research/supporting_research/user_statistics (last accessed 14 October 2014).

Vanderbeck, R.M. (2008) Inner City Children, Country Summers: Narrating American Childhood and the Geographies of Whiteness. *Environment and Planning A* **40**: 1132-1150.

Vanderbeck, R. and J. Johnson (2000) "That's the Only Place Where You Can Hang Out": Urban Young People and the Space of the Mall. *Urban Geography* **21** (1): 5–25.

Vohra, P. (2007) *Q2P*. India, Paromita Vohra/Devi Pictures.

Volkan, A. and J. Rath (eds.) (2012) *Selling Ethnic Neighborhoods: The Rise of Neighborhoods as Places of Leisure and Consumption*. New York, Routledge.

Wacquant, L. (1997) Three Pernicious Premises in the Study of the American Ghetto. *International Journal of Urban and Regional Research* **21** (2): 341–353.

Wacquant, L. (2009) *Punishing the Poor: the Neoliberal Government of Social Insecurity*. Durham, NC, Duke University Press.

Waitt, G. (1999) Playing Games with Sydney: Marketing Sydney for the 2000 Olympics. *Urban Studies* **36**: 1055-1077.

Walker, R.A. and B. Large (1974) The Ecology of Energy Extravagance. *Ecology Law Quarterly* **4**: 963-985.

Walsh, J. (2000) Organising the Scale of Labor Regulation in the United States: Service-Sector Activism in the City. *Environment and Planning A* **32**: 1593–1610.

Ward, D. (1971) *Cities and Immigrants*. New York, Oxford University Press.

Ward, K. (2006) Geography and Public Policy: Towards Public Geographies. *Progress in Human Geography* **30** (4): 495–503.

Ward, K. (2007) Business Improvement Districts: Policy Origins, Mobile Policies and Urban Liveability. *Geography Compass* **1** (3): 657-672.

Ward, K. (2010) Entrepreneurial Urbanism and Business Improvement Districts in the State of Wisconsin: a Cosmopolitan Critique. *Annals of the Association of American Geographers* **100**: 1177-1196.

Ward, K. and A.E.G. Jonas (2004) Competitive City-Regionalism as a Politics of Space: A Critical Reinterpretation of the New Regionalism. *Environment and Planning A* **36**: 2112–2139.

Wassener, B. (2014) Continuing Unrest Could Undermine Thailand's Economy. *New York Times*, 30 January. http://www.nytimes.com/2014/01/31/business/international/continuing-unrest-could-undermine-thailand-economy.html?_r=0 (last accessed 14 October 2014).

Weaver, R. (1977) The Suburbanization of America or the Shrinking of the Cities. *Civil Rights Digest* **9**: 2–11.

Weber, R. (2003) Equity and Entrepreneurialism: the Impact of Tax Increment Financing on School Finance. *Urban Affairs Review* **38**: 619–644.

Weizman, E. (2006) The Art of War. *Frieze* **99.** http://www.frieze.com/issue/article/the_art_of_war/ (last accessed 14 October 2014).

Weizman, E. (2010) Forensic Architecture: Only the Criminal Can Solve the Crime. *Radical Philosophy* **164**: 9–24.

Welby, J. (2013) Payday loans. Archbishop's speech in the House of Lords. http://www.archbishopofcanterbury.org/articles.php/5083/payday-loans-archbishops-speech-in-the-house-of-lords (last accessed 13 October 2014).

While, A.H., A.E.G. Jonas and D.C. Gibbs (2004a) Unblocking the City: Growth Pressures, Collective Provision and the Search for New Spaces of Governance in Greater Cambridge, England. *Environment and Planning A* **36**: 279–304.

While, A.H., A.E.G. Jonas and D.C. Gibbs (2004b) The Environment and the Entrepreneurial City: Searching for a "Sustainability Fix" in Leeds and Manchester. *International Journal of Urban and Regional Research* **28**: 549-569.

Williams, C. and M. Pendras (2013) Urban Stasis and the Politics of Alternative Development in the United States. *Urban Geography* **34**: 289–304.

Wills, J. and B. Linneker (2013) In-work Poverty and the Living Wage in the United Kingdom: A Geographical Perspective. *Transactions of the Institute of British Geographers* **39**(2): 182–194.

Wills, J., K. Datta, Y. Evans, *et al.* (2009) Religion at Work: The Role of Faith-Based Organisations in Living Wage Campaigns for Immigrant Workers in London. *The Cambridge Journal of Regions, Economy and Society* **2**: 443–461.

Wilson D. (2009) Globalization, the Global Trope, and Poor Black Communities: the Recent American Experience. *Global-E: A Global Studies Journal*, **3**. http://global-ejournal.org/2009/05/15/globalization-the-global-trope-and-poor-black-communities-the-recent-american-experience/ (last accessed 14 October 2014).

Wilson, D. and R. Keil (2008) The Real Creative Class. *Social and Cultural Geography* **9** (8): 841–847.

Wirth, L. (1938) Urbanism as a Way of Life. *American Journal of Sociology* **XLIV** (1): 1–24.

Wolch, J. (2007) Green Urban Worlds. *Annals of the Association of American Geographers* **97**: 371–384.

Wood, A. (1998) Making Sense of Urban Entrepreneurialism. *Scottish Geographical Journal* **114** (2): 120–123.

Wood, A. (2014a) Learning through Policy Tourism: Circulating Bus Rapid Transit from South America to South Africa. *Environment and Planning A* **46** (11): 2654–2669.

Wood, A. (2014b) Moving Policy: Global and Local Characters Circulating Bus Rapid Transit Through South African Cities. *Urban Geography* DOI 10.1080/02723638.2014.954459.

World Future Council (2013) *Sharing the Experience of the Food Security System of Belo Horizonte.* http://www.fao.org/fileadmin/templates/FCIT/Meetings/Africites/presentations/WorldFutureCouncil_experience-Belo-Horizonte.pdf (last accessed 14 October 2014).

Worster, D. (1985) *Rivers of Empire: Water, Aridity, and the Growth of the American West.* New York, Pantheon.

Wright, M. (2006) *Disposable Women and Other Myths of Global Capitalism.* New York and London, Routledge.

Wright, M. (2010a) Gender and Geography: Feminism and a Feeling of Justice. *Progress in Human Geography* **34**: 818–827.

Wright, M. (2010b) Gender and Geography II: Bridging the Gap – Feminist, Queer and the Geographical Imaginary. *Progress in Human Geography* **34**: 56–66.

Wyly, E., M. Moos, and D.J. Hammel (2012) Race, Class and Rent in America's Subprime Cities. In: M.B. Albers (ed.) *Subprime Cities: The Political Economy of Mortgage Markets.* Chichester, John Wiley & Sons Ltd, pp. 242–290.

Young, L. (2003) The "Place" of Street Children in Kampala, Uganda: Marginalisation, Resistance, and Acceptance in the Urban Environment. *Environment and Planning D: Society and Space* **21** (5): 607–627.

Zukin, S. (1982) *Loft Living.* Baltimore, MD, Johns Hopkins Press.

Index

Page numbers in *italics* denotes an illustration/figure/table

Urban Geography: A Critical Introduction, First Edition. Andrew E.G. Jonas, Eugene McCann,
and Mary Thomas.
© 2015 Andrew E.G. Jonas, Eugene McCann, and Mary Thomas. Published 2015 by John Wiley & Sons, Ltd.